Framing a Revolution

Rhetorical contests about how to frame a war run alongside many armed conflicts. With the rise of internet access, social media, and cyber operations, these propaganda battles have a wider audience than ever before. Yet, such framing contests have attracted little attention in scholarly literature. What are the effects of gendered and strategic framing in civil war? How do different types of individuals - victims, combatants, women, commanders - utilize the frames created around them and about them? Who benefits from these contests, and who loses? Following the lives of eleven ex-combatants from non-state armed groups and supplemented by over one hundred interviews conducted across Colombia, Framing a Revolution opens a window into this crucial part of civil war. Their testimonies demonstrate the importance of these contests for combatants' commitments to their armed groups during fighting and the Colombian peace process, while also drawing implications for the concept of civil war worldwide.

Rachel Schmidt, PhD, is a senior national security analyst and a research fellow at the Norman Paterson School of International Affairs. She is an expert in armed conflict and human rights and has done fieldwork in Colombia, Ecuador, the UK, and Canada.

T0382341

Framing a Revolution

Narrative Battles in Colombia's Civil War

RACHEL SCHMIDT

CAMBRIDGE
UNIVERSITY PRESS

Shaftesbury Road, Cambridge CB2 8EA, United Kingdom

One Liberty Plaza, 20th Floor, New York, NY 10006, USA

477 Williamstown Road, Port Melbourne, VIC 3207, Australia

314–321, 3rd Floor, Plot 3, Splendor Forum, Jasola District Centre, New Delhi – 110025, India

103 Penang Road, #05–06/07, Visioncrest Commercial, Singapore 238467

Cambridge University Press is part of Cambridge University Press & Assessment, a department of the University of Cambridge.

We share the University's mission to contribute to society through the pursuit of education, learning and research at the highest international levels of excellence.

www.cambridge.org
Information on this title: www.cambridge.org/9781009219518

DOI: 10.1017/9781009219549

First published 2023
First paperback edition 2024

A catalogue record for this publication is available from the British Library

Library of Congress Cataloging-in-Publication data
NAMES: Schmidt, Rachel, author.
TITLE: Framing a revolution : narrative battles in Colombia's civil war / Rachel Schmidt, University of Denver.
DESCRIPTION: New York, NY : Cambridge University Press, [2023] | Includes bibliographical references and index.
IDENTIFIERS: LCCN 2022032356 | ISBN 9781009219556 (hardback) | ISBN 9781009219549 (ebook)
SUBJECTS: LCSH: Peace-building – Columbia. | Civil war – Columbia. | Gender in conflict management – Columbia. | Conflict management – Columbia. | Political violence – Columbia. | Columbia – Politics and government.
CLASSIFICATION: LCC JZ5584.C7 S36 2023 | DDC 303.6/609861–dc23/eng/20221107 LC record available at https://lccn.loc.gov/2022032356

ISBN   978-1-009-21955-6   Hardback
ISBN   978-1-009-21951-8   Paperback

For my beloved father, Rudy Wiebe (1951–2021),
who taught me to live and love with joy.
You are deeply missed.

I wonder what it's like to be talking of killings day in and day out for so many years? What does it do to you, to your understanding of the things in the world?

Michael Taussig, *Law in a Lawless Land: Diary of a Limpieza in Colombia*

Contents

Figures

Tables

Preface

When we spend entire careers thinking and writing about war, it can be easy to lose sight of the individual people inside it. As social scientists, we are generally trained to see patterns, to build and test theories, to be rigorous and scientific – objective, even. War studies often focus on nations, borders, organizations, and balances of power, which can reinforce this (false) sense of objectivity. If we do study people, they are called respondents, participants, subjects, or samples.

But feminist and critical security scholars have long challenged these ideas of scientific objectivity, recognizing that who we are and our position in the world inevitably affect how we analyze and interpret events around us. My work builds on these traditions. Feminist and critical security scholars have challenged the mainstream, engaged with it, *and* contributed to it – things that I strive to do with this book. But there is a tension here. To quote Nimmi Gowrinathan: "Where feminist arguments are generally gathered inside sanctioned space for women on bookshelves, the thinking of men on violence is nestled into a political canon."[1]

While this book is based on empirical social science research methods and theoretical analysis, with the aim of building a theory around framing contests, desertion, and reintegration, my other goal is that people's stories shine through. The book is structured around organizational framing competitions in war, but it is *people* who create and contest these frames. It is people – mothers, fathers, sons, daughters, fighters, peacemakers – who fight and die in these wars, and who try to make sense of them. And the people presented in this book know more about war than I ever will.

---

[1] Nimmi Gowrinathan, *Radicalizing Her* (Boston: Beacon Press, 2021), 57.

The ex-combatants, civilians, and military officers in this book spoke to me because they wanted me to share their stories. They do not care about framing theory or snowball sampling or literature on desertion patterns. Most do not know or care what the academic research says about Colombia's civil war. None of that matters when you are living through it. What matters is that people see you, that they hear you, and that they might even care enough to help you.

I hope, by sharing their stories, that readers will see and hear at least a few of the people inside Colombia's many intersecting conflicts. It is very easy to consider certain people as evil, lost, beyond hope, undeserving of sympathy – until you sit down and share a meal with them, hear their life stories, meet their children, and understand how they got to where they are now. As Kimberlé Crenshaw has said: "We must contextualize any violence of the resistance in the violence they were resisting."[2]

And finally, I hope that the experiences reflected here help us to understand what "post-conflict" life in Colombia – and beyond – really looks like, and what it can teach us about building sustainable peace.

[2] Gowrinathan, *Radicalizing Her*, 66.

Acknowledgments

I wrote this book amid multiple public health lockdowns, while my two children struggled through more months of online schooling during the pandemic than anywhere else in North America. During all of this, my beloved father passed away suddenly while I was working on the final draft. Needless to say, I would not have completed this book without a village of incredible people to hold me up and keep me going.

I will start with my PhD supervisor, Jean Daudelin, whose clarity and feedback made me a consistently better scholar. Thank you for encouraging me to take calculated risks, for finding the gold in my tsunami-like dissertation chapters, and for pushing me to take the time to write this book. I also owe a great deal of thanks to my two postdoctoral supervisors, Marie Berry at the University of Denver and Theo McLauchlin at the University of Montreal. Thank you both for believing in this project and for your understanding and encouragement as I wrote this book amid an avalanche of personal challenges. Marie stepped in to give me a postdoctoral home at the Josef Korbel School of International Studies after the pandemic derailed my plans, and her grace, humor, and compassion meant so much to me. And to Anastasia Shesterinina, who helped me when she had no reason to do so, and without expecting anything in return – you are truly a gem, and I cannot wait to repay you somehow.

The fieldwork for this book was made possible by generous funding from the Social Sciences and Humanities Research Council of Canada (SSHRC) and the IDRC (International Development Research Centre), as well as the Norman Paterson School of International Affairs at Carleton University. I also received postdoctoral funding to finish this book from SSHRC and the University of Montreal.

At Cambridge University Press, Sara Doskow was the first to see potential in my work, and I will always be grateful that. She then passed the reins to Rachel Blaifeder, who patiently walked me through the editing process and tolerated my endless questions. Thank you to all the staff at Cambridge University Press who worked to make this happen. I am also in debt to the anonymous peer reviewers who read my book and provided so much thoughtful feedback – this book is undoubtedly better because of both of you.

In Colombia, there are far too many people to list, but I am very grateful to all the ex-combatants from the FARC, ELN, and AUC who opened their homes, drank coffee and "vino colombiano" with me, and shared their stories, laughter, and tears. Special thanks are due to Cliver, Jorge, and Yina. Thank you to Nancy Amos and Delaney Turner for opening their home to me in Bogotá on my first round of interviews (and for tolerating a surprise visit from the Colombian military at 4.30 am!). I also owe a great deal of thanks to Natalia Herrera and the staff of the two Ministry of Defense safe houses for facilitating my access to these sites, which were the jumping-off points for this work. I am indebted to my hard-working transcribers, Alejandro Reverend and Jorge Soto (without whom I would likely still be transcribing), and to my beloved Spanish teacher, Mauricio Hoyos, and his family, who not only taught me much-needed Colombian slang but also provided a place to rest in the midst of intense fieldwork. And I do not even know how to adequately thank Alejandro Carlosama, who worked beyond all expectations as my research assistant, fixer, and confidante. *Alejo, estoy muy agradecida por lo que has hecho y siempre te tendré a ti y a tu familia en mi corazón.*

Many wonderful friends kept me sane during this process and held me up through a very difficult two years, especially Julie Stonehouse, Maya Dafinova, Gaëlle Rivard Piché, Kailey Zollinger, and my runner girl gang. My dear children, Jesse and Calia, showed incredible courage and tenacity throughout this long process, happily accepted the adventure of going to Colombia, and endured many weekends of my absence while I escaped to finish this manuscript in 2021–2. This all would have been impossible without Jon Schmidt, my husband of nearly twenty years, whose unfailing loyalty, flexibility, and encouragement – even when I made *highly* questionable decisions – allowed all of this to happen. Thank you for being a rock when I was the storm.

This last part is hard to write. My parents, Hilda and Rudy Wiebe, were wonderfully brave enough to homeschool me and my siblings, and they fostered an insatiable curiosity, a love of learning and adventure, and the freedom to be who I am. Without them, I probably never would have been brave enough to do the fieldwork that I did. But on February 5, 2021, while I was working on the final draft of this book, my beloved father died suddenly and unexpectedly at age sixty-nine. This loss ripped a hole in my heart for which I was completely unprepared. I am truly thankful to have had him as a wonderful father for as long as I did. He and my mom came to Colombia to visit while I was doing fieldwork, and he read the first draft of this manuscript. Both of my parents provided so much support for this work, including flying across the country to help care for my children while I finished my PhD. I am so proud of my mom for her resilience and strength, and I cannot wait to hand her the first copy of this book.

Finally, I owe my life to someone whose name I only learned while finalizing this book. In 2012, a young man anonymously donated his bone marrow so that I could survive an aggressive form of acute myeloid leukemia. He gave me back to my family. None of this would have happened if not for him.

Thank you, Helge Garrels. I cannot wait to meet you.

Abbreviations

ACCU	Campesino Self-defense Forces of Córdoba and Urabá
ACR	Colombian Reintegration Agency
ARN	Agency for Reincorporation and Normalization
AUC	United Self-defense Forces of Colombia
BACRIM	emerging criminal group (generally refers to paramilitary successor organizations)
COL$	Colombian peso
DDR	disarmament, disengagement, and reintegration
ELN	National Liberation Army
EPL	Popular Liberation Army
ETCR	Territorial Spaces for Training and Reincorporation
FARC	Revolutionary Armed Forces of Colombia
GAHD	Group for Humanitarian Attention to the Demobilized
IDP	internally displaced person
JEP	Special Jurisdiction for Peace
LGBTQ+	lesbian, gay, bisexual, transgender, queer, plus
M-19	April 19th Movement
NGO	nongovernmental organization
PRVC	Reincorporation Program into Civilian Life
UNHCR	United Nations High Commissioner for Refugees
UP	Patriotic Union

I

What's in a Frame?

Peace is not an absence of war, it is a virtue, a state of mind, a disposition
for benevolence, confidence, justice.

Baruch Spinoza

"They want to make us look like victims," said Mari,[1] the frustration
clear on her face. "We are not victims of the FARC. We are victims of the
state." She landed hard on this last word, visibly annoyed. We had been
talking amicably for a while, until I started asking her about the many
claims of sexual violence within the FARC (Revolutionary Armed Forces
of Colombia) guerrilla ranks. It was clear she had heard this question
many times before, and the way she pressed her lips together in a thin,
hard line indicated that she did not like it at all. We were sitting on two
plastic chairs outside a makeshift hut with a blue tarp for a roof. One of
the members of the FARC Secretariat – the guerrillas' seven-man governing structure – was napping inside. Over lunch the day before, he told me
he was more comfortable there than in the unbearably hot drywall structures built for ex-combatants in the camp. When I asked him questions
about FARC women and the government's narratives about them, he
said that I needed to talk to Mari. Mari would set me straight, he implied.

We were in one of the many ETCR (Territorial Spaces for Reincorporation
and Training) camps scattered across Colombia (see Figure 1). These
camps were meant to be temporary housing for FARC ex-combatants after
the peace accord was signed in late 2016, until they were transferred to
more permanent communities. The buildings were indeed slapdash, with

---

[1] All of the names of research participants in this book are pseudonyms.

FIGURE 1 Research site: FARC reincorporation camp (ETCR).
Photo credit: author.

exposed drywall, concrete floors, and plastic roofs that sucked in the heat
and baked the residents inside. A few lucky residents had fans – most did
not. Each ETCR, I would discover, had unique quirks and design flaws
alongside major humanitarian issues: limited access to healthcare, contam-
inated water, spotty cell phone signals, sewage disposal issues, epidemics
of boredom, and somewhat alarming levels of beer consumption among
the younger men. In one camp, the leaders told me that they had pock-
eted the government money allocated for an engineer and built the houses
themselves. This was why all the roofs were crooked and the walls were
slanted, they explained, laughing with a tinge of embarrassment. This was
two years after the peace accord, even though these camps were designed
for only six months. As I write this several years later, some ex-combatants
that I spoke to are still there, in this "temporary" housing.

But back to Mari. It was hot and we were sheltering in the shade of
several large palm trees. Occasionally, a chainsaw would buzz nearby,
muffling our conversation and causing Mari to laugh when I couldn't

understand her. It was nice to see her laugh, because during most of our conversation she had been intense and guarded. Violence against women comrades, she said, never happened. *Ever*. Those stories were made up by deserters and government infiltrators who were paid to lie. She knew this first hand, she said, because she had been captured and arrested once, and the military offered her money to lie:

The first thing they put in your hands – it's that I also was imprisoned – and the first thing they put in your hands, the justice department, is the following: on the table they can put 200, 300 million pesos.[2] And they say, "you want to leave freely right now?" Knowing that's not going to happen because there are laws already instituted, [criminal] codes that say that, for rebellion, you have to pay many years in prison, for murder you have to pay many years, but nonetheless they trick the people and offer money. Or they do not offer money, they show a package and say, "well, you will collaborate. You will tell me who is the commander, what the commander does, who are the contacts, and in this package that we will give you, we have a house in Europe, you will have private security, we will pay you monthly."

She trailed off, rolling her eyes as if to say, "who would believe such nonsense?" And yet, according to her, many combatants *did* believe it. In fact, deserters' stories are one of the government's key weapons to discredit the FARC. By telling stories of forced contraception and abortion, jungle C-sections, human trafficking, and other serious human rights violations, the Colombian government has worked for decades to discredit the FARC's grievances and invalidate any claim the group has of being an egalitarian "army of the people" fighting for human rights. The more Mari talked about this, the more incensed she became:

At no point was anyone restrained ... like the media always says, that we came into the ranks to prostitute ourselves. This is not true! At least, a person who has all his senses in his head [would understand] that they give a rifle to me to fight the enemy, and the commander is going to grab me and is going to rape me, and I'm not going to use this rifle? *(Laughs)* I mean, I don't understand in what head of what person this makes sense ... Could it be that I am going to let them rape me, I am going to let them abuse me, if I am fighting for those changes [for women's rights] and if I can confront a soldier? I mean, this is where the question remains that people have to discuss: Is it possible that the women were raped *and* venerated in this manner there?

I did not challenge her on the trope that armed soldiers cannot be raped by their peers or superiors, though decades of military history prove this

[2] Roughly equivalent to US$58,000–87,000. This incredibly large sum may have been an exaggeration.

to be untrue. She was so earnest that it made me wonder. *Was* it possible? Could women have been raped *and* venerated in the FARC ranks? By that point, I had heard tear-filled stories of forced abortions, older commanders taking advantage of young girls, teenage boys molested by their mentors, life-threatening escapes, and more.

There were two clear frames here. First, that FARC women were loyal fighters, essential to the cause, feminist saviors who would enlighten poor and abused women. But the contrasting frame, the government's frame, maintained that FARC women were victims who were manipulated, tricked, and subjugated by male commanders. I had heard these stories of abuse first hand from both FARC loyalists and deserters, when they had little reason to lie to me about it. What, then, was the purpose of this and other framing contests, and how did these discursive battles affect ex-combatants and their transitions to civilian life? What did these extended framing contests mean for the quality and stability of the peace agreement?

The longer I stayed in Colombia, the more I saw these framing contests intersecting all around me, and the more I realized how much they might teach us about sustainable peace. Discursive battles were everywhere, in every single conversation. The demobilized FARC loyalists vehemently refused to be called "demobilized", because for them that word implied capitulation to the government. Ex-paramilitaries rejected the word "paramilitary" and instead called themselves "self-defense forces." Deserters rejected the label of "traitor" bestowed on them by loyalist FARC members, with many choosing instead to frame themselves as noble for having left the fight. FARC loyalists talked around the issue of drug trafficking, saying that the so-called "war on drugs" was an American sham. These loyalists said drugs were the scourge of Colombia, that the government was corrupt, and that they were the only ones who cared about "the people." The government, on the other hand, has long called guerrilla groups in Colombia "narco-terrorists," conflating them all as nothing but criminals. And in all of this, deserters claimed to be the "real victims," pointing to the government as the "real terrorist."

In fact, when I started writing this chapter, Colombia's president set off a heated discursive debate when he used the term "collective homicides" to refer to a string of massacres that had recently occurred across the country.[3] His critics derided the president for trivializing the marked

---

[3] Semana, "¿Cuál Es La Diferencia Entre Homicidios Colectivos y Masacres?" *Semana*, August 24, 2020, www.semana.com/nacion/articulo/cual-es-la-diferencia-entre-homicidios-colectivos-y-masacres/696762/.

increase in massacres,[4] arguing that the term "collective homicides" ignores that massacres in Colombia are a systematic criminal phenomenon and not random events.[5]

Rhetorical battles about how to frame the war itself run alongside many armed conflicts. What do these frames and labels achieve, and what is their long-term effect on Colombia's fragile peace? And how do these gendered and racialized framing contests between insurgent groups and the government affect combatants' perceptions of their alternatives and their transitions to civilian life?

EX-COMBATANT TRAJECTORIES

This book contains stories from ninety-nine individual ex-combatants (thirty-seven women and sixty-two men), 39 percent of whom deserted at least one nonstate armed group, though some fled from more than one. These ex-combatants come from two leftist guerrilla groups, the FARC and the National Liberation Army (ELN), and one rightist, state-supporting paramilitary group, the United Self-defense Forces of Colombia (AUC). The AUC officially demobilized in 2003–6, and the FARC demobilized in 2016 – though dissidents from both groups remain active. And, despite multiple rounds of peace talks over the last several years, the ELN was still active at the time of writing this book.

The book follows the stories of twelve of these combatants, using testimonies from the other eighty-seven, alongside fifteen interviews with government reintegration professionals, civilian experts, and military and police officers, to explore the ways in which frames are constructed, debated, and transformed in armed conflict. I chose these twelve for several reasons. First, I wanted to ensure representation from all three of the armed groups, from men and women, from deserters and loyalists, and from various ethnicities and ages. Second, I wanted to illustrate several key post-demobilization trajectories that I saw repeated in the full sample of combatants. Third, I maintained contact with several of these ex-combatants for years after the initial fieldwork, which allowed me to provide a fuller picture of their lives after demobilization.

---

[4] El Espectador, "Las Masacres Aumentaron Un 30% En Los Primeros Dos Años Del Gobierno Duque," *El Espectador*, August 7, 2020, www.elespectador.com/colombia2020/ pais/la-guerra-en-los-dos-primeros-anos-del-gobierno-duque/.

[5] Semana, "¿Cuál Es La Diferencia Entre Homicidios Colectivos y Masacres?"

The first ex-combatant, Mari, has already been partially introduced. Mari was in her early forties when I met her; she joined the FARC when she was fourteen after years of being constantly displaced by violence. She had spent twenty-seven years in the group before the peace agreement. Mari is a staunch loyalist, spent several years in a Colombian prison, and was a clear leader in the camp. From the moment I met her, it was clear that Mari is a person who gets things done and waits for no man. She was grateful for her militant experience and told me that she never once considered leaving the FARC, not even as a teenager.

The second ex-combatant I focus on, also from the FARC, had a very different story. Dayana is an Indigenous woman in her thirties who also joined the FARC at fourteen, but to escape an abusive family. Articulate, kind, and immediately likable, Dayana slowly opened up and told me that she faced the same abuse inside the FARC that she had tried to escape in her own family. After seven years in the ranks, she fled, pregnant and alone, only to reluctantly return to a FARC reincorporation camp years later with her two children in order to claim reintegration benefits.

Pablo, on the other hand, vehemently denied everything that Dayana and other women like her have said. A proud member of the FARC's governing Secretariat, Pablo insisted that the women who told those stories were nothing but spies and paid informants. Despite the fact that there had never been a single woman in the Secretariat, Pablo assured me that the group was truly egalitarian, while pointing to women's lack of "capacity" as the reason that they were not commanders.

Three more FARC ex-combatants round out this group: Mafe, Andrés, and Lina. Mafe never really "joined" the FARC, she says. She was essentially consumed by the organizational structure when the group took over their community. Educated and eloquent, Mafe saw the FARC as the only group doing anything to help her community, and at age twenty she became passionately involved in their work as a political ideologue, educating other communities about the FARC's mission and goals. Ten years later, demobilized but still determined to fight for equality, Mafe was organizing women's meetings at the FARC camp when I met her, trying to educate local women about equality and the need for women's representation in politics.

Andrés, however, was essentially the direct opposite. Full of bravado and a big talker, he cared little for FARC ideology and loved to tell me about all the drug deals he did for the group. He told me that before he demobilized, his mother thought he was dead because the military showed up one day with an unrecognizable body, saying that it was her son. They even held a funeral. (This caused significant problems when he tried to demobilize and the military told him that he was already dead.) Once, when I met up with Andrés in a conflict-affected region, he reassured me with a grin: "Don't worry about being robbed here. The *narcos* keep all that under control." Andrés loved his militia job so much that he refused to demobilize when the FARC signed the peace accord, taking his chances with the dissidents. When that proved too dangerous for his young family, he sought refuge in a government safe house. Now labeled a traitor by both sides – the group he was loyal to for over a decade *and* the dissidents he abandoned – he was constantly on the move, fearing for his life.

Lina was also constantly in hiding. Having deserted the FARC with her militia commander husband over a decade ago, the couple hid their ex-combatant past and registered for benefits with the Colombian Victims' Unit. Eventually discovered, they were forced into the disarmament, demobilization, and reintegration (DDR) program run by the government. This program has its fair share of informants on all sides, and Lina and her husband were soon on the run after receiving death threats from the group they abandoned long ago.

In addition to these ex-combatants from the FARC, the book follows three former members of the ELN: Junior, Michael, and Namona. Junior joined the ELN when he was only eleven, because his entire family was already in the group and, as the son of a top commander, opposition forces were threatening to kill him. He was still a true believer when we met, but after fourteen years in the ranks, he made a fatal error and was forced to run for his life. He had never wanted to leave the group, and he clearly did not want to be in the military safe house either. Michael, however, was a different story: forcibly recruited by the ELN when he was seventeen, Michael was charming, bright, and immensely loveable. He reminded me of my undergraduate students and made me wonder what his life could have been like if he had been born somewhere else. Michael spent three years in the group before he escaped, but then had no idea what to do next. He certainly could not go home, where the group was waiting to kill him, but where could he go, with no money, no legitimate work experience, and no references?

Namona is a bit of an outlier in that she joined the ELN in her late thirties because she needed a job, and to this day she regrets that decision. She says she spent most of her time as a cook for the group but experienced a severe trauma at the hands of her comrades, which precipitated her escape. When I met her again nearly a year later, she and her husband were still on the run, with a reward for their capture (or death) on their heads.

Finally, the book follows three ex-paramilitary members who have been demobilized since 2005–6: Tobias, an intimidating former AUC commander with a crushing handshake, who now writes poetry and makes children's toys; Hugo, a dizzying storyteller who joined the AUC as a young drug-addicted *sicario* ("assassin") and credits the organization for his sobriety; and Nell, a fiercely independent woman who joined the AUC as a single mother of three, when guerrillas destroyed her business and she desperately needed work and protection. While Tobias and Hugo expressed pride in their roles fighting back against the guerrillas, Nell insisted several times that she was never involved in any violence.

Through these twelve stories, this book examines what happens to ex-combatants leading up to their decisions to disengage (or not) from non-state armed groups, what happens afterward, and how ex-combatants interpret and engage with the frames constructed around them and about them. How do deserters manage the constant fear of being caught, the demands of the government to share intelligence, and the stigmatization that prevents them from obtaining jobs and proper housing? How do loyalists manage the post-demobilization struggle of identities as their collective breaks down – one part of them a fighter for justice, and the other part a struggling citizen, trying to put food on the table and navigate the unknowns of civilian life? And how do ex-paramilitaries, demobilized for nearly fifteen years and still facing stigma and rumors, shed these violent identities when the temptation of fast and easy money is all around them?

DESERTION DECISIONS AND REINTEGRATION PATHWAYS

I originally went into the field interested in the puzzle of desertion, but it quickly became clear that how and why insurgent organizations, governments, and individual combatants were framing stories of desertion was critical to understanding the complexity of these individual decisions to fight or flee and the experiences that came afterward. Why rebel groups thrive or disintegrate has long been a puzzle in political science, including questions of why some combatants desert their groups while others stay – but the question of how these trajectories affect reintegration experiences is far less explored. The civil war and insurgency literature has primarily addressed rebel group cohesion at the organizational level, examining how and why different types of groups retain recruits – or not.[6] Individual-level

---

[6] Dora L Costa and Matthew E Kahn, *Heroes and Cowards: The Social Face of War* (Princeton: Princeton University Press, 2010); Francisco Gutiérrez Sanín, "The FARC's Militaristic Blueprint," *Small Wars & Insurgencies* 29, no. 4 (2018): 629–53; Francisco

analysis is more prevalent in terrorism and psychology literature, which offer multiple explanations for desertion, including government pressure, in-group violence, disillusionment in the group's cause, networks, and trauma.[7] This latter body of literature crosses many disciplines and at times is disjointed or often contradictory. Nonetheless, five key variables emerge: types of commitment, ideology, identity, networks, and costs/benefits of membership. Types of commitment to the group – such as economic, personal, or ideological commitment – are significant in weighing one's options to fight or flee, as are ethnic and religious identities, which can hold people firmly inside a group.[8] Indeed, multiple studies conclude

Gutiérrez Sanín and Elisabeth Jean Wood, "Ideology in Civil War: Instrumental Adoption and Beyond," *Journal of Peace Research* 51, no. 2 (2014): 213–26; Stathis N Kalyvas, "Ethnic Defection in Civil War," *Comparative Political Studies* 41, no. 8 (2008): 1043–68; Kevin Koehler, Dorothy Ohl, and Holger Albrecht, "Disaffection to Desertion: How Networks Facilitate Military Insubordination in Civil Conflict," *Comparative Politics* 48, no. 4 (2016): 439–57; Theodore McLauchlin and Wendy Pearlman, "Out-Group Conflict, In-Group Unity? Exploring the Effect of Repression on Intramovement Cooperation," *The Journal of Conflict Resolution* 56, no. 1 (2012): 41–66; Theodore McLauchlin, "Desertion and Collective Action in Civil Wars," *International Studies Quarterly* 59, no. 4 (2015): 669–79; Paul Staniland, "Between a Rock and a Hard Place," *Journal of Conflict Resolution* 56, no. 1 (2012): 16–40.

7 Mary Beth Altier, John Horgan, and Christian Thoroughgood, "In Their Own Words? Methodological Considerations in the Analysis of Terrorist Autobiographies," *Journal of Strategic Security* 5, no. 4 (2012): 85–98; Mary Beth Altier, Christian N Thoroughgood, and John G Horgan, "Turning away from Terrorism: Lessons from Psychology, Sociology, and Criminology," *Journal of Peace Research* 51, no. 5 (2014): 647–61; Mary Beth Altier et al., "Why They Leave: An Analysis of Terrorist Disengagement Events from Eighty-Seven Autobiographical Accounts," *Security Studies* 26, no. 2 (2017): 305–32; Julie Chernov Hwang, *Why Terrorists Quit: The Disengagement of Indonesian Jihadists* (Ithaca, NY and London: Cornell University Press, 2018); Neil Ferguson, Mark Burgess, and Ian Hollywood, "Leaving Violence behind: Disengaging from Politically Motivated Violence in Northern Ireland," *Political Psychology* 36, no. 2 (April 2015): 199–214; M Jacobson, "Terrorist Dropouts: Learning from Those Who Have Left," Washington Institute, 2010, www.washingtoninstitute.org/uploads/Documents/pubs/PolicyFocus101.pdf; John Horgan, *Walking away from Terrorism: Accounts of Disengagement from Radical and Extremist Movements* (Abingdon and New York: Routledge, 2009); Ben Oppenheim et al., "True Believers, Deserters, and Traitors: Who Leaves Insurgent Groups and Why," *Journal of Conflict Resolution* 59, no. 5 (2015): 794–823.

8 Altier, Thoroughgood, and Horgan, "Turning away from Terrorism"; Tore Bjørgo, "Processes of Disengagement from Violent Groups of the Extreme Right," in *Leaving Terrorism behind: Individual and Collective Disengagement*, ed. Tore Bjørgo and John Horgan (New York: Routledge, 2009); Oppenheim et al., "True Believers, Deserters, and Traitors"; Caryl Rusbult, Christopher Agnew, and Ximena Arriaga, "The Investment Model of Commitment Processes," in *Handbook of Theories of Social Psychology*, ed. Paul Van Lange, Arie Kruglanski Higgins, and E Tory (London: Sage Publications, 2012); Jacquelien van Stekelenburg and Bert Klandermans, "The Social Psychology of Protest," *Current Sociology* 61, nos. 5–6 (2013): 886–905; Bryan F

that ideology is especially significant in explaining variations in patterns of violence, troop retention, and operational choices.[9]

In addition, networks both inside and outside the group can influence decisions to leave or stay: strong social bonds with law-abiding people can draw people out, but the reverse is also true when a person's strongest bonds are inside the group. Trauma or high costs of membership might motivate people to leave, but these factors can also make them too scared to leave.[10] The direction and causal mechanisms of many of these variables remain unclear and unsatisfactory, as does the degree of overlap and/or compound effects – with the role of gender(ed/ing) norms in desertion decisions largely unexplored.

GENDER AND ARMED CONFLICT

Feminist and critical security scholars have added an important aspect to research on armed conflict by highlighting that armed group ideologies are highly gendered, with state and nonstate armed groups frequently emphasizing militarized masculinities that reward heterosexual aggression and "toughness," while using feminization of the enemy and

Bubolz and Pete Simi, "Disillusionment and Change: A Cognitive-Emotional Theory of Gang Exit," *Deviant Behavior* 36, no. 4 (2015): 330–45; Helen Rose Fuchs Ebaugh, *Becoming an Ex: The Process of Role Exit* (Chicago: University of Chicago Press, 1988); A Rapoport, *The Origins of Violence: Approaches to the Study of Conflict* (London: Transaction Publishers, 1994); Anne Speckhard, "The Emergence of Female Suicide Terrorists," *Studies in Conflict & Terrorism* 31, no. 11 (2008): 995–1051; Stephen Vertigans, *The Sociology of Terrorism: People, Places and Processes* (London and New York: Routledge, 2011).

[9] Mia Bloom, *Bombshell: The Many Faces of Women Terrorists* (Toronto: Viking Canada, 2011); Dara Kay Cohen, *Rape during Civil War* (Ithaca, NY: Cornell University Press, 2016); Francisco Gutiérrez Sanín and Antonio Giustozzi, "Networks and Armies: Structuring Rebellion in Colombia and Afghanistan," *Studies in Conflict & Terrorism* 33, no. 9 (2010): 836–53; Gutiérrez Sanín and Wood, "Ideology in Civil War"; Thomas Hegghammer, "Should I Stay or Should I Go? Explaining Variation in Western Jihadists' Choice between Domestic and Foreign Fighting," *American Political Science Review* 107, no. 1 (2013): 1–15.

[10] Altier, Thoroughgood, and Horgan, "Turning away from Terrorism"; Bjørgo, "Processes of Disengagement"; Frank Bovenkerk, "On Leaving Criminal Organizations," *Crime, Law and Social Change* 55, no. 4 (2011): 261–76; Chernov Hwang, *Why Terrorists Quit*; Froukje Demant et al., *Decline and Disengagement: An Analysis of Processes of Deradicalisation* (Amsterdam: IMES, 2008); Ferguson, Burgess, and Hollywood, "Leaving Violence Behind"; Koehler, Ohl, and Albrecht, "Disaffection to Desertion"; McLauchlin, "Desertion and Collective Action in Civil Wars"; Dorothy Ohl, "The Soldier's Dilemma: Military Responses to Uprisings in Jordan, Iraq, Bahrain, and Syria," PhD dissertation, George Washington University, 2016.

gender-based violence for troop cohesion.[11] War is, after all, built on gendered narratives that are dependent on particular ideals of masculine and feminine,[12] and it is well established that patriarchal gender norms are exacerbated by armed conflict.[13] Theories of war and rebellion are thus incomplete without a consideration of the gender(ed/ing) norms that structure militaristic groups and the nature of war itself.

Gender norms are always socially constructed, frequently contested, and affect the distribution of power in society – especially those affected by armed conflict. Militarism relies on masculinity to function, and this masculinity depends on the subjugation of the feminine.[14] Literature on women in war also shows that framing women combatants as (bad) mothers, monsters, victims, or "whores" strongly affects how these women are treated both during conflict and afterward, especially when they are labeled as irrational or "crazy" for engaging in violence.[15] Indeed, as Gowrinathan notes, "[t]o consider the decision to choose violence as a momentary lapse of rationality is to dismiss the expansive reservoirs of trauma that shape the makeup of the women who do."[16] Feminist scholars identify many

---

[11] Raewyn Connell and James Messerschmidt, "Hegemonic Masculinity: Rethinking the Concept," *Gender & Society* 19, no. 6 (2005): 829–59; Cohen, *Rape during Civil War*; Claire Duncanson, "Forces for Good? Narratives of Military Masculinity in Peacekeeping Operations," *International Feminist Journal of Politics* 11, no. 1 (2009): 63–80; Cynthia H Enloe, *Maneuvers: The International Politics of Militarizing Women's Lives* (Berkeley: University of California Press, 2000); Joshua S Goldstein, *War and Gender: How Gender Shapes the War System and Vice Versa* (Cambridge: Cambridge University Press, 2001).

[12] Carol Cohn, "Women and Wars: Toward a Conceptual Framework," in *Women and Wars*, ed. Carol Cohn (Cambridge: Polity Press, 2013).

[13] Tsjeard Bouta, Ian Bannon, and Georg Frerks, *Gender, Conflict, and Development* (Washington, DC: World Bank, 2005); Cohn, "Women and Wars"; Sandra Cheldelin and Maneshka Eliatamby, *Women Waging War and Peace: International Perspectives of Women's Roles in Conflict and Post-conflict Reconstruction* (New York: Continuum, 2011); Caron E Gentry and Laura Sjoberg, *Beyond Mothers, Monsters, Whores: Thinking about Women's Violence in Global Politics* (London: Zed Books, 2015); Goldstein, *War and Gender*.

[14] Goldstein, *War and Gender*.

[15] Carol Cohn (ed.), *Women and Wars* (Cambridge: Polity Press, 2013); Gentry and Sjoberg, *Beyond Mothers, Monsters, Whores*; Luz María Londoño and Yoana Fernanda Nieto, *Mujeres No Contadas: Procesos de Desmovilización y Retorno a La Vida Civil de Mujeres Excombatientes En Colombia, 1990–2003* (Bogota: La Carreta Editores, 2006); Yoana Fernanda Nieto-Valdivieso, "The Joy of the Militancy: Happiness and the Pursuit of Revolutionary Struggle," *Journal of Gender Studies* 26, no. 1 (2017): 78–90; Laura Sjoberg and Caron E Gentry, *Mothers, Monsters, Whores: Women's Violence in Global Politics* (New York and London: Zed Books, 2007); Laura Sjoberg and Caron E Gentry, *Women, Gender, and Terrorism* (Athens, GA: University of Georgia Press, 2011); Rachel Schmidt, "Duped: Examining Gender Stereotypes in Disengagement and Deradicalization Practices," *Studies in Conflict & Terrorism*, 2020, https://doi.org/10.1080/1057610X.2020.1711586.

[16] Gowrinathan, *Radicalizing Her*, 55.

such stereotypes of women in war[17] and have discussed how harmful gender norms adversely affect both men's and women's post-conflict experiences.[18] On the other hand, Carpenter argues that some feminist work
overemphasizes women as war's main victims and has failed to consider
the role of masculinity and the targeting of men and boys in war.[19] It is
clear that to understand conflict, we must consider gender from a range of
perspectives, examining how gender(ed/ing) norms arrange, control, and
restrict political and personal choices both during and after war.[20]

FRAMING AND SOCIAL MOVEMENTS

It was not until coding my transcripts (see the next section on methods
and data collection) based on the five key variables influencing desertion decisions noted earlier (i.e., types of commitment, ideology, identity,

[17] Kim Cragin and Sara A Daly, *Women as Terrorists: Mothers, Recruiters, and Martyrs*
(Santa Barbara, CA: Praeger Security International/ABC-CLIO, 2009); Luisa Maria
Dietrich, "Looking beyond Violent Militarized Masculinities: Guerrilla Gender Regimes
in Latin America," *International Feminist Journal of Politics* 14, no. 4 (2012): 489–507;
Anthony King, "The Female Combat Soldier," *European Journal of International Relations* 22, no. 1 (2015): 122–43; Brigitte L Nacos, "The Portrayal of Female Terrorists
in the Media: Similar Framing Patterns in the News Coverage of Women in Politics and
in Terrorism," *Studies in Conflict and Terrorism* 28, no. 5 (2005): 435–51; Gentry and
Sjoberg, *Beyond Mothers, Monsters, Whores*.
[18] Myriam Denov, "Girl Soldiers and Human Rights: Lessons from Angola, Mozambique,
Sierra Leone and Northern Uganda," *The International Journal of Human Rights* 12, no. 5
(2008): 813–36; Susan McKay and Dyan E Mazurana, *Where Are the Girls? Girls in Fighting Forces in Northern Uganda, Sierra Leone and Mozambique: Their Lives during and after
War* (Montréal: Rights & Democracy, 2004); Mendez, "Militarized Gender Performativity:
Women and Demobilization in Colombia's FARC and AUC," PhD dissertation, Queen's
University, 2012; Kathleen M Jennings, "The Political Economy of DDR in Liberia: A Gendered Critique," *Conflict, Security & Development* 9, no. 4 (2009): 475–94; Kimberly Theidon, "Reconstructing Masculinities: The Disarmament, Demobilization, and Reintegration
of Former Combatants in Colombia," *Human Rights Quarterly* 31, no. 1 (2009): 1–34.
[19] R Charli Carpenter, "Gender Theory in World Politics: Contributions of a Nonfeminist
Standpoint?" *International Studies Review* 4, no. 3 (2002): 153–65; R Charli Carpenter,
"'Women, Children and Other Vulnerable Groups': Gender, Strategic Frames and the
Protection of Civilians as a Transnational Issue," *International Studies Quarterly* 49, no.
2 (2005): 295–334.
[20] Miranda Alison, *Women and Political Violence: Female Combatants in Ethno-National
Conflict* (New York and London: Routledge, 2009); Cheldelin and Eliatamby, *Women
Waging War and Peace*; Cragin and Daly, *Women as Terrorists*; Swechchha Dahal, "Challenging the Boundaries: The Narratives of the Female Ex-combatants in Nepal," in *Female
Combatants in Conflict and Peace: Challenging Gender in Violence and Post-conflict Reintegration*, ed. Seema Shekawat (Basingstoke: Palgrave Macmillan, 2015); Reed M Wood
and Jakana L Thomas, "Women on the Frontline: Rebel Group Ideology and Women's
Participation in Violent Rebellion," *Journal of Peace Research* 54, no. 1 (2017): 31–46.

networks, and costs/benefits of membership) that patterns of discursive battles – and the impact these contests were having on individual people and their disengagement and reintegration trajectories – became clear. That is, although the puzzle of desertion was my initial academic pursuit, what emerged organically from the field was something much more nuanced and, to me at least, far more interesting.

Frames appear critical to mobilizing combatants and to our understanding of armed conflict. Yet, while frame analysis is prolific in the study of social movements, it has been far less influential in the disengagement literature.[21] In very broad strokes, the literature on desertion and disengagement treats the puzzle of desertion either as an individual problem (e.g., what makes certain people fight or flee?) or as a collective action problem (e.g., what types of armed groups face higher desertion rates?). My aim here is to connect these two aspects of rebel group cohesion and examine how these choices affect what comes next for ex-combatants.

Framing theory focuses on how organizations and their members understand, organize, and convey information about hierarchies of identity and the costs/benefits of group membership.[22] Utilizing the concept of frames focuses the analysis on how people and groups organize and interpret knowledge.[23] That is, frames are social objects that are both inside people's minds and embedded in social routines, discourses, practices, and institutions; they can involve ideologies, assumptions, paradigms, and shared definitions.[24] Frames can be communicated with slogans, posters, songs, stories, advertisements, articles, and other mediums of communication.

Who is communicating the frame, and to what audience, are critical elements to understanding both the goal of the frame and the true impact of

---

[21] For example, Chernov Hwang, *Why Terrorists Quit*; Jason Lyall, *Divided Armies: Inequality and Battlefield Performance in Modern War* (Princeton, NJ: Princeton University Press, 2020); Theodore McLauchlin, *Desertion: Trust and Mistrust in Civil Wars* (Ithaca, NY: Cornell University Press, 2020); Vera Mironova, *From Freedom Fighters to Jihadists: Human Resources of Non State Armed Groups, Causes and Consequences of Terrorism* (New York: Oxford University Press, 2019).

[22] Erving Goffman, *Frame Analysis: An Essay on the Organization of Experience* (Cambridge, MA: Harvard University Press, 1974); Robert D Benford and David A Snow, "Framing Processes and Social Movements: An Overview and Assessment," *Annual Review of Sociology* 26, no. 1 (2000): 611–39.

[23] Séverine Autesserre, "Hobbes and the Congo: Frames, Local Violence, and International Intervention," *International Organization* 63, no. 2 (2009): 249–80; Benford and Snow, "Framing Processes and Social Movements"; Goffman, *Frame Analysis*.

[24] Autesserre, "Hobbes and the Congo"; Robert Jervis, "Understanding Beliefs," *Political Psychology* 27, no. 5 (2006): 641–63; Karl E Weick, *Sensemaking in Organizations* (Thousand Oaks, CA: Sage, 1995).

framing efforts. The social movement literature identifies four key characteristics to frames: (1) flexibility and rigidity (i.e., frames vary in elasticity and
the number of themes/ideas they incorporate); (2) inclusivity and exclusivity
(i.e., what is the inclusion criteria for who is part of the frame); (3) variation
in interpretive scope and influence (i.e., frames can be very broad, such as a
"master frame," or the scope can be quite narrow); and (4) resonance (i.e.,
the consistency and credibility of the frame).[25] This last factor has received
the least amount of empirical research, especially in the study of armed
movements, and is a core analytical component of this book.

   The resonance of a frame depends on its credibility and its salience.[26]
Overall credibility comes from three sources: frame consistency, empirical credibility (i.e., the evidence-base for the frame), and the credibility of
the frame-makers themselves. Salience relies on how essential the beliefs,
values, and ideas of the frame are to the target population.[27] Salience also
relies on whether the frame resonates with the daily lives of the population, and, finally, on whether the frame resonates with cultural narratives
or "myths."[28] This resonance is critical to the identity formation that is a
key feature of many constructed frames.

   In political science, scholars have used frame analysis to investigate
and explain development and humanitarian interventions, refugee policy, peacekeeping action, and human rights strategies, among others.[29]
Frames can preexist a movement (such as the historic discrimination of
a marginalized group) or they can emerge from practice (such as specific
group norms, including gender norms, rules, and behavioral expectations).[30] Perhaps most critical, the literature on frames illustrates that

[25] Benford and Snow, "Framing Processes and Social Movements."
[26] Benford and Snow, "Framing Processes and Social Movements."
[27] David A Snow and Robert D Benford, "Ideology, Frame Resonance, and Participant
    Mobilization," *International Social Movement Research* 1 (1988): 197–217.
[28] Benford and Snow, "Framing Processes and Social Movements"; Alena Heitlinger,
    "Framing Feminism in Post-Communist Czech Republic," *Communist and Post-
    Communist Studies* 29, no. 1 (1996): 77–93; Alvin Ward Gouldner, *The Coming Crisis
    of Western Sociology* (New York: Basic Books, 1970).
[29] Autesserre, "Hobbes and the Congo"; Michael Barnett et al., "Peacebuilding: What Is in
    a Name?" *Global Governance* 13, no. 1 (2007): 35–58; Michael N Barnett and Martha
    Finnemore, *Rules for the World: International Organizations in Global Politics* (Ithaca,
    NY: Cornell University Press, 2004); Margaret E Keck and Kathryn Sikkink, *Activists
    beyond Borders: Advocacy Networks in International Politics* (Ithaca, NY: Cornell Uni-
    versity Press, 1998); Ibrahim Seaga Shaw, "Historical Frames and the Politics of Human-
    itarian Intervention: From Ethiopia, Somalia to Rwanda," *Globalisation, Societies and
    Education* 5, no. 3 (2007): 351–71.
[30] Autesserre, "Hobbes and the Congo."

problems have to be socially constructed; that is, frames shape whether or not people view something as a problem, and they also determine what events are noticed and how they are interpreted.[31] To illustrate, whether gender-based violence is considered an urgent social problem needing political intervention depends on how it is framed (i.e., as a "private" issue or a "public" problem), and the credibility of those framing it. Power also matters, especially in emerging frames – the influence of the frame-makers will affect how robust and convincing the frame becomes. For example, framing women in armed groups as camp followers, "bush wives," brainwashed victims, or combatants with agency affects what disengagement options are available to them and whether political actors consider them to be important in peace negotiations. Similarly, government and media framing of a rebel group as an insurgency, a criminal organization, or a terrorist faction affects the policy options available to a government and to the international community.

Applying framing theory to civil war studies potentially provides the "missing link" between understanding macro-level context factors and individual choices to participate in rebellion.[32] In intrastate conflicts worldwide, governments and insurgent groups invest considerable effort in discursive battles to win support[33] and authoritarian governments use framing to legitimize repression.[34] Framing theory has the potential to improve our understanding of individual choices to leave rebellion and the trajectories that follow this choice. For example, Shesterinina's case study of the Georgian–Abkhaz war shows how the collective framing of threats in civil war affects individual decisions to fight or flee.[35] A credible and highly resonant frame might retain recruits even in the face of significant cognitive dissonance, but a weak frame, especially if the frame-makers lose credibility, could threaten an entire movement.

[31] Barnett and Finnemore, *Rules for the World*; Weick, *Sensemaking in Organizations*.
[32] Anne Theobald, "Successful or Failed Rebellion? The Casamance Conflict from a Framing Perspective," *Civil Wars* 17, no. 2 (2015): 181–200, 184.
[33] Laura A Bray, Thomas E Shriver, and Alison E Adams, "Framing Authoritarian Legitimacy: Elite Cohesion in the Aftermath of Popular Rebellion," *Social Movement Studies* 18, no. 6 (2019): 682–701; David Drissel, "Reframing the Taliban Insurgency in Afghanistan: New Communication and Mobilization Strategies for the Twitter Generation," *Behavioral Sciences of Terrorism and Political Aggression* 7, no. 2 (2015): 97–128; Theobald, "Successful or Failed Rebellion?"
[34] Mirjam Edel and Maria Josua, "How Authoritarian Rulers Seek to Legitimize Repression: Framing Mass Killings in Egypt and Uzbekistan," *Democratization* 25, no. 5 (2018): 882–900.
[35] "Collective Threat Framing and Mobilization in Civil War," *The American Political Science Review* 110, no. 3 (2016): 411–27.

Framing is thus an active and contentious process, and identity construction is a critical factor in creating resonant frames that mobilize collective action.[36] Framing, therefore, not only links individuals with their groups ideologically, but it also creates and embellishes identities ranging from collaborative to conflictual.[37] In militant structures in particular, these identities are built along both ideological and gendered lines. In this book, I combine framing theory with gender-based analysis to assess the impact of gender norms and gender(ed/ing) frames on individual combatants' demobilization decisions and reintegration trajectories. Building on the work of feminist and critical security scholars, I use gender-based analysis to examine how socially constructed and contested gender(ed/ing) norms interact with other factors – such as age, race, and social class – and how these contested interactions affect and organize personal, political, and intellectual life.[38] Indeed, gender is often employed as a strategic frame but is not always recognized as such. And, like other frames, gender is an evolving and contested process.

Using data from 114 in-depth interviews and months of participant observation across Colombia, I contend that framing contests and related identity constructions are essential in insurgencies and civil war, and that the outcome of these contests influences individual commitment to an armed group and the experiences of ex-combatants after demobilization. Second, I argue that how these competing frames operationalize gender norms – including narratives of brotherhood and masculinity, of women as victims, and of gender equality – influence not only troop cohesion but also the way combatants perceive their investments and possible alternatives, and the way they experience post-demobilization life.

METHODS AND DATA COLLECTION

For many people who have never been to Colombia, the two main things they associate with the country are violence and drugs – and Colombians are acutely aware of this. Many of my hosts went out of their way to

---

[36] Autesserre, "Hobbes and the Congo"; Benford and Snow, "Framing Processes and Social Movements"; Scott Hunt and Robert D. Benford, "Identity Talk in the Peace and Justice Movement," *Journal of Contemporary Ethnography* 22, no. 4 (1994): 488–517; Snow and Benford, "Ideology, Frame Resonance, and Participant Mobilization."

[37] Hunt and Benford, "Identity Talk in the Peace and Justice Movement."

[38] Cohn, "Women and Wars"; Kimberlé Crenshaw, "Demarginalizing the Intersection of Race and Sex: A Black Feminist Critique of Antidiscrimination Doctrine, Feminist Theory and Antiracist Politics," *University of Chicago Legal Forum* 1 (1989); Luisa Maria

show me different sides of their beautiful country, and through them I swam in Amazonian rivers, walked on riverbanks among swarms of butterflies, dined in elegant restaurants and ate *arepas* from street carts, drank what my Colombian friends laughingly called "Colombian wine" (i.e., beer), played soccer with children, and had fascinating conversations about politics, families, travel, fashion, war, and everything in between. Perhaps unsurprisingly, many of my respondents became the most animated when we stopped talking about war and started talking about the future, or Canada, or nature, or any number of things that were not related to violence or drugs.

As the majority of ex-combatant studies in Colombia have historically taken place in urban centers (for many reasons, including security and high levels of ex-combatants concentrated in those areas), I wanted to speak to a larger cross section of the ex-combatant population. At the time of my fieldwork, less than two years after the peace agreement, researchers and media were swarming the country and I wanted to avoid speaking to the same groups of ex-combatants that everyone seemed to be speaking to. To avoid this research fatigue, I needed to travel the country and experience more of Colombia than I had before.

I was unexpectedly pushed further in that direction than I had planned when my year-long effort to collaborate with Colombia's reintegration agency, now known as the Agency for Reincorporation and Normalization (ARN), dissolved into nothing. While this slamming of what I saw as an essential door first seemed like a crisis, being forced to consider alternative fieldwork options meant that I went to locations where few researchers had been and worked with local fixers and research assistants, many of whom were ex-combatants themselves and were not interested in shaping my findings to fit the government narrative. As a result, the majority of my respondents had never been interviewed by a researcher before, domestic or foreign.

When I got off the plane the first time I went to Putumayo, a rural department rich in natural resources and known for its high coca production and widespread armed violence, I checked my phone to see a WhatsApp message from my research assistant, himself an ex-combatant: "Running late. Do *not* leave the airport until I get there. Be there soon." This particular

Dietrich, "La Compañera Guerrilla as Construction of Politicised Femininity: A Comparative Study of Gender Arrangements in Latin American Insurgencies and New Paths for Gender Responsive Demobilisation of Combatants," PhD dissertation, University of Vienna, 2017; Enloe, *Maneuvers*.

research assistant was born and raised in Putumayo and was well versed in the clashes between armed groups there – I knew better than to question his judgment. I also knew that "soon" can mean anything in Colombia.

I waited in that tiny airport for nearly three hours.

When my assistant finally did show up, I am sure the entire town already knew I was there. I had certainly raised the curiosity of airport security guards and the woman serving coffee at the airport kiosk. The mini-van taxi pulled up across the street and my assistant waved me into it, with a look of deep concern. Once inside, he said to me: "Okay, if anyone asks, you're researching Indigenous plants, understand?" I opened my mouth to protest. First, we obviously should have discussed any type of "cover" long before I landed so I had time think about what to say if anyone asked. And second, did I even need a cover? I had no intention of deceiving anyone about my research, though I was of course careful about how much I said, and to whom. Third, this supposed cover was only one layer deep – I knew nothing about Indigenous plants in Putumayo (or anywhere else, for that matter). The story would break down if someone asked even one follow-up question. But my assistant stopped me before I could get a word out: "Raquel, this is *Putumayo*." He emphasized the word slowly to make sure I understood. The driver smirked at me in the rearview mirror, nodding. "We don't know who anyone is around here. If the wrong people think you're working on the peace process or that you are human rights defender, pfffft!" He drew a finger across his throat. (He was always quite dramatic, and I think he liked to scare me.) "We have to pick something that isn't political." He gave me a wink and a grin as we rumbled off. "Like plants!"

I chose Colombia as an ideal case in which to generate and explore theories around desertion decisions and resulting reintegration trajectories, as tens of thousands of men and women have disengaged from various nonstate armed groups or demobilized collectively during Colombia's long history of conflict. As a result, the ability to compare men and women's disengagement processes, and to compare differences between deserters and nondeserters, were both highly feasible in the Colombian case. While case studies within a single country can be limited in terms of generalizability, the range of armed actors in Colombia and the varied demobilization programs, as well as the high number of women combatants, offer rich narratives from which to generate theories that can then, ideally, be tested in other cases.

I had also been to Colombia before: I conducted my master's degree fieldwork there in 2006. At that time, I was working in Soacha, a low-income neighborhood with high levels of displaced families just south of Bogotá. Though few knew it yet, at that time Soacha was already the epicenter of the so-called "false positives" scandal, where the military had been executing vulnerable teenage boys and young men, and dressing them up in guerrilla fatigues post-mortem to increase the appearance of combat body counts.[39] This story did not hit the Colombian media until 2008, but I distinctly remember mothers protesting in the town square two years prior, holding pictures of their missing sons. I remember a man who worked for a nonprofit organization showing me a list of over 400 names that they had collected, lamenting that they did not know who they could trust with that information.

That was my first experience in Colombia, and my first direct experience with the country's politics of framing – though I did not see it that way at the time. When the story hit the media years later, the government repeatedly called these state-sanctioned murders "false positives" until that phrase stuck in the collective consciousness: *falsos positivos*. But this term, like "collective homicides," conveniently erased the systematic violence of those murders and the widespread government corruption involved to cover them up.

Colombia had wedged its way under my skin.

When I returned to academia to complete my PhD, the signing of the peace agreement in 2016 presented a unique opportunity to go back. As noted earlier, an inability to study loyalist fighters in comparison to deserters has long been a limiting factor in studies on desertion from armed groups. In Colombia, once the FARC disarmed, it became possible to study both groups of combatants and to look at the differences in their reintegration trajectories.

This project uses in-depth interviews with men and women ex-combatants from three different armed groups, including deserters and loyalists. As this is a vulnerable, hard-to-reach population (especially in the case of deserters, who often wish to remain hidden), in-depth, face-to-face interviews allowed for the investigation of important nuances that are easily missed in large-scale survey interviews with multiple researchers. In addition, quantitative analysis on desertion and disengagement has often obscured the interaction of key variables by only coding one reason for exit, when the reality of leaving violent groups is far more complex and

---

[39] Omar Rojas Bolaños and Fabian Leonardo Benavides, *Ejecuciones Extrajudiciales En Colombia, 2002–2010: Obedencia Ciega En Campos de Batalla Ficticios* (Bogotá: Universidad Santo Tomás, 2017); Semana, "Las Cuentas de Los Falsos Positivos," *Semana*, January 29, 2009, www.semana.com/nacion/justicia/articulo/las-cuentas-falsos-positivos/99556-3.

usually involves a process of several interacting factors.[40] While staying in the FARC reintegration camps and visiting the government safe houses, I also recorded detailed observations of behavior, meetings, and activities in my field notes. Notably, I would not have collected nearly as much nuanced information if I had needed an interpreter; some of the best stories I heard happened in informal situations, over meals or drinks, in taxis, on motorcycles, or spoken in confidence while walking around the camps. In this way, I also learned a long list of guerrilla slang during my fieldwork, which helped immensely when I was later analyzing interview transcripts.

For the interviews, participants were located primarily through referral chain ("snowball") sampling. The first two points of contact with ex-combatants for two distinct snowballs were obtained from (1) a cold contact to an ex-FARC commander located online; and (2) a contact at the Ministry of Defense who facilitated permission to enter the safe houses for individually demobilized ex-combatants. For certain translation issues from transcripts (e.g., the guerrillas have a specific vocabulary and expressions that sometimes even my Colombian transcribers did not understand), I consulted with two ex-combatants with whom I remained in contact, to ensure accuracy in translation.[41]

Interview Settings

Studies on civil war have long been plagued by an "urban bias" – often due to issues of security and access – even though armed conflict usually takes place in rural areas.[42] This study aims to at least partially circumvent the urban bias by deliberately seeking out interviews in both urban and rural areas, including areas with ongoing armed violence where reasonable risk mitigation was possible. Overall, my interviews took place in seven different departments of Colombia: Cundinamarca, La Guajira, Meta, Putumayo, Quindío, Tolima, and Valle del Cauca (see Figure 2).

The first individual interview took place over WhatsApp in December 2017, with an ex-combatant who was living in Chile at the time to hide

---

[40] Altier, Thoroughgood, and Horgan, "Turning Away from Terrorism"; Hwang, *Why Terrorists Quit*; Ebaugh, *Becoming an Ex*.

[41] To protect the confidentiality of respondents, when I was confirming a translation, I would only send a single sentence from the transcript, explaining the context if necessary, when asking for clarification. No information on the particular respondent was provided to the assistants and they did not have access to the recordings or transcripts.

[42] Stathis N Kalyvas, *The Logic of Violence in Civil War* (Cambridge: Cambridge University Press, 2006), 38–48.

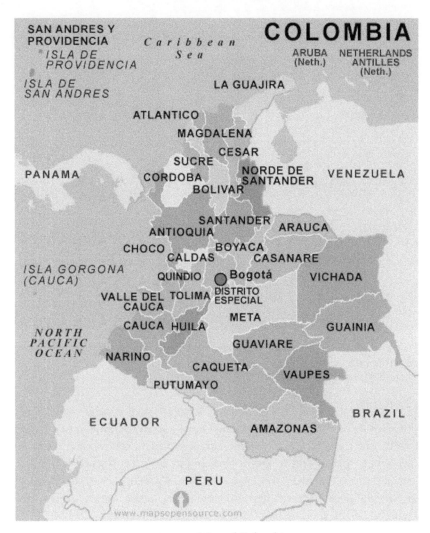

FIGURE 2 Map of Colombia.

from the dissidents allegedly hunting him. The first set of on-site fieldwork interviews took place in two government safe houses in undisclosed locations in Colombia in February 2018. All in-country interviews were completed by December 2018, though informal conversations with several ex-combatants continued for years after this point. In addition to the safe houses, interviews took place in the following locations: two paramilitary reintegration compounds in rural areas, three FARC reincorporation camps

FIGURE 3 Research site: compound for former paramilitaries (formerly the estate of a drug cartel leader).
Photo credit: author.

(ETCRs) in rural areas, as well as urban locations such as cafés, government offices, hotel lobbies, and participants' homes in several different cities and towns. The three ETCRs I visited were in southern, central, and northern Colombia, in areas still facing violent conflict and the presence of multiple armed groups. The two paramilitary compounds were in central Colombia, in two different departments also containing active armed groups (see Figure 3). These sites are described in more detail throughout the book.

In addition to interviews, I took extensive field notes based on informal conversations and observations. I was able to observe community meetings and school lessons in two of the three ETCRs, including one meeting on women's rights led by women in the FARC, and I took part in meals and activities with ex-combatants and their families in all three. Due to security concerns of the participants and promises of confidentiality, the exact locations of these safe houses, compounds, and reincorporation camps will not be disclosed.[43]

---

[43] For example, in some departments there is only one ETCR, and respondents expressed concern that they could be identified simply by linking their interview to a specific department.

After my first visit to an ETCR, the leaders in that camp called ahead to another ETCR to provide a referral and recommend that I be allowed to enter. Even so, on my first day there, I had to go through the same lengthy verification process with commanders. The leaders at this ETCR then gave us a referral to a third camp. In this third camp, we arrived with a United Nations representative, who introduced us to the main leader there (a FARC Secretariat member), where I once again explained my study, shared the documentation, and received permission to return the next day to begin interviews. This third camp was the most organized overall and also the least rigid in terms of how long I was allowed to stay.

From Coding Variables to Recognizing Framing Contests

As noted earlier, this work initially focused on desertion decisions before framing mechanisms became clearly relevant in interview transcripts. Qualitative research has two main coding approaches: (1) emergent coding, which is inductive; and (2) a priori coding, where the researcher establishes codes in advance.[44] This research blends both approaches. While systematically coding my initial five variables of interest (e.g., networks, costs/benefits of memberships, identity, ideology, and types of commitment), patterns began to emerge suggesting that the ways in which ex-combatants assessed and understood these variables, and made their decisions to fight or flee, were deeply affected by the frames in which they had organized their experiences. I then established new coding categories based on the frames, identities, and labels that respondents were repeatedly using. I then used discourse analysis to identify and analyze the three main framing contests examined in this book.

Positionality

Applying reflexivity, or being "methodologically self-conscious," in qualitative work is extremely important to maintain the validity of the data, especially in complicated contexts of ongoing armed violence.[45]

---

[44] Steve Stemler, "An Overview of Content Analysis," *Practical Assessment, Research & Evaluation* 7, no. 17 (2001): 1–6.
[45] Erik Blair, "A Reflexive Exploration of Two Qualitative Data Coding Techniques," *Journal of Methods and Measurement in the Social Sciences* 6, no. 1 (2016): 14–29; Michael Lynch, "Against Reflexivity as an Academic Virtue and Source of Privileged Knowledge," *Theory, Culture & Society* 17, no. 3 (2000): 26–54.

I am acutely aware that who I am as a researcher undoubtedly affected my data collection, research experience, and data analysis. As an obvious foreigner (tall, with blonde hair and blue eyes), Colombians were curious about me wherever I went – especially in rural areas where foreign visitors are still quite rare. In some ways, this identity helped make connections, as most people wanted to talk to me, at the very least to find out where I was from. It was also helpful in overcoming suspicion and mistrust, because as an obvious foreigner it was unlikely that I was working with an opposing armed group, dissidents, or the Colombian government. Being Canadian also helped in unexpected ways, as ex-combatants were wary when they thought I was American (e.g., anti-American sentiment is particularly high among the FARC loyalists) and their attitude changed completely when they discovered I was from Canada. I did encounter some resistance in the first ETCR, as the leaders in that camp were very concerned that I was a journalist posing as a student. This fear was not unfounded, as only weeks before I corresponded with a journalist who told me he had lied his way into a different ETCR, posing as a maintenance worker. I showed them all of my university documentation, as well as my official letter of permission from the Colombian Ministry of Defense, and they questioned me for an hour about my research before they would grant permission to enter the camp. Even then, I was only permitted to stay for three days.

In the paramilitary sites, I heard many stories of how the government had sent in agents pretending to be someone else and had tricked them into signing papers they did not understand. Several participants explained that this, combined with their experiences in the AUC ranks, had caused them to distrust everyone. They explained that they were more comfortable talking to me because my obvious foreigner status made it clear that I was not working for the Colombian government. They were less certain of my Colombian assistant, but he was not present during interviews, and I explained that he was not permitted to listen to the recordings or view transcripts, nor did I ever discuss interview content with him.

Because there is a clear imbalance of power in this type of interview situation (i.e., a foreign, university-educated researcher with the implied economic resources), I tried to find ways to give more power to the participants. Specifically, I was not rigidly committed to my interview questions and largely allowed participants to control the direction of our conversations. While I had my list of questions, I made it clear that I wanted to hear what *they* thought was important. I also made it clear that all questions were optional, that they could stop the interview at any time, and that the recorder was also optional. I positioned myself not as an "expert" but as someone ignorant of the realities of their lives, inviting them to teach me what they knew. I also used the fact that my Spanish was not perfect to put participants at ease, and my honest language mistakes created many comical moments that, I hope, made me more relatable and less intimidating. I asked them to teach me new words, especially "guerrilla vocabulary" or Colombian slang; we would laugh when I would mispronounce something or when they could not understand me, and I would admit when I could not find the right word for something. They also delighted in the fact that I did not mind eating the same food as they did, although this too created some humorous situations. In one ex-AUC compound, for example, we were walking down the hill to our host's house for lunch when my research assistant told me that they were serving something special, but I could not ask what it was in advance.

"Is it rat?" I asked, laughing nervously and only half-joking. I had eaten a fair share of mystery meat already in rural Colombia, and on our last trip, a rat had fallen from a hole right above us in a restaurant ceiling, landing on the seat beside my assistant before scuttling across the floor. The restaurant staff had laughed uproariously. I had not.

"No, no, no, no – it's not rat. But just ... don't ask, okay? It's a very *special* meal." His eyes twinkled, like I was about to be the victim of a practical joke. A Colombian practical joke, no less.

We ate lunch, and I dutifully ate the unrecognizable roasted meat placed in front of me. Nell – a former paramilitary woman and entrepreneur, the host who had cooked the meal, and one of the most fascinating people I have ever met – kept grinning at me, her eyes holding that same twinkle. After we finished, I finally asked: "Okay, please tell me – what did I just eat?"

"Come back here, I'll show you!" she said, excited.

We went into their backyard, followed closely by several giggling children, and there, in a pen beside the chickens, were dozens of fluffy, adorable guinea pigs. I tried not to look as horrified as I was.

"These are *pets* in Canada," I exclaimed balefully, and they all burst into gales of laughter.

These types of exchanges went a long way in building trust and rapport in the communities I stayed in, and most respondents loved to ask me questions about Canada, inquiring about everything from food to fashion to the infamous Canadian winters. They clearly loved talking about something other than the war, something other than their past lives.

However, I recognize that because I was giving small gifts or cash in thanks for these interviews, there was still a clear imbalance of power. But because several participants commented that they had felt exploited or misrepresented by researchers and/or journalists, I felt that it was necessary to compensate participants for their time – especially as, since the peace process, there has been a massive influx of researchers into Colombia, and quite a few ex-combatants commented with resentment about how they get little out of these studies. In the ETCRs where women often stated they were too busy to participate, this offering of compensation (equivalent to about US$5) – which I explained was not my own money but from a Canadian nonprofit research organization – was critical, and it was always received with immense gratitude. The rare exception was that a few potential participants in one ETCR asked for large sums of money for their interviews, which I could not agree to, and these people then refused to participate. This only happened once, however, and many participants agreed to be interviewed before knowing that they were going to receive compensation.

Finally, the fact that I am a mother myself helped immensely in speaking with women ex-combatants – many of whom now have children or were pregnant when we spoke. While the women were more wary of me than the men, once I showed them pictures of my own children, they warmed quickly as we swapped stories of pregnancy and motherhood. I am sure that this identity – woman, foreigner, doctoral student, mother – affected the answers that I received, and another researcher speaking to the same people might obtain different responses, and in turn might interpret those responses differently. However, I took all measures possible to build trust with participants, to give them power over the interviews, to give them space to ask questions, and to respect their roles and choices. I also asked every participant at the end of each interview if there was something that they wanted to talk about that I did not ask – and many (especially the loyalists) had a lot to add.

Participant Overview

While I conducted 114 official interviews,[46] over the course of the fieldwork and beyond, I had repeated conversations with five of the participants (two deserters from the ELN, and three deserters from the FARC), who provided substantial information about their experiences through the DDR processes, as well as information about the two guerrilla groups' operations, rules, and strategies.[47] This sample includes

---

[46] Appendix A contains further details on these participants while protecting their identities.
[47] These conversations took place after the initial interviews with these participants – usually over meals or coffee – and were not recorded nor remunerated.

thirty-seven women and sixty-two men from the FARC, the ELN, and the AUC, and ex-combatant respondents originated from twenty-five out of thirty-two departments, with one from Venezuela.[48] Within this breakdown are sixty nondeserters ("loyalists") of the FARC and AUC, thirty-five deserters from the FARC and the ELN, and four ex-combatants who were in both categories (i.e., they deserted one group and then stayed with another until ordered to demobilize). Some had switched sides to join another group, and some had deserted from more than one group. Ages of enlistment ranged from 10 to 45, with an average enlistment age of 19.5 (median: 17). In addition, thirty-seven of the ninety-nine respondents joined at age 15 or younger, with thirteen that joined between the ages of 16 and 17; thus, over 50 percent of the sample joined as minors, and most of these underage recruits were FARC and ELN. Participants were invited to self-identify their ethnicity through this question: "Do you identify with any type of ethnicity or race?"[49] Sometimes participants did not understand this question, in which case I provided examples such as Indigenous, Afro-descendant, *mestizo*, and mulatto. Seven participants identified as Afro-descendant, eighteen identified as Indigenous, one as Creole, and one as mulatto.[50] The rest identified as *mestizo* ("mixed race") or did not identify with any ethnicity.

The overall average time spent in the group was 12.72 years (median: 10 years). Deserters' time ranged from 6 months to 25 years, with an average of 8.8 years (median: 6.5 years). In this category, four respondents did not know (or did not want to disclose) the amount of time in the group. The time loyalists spent in the group also ranged widely, from 4 months to 47 years, with an average of 15 years (median: 11 years).[51] In this category, at least four paramilitary respondents reported a duration that was significantly shorter than their actual time in the group, so the

---

[48] The aim was to have at least 50 percent women, but this became impossible within the paramilitary population due to the difficulty in locating ex-AUC women who were willing to speak. See Appendix A for an anonymized list of interviewees.

[49] Self-identification has become standard practice for collecting racial and ethnic data, and is the primary criterion for counting Indigenous people per Convention 169 of the International Labour Organization. Edward Eric Telles, *Pigmentocracies: Ethnicity, Race, and Color in Latin America* (Chapel Hill: University of North Carolina Press, 2014).

[50] For statistical purposes, in the demographic tables the percentage of Afro-descendants includes the mulatto and Creole respondents.

[51] As discussed later in more detail, some respondents, particularly AUC respondents, openly lied about the length of time they had been in the group to stay consistent with what they had told the government. Some later disclosed the truth.

average and median for this category are almost certainly higher.[52] Ranks in both groups ranged from basic foot soldier to top-level commander, including one member of the FARC Secretariat. In addition, 31 percent of this sample had reached some level of command (from the first rank of squad commander – commanding twelve people – to the top rank of Secretariat). While broad, this sample was not randomly collected, and I do not claim that it is statistically representative of the entire demobilized population (see Tables 1 and 2).

In addition to interviews, I also took detailed field notes from my interactions with participant populations. In fact, in this type of complicated environment, where building trust is critical to collecting quality information, engaging in community activities such as children's games, group meals, cooking, washing dishes, sitting in on community meetings and group classes, drinking beer and coffee, listening to poetry, taking guided walks, and playing billiards were all key activities in building trust. In many of the interview sites, well before I requested interviews, I simply walked around or sat in a gathering place to talk to the locals or asked for a tour of the camp or farm, and curious residents (often their children first) would stop to chat with me and ask where I was from (see Figure 4). In this manner, I had far more than 114 conversations, many with people who did not formally participate in interviews (such as servers, street vendors, bus passengers, and Uber drivers) but were eager to share their expertise or opinions about the conflict, the reintegration process, and/or the government. This cumulative observation and informal conversation provided an increased understanding of local views that I may not have had if I had relied strictly on interviews alone.

Misinformation and Lies

With several of the research participants, I was able to maintain contact and have repeated conversations in person and through WhatsApp over the course of 2018 and all the way into 2022. During these conversations, I received admissions that some respondents had lied in their initial interviews. For example, after several extended conversations, one participant that I had interviewed in February 2018 later admitted that he had lied

---

[52] Respondents either disclosed a short time in the group (e.g., six months) but then shared stories and experiences that did not correspond to this time frame, or another respondent's information indicated that the person had spent far more time in the group than they disclosed.

TABLE 1 *Ex-combatant sample, demographic information*

Female	37%
Deserted at least one group	39%
Indigenous[53]	18%
Afro-descendant	9%
Average age at recruitment	19.5*
Joined as a minor (age 17 or younger)	50%
Average time (years) in armed group	13
Median time (years) in armed group	10
Minimum time in armed group	4 months
Maximum time in armed group	47 years
Married or common-law	35%
One or more living children	66%
Attained some formal secondary education (i.e., above sixth grade) *before* demobilization	3%
Served time in prison	14%
Forcibly recruited	5%
Membership in more than one armed group	13%
Reached a commander rank (mid to high)	31%
Militia (urban operative)	10%

*Lowest enlistment age: 10; highest enlistment age: 45; standard deviation: 8.

TABLE 2 *Demographic breakdown by gender*

	Women	Men
Indigenous	22%	15%
Afro-descendant	5%	15%
Joined as a minor	54%	45%
Average time (years) in armed group	12	13.2
Median time (years) in armed group	7	10
One or more living children	70%	63%
Reached a commander rank of any kind	19%	42%
Advanced beyond lowest level of command	3%	21%
Militia	16%	8%

to me about his rank because he felt that his answer had to match the answer he gave to the government when he demobilized, where he had downplayed his high rank to avoid legal repercussions. Another woman

---

[53] Indigenous peoples make up approximately 3.4 percent of Colombia's population while Afro-descendants make up 10.4 percent. See: Departamento Administrativo Nacional de Estadística, "Censo General 2005," DANE, 2005, www.dane.gov.co/index.php/ estadisticas-por-tema/demografia-y-poblacion/censo-general-2005-1.

FIGURE 4 Respondent walking through her neighborhood in Usme, Bogotá.
Photo credit: author.

in a FARC ETCR was evasive when I asked her what her roles had been
in the group. After a long silence, she finally told me that she had been a
cook for a member of the Secretariat – for nearly twenty years. This does
not match testimony from the majority of FARC ex-combatants who
said that everyone shared in cooking, standing guard, cleaning, laundry,
and so on. This woman later admitted to my assistant that she had been
a member of that commander's personal bodyguard squad (*esquema*).
Several other women told me that, despite being in the FARC for over
twenty years, they had never once been in combat – although perhaps
possible, in comparison with other testimonies from their comrades this
too seemed unlikely.

In the paramilitary interviews, many of the respondents, including
Tobias, openly lied about their rank and time spent in the group, saying for example that they had only spent one year in the AUC but then
sharing stories and details that did not match such a brief experience.
One participant first told me he had spent eighteen months in the group,

then later admitted it was actually five years, and told me that most para-militaries lied to the government about their time in the group to avoid prison sentences. Nell told me that no one from the AUC would tell me the full truth, while others said that they desperately wanted to tell the truth because they had not been able to tell anyone else.

With all these instances of lying, despite my various efforts to build trust, I had to question the validity of my research data. How many times had people lied to me, and why? I have previous fieldwork experience, and it is often not difficult to spot a lie – hesitation, avoiding eye contact, or information during an interview will contradict previous information a person shared, or other people will say things about the participant that do not match what they said. While it is impossible to know with certainty if people are telling the truth, what they shared was how they wanted to represent themselves, and what people lie about reveals as much as what they are truthful about. Indeed, when lies can be identified, they add information and understanding to the topic under discussion. As Lee Ann Fujii wrote: "the value of oral testimonies researchers collect in places that have recently suffered violence does not lie solely in the truthfulness of their content."[54] In fact, Fujii argued that "silences, rumors, and invented stories" are as valuable as the testimonies themselves because they indicate how social and political factors shape what people say to a researcher.[55]

The fact that so many respondents lied to downplay their rank indicates, for instance, that even though my sample is 31 percent mid- to high-ranking commanders, this is likely not because some people claimed to be commanders when they were not. It suggests that commanders were heavily represented – and possibly overrepresented – in the sample. In fact, it is possible that the percentage of commanders is even higher than presented here because of the observed tendency of respondents to lie to downgrade actual ranks – especially among women and paramilitaries. So few women in the sample claimed to be commanders that at first I questioned whether they were lying to downplay their roles in violence (which for some may be true, like the woman who lied about being a bodyguard); however, many ex-combatants confirmed that even though women commanders did exist, especially in the FARC ranks, it was still relatively rare.

---

[54] Lee Ann Fujii, "Shades of Truth and Lies: Interpreting Testimonies of War and Violence," *Journal of Peace Research* 47, no. 2 (2010): 231–41, 232.
[55] Fujii, "Shades of Truth and Lies," 232.

One important note: when a person asks a question, how that question is phrased unavoidably influences the type of answer a researcher will get, and this was a critical part of my interview strategy. For example, instead of asking *why* a participant left, I asked "when did you start thinking about leaving?" to get a better sense of the process leading up to the decision. But this question came well into the conversation, when rapport had been established and the respondent was more comfortable. Then, because participants had likely rehearsed and repeated why they had left in many military interviews, instead of asking them why, I asked *how* they left. Because this is a process-oriented question – rather than asking about motivations sometimes years or even decades after the fact – it is less likely to be rehearsed but still provides critical insights as to the motives, networks, and resources around that person's disengagement.[56] It can also present a much longer story, with richer information, than a motivation-oriented explanation. For example, in my first conversation with one FARC ex-commander, he told me that he had deserted because he was "tired of war" (and, in fact, this is one of the most common reasons that deserters report to the military). But, after several conversations, when we finally had our official interview, I asked him *how* he had deserted, and he proceeded to give me a detailed account about discovering that one of his comrades was a government informant, and he became scared for his life after hearing about a plot to kill him. He then made a plan and escaped at night while everyone else was having their annual Christmas party. This is indeed a very different answer than simply being "tired of war."

Overall, however, respondents appeared grateful for the experience to share their expertise and stories, and whenever possible – especially when deceit was suspected about verifiable information like rank – I worked to triangulate this information with other sources. Many stated openly when they could not or would not tell me something (e.g., what they did in the group), but were happy to talk about other subjects, while others were quite proud to share their experiences. Many respondents became emotional while recounting their stories, and the majority thanked me for allowing them to share their experiences and insights. Several told me that I was the first person in their lives who had ever just sat and listened to them. Thus, while it is certainly possible that there were other lies that I did not detect, what they shared – true or not – revealed a lot about the function of framing and constructed identities.

---

[56] I am indebted to Dr. Katherine Brown (University of Birmingham) for this advice on asking "how" rather than "why" in my interviews.

Ethical Considerations

While this project received university ethics clearance,[57] such clearance does not absolve researchers from considering the range of ethical implications of such work, especially given the reliance on interviews with a highly vulnerable population – many of whom are still afraid of being tracked down and killed. These considerations include (but are not limited to): retraumatizing people by asking them to recount their life histories, exposing ex-combatants to unwanted attention, putting both myself and the participant in danger if the purpose of our conversation is misunderstood by others, and/or inadvertently reinforcing harmful gender dynamics by working through primarily male gatekeepers.

While I have tried to address all of these considerations, the dynamic of a white, Western, university-educated researcher and a Colombian participant with limited education and resources does give rise to power dynamics that are sometimes difficult to avoid, even with the best of intentions for participatory research. For example, one outcome of giving small sums of money to compensate research participants for their time is that it left the impression that I was immensely wealthy (despite my repeated explanations that the money for the interviews was not my own). As a result, some participants continued to contact me for months afterward, asking for money for their children, for sick relatives, or for whatever crisis had arisen. Many asked for my help in obtaining a visa to come to Canada, and others asked for help in improving their security situation because they were receiving death threats. Obviously, none of these requests were within my power to grant, but they did raise the question of how, or even if, this research had the ability to improve the lives of those who made it possible. It also raised the question, for me, of whether helping participants once a study is over is unethical, or if it is more unethical *not* to help.[58] This book does not purport to answer that question, but it is one worth raising for other researchers embarking on similar work.

In terms of retraumatizing participants, this was an ongoing concern as many participants shared violent and traumatic stories, and some became quite emotional during the interviews. In my former therapeutic work in the cancer and brain injury communities, I have been trained to work with people recovering from trauma, including what types of language to use and what to avoid, and how to provide a safe and nonjudgmental

[57] Carleton University Ethics Review Board #106973.
[58] Rachel Schmidt, "When Fieldwork Ends: Navigating Ongoing Contact with Former Insurgents," *Terrorism and Political Violence* 33, no. 2 (2020): 312–23.

space when people are sharing intimate and/or traumatic details of their lives, in order to avoid retraumatizing people. Participants were reminded throughout the interview that all questions were optional, that they did not have to share stories that were emotionally difficult, and that they were free to end the interview at any time. While some said that their participation had been cathartic, it is difficult to know without ongoing contact what the later effects of this sharing may have been. While most participants had access through the reintegration program to psychologists and social workers, many of them felt that this assistance was wholly inadequate, while others were not interested in accessing such help.

Finally, as with all research involving human subjects, and especially in conflict-affected areas, there was a degree of risk to both the participants and to myself in this research. There were times when I took a leap of faith in more conflict-prone areas of the country that, when looking back, could have gone horribly wrong. I took all precautions to minimize risk as much as possible and to allow the participants to guide the subject of the conversations. Nonetheless, as I have written about elsewhere,[59] there is still much improvement in this field that researchers can make to ensure their projects are not exploitative and instead become truly participatory. I hope that this book is another step forward in that direction.

MAPPING OUT THE BOOK

Following the stories of the twelve ex-combatants noted earlier, this book moves through three different archetypal framing contests that emerged in the interviews and then became prominent during the coding process: *victims versus perpetrators*, *revolutionaries versus narco-terrorists*, and *loyalists versus deserters*. Despite how I have laid out these dichotomies for analytical clarity, respondent interviews will show that these narratives are not nearly as binary as they first appear. While I was not initially looking for these frames, in the life history interviews that I conducted almost everyone was framing their experiences and decisions in a particular way. This is not surprising – we all do this to some extent. We all try to convince ourselves and others that we are the "good guys." But these narratives went beyond personal justification of choices. When coding for both pre-established variables and ones that emerged from the text, these narratives surfaced as collective, strategic, and highly combative – the result of a combined inductive and deductive approach. Individual

---

[59] Schmidt, "When Fieldwork Ends."

narratives converged as a collective of competing frames. While the three narrative contests examined in this book are surely not the only ones apparent in Colombia or other conflicted-affected places, they are the ones that emerged most clearly in my interviews as collectively adopted and highly strategic frames with targeted audiences.

First, Chapter II provides a background to the Colombian conflict, including an overview of gender norms in Colombia and brief descriptions of the three main armed groups under examination – the FARC, the ELN, and the AUC. Next, in Chapter III, I describe the evolution of various demobilization and reintegration programs in Colombia, looking at how the government has addressed (or failed to address) the guerrillas' emphasis on gender equality and how the framing of women as victims has affected women's perceived alternatives and their reintegration experiences.

The following six chapters analyze the three key framing contests that I argue affect rebel decisions to desert and the resulting reintegration trajectories. In Chapter IV, I introduce the first highly salient guerrilla frame that emerged from interviews: collective victimhood. In this chapter, I analyze how and why the FARC and ELN have constructed a frame of victimhood to recruit and retain members, relying heavily on their rural, *campesino*[60] identity and the construction of the government as the "real terrorists." Then, in Chapter V, I discuss how the government and many deserters reject this victimhood frame, often conflating *campesinos* with guerrillas and painting the guerrillas as perpetrators of violence against their own troops – emphasizing forced abortions and violence against women guerrillas in particular.

In Chapter VI, I introduce the contest of *revolutionaries versus narco-terrorists*, in which the guerrillas – and particularly the FARC – have framed their revolution as something they are doing both in self-defense and "for the people," with an emphasis on identities as revolutionaries and "insurgent feminists." In Chapter VII, I analyze how and why the government has contested this revolutionary frame with a narrative of the guerrillas as narco-terrorists, which not only affects the government's policy approaches but also affects combatants' perceived alternatives and

---

[60] While *campesino* generally translates to the English "peasant," I choose to retain the Spanish word throughout this book, as the word "peasant" is both pejorative and does not adequately capture the unique racial and cultural history of Colombia's *campesino* population. See: Gwen Burnyeat, *Chocolate, Politics and Peace-Building: An Ethnography of the Peace Community of San José de Apartadó, Colombia* (London: Palgrave Macmillan, 2018); Christopher Courtheyn, "De-Indigenized but Not Defeated: Race and Resistance in Colombia's Peace Community and Campesino University," *Ethnic and Racial Studies* 42, no. 15 (2018): 1–20.

their post-conflict experiences. This contest is, of course, archetypal and appears in many armed conflicts across the world. These two chapters thus explore what we can learn from the people inside such contests, and how these narrative battles not only affect individual decisions to fight or flee but also might impede societal transitions to peace.

In Chapter VIII, I present the first part of the last framing contest, that of *deserters versus loyalists*. Unlike the other two contests, this one is not between the government and the nonstate armed groups but between the various groups of ex-combatants, including deserters, loyalists, and "would-be" deserters. This chapter explores how the FARC in particular has framed deserters from their group as liars, traitors, and spies, and discusses the highly gendered nature of this framing. Chapter IX then looks at how deserters contest this framing and try to portray themselves as courageous and noble for making the decision to abandon violence. Finally, the book concludes with Chapter X, examining how all these framing contests are linked together and their cumulative impact on disengagement and reintegration trajectories. Where are these former combatants now, and how did these framing contests affect their specific reintegration experiences?

Depending on the outcome of framing contests, even recruits that are not fully committed may see no possible alternative to their membership in the group. Conversely, some recruits may buy into the government narrative and attempt to leave, only to face the stigmatizing consequences of that narrative and the impossibility of the state's economic promises in civilian life. This book examines what variables produce these and other possible outcomes, emphasizing how ignoring gender in the examination of rebel group cohesion and individual commitment to armed groups has left a blind spot in our understanding of both desertion and post-conflict reintegration.

A NOTE ON TERMINOLOGY

In the building and contesting of frames in war, language and labels are central. These are discursive battles, after all, about how to represent reality. The language choices in this book are deliberate and carefully considered, in order to best convey what respondents said to me. Throughout this book, I refer to "loyalists" (i.e., combatants who stayed in their group until ordered to demobilized) and "deserters" (i.e., combatants who fled their group without permission). While these simplified categories certainly contribute to analytical clarity, they also imply an availability of meaningful choices that do not always exist in war. "Loyalists" may stay in their group for a variety of reasons, including economic benefits, basic survival, or personal relationships, or they may want to leave but be unable to do so. In this book, those referred to as FARC "loyalists" professed a high commitment to both the group and its ideology, vehemently rejecting any implication that they had been forced to stay. They considered themselves as still part of the FARC – now the political party rather than the armed group. For this reason, I quote these respondents as "FARC" rather than "ex-FARC."

Those referred to as paramilitary "loyalists" were simply those who stayed in the group until ordered to disarm. They were not all uniformly "loyal" to the leaders, but they were not deserters either. I quote these respondents as "ex-AUC" because the AUC as a collective group no longer exists, even though successor paramilitary groups remain.

Respondents referred to as "deserters" are ex-combatants who deliberately fled their armed group without permission. While some are not true deserters (i.e., they were captured by state forces and coerced to "desert" their groups in order to avoid lengthy prison sentences), in this study there were only four such cases. And regardless of the pressures around their so-called desertion, FARC loyalists shunned them as deserters anyway. The rest of the "deserter" category respondents had deliberately fled their groups at great risk – even though some still remained ideologically loyal.

As Chapters VIII and IX explore in detail, the label of deserter is especially problematic in Colombia's fraught attempts to reintegrate ex-combatants and transition to a "post-conflict" society. The Colombian government has used deserters' stories to discredit the FARC and the ELN, which has heightened tensions between loyalists and deserters now that the FARC has officially disarmed. FARC loyalists blame deserters for creating a falsely negative image of them, calling them traitors and liars. These loyalists refused to be called *desmovilizados* ("demobilized") because that was a derogatory term that they reserved for deserters and ex-AUC paramilitaries. Indeed, as subsequent chapters illustrate, what ex-combatants called themselves was deeply affected by organizational framing and by external contestations of how they defined themselves. In fact, the FARC negotiated their reintegration program to be defined as transforming the guerrillas into disarmed *political actors* – and not simply as disarming and returning to civilian life.[61] The government's use of deserters' stories has exacerbated the divide between groups of

---

[61] Erin McFee and Angelika Rettberg, eds., *Excombatientes y Acuerdo de Paz Con Las FARC-EP En Colombia: Balance de La Etapa Temprana* (Bogotá: Universidad de los Andes, 2019).

ex-combatants who are all supposed to be peacefully coexisting as civilians. Labeling and language choices matter a lot in this context – and in Colombia I sometimes learned this the hard way.

Finally, throughout this book I retain one Spanish word that does not have a sufficient translation in English: *campesino*. While *campesino* is generally considered to be a "nonethnic" designation in Latin America and is typically translated to "peasant" or "small-scale farmer," this translation is problematic due to the pejorative connotations of the former and lack of cultural identity in the latter.[62] I retain the term *campesino* throughout the book to describe a "social identity category of someone whose customs, beliefs, lifestyle and social, economic political and cultural practices are linked to rural land and economy."[63] As Chapter IV describes in more detail, *campesinos* are at the heart of Colombia's conflict – a rural and mixed-race population, they not only make up the majority of internally displaced persons (IDPs), coca farmers, and official victims of the conflict, but they are also the main population from which rebel group members are recruited.

---

[62] Burnyeat, *Chocolate, Politics and Peace-Building.*
[63] Claudia Maria López, "Contesting Double Displacement: Internally Displaced Campesinos and the Social Production of Urban Territory in Medellín, Colombia," *Geographica Helvetica* 74, no. 3 (2019): 249–59, 250

II

A History of (Gendered) Violence in Colombia

Look how the organization FARC-EP was the only organization that voluntarily resisted and confronted the Colombian government, and not only the Colombian government, but also the government of the United States. Because it was not only here in Colombia but with all of their high-end technology, they fought us, men and women *campesinos*, many of whom did not know how to write nor read, but who had the capacity and the clarity to say: this is the only road we have left, to achieve change in this country one day.

> Reina, FARC (B40)

This war, son of a bitch, well, we're killing ourselves, between soldiers and guerrillas ... a soldier is the son of whom? The same *campesino*.

> Junior, ex-ELN (B17)

The history of Colombia, especially around the origins of the current conflict, can vary significantly depending on who is telling it – or, to be more precise, on who is framing it. The government points to the "narco-guerrillas" as the root of the problems, erasing decades of sectarian violence and government neglect that laid the foundations in which the guerrillas could thrive. The guerrillas point to the government as the "real terrorist," whose persecution and violence forced them to take up arms to defend themselves and the Colombian people. But many of these same Colombian people want nothing to do with the guerrillas, saying that no one has protected them, and that the ongoing violence has destroyed their country and their lives. Many guerrillas also blame the United States for exacerbating the conflict with millions of dollars of military funding for the "war on drugs," and later the "war on terror." And the paramilitaries, at least the ones that I spoke to, blamed everyone except themselves: the politicians, the government, the guerrillas – all were at fault for the current situation. If it were not for the paramilitaries, they told me, the situation would be a lot worse. As Lina's husband said to me wryly one day, reflecting on all the conflicting stories about Colombia: "There is no truth here."

FALSE PROMISES AND DETERIORATING TRUST

> I have told the government that I do not want anything to do with the prosecutor's office and [all] that, because ... one cannot trust the government now, because they will come and sell us for anything.
>
> Namona, ex-ELN (B06)

> Well, the most difficult thing is, no, right now the most difficult of all for me ... is to trust the state.
>
> Jhon, FARC (B35)

When I asked ex-combatants about the peace accord, I received many conflicting responses – sometimes from the same person. Many FARC deserters were relieved, because they hoped it meant that the group would stop hunting them. But they were also frustrated because the collectively demobilized FARC loyalists were receiving higher monthly reintegration benefits than they were. Most of the former AUC combatants were cautiously optimistic: they were hopeful about the potential for less violence in Colombia, but many were skeptical that the FARC had actually laid down their arms. As some of them were hardly concealing their involvement in ongoing drug operations, I suspect that these ex-combatants also may have been hopeful about getting control of a larger share of the market. In fact, one ELN deserter told me that before he deserted, he was happy about the peace agreement because it meant "more territory for the ELN."

FARC loyalists gave perhaps the most mixed responses: most said that they were happy because they finally got what they wanted (i.e., a peace deal and land reform), but then in almost the same breath they would say that the government had lied, that the whole thing was a scam, and that President Duque was reneging on key aspects of the deal. Many told me that they would never be able to trust the government. More than a few said they wished that they had never demobilized.

Indeed, despite the historic peace agreement signed with the FARC guerrillas in 2016 – ending the longest-running insurgency in the world – there are still thousands of armed actors operating throughout Colombia, including the ELN and dissidents from at least two formerly demobilized groups: the FARC and the EPL (Popular Liberation Army). As post-plebiscite surveys and the massive failure of FARC politicians in congressional elections demonstrate, stigma against ex-combatants continues to be high in Colombian society.[1] In addition, due to massive publicity over political corruption in the last two decades – including multiple members of Congress being indicted for colluding with paramilitary death squads, and thousands of extrajudicial executions of civilians by the military – overall trust in the government is low, especially among poor populations and ex-combatants.[2] Compounding the problem are Mexican drug cartels reportedly taking advantage of the power vacuum left by the FARC's absence and moving into prime coca-growing regions, clashing with FARC dissidents and ELN factions for control of territory.[3]

The complex history of political conflict in Colombia dates back over a hundred years, although this too can vary, depending on the source. The most recent cycle of violence began in the mid-1960s with the emergence of several leftist guerrilla movements, the most prominent being the FARC, the ELN, April 19th Movement (M-19), and the EPL. These guerrilla movements rose up largely in reaction to extreme inequality, sectarian violence, and the domination of land ownership in the hands of a few wealthy families. But even before this, communists had been organizing with rural peasant families since the 1930s to occupy public lands or *haciendas* where landlords were absent, where they would set up militias to protect themselves from eviction.[4] During the onslaught of sectarian violence between Liberals and Conservatives in 1950–3, Communist and Liberal guerrilla-militias once again formed these "resistance communities" as a method of self-defense, to which Liberal peasants from other areas migrated.[5] Over the years, more organized guerrilla armies emerged from these

[1] Nicolás Galvis et al., "Barómetro de Las Américas Colombia 2016" (Bogota, 2016), https://obsdemocracia.org/uploads/related_file/Informe_Paz_2016.pdf; Semana, "ELN, El Nuevo Enemigo," *Semana*, February 17, 2018, www.semana.com/nacion/articulo/eln-en-venezuela-el-nuevo-enemigo/557445.

[2] Ariel Ávila, "Bacrim, Neoparamilitares y Grupos Post-Desmovilización Paramilitar," *Semana*, March 30, 2016, www.semana.com/opinion/articulo/ariel-avila-bacrim-neoparamilitares-y-grupos-post-desmovilizacion-paramilitar/467330; Semana, "Las Cuentas de Los Falsos Positivos."

[3] El Tiempo, "En Estos Diez Departamentos Hacen Presencia Los Carteles Mexicanos," *El Tiempo*, January 28, 2018, www.eltiempo.com/justicia/investigacion/fiscalia-alerta-de-presencia-de-mafia-mexicana-en-10-zonas-de-colombia-175974.

[4] Grace Livingstone, *Inside Colombia: Drugs, Democracy, and War* (New Brunswick, NJ: Rutgers University Press, 2004).

[5] Livingstone, *Inside Colombia.*

resistance communities. Since that time, many different guerrilla and paramilitary organizations have formed and fought against each other and against the government, and decades of conflict have left millions of victims of forced displacement, homicide, sexual violence, threats, and kidnapping, including 340,000 refugees that have fled to neighboring countries, and more than 7.7 million IDPs – the largest IDP population in the world at the time of writing.[6]

In the 1980s, the rise and consolidation of drug-trafficking cartels and coca production contributed to the territorial presence and resources of the guerrilla groups. At this time, President Belisario Betancur initiated a peace agreement with the FARC, and the Patriotic Union (UP) political party was then co-founded by the FARC and the country's Communist Party.[7] However, many members of the UP were violently attacked and assassinated by drug traffickers and paramilitaries, with many of the survivors returning to armed conflict or going into hiding. In fact, many FARC loyalists that I interviewed were children when these attacks happened, and they distinctly remembered the terror of those targeted assassinations, as the victims were their parents, relatives, and neighbors. A few participants recalled being constantly on the run because their parents were UP members, while others' parents were murdered for being part of the UP – life-altering events that precipitated their entry into the FARC.

This history of FARC political members being targeted and murdered would have a significant impact on future peace agreements and trust between the government and the guerrillas. After these murders, the FARC distanced itself from politics and returned to violent tactics.[8] Betancur's agreement with the FARC failed, and during the next two decades the FARC increased its membership to nearly 20,000[9] – though this figure does not include significant numbers of urban militia forces

[6] Centro Nacional de Memoria Historia, "Exilio Colombiano: Huellas Del Conflicto Armado Más Allá de Las Fronteras" (Bogota, 2018), www.centrodememoriahistorica .gov.co/informes/informes-2018/exilio-colombiano; Human Rights Watch, "World Report 2018: Colombia," New York, 2018, www.hrw.org/world-report/2018/country-chapters/colombia#84a68b; UARIV, "Registro Único de Víctimas (RUV): Unidad Para Las Víctimas," Unidadvictimas.gov, 2018, www.unidadvictimas.gov.co/es/registro-unico-de-victimas-ruv/37394; UNHCR (United Nations High Commissioner for Refugees), "ACNUR – Colombia," 2018, www.acnur.org/5b97f3154.pdf.
[7] Diana Jean Schemo, "Colombia's Death-Strewn Democracy," *New York Times*, July 24, 1997, www.nytimes.com/1997/07/24/world/colombia-s-death-strewn-democracy.html.
[8] Cristina Rojas, "Securing the State and Developing Social Insecurities: The Securitisation of Citizenship in Contemporary Colombia," *Third World Quarterly* 30, no. 1 (2009): 227–45.
[9] Elizabeth Reyes le Paliscot, "La Oportunidad de La Paz," Fundación Ideas para la Paz, 2015, https://doi.org/10.15713/ins.mmj.3.

nor "reserves." In fact, the creation of a demilitarized zone in southern Colombia between 1999 and 2002 – authorized by President Andrés Pastrana's government to facilitate peace talks – likely contributed to the increased enlistment into FARC ranks during this time.[10] Rightwing paramilitary forces also increased rapidly in this period: by 2002, the paramilitaries outnumbered the guerrillas by an estimated 27,000 people.[11]

Many of the country's elites – primarily landowners and established drug traffickers – opposed Betancur's efforts to make peace with the guerrillas and began their own formation of civilian *autodefensas* ("self-defense groups") to defend themselves against guerrillas who were "taxing" land, shipping routes, and crops.[12] Many ex-paramilitaries in this study still preferred the term *autodefensa*, resenting the term "paramilitary," which they said implied they were working for the military. The rise and consolidation of these paramilitary groups marked a notable shift and further complicated the Colombian war, with the founding of the Campesino Self-defense Forces of Córdoba and Urabá (ACCU) in 1994, which merged into the AUC in 1997. Despite admitted connections to drug trafficking and other illegal business, the AUC generally eschewed political motivations, and its commanders repeatedly insisted that their original role was to fill security gaps left by the state.[13] The rise of these often brutal forces – known for large massacres, widespread sexual violence, and attacking anyone suspected of supporting leftist ideals associated with the guerrillas – quickly polarized the country and further deteriorated trust in the state.[14] The Colombian police and military became increasingly involved in paramilitary activities, using these unofficial forces when they needed additional numbers, or to do things the military could not do.[15] While the government was publicly "against" the vigilante violence of the

---

[10] Juan Esteban Ugarriza and Rafael Camilo Quishpe, "Guerrilla Sin Armas: La Reintegración Política de La FARC Como Transformación de Los Comunistas Revolucionarios En Colombia," in *Excombatientes y Acuerdo de Paz Con Las FARC-EP En Colombia: Balance de La Etapa Temprana*, ed. Erin McFee and Angelika Rettberg (Bogotá: Ediciones Uniandes, 2019).

[11] Rojas, "Securing the State and Developing Social Insecurities."

[12] Mauricio Romero, *Paramilitares y Autodefensas* (Bogotá: IEPRI, 2003); G L Simons, "Colombia: A Brutal History" (London: SAQI, 2004).

[13] Salvatore Mancuso, "Discurso de Salvatore Mancuso Ante El Congreso de La República" (Bogotá, 2004), www.telam.com.ar/advf/documentos/2013/11/52966a9d7950c.pdf.

[14] Romero, *Paramilitares y Autodefensas*.

[15] Human Rights Watch, "The Ties That Bind: Colombia and Military–Paramlitary Links" (New York, London, Washington, Brussels, 2000), www.hrw.org/reports/2000/colombia/; Human Rights Watch, "The 'Sixth Division': Military–Paramilitary Ties and

paramilitaries, multiple paramilitary respondents in this study stated that they often fought alongside the Colombian army, and never against them (except by mistake). Indeed, mounting accusations of government collusion with paramilitary forces – which would become official indictments in 2006 – further damaged already weak civilian trust in the state.[16]

In 1999, President Pastrana once again attempted to negotiate a peace agreement with the FARC, including the creation of the above-mentioned demilitarized zone, but both the state and the FARC increased their military capacity during the negotiations, forcing a stalemate.[17] Álvaro Uribe won the subsequent elections with the opposite promise – to abandon any talk of compromise and toughen the fight against the FARC. The professionalization and fortification of Colombia's military continued throughout this period with the financial support of the United States through a program called "Plan Colombia." This American funding also helped to prove the links between drug trafficking and FARC leadership.[18] Despite the persistent lack of transparency, Uribe's combination of individual demobilization (i.e., encouraging desertion) and military pressure was relatively effective in reducing some violence in the country and diminishing FARC military capacity and territorial presence: government estimates indicate that FARC troops diminished from 20,000 to about 7,000 by 2015 in a combination of combat deaths and desertions.[19] However, government numbers of FARC deaths and desertions must be interpreted carefully. Given the military's use of "false positives" to increase the appearance of battle deaths during this same period (discussed shortly), it is highly questionable as to whether the reduction in FARC numbers was as great as the military claims. Indeed, by August 2017 the FARC had submitted a list of over 14,000 former members for demobilization benefits, and by

U.S. Policy in Colombia" (New York, London, Washington, Brussels, 2001), www.hrw .org/reports/2001/colombia/; Rojas Bolaños and Benavides, *Ejecuciones Extrajudiciales En Colombia, 2002–2010.*

[16] Sibylla Brodzinsky, "Colombia's 'Parapolitics' Scandal Casts Shadow over President," *The Guardian,* April 23, 2008, www.theguardian.com/world/2008/apr/23/colombia; Enzo Nussio, "Learning from Shortcomings: The Demobilisation of Paramilitaries in Colombia," *Journal of Peacebuilding & Development* 6, no. 2 (2011): 88–92.

[17] Luis Eduardo Celis, "Diez Años de Enfrentamientos Con Las Farc," *El Espectador,* August 7, 2008, www.elespectador.com/impreso/politica/articuloimpreso-diez-anos-de-enfrentamientos-farc-o.

[18] Javier Alberto Castrillón Riascos and René Alonso Guerra Molina, "A Deep Influence: United States–Colombia Bilateral Relations and Security Sector Reform (SSR), 1994–2002," *Opera,* no. 20 (2017): 35–54.

[19] Castrillón Riascos and Guerra Molina, "A Deep Influence"; Reyes le Paliscot, "La Oportunidad de La Paz."

December of that year the Office of the High Commissioner for Peace had verified approximately 11,900 members on that list.[20]

During the early 2000s, further information began to surface on deep ties between politicians – primarily in the Uribe administration – and paramilitaries. President Uribe began talks around demobilization with AUC commanders in 2003, and the demobilization of AUC ranks was officially completed by 2006. Notably, this demobilization occurred when international actors, including various donor organizations and countries, began to play a key role in Colombian DDR efforts.[21] While the involvement of international actors lent credibility to the endeavor, the legitimacy of this DDR process remains contested, as many former AUC combatants simply rearmed and regrouped under different names, with their criminal networks intact.[22] At the same time, indictments started to come down for high-ranking politicians in relation to illegal AUC activities, which was dubbed the *para-política* ("para-politics") scandal. When Uribe's own cousin was indicted, along with Uribe's director of intelligence and his foreign relations minister, many people in Colombia and abroad openly mused about Uribe himself having direct ties to the paramilitaries.[23] While in other circumstances such allegations may have further deteriorated public trust in the president, many Colombians saw Uribe's hardline policies as the key to defeating the guerrillas – this view was perhaps bolstered by Uribe's infamous claim before the election that Colombia was facing a terrorist threat and not an armed conflict.[24]

---

[20] Antonio Guterres, "United Nations Verification Mission in Colombia: Report of the Secretary General, April 2018" (New York, 2018), https://reliefweb.int/sites/reliefweb .int/files/resources/N1808241.pdf.

[21] Juana García Duque and Juan David Martínez, "Cooperación Internacional, DDR y Los Retos de La Reincoporación," in *Excombatientes y Acuerdo de Paz Con Las FARC-EP En Colombia: Balance de La Etapa Temprana*, ed. Erin McFee and Angelika Rettberg (Bogotá: Universidad de los Andes, 2019).

[22] Nussio, "Learning from Shortcomings: The Demobilisation of Paramilitaries in Colombia"; Human Rights Watch, "Smoke and Mirrors: Colombia's Demobilization of Paramilitary Groups," New York, 2005, www.hrw.org/report/2005/07/31/smoke-and-mirrors/ colombias-demobilization-paramilitary-groups; Human Rights Watch, "Paramilitaries' Heirs: The New Face of Violence in Colombia" (New York, 2010), www.hrw.org/sites/ default/files/reports/colombia0210webwcover_0.pdf; Deborah Sontag, "Colombia's Paramilitaries and the U.S. War on Drugs," *New York Times*, September 10, 2016, www.nytimes.com/2016/09/11/world/americas/colombia-cocaine-human-rights.html.

[23] Brodzinsky, "Colombia's 'Parapolitics' Scandal Casts Shadow over President."

[24] Semana, "Sí Hay Guerra, Señor Presidente," *Semana*, February 6, 2005, www.semana .com/portada/articulo/si-guerra-senor-presidente/70763-3.

Indeed, this claim was central to the Colombian government's framing of the guerrillas, of the armed forces, and of the conflict itself. And it was, apparently, a highly resonant frame with voters, as Uribe was reelected in 2006 in a landslide and continued his offensive against the guerillas.[25] Many FARC respondents in this study spoke of this "Uribe offensive" as one of heightened violence and constant attacks, with the loss of many friends and comrades. During this same period, new criminal groups were already emerging in territories previously controlled by the AUC, dubbed "BACRIMs" ("emerging criminal groups") – a term widely used by the government in another strategic framing that omitted the ties of these emerging groups to demobilized AUC paramilitaries.[26]

But the *para-política* indictments that emerged in 2006 were not the only scandal to hit the Uribe administration. In 2008, news broke that the Colombian military and national police had been involved in thousands of extrajudicial executions of civilians, in what were dubbed *falsos positivos* ("false positives").[27] These executions had a highly gendered element, as the military lured predominantly young men into the countryside with promises of jobs, whereupon these men and teenage boys were executed and dressed in guerrilla fatigues, photographed, and logged as combat deaths. Officers – who were also almost entirely men – received bonuses, vacations, and promotions for these increased body counts.[28] Evidence now shows that paramilitaries were also sometimes involved in these executions by handing over bodies from civilian massacres to the army, who would then dress the bodies in camouflage fatigues and present them as "combat deaths."[29] This practice was not simply a few "bad apples" as military commanders originally claimed; in fact, investigations revealed that the practice was institutionalized and widespread throughout the military and police, up to the highest levels of command, and included the prosecutor's office, judges and magistrates, and politicians.[30] These high body counts were also presented as evidence to the United States that

---

[25] BBC, "Colombia's Uribe Wins Second Term," *BBC News*, May 29, 2006, http://news.bbc.co.uk/2/hi/americas/5024428.stm.

[26] Human Rights Watch, "Paramilitaries' Heirs: The New Face of Violence in Colombia."

[27] Rojas Bolaños and Benavides, *Ejecuciones Extrajudiciales En Colombia, 2002–2010.*

[28] Rojas Bolaños and Benavides, *Ejecuciones Extrajudiciales En Colombia, 2002–2010*; Semana, "Ya Son 46 Los Jóvenes Desaparecidos Que Fueron Reportados Como Muertos En Combate," *Semana*, September 26, 2008, www.semana.com/nacion/conflicto-armado/articulo/ya-46-jovenes-desaparecidos-fueron-reportados-como-muertos-combate/95578-3; Semana, "Las Cuentas de Los Falsos Positivos."

[29] Rojas Bolaños and Benavides, *Ejecuciones Extrajudiciales En Colombia, 2002–2010.*

[30] Rojas Bolaños and Benavides, *Ejecuciones Extrajudiciales En Colombia, 2002–2010.*

Uribe was winning the "war on drugs" and thus used to justify additional American military aid.[31] Notably, Juan Manuel Santos, the president who later won the Nobel Peace Prize for the agreement with the FARC, was the minister of defense during most of these military-perpetrated murders. He was never indicted. While the Colombian public is arguably used to a certain level of corruption in its politicians, and Colombian citizens are less likely to claim their political rights than they are to obey leaders in exchange for protection,[32] this proof of public forces deliberately killing civilians for their own enrichment sent shock waves through the public. Why Santos was never held directly responsible for the thousands of murders that happened under his watch remains unclear.

In fact, Santos later won the presidential election on the public's expectation that he would continue the hardline direction of his predecessor against the guerrillas. Despite being the minister of defense at the time of two massive scandals involving the military, Santos somehow emerged unscathed from both the *para-política* and the "false positives" events. It is uncertain whether he knew of the extrajudicial executions that were happening under his watch, but it seems highly unlikely that, as minister of defense, he could not have known. To my knowledge, no hard evidence has been made public in that regard.

In August 2012, and against public expectations, Santos announced the start of peace negotiations with the FARC. Despite extensive controversy, including Uribe's very public and effective campaign against the accord and a failed public plebiscite on the process, the two sides put a final peace agreement in place in late 2016.[33] Santos later won the Nobel Peace Prize for his efforts – an award some critics felt was premature.

As the following sections illustrate, the peace agreement polarized the country and is an ongoing source of discontent among the Colombian public. The failure to follow through on key aspects of the accord appears to have heightened public distrust in the government, especially among rural citizens and ex-combatants from all groups. The implementation of transitional justice processes, such as truth-telling and reparations, amid ongoing armed conflict also raises myriad security concerns, especially

---

[31] Rojas Bolaños and Benavides, *Ejecuciones Extrajudiciales En Colombia, 2002–2010*.

[32] Rojas, "Securing the State and Developing Social Insecurities."

[33] Alto Comisionado para la Paz, "Acuerdo Final de Paz," 2016, www.altocomisionadoparalapaz .gov.co/procesos-y-conversaciones/Documentos compartidos/24-11-2016NuevoAcuerdo Final.pdf; El Universal, "Cronología Del Proceso de Paz Con Las Farc En La Habana," *El Universal*, November 6, 2013, www.eluniversal.com.co/colombia/cronologia-del-proceso-de-paz-con-las-farc-en-la-habana-cuba-140970.

of witnesses and victims being targeted.[34] Research also shows that violence against women frequently goes up after a peace agreement – which some scholars have argued is due to war's disruption of gender norms.[35] Indeed, one study reported that women in particular had far *less* safety and security when paramilitary combatants demobilized and returned to their communities.[36] In addition, civilian life in Colombia – and indeed in most conflict-affected countries – is underscored by violence, corruption, impunity, and vigilante justice, making ex-combatants feel extremely vulnerable when they relinquish their weapons.[37] And many ex-combatants are justifiably nervous: as of December 2021, 303 FARC ex-combatants (ten of them women) had been murdered, with the killings largely attributed to illegal armed groups, in addition to twenty-five disappearances and seventy-nine attempted homicides.[38] In addition, the Office of the United Nations High Commissioner for Human Rights has verified 412 murders of civilian social leaders and human rights defenders since the agreement was signed.[39] This number does not account for the deserters of various armed groups that have gone through the demobilization process and have been subsequently tracked down and killed by their former groups.[40] In addition, while at least 97 percent of families that received substitution benefits have voluntarily eradicated their coca crops, the UN initially stated that these families would only be able to transition away from illicit crops if sustainable opportunities reach them quickly.[41] Indeed, areas under coca cultivation in Colombia had hit an all-time high by the end of 2017.[42] Five years after the accord was signed, civil society leaders and members of Congress continued to raise concerns about the glacial pace of the implementing these projects. Clearly, Colombia continues to face complex implementation challenges regarding the peace accord, with ongoing disputes about who is to blame.

---

[34] Laura K Taylor, "Transitional Justice, Demobilisation and Peacebuilding amid Political Violence: Examining Individual Preferences in the Caribbean Coast of Colombia," *Peacebuilding* 3, no. 1 (2015): 90–108.

[35] Bouta, Bannon, and Frerks, *Gender, Conflict, and Development*.

[36] Taylor, "Transitional Justice, Demobilisation and Peacebuilding amid Political Violence."

[37] María Clemencia Castro and Carmen Lucía Díaz, *Guerrilla, Reinserción y Lazo Social* (Bogota: Almudena Editores, 1997).

[38] Antonio Guterres, "United Nations Verification Mission in Colombia: Report of the Secretary General, December 2020" (New York, 2020).

[39] Guterres.

[40] Deserters in this study repeatedly stated that they were being hunted down and killed by their former groups (or by dissidents) and that the government was not doing anything about it.

[41] Guterres, "United Nations Verification Mission in Colombia: December 2020."

[42] Antonio Guterres, "United Nations Verification Mission in Colombia: Report of the Secretary General, December 2019" (New York, 2019).

GENDER NORMS AND CONFLICT IN COLOMBIA

[V]iolence is about control – but not solely for the domination of men over women. It is embedded in a masculine state apparatus that seeks to establish supremacy over "the others," where militaries enforce the desires of an executive, democratically elected or not. When the state seeks control through violence, the resistance fights for self-determination – for the intrinsic desire to control one's own life – in the same way.

Nimmi Gowrinathan, *Radicalizing Her*

Colombia's history is replete with complex networks of armed groups, multiple attempts at peace negotiations, and many different forms of demobilization agreements and programs, all of which are heavily gendered. The overall social climate in Colombia around gender equality, women's rights, and patriarchal gender norms must be taken into consideration when examining the demobilization and reintegration of both men and women combatants, as well as combatants along the gender spectrum. In Colombia, there are two predominant and interrelated Latin American traditions of gender norms: *machismo*, which emphasizes the masculine warrior/protector/provider and the dominance of men; and *marianismo* for women, which emphasizes fertility, domesticity, subordination, and self-sacrifice.[43] Women in Colombia have, historically and currently, faced both social and political exclusion, with intersecting factors such as race, class, and geography exacerbating these inequalities. The country also has a history of marketing Colombian women's beauty as a key national symbol, with the accompanying *machismo* that privileges militarized male power, and a strong tradition of Catholicism, which emphasizes patriarchal gender norms where men are the breadwinners and heads of the family and women are caretakers and child bearers.[44] Due to the long history of armed conflict in Colombia, militarized masculinities – which link military service to manhood and prioritize *machismo* and the use of armed violence to dominate others[45] – is particularly prevalent. And, unsurprisingly, there is little to no room for gender nonbinary individuals in this discourse.

---

[43] Sylvia Chant and Nikki Craske, *Gender in Latin America* (New Jersey: Rutgers University Press, 2003).

[44] Virginia M Bouvier, "Gender and the Role of Women in Colombia's Peace Process," 2016, www.peacewomen.org/sites/default/files/Women-Colombia-Peace-Process-EN.pdf; Michael Edward Stanfield, *Of Beasts and Beauty: Gender, Race, and Identity in Colombia* (Austin: University of Texas Press, 2013).

[45] Connell and Messerschmidt, "Hegemonic Masculinity"; Raewyn Connell, "Masculinities in Global Perspective: Hegemony, Contestation, and Changing Structures of Power," *Theory and Society* 45, no. 4 (August 2016): 303–18.

Colombian feminists have made concerted efforts to challenge this status quo, and Colombia has made some significant strides in terms of women's presence in the workforce and in higher education, including progressive legislation, judicial rulings, and executive decrees to support women's rights and to address gender-based violence.[46] However, the reality for many Colombian women – especially Indigenous, Afro-descendant, and *campesino* women – does not reflect these legislative changes. For example, women who do hold political office and other positions of power generally all come from the same elite (and very white) social circles; at the local political levels, women remain vastly underrepresented, especially racialized women.[47] Intimate partner violence – including marital rape – is particularly widespread: 33.33 percent of Colombian women report having experienced physical and/or sexual intimate partner violence over their lifetime.[48] Access to justice and health care for victims of sexual violence continues to be a challenge, especially for women and lesbian, gay, bisexual, transgender, and queer (LGBTQ+) persons in rural areas – where many Indigenous and other ethnic minority populations live.[49] Sexual abuse against children (most commonly female children) is also widespread: in the last twenty years, according to the medical examiner's office, official rates of rape have tripled, and 83 percent of those cases were children under fifteen.[50] Considering that sexual violence is generally underreported, often due to fear of stigma or retribution, it is likely that the actual rates of sexual assault in Colombia are much higher; for example, in 2018, the National Victims Unit registered 97,916 victims of the armed conflict overall, but only 254 registered specifically as victims of sexual violence.[51] Relatedly, while the country's rate of adolescent pregnancy has been going down overall, these rates are higher among rural adolescents (22.2 percent compared to 13.8 percent), and the fertility rates of male adolescents

---

[46] Bouvier, "Gender and the Role of Women in Colombia's Peace Process."

[47] Bouvier, "Gender and the Role of Women in Colombia's Peace Process."

[48] UN Women, "Global Database on Violence against Women: Colombia," Global Database on Violence against Women, 2020, https://evaw-global-database.unwomen.org/en/countries/americas/colombia.

[49] Antonio Guterres, "Conflict Related Sexual Violence: Report of the Secretary General S/2019/280" (New York, 2019), www.un.org/sexualviolenceinconflict/wp-content/uploads/2019/04/report/s-2019-280/Annual-report-2018.pdf.

[50] Adriaan Alsema, "Rape in Colombia Tripled over Past 20 Years; 87% of Victims Are Minors," *Colombia Reports*, 2019, https://colombiareports.com/rape-in-colombia-tripled-over-past-20-years-87-of-victims-are-minors/.

[51] Miguel Salazar and Mariana Araujo Herrera, "The Silences of Sexual Violence: Commission Faces Truth Deficits in Colombia," Council on Hemispheric Affairs, 2015, www.coha.org/the-silences-of-sexual-violence-commission-faces-truth-deficits-in-colombia/.

are much lower than those of female adolescents, indicating that many adolescent pregnancies are fathered by adult men.[52]

The complexities of Colombia's armed conflict have reinforced the gender norms of militarized masculinity and exacerbated systemic violence against women and sexual/gender minorities. For example, opposing armed groups have targeted women for being relatives of the "other side," and right-wing paramilitaries in particular have used rape to terrorize the civilian population; in addition, forced contraception, sterilization, forced prostitution, and sexual enslavement have all been reported during the armed conflict.[53] The history of Colombia's peace negotiations also reflects an overall dominance of men and a related devaluation of women and LGBTQ+ communities. This male dominance continues to reproduce multiple gender inequalities throughout Colombia (see Figure 5) and is a critical element to understanding the armed conflict and the "post-conflict" lives of ex-combatants of all genders.

Of course, not all people in Colombia (or elsewhere) who advocate for women's equality are also supportive of LGBTQ+ rights – even though the two are often conflated under "gender issues." Despite many protective laws, a large segment of the Colombian population is still fairly homophobic, and all sides – including the state – have perpetrated violence against the LGBTQ+ community.[54] Indeed, as the earlier statistics indicate, violence against women and the LGBTQ+ community has been normalized in many parts of the country.[55] In paramilitary-held territories in particular, traditional gender roles have been enforced with violence,[56] and several informants in this study said that homosexual relationships were strictly forbidden in the FARC. Jokes and slurs against gay men were especially common in the ex-combatant populations where I spent time. Indeed, the paramilitary manipulation of gender norms and violence against homosexuals and transgender persons – continued by many of their successor organizations – have made many communities complicit in the ongoing prejudice and violence against LGBTQ+ communities.[57] Underpinning this

[52] Monica Alzate, "Adolescent Pregnancy in Colombia: The Price of Inequality and Political Conflict," in *International Handbook of Adolescent Pregnancy*, ed. Andrew Cherry and Mary Dillon (New York: Springer, 2014).

[53] Guterres, "Conflict Related Sexual Violence"; Grupo de Memoria Histórica, "Basta Ya! Colombia: Memorias de Guerra y Dignidad" (Bogotá, 2016).

[54] Grupo de Memoria Histórica, "Basta Ya! Colombia."

[55] Grupo de Memoria Histórica, "Basta Ya! Colombia."

[56] Bouvier, "Gender and the Role of Women in Colombia's Peace Process"; Rachel Schmidt, *No Girls Allowed? Recruitment and Gender in Colombian Armed Groups* (Ottawa: ProQuest Dissertations Publishing, 2007).

[57] Bouvier, "Gender and the Role of Women in Colombia's Peace Process."

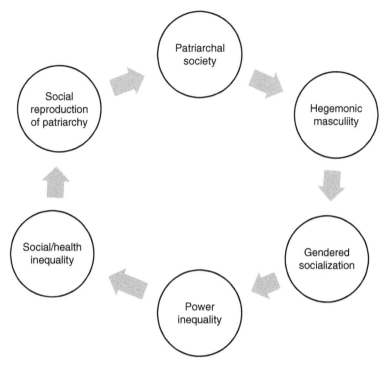

FIGURE 5 The dynamics of gender inequalities.
Image credit: Alex Scott-Samuel, "Patriarchy, Masculinities and Health Inequalities" (Liverpool: University of Liverpool, 2008), https://scielosp.org/article/gs/2009.v23n2/159-160/.

emphasis on patriarchal gender norms is the widespread influence of conservative Christianity, as Colombia remains a majority Catholic country with rising numbers of Pentecostal congregations.[58]

OVERVIEW OF THE ARMED GROUPS (FARC, AUC, AND ELN)

FARC

In our case, with the government of Uribe with the famous "democratic security" ... the "democratic security," well, it consists of all possible forms of war to end the organization and the foundations of our organization. And for them, who was the foundation of the organization? *Campesinos*, those

[58] For example, according to the Pew Research Center, 92 percent of Colombians say they were raised Catholic and 79 percent currently identify as Catholic.

who supported us ... The *campesinos*. The ones who helped us. It is because they are human beings and if one arrives in the region and shares with them ... these are regions where there is no government present ... where there are no roads, where there is no energy, where there are no means, and the only possible force is the organization that arrives there. So, then people become very close friends with us. But they are not to blame that they are abandoned by the state. Because of course they will give you support.

Mari, FARC (B58)

Officially founded in 1966 and now in an ongoing reintegration process after signing a peace agreement with the Colombian government in 2016, the FARC (also known as the FARC-EP) was one of the oldest and most powerful guerrilla armies in the world before it disarmed. The precursor of this rebel group began in 1964 with forty-six men and two women intent on overthrowing the government to radically restructure society.[59] The original FARC recruits came primarily from rural areas, where poor *campesino* farmers were fleeing sectarian violence and forming self-defense groups. The FARC consolidated power and legitimacy in rural areas by offering protection to *campesino* farmers in return for a tax on their coca crop earnings.[60] The pull of rising profits from Colombia's thriving drug trade, as well as funding shortages brought on by the end of the Cold War and the FARC's break from the Colombian Communist Party, drew the group into increasing involvement in coca production, cocaine trafficking, and kidnapping to fund their rebellion.[61] In the early 2000s, in a move away from previous practices, the FARC also threatened, kidnapped, and killed political candidates in order to "free" certain areas from politics.[62] While the FARC's highest levels of command have repeatedly condemned the drug trade as one of the Colombia's greatest ills (including in my interviews), the links of the FARC to drug trafficking have long been established,[63] and several ex-FARC militia commanders in this study provided detailed information on how they trafficked narcotics for the group. In addition, while the FARC claimed to be fighting on behalf of Colombian *campesinos* – and later, also on behalf of Indigenous rights – my respondents suggested that

---

[59] Simons, "Colombia."
[60] Livingstone, *Inside Colombia*.
[61] Steven Monblatt, "Terrorism and Drugs in the Americas: The OAS Response," OAS, 2004, www.oas.org/ezine/ezine24/Monblatt.htm; Angel Rabasa and Peter Chalk, *Colombian Labyrinth* (Santa Monica: RAND Corporation, 2001), www.rand.org/pubs/monograph_reports/MR1339.html.
[62] Rojas, "Securing the State and Developing Social Insecurities."
[63] Castrillón and Guerra Molina, "A Deep Influence."

treatment of civilians and relationships with Indigenous peoples varied significantly depending on individual commanders. As subsequent chapters show, misinformation, propaganda, and mistrust on all sides have been key characteristics of Colombia's conflict.

The FARC was significantly more regimented and "army-like" than the paramilitaries, with a high percentage of both *campesinos* and women in its forces, and its troops were younger and less educated overall compared to the paramilitaries, whose recruits were generally older and commonly had military experience.[64] Historically, FARC recruits were never paid directly (though there is evidence of personal enrichment at higher levels of command) and most recruits were indoctrinated with ideological training to ensure their commitment to the cause.[65] However, respondents indicated that not all recruits received the same level of indoctrination – especially urban militia members.

FARC members in this study and others cite a wide range of reasons for joining the ranks, from fleeing violence to being fascinated with weapons, to following romantic partners (both men and women), to being inspired by the FARC's fight against injustice, among many other reasons. As discussed in subsequent chapters, some women also cited fear of sexual violence from the military and paramilitaries as a reason for joining.

In terms of female membership, estimates of women in the FARC guerrilla forces, including FARC commanders' claims, range widely from 20–50 percent, though most credible estimates land between 30–40 percent.[66] The FARC has long claimed a platform of gender equality in a direct and explicit challenge to Colombia's patriarchal norms, and their former website linked to a separate *Mujer Fariana* page created by the women of the FARC in 2013, which contained feminist manifestos and proclamations about women's rights and gender equality.[67] When considering the group's utilization of women's rights and gender equality discourse as a political tool, the timing of the original *Mujer Fariana* website is important, as it went up approximately one year after the peace talks started in 2012. The FARC political party now has a Gender Committee, which co-hosted a workshop with the UN Mission in 2018 to ensure

---

[64] Taylor, "Transitional Justice, Demobilisation and Peacebuilding amid Political Violence."

[65] Francisco Gutiérrez Sanín, "Telling the Difference: Guerrillas and Paramilitaries in the Colombian War," *Politics & Society* 36, no. 1 (2008): 3–34.

[66] Gutiérrez Sanín, "Telling the Difference"; Human Rights Watch, "'You'll Learn Not to Cry': Child Combatants in Colombia" (New York, 2003), www.hrw.org/reports/2003/colombia0903/colombia0903.pdf.

[67] At the time of writing much of this information could still be found on FARC's political site: https://partidofarc.com.co.

a gender-sensitive approach in reintegration projects.[68] The successes of these efforts are still unclear, however, with many female ex-combatants in this study reporting that gender equality in the guerrilla ranks was better than in Colombian society.

Indeed, despite evidence and testimony of gender-based violence, sexual exploitation of minors, and forced abortions in the ranks, the FARC has created a public framing of being not only egalitarian but explicitly feminist. Rape and other forms of sexual violence were strictly forbidden in FARC regulations, and unlike their paramilitary opponents, the FARC did not use sexual violence as a strategy to control territory.[69] Reports exist of opportunistic sexual violence by FARC troops, but in general sexual violence was not used by the FARC as a war strategy and forced recruitment by the FARC was rare.[70] And, as subsequent chapters will demonstrate, many female ex-combatants in this study proclaimed a staunch commitment to women's rights and gratitude to the FARC for their militant experiences.

While an estimated 14,000 FARC combatants demobilized collectively after the 2016 peace agreement, thousands have since left the demobilization and reintegration sites (ETCRs) and many of these departing ex-combatants are not being adequately tracked, leaving unanswered questions about the efficacy of the program and rates of recidivism.[71] Indeed, in late 2019, amid dual accusations that neither side was fulfilling the peace agreement, three of the key FARC negotiators of the peace accord – Jesús Santrich, Iván Márquez,[72] and Hernán Darío Velázquez (aka "El Paisa") – appeared in a video announcing that they were returning to arms due to the government's failure to implement its promises.[73] This dramatic rejection of the peace accord set off another firestorm of discursive battles.

---

[68] Guterres, "United Nations Verification Mission in Colombia: April 2018."

[69] Bouvier, "Gender and the Role of Women in Colombia's Peace Process."

[70] Bouvier, "Gender and the Role of Women in Colombia's Peace Process"; Grupo de Memoria Histórica, "Basta Ya! Colombia."

[71] Guterres, "United Nations Verification Mission in Colombia: December 2019"; Antonio Guterres, "United Nations Verification Mission in Colombia: Report of the Secretary General, March 2020" (New York, 2020).

[72] Márquez (aka Luciano Marín) led the FARC's negotiating team during the four-year peace talks; he resigned his seat in the Colombian Senate and went into hiding shortly after Santrich was arrested. He later reappeared in a video saying that the FARC had made a critical error in laying down their weapons too early before establishing clear guarantees. Guterres, "United Nations Verification Mission in Colombia: December 2019."

[73] EFE, "El Ex Número Dos de Las FARC, Iván Márquez, Anuncia Que Retoma Las Armas," *La Vanguardia*, August 29, 2019, www.lavanguardia.com/internacional/20190829/4734958577/farc-guerrilla-vuelta-armas-ivan-marquez.html.

AUC

If we [the AUC] had not existed, the country would not be like this, it would be even worse, it would be worse because we were the ones who sought out the guerrillas to attack them, to prevent them from shooting up the villages.

Pedro, ex-AUC (B77)

As stated earlier, the AUC formally organized in 1997 out of small groups of *autodefensas* ("self-defense forces") composed of landowners and elite drug cartels.[74] Paramilitary forces in Colombia are infamous for being particularly brutal, using gender-based violence against LGBTQ+ peoples and women as a specific form of social control.[75] During fieldwork for this study, this reputation was readily apparent: respondents would discuss and name the FARC quite openly, but when discussions moved to the AUC, most respondents would lower their voices or use euphemisms rather than the group's actual name. Once, while having coffee at an upscale mall in northern Bogotá, I casually used the word *paraco* (common slang for "paramilitary") and one of my Colombian research assistants – himself a FARC deserter – gaped at me in horror and hissed at me to keep my voice down. The specter of paramilitary violence looms large in Colombia.

Indeed, the former paramilitaries that I spoke to always referred to themselves as *autodefensas*, rejecting the stigma attached to the word "paramilitaries." Data from the Colombian Victims' Unit confirm that paramilitaries were responsible for more massacres and direct attacks on civilians than the FARC, while the FARC was more likely to use landmines and kidnappings and to cause forced displacement.[76] The AUC was known for using sexual violence as a tactic, including specifically targeting pregnant women and killing fetuses to spread terror.[77] The group used sexual violence to control territory, to punish and humiliate opposing forces by assaulting the wives and girlfriends of commanders, to stigmatize women suspected of being associated with guerrillas, and to build troop cohesion around a shared identity of violent masculinity.[78] Indeed, some segments of the Colombian public – particularly ones displaced by paramilitary violence – saw the guerrillas as more "humane" and

---

[74] Romero, *Paramilitares y Autodefensas.*
[75] Bouvier, "Gender and the Role of Women in Colombia's Peace Process."
[76] Gutiérrez Sanín, "Telling the Difference."
[77] Rojas, "Securing the State and Developing Social Insecurities"; Bouvier, "Gender and the Role of Women in Colombia's Peace Process."
[78] Grupo de Memoria Histórica, "Basta Ya! Colombia."

less *machista* than the paramilitaries,[79] and macabre stories of paramilitary violence were rampant during my fieldwork among both ex-combatants and civilians. One research assistant told me several times about a pond of alligators near his childhood home into which the paramilitaries used to throw their victims. Another popular and oft-repeated story was that of AUC combatants playing soccer with the heads of their victims. Whether true or not, these gruesome stories all served the purpose of breeding fear in the population, often in a highly gendered manner.

While the FARC, ELN, and AUC all benefited or continue to benefit from the drug trade, the paramilitaries differed from the guerrillas in that they were very open about their source of profits. One of the group's founders, Carlos Castaño, stated in a television interview that 70 percent of the group's revenue was from the drug trade, but in an open letter to Congress he also stated that the group was supported by national and international businesses.[80] While the group officially demobilized in 2003–6 as part of an agreement with the Colombian government, this "peace" process was largely criticized by human rights actors as being too lenient and not adequately dismantling paramilitary power and networks.[81] Many citizens, especially those displaced by paramilitary violence, felt that the government's conditional amnesty was prioritizing ex-combatants over their victims.[82] Indeed, these programmatic weaknesses helped lead to the emergence of BACRIMs, which are now considered a key threat to security and to the ongoing peace process.[83] These groups, such as the Black Eagles and the Autodefensas Gaitanistas de Colombia (aka the "Gulf Clan"), largely grew out of "demobilized" paramilitaries and are now some of the leading drug cartels in Colombia, with known ties to Mexican drug traffickers like the Sinaloa cartel.[84]

---

[79] Luis Alberto Arias, "Familias En Situación de Desplazamiento En Altos de Cazucá" (Bogotá, 2003); Schmidt, "No Girls Allowed?"

[80] Reuters, "Colombian Paramilitary Chief Admits Getting Backing from Businessmen," *CNN*, September 6, 2000, www.cnn.com/2000/WORLD/americas/09/06/colombia.paramilitary .reut/.

[81] Reuters, "Colombian Paramilitary Chief."

[82] Jose E Arvelo, "International Law and Conflict Resolution in Colombia: Balancing Peace and Justice in the Paramilitary Demobilization Process," *Georgetown Journal of International Law* 37, no. 2 (2006): 411.

[83] Alzate, "Adolescent Pregnancy in Colombia."

[84] León Valencia and Ariel Avila, "La Compleja Estructura Detrás Del 'Clan Del Golfo,'" *El Tiempo*, July 14, 2018, www.eltiempo.com/justicia/conflicto-y-narcotrafico/como-funciona-la-estructura-del-clan-del-golfo-243522; José Meléndez, "Increasing Presence of Mexican Drug Cartels in Colombia," *El Universal*, October 2018, www.eluniversal .com.mx/english/increasing-presence-of-mexican-drug-cartels-colombia.

Such groups have clashed with the ELN and dissidents from the FARC in some areas, while collaborating with them in others.[85] In fact, many ex-paramilitaries in this study said they personally knew demobilized AUC members who had returned to armed activities and that they themselves had received multiple offers to work with these groups. The pull for these ex-combatants to return to illegal activity, whether through peer pressure or financial incentives, remains very high.

Estimates of women active in the AUC ranks are low, with several databases showing averages of less than 1 percent,[86] while others claim it is as high as 10 percent.[87] The lack of female presence can be partly attributed to the fact that the AUC was working to maintain the status quo in a highly *machista* society against a leftist (and purportedly feminist) guerrilla army. Indeed, several participants in this study told me that the AUC wanted men with military experience and generally avoided recruiting women and children. One told me that he threatened to quit if the group ever put women in command positions. The AUC also enforced highly gendered codes of conduct in areas under their control, such as not allowing men to have long or dyed hair or earrings, insisting that women be accompanied by male partners, and determining behaviors that differentiated "decent" and "indecent" women – with severe punishments for women who deviated from acceptable norms.[88] The AUC's so-called social cleansing raids (i.e., executions of neighborhood "undesirables" such as street kids, drug addicts, and prostitutes) also violently targeted homosexuals in particular, and there is evidence of off-duty police and military officers supporting these raids.[89]

Nonetheless, the low estimates of female AUC members do not usually take into consideration women living in paramilitary zones (and/or with male paramilitary fighters) who may have assisted with storing weapons, moving drugs, contributing intelligence, and other critical support operations. In fact, some female ex-paramilitaries in this study noted that many more women were involved than official numbers indicate, such as women who were sent to join the guerrillas as spies.[90] Notably, the wives of ex-paramilitaries in the collective compounds where I conducted interviews declined to participate in this study on the grounds that they were never

---

[85] Valencia and Avila, "La Compleja Estructura Detrás Del 'Clan Del Golfo.'"

[86] Author interview C13; Gutiérrez Sanín, "Telling the Difference."

[87] Bouvier, "Gender and the Role of Women in Colombia's Peace Process."

[88] Bouvier, "Gender and the Role of Women in Colombia's Peace Process"; Schmidt, "No Girls Allowed?"

[89] Grupo de Memoria Histórica, "Basta Ya! Colombia"; Schmidt, "No Girls Allowed?"; Simons, "Colombia."

[90] Author interviews B87, B99.

"combatants," despite repeated statements that I was interested in talking to anyone even tangentially involved. Several of the men respondents stated multiple times, and firmly, that their wives were *never* involved in the AUC, implying that women involved with the group were not respectable. As one man said: "No, I never let her. I never let [my wife] enter into that."[91] Another man said women should not be in the ranks because they are weak and cause trouble.[92] Indeed, some ex-AUC men told me that women paramilitaries were especially "crazy" and frighteningly violent. (Notably, I never heard women discussed in this way in any FARC or ELN interviews.) As Tobias once told me: "No one is more violent in war than women. People do things in war you would never believe." This common trope assigned to women in armed groups conveniently maintains patriarchal hierarchies by reaffirming that women willingly involved in violence are gender deviants, possibly psychotic, and definitely not to be be trusted.

In terms of recruitment, the AUC openly recruited members through flyers and public gatherings and paid their recruits fairly well – a key aspect of their rapid membership growth, especially as Colombia's unemployment reached record highs in the late 1990s. They were also successful at recruiting ex-guerrillas whose families had suffered due to FARC activities.[93] Indeed, several participants in this study had been members of multiple groups, with some switching from guerrillas to paramilitaries (more common) or vice versa (less common). While some paramilitaries demobilized individually, the majority in this study – and in general – did so through the obligatory group demobilization process in 2003–6. But, as this demobilization process illustrates, failing to adequately address an armed group's underlying criminal networks, political ties, and financial assets wreaked havoc on this supposed "peace" deal.

ELN

The government says, "the guerrillas are terrorists," because they kill one or two people. And so, if the guerrillas are terrorists, when we were bombarded and [the army] killed fifteen, sixteen, and seventeen people, or eighteen, twenty to thirty people, they aren't terrorists? So, what are they? Good guys? They say, Colombian justice says: if you kill a person, you must pay. So, then what of those people who bomb [us]? Because they don't pay for all of the guerrillas they kill. If they kill twelve, twenty, thirty, forty, it's because there is no justice.

Junior, ex-ELN (B17)

[91] Author interview B76.
[92] Author interview B81.
[93] Livingstone, *Inside Colombia.*

Due to their lack of territory, size, power, and impact, much less research has been conducted on the ELN compared to the other two groups examined in this book. Nonetheless, they remain an active guerrilla faction that is potentially recruiting ex-combatants from other groups and is certainly clashing with dissidents of the FARC in some areas while collaborating with them in others.[94]

The ELN formed in 1964 and was originally made up of middle-class students, Catholic radicals, and leftist intellectuals inspired by Che Guevara and Catholic liberation theology.[95] After decades of eschewing the drug trade, by the late 1990s the group began taxing trafficking routes to finance its operations.[96] In 1998 the government attempted to negotiate a peace agreement with the ELN but controversy erupted when the government refused to set up a second demilitarized zone for the ELN similar to the one created for the FARC, and the ELN responded with a series of mass kidnappings.[97] In 2009, the ELN and FARC negotiated a ceasefire agreement and even allegedly cooperated in military operations.[98] Colombia has also accused Venezuela of harboring ELN combatants and funding their operations,[99] and several ex-combatants from the ELN in this study confirmed that they had often gone back and forth between the two countries.

In 2016, the government and the ELN announced that they would begin peace negotiations again,[100] but at the time of writing this process had been called off due to increasing violence and kidnappings on behalf of the ELN. In fact, in February 2018, the ELN reportedly signed an agreement with FARC dissidents to fight the Colombian armed forces in the department of Arauca in order to maintain joint control of the Venezuelan border in that area.[101] In early 2019, shortly after I left the country, the ELN shocked Colombians by detonating a car bomb at

---

[94] Alicia Liliana Méndez, "Eln y Disidencias Se Unieron En Arauca Para Controlar La Frontera," *El Tiempo*, February 18, 2018, www.eltiempo.com/justicia/conflicto-y-narcotrafico/eln-y-disidencias-firman-pacto-de-control-en-arauca-327990.

[95] Livingstone, *Inside Colombia*.

[96] Mapping Militants Project, "National Liberation Army (Colombia): Mapping Militant Organizations," Stanford, 2015, http://web.stanford.edu/group/mappingmilitants/cgi-bin/groups/view/87.

[97] Livingstone, *Inside Colombia*.

[98] InSight Crime, "ELN Profile," 2017, www.insightcrime.org/colombia-organized-crime-news/eln-profile.

[99] Semana, "ELN, El Nuevo Enemigo."

[100] Human Rights Watch, "World Report 2017: Colombia," New York, 2017, www.hrw.org/world-report/2017/country-chapters/colombia.

[101] Méndez, "Eln y Disidencias Se Unieron En Arauca Para Controlar La Frontera."

a police academy in Bogotá, killing twenty-one people (mostly young police cadets) and injuring dozens more – the first such attack in many years.[102] The ELN claimed that the bombing was in retaliation for the government breaking the ceasefire and bombing one of their camps on December 25, 2018, and that the police academy was a legitimate military target.[103] The government labeled the bombing a terrorist attack because most of the victims were civilian cadets in training and were not yet official police officers.[104] The bombing renewed governmental condemnation of the group and destroyed any hope that the Colombian public might have another peace accord in the near future. During the Covid-19 pandemic, the ELN initially agreed to a ceasefire in April 2020, but then declined to extend the ceasefire, saying that it had not been reciprocated by the government.[105]

While the ELN has been less overtly feminist compared to the FARC in terms of public declarations and propaganda, some estimates put the group at a quarter to a third women.[106] Junior told me that the ELN were the "real" revolutionaries, unlike the FARC, who he said were just drug traffickers and criminals – a familiar echo of the government's narco-terrorist framing. The ELN's official website has statements around a "gender focus," one of which ties capitalism to *machismo* and discusses the importance of creating a new Colombia where divisive identities such as man, woman, Black, white, or Indigenous do not matter.[107] This same publication discusses how it is not only women's responsibilities to fight for gender equality, while admitting that very few women are commanders and some guerrilla roles are more "suitable" for women.[108] Indeed, many ex-ELN participants in this study repeatedly stated that everyone was treated "equally" in terms of roles and responsibilities, regardless of gender. However, as subsequent chapters show, the guerrilla concept of gender equality is often utilitarian and limited in scope.

[102] El Tiempo, "Cuatro Fichas Claves En El Plan Contra La Escuela de Cadetes," *El Tiempo*, January 20, 2019, www.eltiempo.com/justicia/conflicto-y-narcotrafico/los-hombres-del-eln-tras-atentado-con-carro-bomba-en-escuela-general-santander-316580.
[103] ELN, "El Camino Es La Solución Política Del Conflicto," eln-voces.com, 2019, https://eln-voces.com/el-camino-es-la-solucion-politica-del-conflicto/.
[104] El Tiempo, "Cuatro Fichas Claves En El Plan Contra La Escuela de Cadetes."
[105] Antonio Guterres, "United Nations Verification Mission in Colombia: Report of the Secretary General, June 2020" (New York, 2020).
[106] Bouvier, "Gender and the Role of Women in Colombia's Peace Process."
[107] ELN, "El Enfoque de Género y La Equidad," 2016, https://eln-voces.com/el-enfoque-de-genero-y-la-equidad/.
[108] ELN, "El Enfoque de Género y La Equidad."

COLOMBIA'S REPEATED ATTEMPTS AT PEACE

Many different administrations in Colombia have attempted peace with various armed groups, with consistent prioritization of disarmament and demobilization.[109] This focus has often been at the expense of effective and sustainable reintegration, which has left many ex-combatants and civilians disillusioned, resentful, and at risk. For example, of the total combatants that have ever entered the government's formal reintegration program (i.e., demobilized AUC members and guerrilla deserters), at least 3,209 (6 percent) have since been murdered, 5,778 (11 percent) have been registered as "at risk" (i.e., credible threats have been made against them), and at least 6,833 (13 percent) are known to have returned to an armed group.[110] That is a total of at least 30 percent of registered ex-combatants outside the FARC peace agreement who have either been murdered, are living in situations of serious threat, or have returned to armed activity – and the real number is almost certainly far higher. These statistics do not, for example, include the deaths and recidivism of ex-combatants who never registered with the government, nor of deserters whose deaths are not being reported and/or tracked. In fact, independent research has estimated recidivism rates closer to 24 percent.[111]

In addition, receiving communities have historically not been adequately consulted before ex-combatants return, contributing to distrust and insecurity in these areas, with some civilians resentful of the benefits that ex-combatants receive.[112] Many ex-combatants in this study, particularly ex-paramilitaries, said that once an employer found out they were ex-combatants, they would immediately lose their jobs – for some, insecurity and the need to hide their past continued to follow them over a decade after disarming. Also, as the demobilization and reintegration programs are largely funded by taxpayer dollars, they remain fairly controversial among the Colombian public, fueling public resentment toward ex-combatants and overall polarization in Colombian society.[113]

---

[109] Eduardo Pizarro Leongómez, *Cambiar El Futuro: Historia de Los Procesos de Paz En Colombia (1981–2016)* (Bogotá: Penguin Random House, 2017).

[110] ARN, "La Reintegración En Colombia – Cifras" (Bogotá, 2019), www.reintegracion .gov.co/es/la-reintegracion/Paginas/cifras.aspx.

[111] FIP, "Retorno a La Legalidad o Reincidencia de Excombatientes En Colombia: Dimensión Del Fenómeno y Factores de Riesgo" (Bogota, 2014), http://cdn.ideaspaz.org/ media/website/document/53c8560f2376b.pdf.

[112] Mendez, "Militarized Gender Performativity"; Taylor, "Transitional Justice, Demobilisation and Peacebuilding amid Political Violence."

[113] Author interview C07; Galvis et al., "Barómetro de Las Américas Colombia 2016."

Between 2001 and 2021, the government reported that of the total 76,440 demobilized combatants (approximately 15 percent women), 51,682 of these combatants (approximately 14 percent women) entered an ARN reintegration program; this is not including the collectively demobilized FARC (approximately 23 percent women).[114] However, the government's history of peace agreements with armed groups and guerrilla and paramilitary demobilizations actually goes back to at least 1982, with the presidency of Belisario Betancur (1982–6).[115] But Betancur's insistence on creating numerous new organizations to deal with the peace process and related reforms ultimately led to a confusing and ineffective process.[116] In 1989, President Virgilio Barco's government successfully negotiated the transformation of the guerrilla group M-19 into a legal political party.[117] But many M-19 guerrillas disagreed with this process and abandoned the demobilization, with some joining the FARC or M-19 dissidents. One ex-FARC commander that I interviewed had been in all three of these groups before he finally deserted the FARC.[118] In this same period, several Liberal and UP presidential candidates were murdered, along with thousands of other UP members, allegedly on the command of drug cartels. Indeed, former president Alfonso López Michelsen noted that Barco was facing a "double war" against both increasingly powerful drug cartels and insurgent groups.[119]

In the early 1990s, the government of César Gaviria embarked on peace talks with three guerrilla groups: the FARC, ELN, and the EPL, who were operating jointly under an umbrella organization called the Simon Bolivar Guerrilla Coordinator.[120] The EPL officially signed a peace agreement with the government in 1991 along with several smaller guerrilla groups; however, some EPL members still remain active.[121]

With this background of multiple failed or only partially implemented peace negotiations, Ernesto Samper came to office in 1994 with

---

[114] ARN, "La Reintegración En Colombia – Cifras"; Colombian Ministry of Defense, "15 Años Transformando Historias," *Las Fuerzas: Periódico Del Comando General de Las Fuerzas Militares de Colombia* 47, September 2017.
[115] Leongómez, *Cambiar El Futuro*.
[116] Leongómez, *Cambiar El Futuro*.
[117] Leongómez, *Cambiar El Futuro*; BBC, "BBC Colombia Timeline," BBC News, 2018, www.bbc.com/news/world-latin-america-19390164.
[118] Author interview B01.
[119] Leongómez, *Cambiar El Futuro*.
[120] Harvey F Kline, *State Building and Conflict Resolution in Colombia: 1986–1994* (Tuscaloosa: University of Alabama Press, 2002).
[121] Daniel Mendendorp Escobar, "Colombia Guerrilla Group EPL Wants to Join Peace Dialogues," *Colombia Reports*, 2014, https://colombiareports.com/colombia-guerrillla-group-epl-wants-join-peace-dialogues/.

declarations that he too would pursue peace with the rebels; however, Samper accomplished little in this regard, as his presidency was plagued by accusations that he had received donations from the Cali drug cartel.[122] During Samper's administration, the FARC took advantage of internal political unrest and mounted major offensives against the military that allowed the group to consolidate territory and dramatically increase troop size. By 1998, the FARC had reached the peak of its power and the US Defense Intelligence Agency warned that the group could defeat the Colombian military within five years.[123]

In that same year, Andrés Pastrana was elected and began discussions with the FARC, where he granted the group a large safe haven of territory that was off-limits to the military.[124] But after three years of stop-and-go peace talks, during which Pastrana repeatedly extended the safe haven, the president ordered the FARC out of the demilitarized zone after they hijacked a plane. In response, the FARC stepped up attacks and the government subsequently declared a war zone in the south of the country, closing any further discussion of peace at that time.[125] In the middle of these conflicts, US President Bill Clinton announced "Plan Colombia": nearly US$1 billion in aid primarily focused on the military and earmarked specifically to fight drug trafficking.[126] Many of the FARC loyalists that I interviewed spoke about Plan Colombia with great disdain, arguing that this money could have been much better spent addressing poverty, inequality, human rights, and land reform.

Álvaro Uribe was then elected in 2002 on promises to crack down even harder on the rebels. And he did not disappoint. Many former guerrillas that I interviewed spoke of Uribe's "Democratic Security," a policy he launched with the help of Israeli security consultants, which essentially subsumed democracy to security.[127] The goal of this policy was to invest in security and restore the government's authority across Colombia, in

[122] Simons, "Colombia."
[123] Garry M Leech, *The FARC: The Longest Insurgency* (London, New York, Halifax: Fernwood, 2011).
[124] BBC, "BBC Colombia Timeline"; Scott Wilson, "Colombian Rebels Use Refuge to Expand Their Power Base," *The Washington Post*, October 3, 2001, www.washingtonpost .com/archive/politics/2001/10/03/colombian-rebels-use-refuge-to-expand-their-power-base/88d8f638-24ea-4607-ac19-c4293bdac97e/?utm_term=.3e6fcb073e3c.
[125] BBC, "BBC Colombia Timeline."
[126] BBC, "BBC Colombia Timeline"; Castrillón Riascos and Guerra Molina, "A Deep Influence."
[127] Alexander F Fattal, *Guerrilla Marketing: Counterinsurgency and Capitalism in Colombia* (Chicago: University of Chicago Press, 2018).

the hopes that citizens would see the state as legitimate and thus cooperate with counterinsurgency efforts.[128] However, that investment in security took priority over social security, health infrastructure, land reform, and poverty reduction, and the resulting violence affected poor communities the most. From the guerrilla point of view, Uribe's "Democratic Security" was nothing more than a massive military offensive launched to kill them all – with many civilians getting caught in the crossfire or accused of being guerrilla sympathizers.

In 2003, Uribe began demobilization negotiations with the right-wing AUC paramilitaries, and in 2005 the government began exploratory peace talks with the ELN in Cuba.[129] As part of these negotiations, the government introduced the highly controversial Law 975, known as the "Justice and Peace Law," which some critics dubbed the "Impunity for Mass Murderers, Terrorists, and Major Cocaine Traffickers Law."[130] This law established sentences of five to eight years in prison for ex-combatants in exchange for their commitment to the truth and reparation of the victims; while it was originally implemented for AUC commanders, it was later extended to include demobilized guerrillas.[131] Thus, some former AUC commanders have since completed their sentences for serious crimes – including civilian massacres and child recruitment – and are now free.[132] During this time the government created an agency called the Reincorporation Program into Civilian Life (PRVC) to assist in the reintegration of ex-combatants (now called the ARN, as discussed in Chapter III). Although Uribe hailed the AUC demobilization as a success, in 2006 the *para-política* investigation began on high-ranking politicians, and by late 2006, detained paramilitary leaders announced that they would pull out of peace talks.[133] In 2011, Uribe's close ally and former chief

[128] Fattal, *Guerrilla Marketing*.
[129] BBC, "BBC Colombia Timeline."
[130] New York Times, "Colombia's Capitulation," *New York Times*, July 6, 2005, www
.nytimes.com/2005/07/06/opinion/colombias-capitulation.html.
[131] Congreso de la Republica de Colombia, "Ley 975 de 2005," Pub. L. No. 45.980, 1 (2005),
www.fiscalia.gov.co/colombia/wp-content/uploads/2013/04/Ley-975-del-25-de-julio-
de-2005-concordada-con-decretos-y-sentencias-de-constitucionalidad.pdf.
[132] Bluradio, "Nueve Exjefes 'Paras' Que Estuvieron Presos En Colombia Ya Están
Libres,"*Blueradio*, 2016, www.bluradio.com/nacion/nueve-exjefes-paras-que-estuvieron-
presos-en-colombia-ya-estan-libres-119450.
[133] Élber Gutiérrez Roa, "Guía Práctica Para Entender El Escándalo de La 'Para-
Política,'" *Semana*, April 10, 2007, www.semana.com/on-line/articulo/guia-practica-
para-entender-escandalo-para-politica/84455-3.

of intelligence, Jorge Noguera, was sentenced to twenty-five years in prison for collaborating with paramilitary death squads.[134] This, along with multiple subsequent convictions of high-ranking politicians also linked to the paramilitaries, seriously damaged the government's credibility in terms of potential peace deals with the guerrillas. In addition, many human rights groups and analysts were skeptical of the AUC demobilization plan as it failed to dismantle paramilitary financial resources, political ties, and criminal networks.[135]

In 2007, Uribe released dozens of FARC prisoners in the hope that the FARC would reciprocate by releasing hostages. Instead, the rebels demanded a new demilitarized zone, and later that year, Venezuelan leader Hugo Chavez stepped in as a mediator, eventually able to secure the release of two high-profile political hostages.[136] In 2009, Uribe finally offered peace talks to the FARC in exchange for a ceasefire and the cessation of all criminal activities. But at the end of this same year, the FARC and ELN declared that they would stop fighting each other and would focus only on fighting the armed forces.[137] A few months after Juan Manuel Santos succeeded Uribe in 2010, the FARC increased violent attacks. Nonetheless, only one year later, the FARC announced a ceasefire as peace talks with the Santos administration began in Cuba. After four years of negotiations and a public referendum that failed by a very close margin (50.21 percent voted against the peace agreement, with only 37.4 percent of eligible voters casting a ballot), the FARC and the Colombian government finally signed a revised peace deal. In June 2017, the FARC formally ended its existence as an armed group after more than fifty years of insurgency.[138] But, as subsequent chapters show, the reintegration aspect of this latest demobilization process continues to face significant challenges that threaten lasting peace.

[134] BBC, "BBC Colombia Timeline"; Semana, "La Fiscalía Acusa a Jorge Noguera de Haber Puesto El DAS Al Servicio de Los Paras," *Semana*, February 1, 2008, www.semana.com/on-line/articulo/la-fiscalia-acusa-jorge-noguera-haber-puesto-das-servicio-paras/90753-3.
[135] Human Rights Watch, "Smoke and Mirrors"; Human Rights Watch, "Paramilitaries' Heirs"; Nussio, "Learning from Shortcomings"; Sontag, "Colombia's Paramilitaries and the U.S. War on Drugs."
[136] BBC, "BBC Colombia Timeline."
[137] BBC, "BBC Colombia Timeline."
[138] BBC, "BBC Colombia Timeline"; El Tiempo, "La Del Plebiscito Fue La Mayor Abstención En 22 Años," *El Tiempo*, October 2, 2016, www.eltiempo.com/politica/proceso-de-paz/abstencion-en-el-plebiscito-por-la-paz-36672.

THE BATTLE OVER "GENDER IDEOLOGY"
IN THE 2016 PEACE PLEBISCITE

So, we the women, our mothers, our grandmothers, our women ancestors, have been the ones who have suffered most in this war, and that have suffered most because we are widows. Here there are widows, women who lost their parents, women without children, because their children were killed, women victims of displacement, human rights violations, rape, total psychological violation ... you cannot be peaceful due to the fact that you are a woman because, because you know that the time could return where a husband has to watch how they raped his wife and he could not do anything, his mother raped, his daughters, and the mother too, and no. I mean, that is something crazy, and I mean, I say that no, no, no, no one resists.

Mafe, FARC (B29)

In the peace negotiations between the Colombian government and various different armed groups between 1990 and 1994, only one woman was a signatory – including among all the witnesses, guarantors, and negotiators.[139] There were no women present in the negotiations with the AUC.[140] In the four sets of peace negotiations with the FARC, the small number of women that were present on both sides used their position to make issues of gender inequality more visible and push for more female representation.[141] But the significant gender focus in the 2016 peace agreement was not necessarily due to the FARC's leftist ideology. At the beginning of negotiations in 2012, despite initial promises from the guerrillas and the government to include women in the process, there were no women involved on either side and there was no mention of gender or women's participation in the framework agreement.[142] During the next round of talks in Cuba, only one negotiator was a woman: Tanja Nimeijer, a Dutch national who joined the FARC in 2002 and became a leading figurehead for the group. Arguably, Nimeijer's position at the table – as a white, European, FARC "celebrity" – was not representative of the average Colombian woman guerrilla.

Nevertheless, from the inception of the agreement, women's groups in Colombia had been insisting on their inclusion, and in 2013 these

---

[139] Londoño and Nieto, *Mujeres No Contadas.*
[140] Bouvier, "Gender and the Role of Women in Colombia's Peace Process."
[141] Bouvier, "Gender and the Role of Women in Colombia's Peace Process."
[142] Hilde Salvesen and Dag Nylander, "Towards an Inclusive Peace: Women and the Gender Approach in the Colombian Peace Process," Reliefweb.int, 2017, https://reliefweb .int/sites/reliefweb.int/files/resources/Salvesen_Nylander_Towards an inclusive peace_ July2017_final.pdf.

groups organized a summit on women and peace, which was the beginning of sustained pressure from civil society and international bodies to include women's rights and a gender focus in the agreement.[143]
Throughout the negotiations, various coalitions of civil society organizations attempted to include the concerns of a wide range of people in the
peace accord, emphasizing the fact that the conflict-affected people dif-
ferentially depending on gender, age, race, social class, geography, and
sexual orientation, among other factors.[144] For example, men and boys
make up the majority of both combatants and noncombatants killed
in the internal conflict and are much more likely to be kidnapped, tortured, arbitrarily detained, and/or forcibly recruited by various armed
actors.[145] Women and girls, on the other hand, are more likely to suffer
from sexual violence, forced displacement, forced prostitution, forced
abortions, and enslavement – in addition to relying on health services
more than men do.[146] As their sons, husbands, and other male family
members are killed or wounded, women are also more likely to be care-
givers of those disabled by war and to be single heads of households –
often facing extreme poverty, displacement, gender-based violence, and
loss of family members all at the same time.[147]

The concerted effort from Colombian women's civil society groups
around these issues lobbied international allies such as UN-Women,
OXFAM, Norway, and Spain, and pushed the Colombian government to
appoint two women negotiators and to increase focus on women's human
rights. By 2015, the FARC delegation in Havana was approximately 40
percent women – a much more accurate representation of the gender composition of the FARC itself.[148] A few women that I interviewed talked
about the terror and excitement they felt when flying to Cuba during these
negotiations, as they had never been on a plane before. Yet despite this
apparent success, the lead negotiating teams remained overwhelmingly
male, and the ex-FARC commanders now holding political positions
or other positions of influence are also predominantly male. The FARC
Secretariat remains entirely male and in 2018–19 still held a significant

[143] Salvesen and Nylander, "Towards an Inclusive Peace."
[144] Bouvier, "Gender and the Role of Women in Colombia's Peace Process"; Grupo de Memoria Histórica, "Basta Ya! Colombia."
[145] Bouvier, "Gender and the Role of Women in Colombia's Peace Process."
[146] Bouvier, "Gender and the Role of Women in Colombia's Peace Process."
[147] Arias, "Familias En Situación de Desplazamiento En Altos de Cazucá"; Bouvier, "Gender and the Role of Women in Colombia's Peace Process."
[148] Bouvier, "Gender and the Role of Women in Colombia's Peace Process."

amount of influence over its members, especially those in the collective reincorporation zones.

Despite the gendered aspects of the agreement and increasingly strong laws to protect minority groups, a large segment of Colombia's conservative Christian population has made it very clear that it does not agree with government initiatives to protect the LGBTQ+ community. One event in particular influenced the public vote on the FARC peace accord. In 2015, in response to the suicide of a homosexual student, the Constitutional Court ruled that Colombia's schools had to implement measures to strengthen students' human, sexual, and reproductive rights.[149] When the Ministry of Education released a manual on gender diversity and sexual orientation, aiming to reduce discrimination in schools, massive crowds – roused primarily by Pentecostal and Catholic leaders – took to the streets in protest.[150] Protest leaders accused the minister of education, an open lesbian, of trying to dissolve families and corrupt children.[151] These leaders adopted the term "gender ideology," a derisive term used increasingly by conservative religious leaders to stir up moral panic that links gender equality with social deterioration.[152] Indeed, using the words "gender" and "ideology" together taints all feminist and queer scholarship with the insinuation of falsehood and/or indoctrination.[153] In Colombia, it also unavoidably suggests links to guerrilla ideology. "Gender ideology" thus became an effective and convincing frame for a large portion of the population. In fact, the protests and discourse around this gender ideology framing were so effective that the government eventually pulled the manual from the curriculum.[154]

In that same year, the Constitutional Court legalized same-sex marriage despite the opposition from religious conservatives, and amid all of this political controversy the final peace agreement arrived with a substantial section on gender, women's rights, and LGBTQ+ rights. The stated purpose of this section of the agreement was to recognize the disproportionate effect the conflict had on women, especially in terms of sexual violence,

---

[149] "Sentencia T-478 de 2015" (2015), www.corteconstitucional.gov.co/inicio/T-478-15 ExpT4734501 (Sergio Urrego).pdf.

[150] William Mauricio Beltrán and Sian Creely, "Pentecostals, Gender Ideology and the Peace Plebiscite: Colombia 2016," *Religions* 9, no. 12 (2018): 418.

[151] Beltrán and Creely, "Pentecostals, Gender Ideology and the Peace Plebiscite."

[152] Beltrán and Creely, "Pentecostals, Gender Ideology and the Peace Plebiscite"; Mara Viveros Vigoya and Manuel Alejandro Rondón Rodríguez, "Hacer y Deshacer La Ideología de Género," *Sexualidad, Salud y Sociedad* 27 (2017): 118–27.

[153] Beltrán and Creely, "Pentecostals, Gender Ideology and the Peace Plebiscite."

[154] Humberto de la Calle, "Enfoque de Género," *El Tiempo*, October 15, 2016, www .eltiempo.com/archivo/documento/CMS-16727692.

and on the LGBTQ+ community.[155] This gender focus was also supposed to address that women were less likely to hold land titles and to address the historical political exclusion of both women and the LGBTQ+ community.[156] But the leaders who rallied against the Ministry of Education also rallied against the peace accord, quickly labeling the agreement's language of LGBTQ+ rights as "gender ideology" that directly threatened traditional families and put Colombia at risk of "homosexual colonization," despite the fact that the agreement did not discuss same-sex marriage at all.[157] Some Pentecostal leaders argued that the LGBTQ+ community was using the peace agreement as a political platform to advance their interests.[158] A few Protestant denominations did support the "yes" campaign and disagreed with the mischaracterization of the gender focus, but these leaders had far fewer followers.[159] In the end, the FARC negotiators and government representatives met with religious leaders and agreed to revise the section on gender in order to finalize the accord.[160] The final text of the agreement explicitly mentions the traditional family as the "fundamental nucleus of society," and many references to "gender" were removed.[161] For example, in terms of political participation, instead of "gender equity" the accord now refers to the "equitable participation between men and women," and similar changes are found in the land restitution section.[162]

Another issue here was that some Colombians felt that any discussion of gender was linked to international discourses and politics, as the UN had played a role in the earlier gender manual for schools.[163] This feeling was not unfounded: the creation of a gender subcommission in 2014 during the peace negotiations was partly influenced by civil society, UN bodies, and guarantor countries such as Norway, which had identified gender as one of its three key priorities from the outset of negotiations.[164] When the

---

[155] Beltrán and Creely, "Pentecostals, Gender Ideology and the Peace Plebiscite"; de la Calle, "Enfoque de Género."

[156] Beltrán and Creely, "Pentecostals, Gender Ideology and the Peace Plebiscite"; de la Calle, "Enfoque de Género."

[157] Beltrán and Creely, "Pentecostals, Gender Ideology and the Peace Plebiscite"; de la Calle, "Enfoque de Género."

[158] Beltrán and Creely, "Pentecostals, Gender Ideology and the Peace Plebiscite."

[159] Beltrán and Creely, "Pentecostals, Gender Ideology and the Peace Plebiscite."

[160] El Espectador, "Cristianos y Farc 'Solucionan' El Tema Del Enfoque de Género En Los Acuerdos," *El Espectador*, October 29, 2016, www.elespectador.com/noticias/paz/cristianos-y-farc-solucionan-el-tema-del-enfoque-de-gen-articulo-663030.

[161] Alto Comisionado para la Paz, "Acuerdo Final de Paz."

[162] Salvesen and Nylander, "Towards an Inclusive Peace."

[163] Beltrán and Creely, "Pentecostals, Gender Ideology and the Peace Plebiscite."

[164] Salvesen and Nylander, "Towards an Inclusive Peace."

gender subcommission was formed, Cuba and Norway each provided a gender expert and Norway also supplied an international gender expert.[165] This assumption of foreign influence allowed some religious leaders to play into anti-colonial anxieties by claiming that the gender focus in the peace accord did not reflect Colombian values.[166] This angle, however, obscures the fact that while Norway, other countries, and international organizations certainly played a role, the gender focus largely arose out of a concerted grassroots effort of Colombian feminist organizations and local LGBTQ+ groups to be included in the process.[167] Unfortunately, parsing off the gender subcommission from the primary political negotiations in many ways separated the demands of women from the demands of the collective and contributed to the depoliticization of women fighters.[168]

Another key sticking point in the public referendum was the concept and mechanisms of transitional justice, and the Special Jurisdiction for Peace (JEP) was perhaps the most confusing and controversial. The JEP was the judicial entity created to administer the restorative justice clauses in the agreement; however, it quickly became central to the referendum debate. The JEP was highly technical and difficult to explain, and many Colombians assumed it would create a general amnesty for especially serious guerrilla crimes, such as child recruitment and sexual exploitation.[169] It was also unclear whether the JEP would apply to other actors beyond ex-FARC combatants in the collective demobilization (e.g., many guerrilla deserters that I spoke to were very confused about this). Finally, some critics argued that Colombia had sufficient justice mechanisms to handle the peace agreement and did not need a new judiciary.[170]

These controversies, particularly the fury around gender discourse and stigmatization against ex-combatants, profoundly affect the environment into which ex-combatants are trying to reintegrate. Women ex-guerrillas are demobilizing into a highly conservative and patriarchal environment from a group in which many of them had agency, respect, and some level of gender equality – even if their true equality with men in the groups remains

---

[165] Salvesen and Nylander, "Towards an Inclusive Peace."

[166] Beltrán and Creely, "Pentecostals, Gender Ideology and the Peace Plebiscite."

[167] Salvesen and Nylander, "Towards an Inclusive Peace"; Beltrán and Creely, "Pentecostals, Gender Ideology and the Peace Plebiscite."

[168] Gowrinathan, *Radicalizing Her.*

[169] Rachel Anne Schmidt and Paulo Tovar, "A 'Post-conflict' Colombia? Analyzing the Pillars (and Spoilers) of Peace," in *Post-conflict Peacebuilding*, ed. Monika Thakur (Montreal: McGill-Queen's University Press, forthcoming).

[170] Schmidt and Tovar, "A 'Post-conflict' Colombia?"

debatable. In addition, there is a broadly shared perception in Colombia (and beyond) that women in the guerilla and paramilitary groups were sexually abused. This stigma – whether true or not – follows demobilized women when they leave and has long-lasting effects.[171] Women ex-combatants worldwide have historically expressed concerns that they are expected to return to traditional gender roles once they demobilize,[172] and many women fighters in this study voiced the same concerns.

CONCLUSION

Any peace process is fraught with challenges – in that regard Colombia is not unique. But this agreement marked the end of over fifty years of insurgency and decades of failed peace talks, brought with it a Nobel Peace Prize for President Santos, and may have raised national and international hopes a bit too high. Now some rural Colombians in former FARC strongholds are facing more violence than they were before the peace deal,[173] and most ex-combatants in this study continue to live in constant fear, facing both physical and economic insecurity. In addition, vast swathes of the population are suffering from high levels of trauma and inadequate access to resources in order to deal with what they have done, experienced, or witnessed. In many cases, the lines between victim and perpetrator are blurred, with most ex-combatants in this study also being a victim of the conflict or of abuse, neglect, or poverty in their childhood.

This chapter also illustrates how the historical and current processes of Colombia's peace negotiations and demobilization programs are both complex and highly gendered. While the Colombian government has lauded its successes in demobilization and wants to share those lessons with the world,[174] the rates of recidivism, high reintegration program

[171] Mendez, "Militarized Gender Performativity."
[172] Megan Alpert, "To Be a Guerrilla, and a Woman, in Colombia," *The Atlantic*, September 2016, www.theatlantic.com/international/archive/2016/09/farc-deal-female-fighters/501644/; Priscyll Anctil Avoine and Rachel Tillman, "Demobilized Women in Colombia: Embodiment, Performativity and Social Reconciliation," in *Female Combatants in Conflict and Peace: Challenging Gender in Violence and Post-conflict Reintegration*, ed. Seema Shekhawat (Basingstoke: Palgrave Macmillan, 2015); Dietrich, "La Compañera Guerrilla as Construction of Politicised Femininity"; Mendez, "Militarized Gender Performativity."
[173] Joe Parkin Daniels, "Peace Is War as Armed Groups Roil Colombia's Lawless Border Region," *The Guardian*, July 20, 2019, www.theguardian.com/world/2019/jul/20/colombia-guerrillas-peace-war-catatumbo.
[174] This goal was expressed to me multiple times by government officials during this fieldwork.

dropout rates, alongside government corruption, falsified statistics, and ongoing criminal activity of various armed groups, make those successes far less credible. Stigmatization against ex-combatants remains high, and a large segment of the population still ascribes to patriarchal values that challenge the feminist aspirations of both civilians and ex-combatants. In addition, as subsequent chapters illustrate, the high rates of informal employment in Colombia and the lack of economic projects for FARC ex-combatants have put the entire reintegration aspect of the peace process into jeopardy.

While this overview paints a fairly bleak picture of Colombia's "post-conflict" situation, many respondents in this study argued that life is better now than during the war, and many FARC loyalists said that their decades-long struggle had been worth it. Deserters, however, rarely shared this latter view, saying that their time in the guerrillas was "lost time" that they could never get back. The situation on the ground continues to change rapidly and is rife with tension, especially with the massive influx of Venezuelan refugees over the last few years.[175] In fact, several ex-combatants in the ETCRs, still waiting for their promised government benefits, expressed resentment that Venezuelan refugees had received expedited work permits and their children had been fast-tracked into school, when as Colombians they still did not have work, nor good quality schools or daycares for their children. In addition, while some aspects of Colombian life may be better than they were before, the drug trade is still thriving and social leaders remain at risk, with multiple armed groups clashing with each other in prime coca-growing regions.[176] The country is not yet in a post-conflict era, and if the government does not adequately address ex-combatants' growing unrest and resentment, it may never get there.

---

[175] The Guardian, "One Million Fled Economic Crisis-Hit Venezuela for Colombia in Past Year," *The Guardian*, May 9, 2018, www.theguardian.com/world/2018/may/09/one-million-refugees-entered-colombia-after-economic-crisis-hit-venezuela.

[176] Daniels, "Peace Is War as Armed Groups Roil Colombia's Lawless Border Region."

III

Navigating Disarmament, Demobilization, and Reintegration in Colombia

> We were a true pilot program, and they made many mistakes with us.
> Nell, ex-AUC (B87)

> Well, really, it's that peace ... there is still no peace. It is an agreement that
> our comrades signed, but there is still a long way to go to cultivate that.
> The illusion of Colombians is that there is peace, that there will be no more
> war. But the other illusion is that things are better now ... That there is
> healthcare, decent housing, schools.
> Jasmine, FARC (B45)

In every interview for this book, I asked ex-combatants near the end of
our conversation what they would change about the DDR program(s)
if they could. This is when I learned that many ex-combatants – especially ones who had recently demobilized – struggled with hypothetical
questions. As one reintegration psychologist explained to me, ex-
combatants had difficulty thinking about the future because they spent
so much of their lives taking orders and living one day at a time, often
in imminent danger. They had a saying for that: "Today I'm alive,
tomorrow who knows."[1] The transition of making a plan for their own
lives, after years of following orders and rarely thinking ahead, was
extremely difficult.

"Yes, I know you can't actually change the program," I would say.
"But just *pretend* that you were the boss here – what would you change?"

"But ... I'm not the boss," came the common reply, often with a confused expression.

---

[1] Author interview C01.

When I learned not to ask hypothetical questions, many ex-combatants replied that they wished the government would help them find jobs, instead of giving them a monthly allowance that was insufficient anyway. They did not want charity, they explained, but they could not live without it if they could not find sustainable employment. As Nell said to me once:

> And I say that to change, to change the program ... for me there would be many things, for sure ... . I say that what would be the best, the best [thing] for when a person demobilizes is to arrive with a job ... a sustainable job, because after [demobilization] one has to provide for a family. I think that this is, this is the best, the best gift that one could give, definitely. (Nell, ex-AUC, B87)

Responses about the quality of the program, however, varied widely depending on what stage of the process the person was in. Most people in the government safe houses, having only recently fled their groups, were so relieved to be safe and fed that they rarely had complaints – or they were too afraid to complain. A common guerrilla narrative is that the demobilization program is a merely a trick to lure guerrillas to their deaths, so many deserters in the safe houses were enormously relieved that they had not been killed at the moment of their surrender. Indeed, many of these respondents expressed gratitude for being able to start over.

However, ex-combatants who had left these temporary safe houses and were now fending for themselves, trying to find jobs and pay rent, exposed daily to threats, stigmatization, and violence, had a lot to say about the program's failings. And paramilitary respondents, who were nearly fifteen years post-demobilization, were uniformly cynical about their DDR experiences, feeling that the government had used and then abandoned them, failing to deliver on its many promises. Rancor against the government was widespread in the ETCRs as well, where loyalist FARC members were repeatedly critical of the government's failure to fulfill the promises set out in the peace accord. These respondents were especially bitter about the lack of permanent housing, the absence of gainful economic projects, and the inability to access land for farming. In fact, while tens of thousands of combatants have entered Colombia's various reintegration programs, large numbers of ex-combatants regularly leave these programs without completing them, while some combatants demobilize but do not enter a reintegration program at all.[2] The ongoing conflict and constantly evolving dynamics into which ex-combatants demobilize certainly create myriad programmatic challenges.

[2] ARN, "La Reintegración En Colombia – Cifras."

Nonetheless, the Colombian government prides itself on its DDR programs. Indeed, the Ministry of Defense celebrated its fifteenth anniversary of formal demobilization programming in 2017, calling it "fifteen years of transforming histories."[3] But Lina's husband had a different name for it: "Why did I want to talk to you? Because I was there last year, at the symposium where they celebrated fifteen years of demobilization programming here in Colombia. Those are fifteen years of hoaxes and lies, because the only ones who are going to win are the bosses, right?" (Johan, ex-FARC, B31). Colombia therefore presents a unique study of DDR due to the ongoing efforts to demobilize and reintegrate combatants in the face of continuing armed conflict and recruitment into armed groups.

In addition, unlike other DDR programs, which are usually run by third (purportedly neutral) parties after the hostilities are over, Colombia has tried to insert what is normally a post-conflict endeavor into an ongoing conflict environment – what other scholars have termed "pre-post-conflict."[4] Inserting a post-conflict program amid ongoing armed hostilities – and investing considerable funds into sharing their "successes" with the world[5] – reinforces the government's repeated framing that there is no armed conflict in Colombia and only narco-terrorism.

In addition, deserters' participation in government demobilization programs in Colombia implies cooperation with the enemy, as deserters must participate in military intelligence interviews before receiving benefits. This forced cooperation means that participation in these programs comes with life-threatening costs. But many deserters that I spoke to did not consider or even realize that they would be compelled to give intelligence to the military in order to demobilize and reintegrate. Michael, the deserter from the ELN introduced in Chapter I, told me that when he first surrendered to the military he had not expected to be grilled for days:

And I said to them, "why are you giving us so much paperwork? Why are you asking so many questions?" Then they said: "No, it's because you know a lot about it there [in the ELN], you know many people." And so, of course we know many people there! And we had to give a physical description of each one, imagine it! Every day we had to give a physical description of each one, and it was very difficult, imagine. At the end, I was very bored, tired. Every day you sit down and say the same thing: "Do you know this man? Yes, give me a physical description, and the hair is this color, the eyebrows, the feet, he wears boots, hm!" Of everything! Then, no, I was very stressed by then. (Michael, ex-ELN, B08)

---

[3] Colombian Ministry of Defence, "15 Años Transformando Historias."
[4] Fattal, *Guerrilla Marketing.*
[5] Fattal, *Guerrilla Marketing.*

As a result of this unexpected questioning, many ex-combatants, including Michael, felt that they were in now in greater peril by surrendering to the government than they would have been if they had just run away somewhere and found a job. Not only did they remain uncertain as to whether the government would arrest and imprison them for what they shared, they also knew that by sharing intelligence with the military, they had exacerbated the risk that they would be hunted down by their former group. They knew that informants were everywhere, including in the safe houses.

THE EVOLUTION OF DDR IN COLOMBIA

From Ad Hoc Demobilization to Formalized DDR

In the Colombian Reintegration Agency's institutional review of 2016, the agency lists the four stages of DDR as: (1) disarmament (collecting weapons), (2) demobilization (bringing disarmed actors into secure areas of concentration), (3) reinsertion (the preliminary phase of reintegration, where ex-combatants receive assistance packets, clothes, shelter, healthcare, and training), and (4) reintegration, which encompasses both the initial reinsertion phase and long-term reintegration.[6] But after the 2016 peace process was finalized, the reintegration agency split into two distinct programs: (1) "reintegration" for ex-combatants who demobilized individually (i.e., deserters) as well as AUC ex-combatants who demobilized collectively, and (2) "reincorporation" for FARC ex-combatants who demobilized collectively as part of the peace accord (see Table 3). The reintegration side, however, contains two separate streams: one for deserters and one for the collectively demobilized AUC. The AUC process is considered complete because the benefits time frame has terminated – not necessarily because ex-combatants have reintegrated successfully. Each of these streams (i.e., deserters, collective AUC, and collective FARC) offers different benefits and different forms of amnesty, and, based on the legal documents, many of the benefits are highly complex and extremely difficult for someone with marginal literacy to understand. Within each stream, ex-combatants receive the same monthly stipend and access to the same benefits as others in the same stream – in theory. However, as respondents made abundantly clear, being able to access certain benefits depends heavily on a person's existing skillset, literacy and numeracy,

[6] ACR, "Reseña Historíca Institucional" (Bogota, 2016), www.reincorporacion.gov.co/es/agencia/Documentos de Gestin Documental/Reseña_Historica_ACR.pdf.

TABLE 3 *The evolution of Colombia's demobilization processes*

Year	Process	Agency/ministry	Focus	Armed group
Late 1980s, early 1990s	Individual deserters accepted by the government M-19 group demobilization (1989) EPL group demobilization (1991)	Ministry of Interior CODA (Operational Committee for Disarmament)	Disarmament and demobilization M19 and EPL convert into political parties (no formal reintegration strategy at this time)	Various, mostly guerrilla (EPL, M-19, FARC, ELN) M19 and EPL dissidents persist
2003	PRVC begins	Ministry of Interior and Justice	Short-term reinsertion only; no focus on long-term reintegration	Primarily guerrilla deserters
2006	Mass demobilization of paramilitaries requires a more official process	High Presidential Council for Reintegration	Reinsertion and reintegration	Collectively demobilized AUC paramilitaries Ongoing demobilization of guerrilla deserters
2011	Official Colombian Reintegration Agency (ACR) is formed GAHD is formed within Ministry of Defense to accept deserters	Group for Humanitarian Attention to the Demobilized (GAHD) ACR	Demobilization and reinsertion (GAHD); reintegration (ACR)	Primarily deserters from ELN and FARC, but also other smaller guerrilla factions and BACRIMs
2017	ACR is renamed and split into two streams: reintegration and reincorporation	ARN	Demobilization (GAHD); reinsertion and reintegration (ARN)	Primarily collectively demobilized FARC Ongoing desertions from active groups

TABLE 4 *Total registered ex-combatants*

Type of program	Number of registered ex-combatants	Women (%)
Collective AUC program	36,455	7
Individual program (deserters)	25,961	21
Collective FARC program	14,024	23
Total confirmed demobilized	76,440	est. 14–20

experiences of trauma, willingness to study, existing social support, number of dependents, and access to childcare. By attempting to be nondiscriminatory, the program has actually created blind spots where the most vulnerable ex-combatants – particularly those with low literacy skills, post-traumatic stress, and/or single parents with multiple dependents – lack the additional assistance they need in order to successfully transition to civilian life.

Of course, in many post-conflict countries there is one additional stream of reintegration: that of elites.[7] While the political reintegration of elite members of the FARC is not the primary focus of this book, it is worth noting that the collective reintegration of rank-and-file FARC members was very different to the political reintegration of elite members of the FARC. And, as subsequent chapters show, this generated a fair share of resentment among lower-ranking members of the FARC and damaged the overall credibility of the FARC leadership's framing efforts. Indeed, explicit analysis on elite reintegration as a separate category from collective political reintegration of an insurgent group has received relatively little scholarly attention.[8] But in the Colombian case these differences are essential to understanding what has worked since the 2016 peace agreement – and what has gone terribly wrong.

As shown in Table 4, as of November 2021, over 76,440 combatants (approximately 17 percent women) officially demobilized between 2001 and 2021.[9] Of this total, 36,455 (approximately 7 percent women) are recorded as collectively demobilized paramilitaries of the AUC, and 14,024 (approximately 23 percent women) are collectively demobilized FARC

[7] Johanna Söderström, *Peacebuilding and Ex-combatants: Political Reintegration in Liberia* (London: Routledge, 2015).
[8] Söderström, *Peacebuilding and Ex-combatants.*
[9] ARN, "La Reintegración En Colombia – Cifras."

combatants certified by the High Commission for the Peace.[10] This figure does not, of course, include combatants who abandoned their groups without reporting to the government; nor does it include combatants who demobilized while still minors, who are tracked and reintegrated separately. Based on responses in this study, there are hundreds (likely thousands) of ex-combatants who deserted armed groups but did not seek any form of government assistance for reintegration, but virtually no data exist for this hidden population. Notably, more granular data exist for the demobilized population and used to be publicly accessible. However, at some point in 2021, the ARN began to require login credentials to access this information. The estimates of women combatants listed here were accurate as of December 2020, when detailed statistics were still available online.

When excluding the collectively demobilized FARC combatants, an estimated 18 percent of all registered demobilized combatants did not enter an ACR/ARN reintegration program at all, and approximately 50 percent (30,840) of total demobilized combatants did not access the program for various reasons (e.g., they never enrolled, dropped out, died, disappeared, were imprisoned, or violated the terms).[11] For a government that purportedly wants to share its DDR successes with the world, a 50 percent noncompletion rate should be raising many questions.

As illustrated by Table 3, the ARN and its related programs have gone through many reinventions over the years, starting with the PRVC, formed as part of the Ministry of Interior and of Justice in 2003.[12] The PRVC was only a short-term "reinsertion" program, and because the initial size of the demobilized population was small, the approach was not viewed as problematic at the time.[13] However, during the mass demobilization of the AUC in 2003–6, the government needed something much larger for long-term planning, so they created the High Presidential Council for Reintegration to confront the complexities of running a massive demobilization program alongside an ongoing conflict.[14] For this reason, many ex-paramilitaries considered themselves the "pilot project" in Colombia's DDR programming – often with no shortage of resentment. Indeed, because of the ongoing violence, the Colombian government has long been running two or more types of DDR simultaneously – the

[10] ARN, "Reincorporacion En Cifras," ARN, 2020, www.reincorporacion.gov.co/es/reincorporacion/Paginas/La-Reincorporación-en-cifras.aspx.
[11] ARN, "La Reintegración En Colombia – Cifras."
[12] ARN, "Reseña Histórica," 2019, www.reincorporacion.gov.co/es/agencia/Paginas/resena.aspx.
[13] ARN, "Reseña Histórica."
[14] ARN, "Reseña Histórica."

collective DDR of groups that have made an agreement with the government (i.e., primarily combatants ordered by superiors to demobilize), and the individual DDR of people who deserted their groups.

In 2011, under President Santos, the High Council – which had been designated as a "special administrative unit" – was transformed into the Colombian Reintegration Agency (ACR) and given more permanent status within the administration.[15] In 2017, the ACR was given a leading role in implementing the peace agreement with the FARC, and the agency was renamed the Agency for Reincorporation and Normalization (ARN) – partly due to the FARC's insistence that they not be included in the same programming category as deserters and paramilitaries.[16] Since then, representatives of the ARN have emphasized the differences between "reintegration" (which involves the prior AUC collective demobilization process, plus all deserters past and present) and "reincorporation" (which exclusively refers to the FARC collective reintegration process).

Because different streams have varying benefits available to ex-combatants, and because word of mouth among ex-combatant networks has distorted the perception of inequality in these benefits (i.e., rumors about benefits that "others" are receiving are often inaccurate), there is some tension between ex-combatants in different streams. As one example, several ex-guerrillas in the individual demobilization program told me, with significant resentment, that ex-paramilitaries received two million Colombian pesos per month (approximately US$615) as part of their demobilization agreement. But that figure matched a one-time payment per person of start-up capital for a small business, not an ongoing monthly payment. This misunderstanding was illustrative of how rumors and misinformation spread quickly in the ex-combatant population.

Incorporating "Gender" into Colombia's DDR

The program for women is equal: if a woman is in a couple, we'll respect that, if a woman is single, we'll treat her the same as a man.
GAHD military officer, C05

Toward the end of my fieldwork, I went to the home of Lina's friend, an Indigenous ex-ELN woman in a very poor area of Bogotá. When I arrived with Lina, however, the woman was not at home. She had left for work, her

---

[15] ARN, "Reseña Histórica."
[16] Information obtained during meetings with ARN officials, Bogotá, October 2018.

daughter said, giving us a shy smile and staring at me. This girl, left home alone, could not have been more than four years old. Lina seemed nonplussed by this, as if it were a regular occurrence (which it probably was). I was seeing firsthand what many of the female ex-combatants had complained about – the complete lack of childcare options in the reintegration program:

> [I]f I have a place for my son, I can free myself and I can continue working and studying. In other words, how am I going to go to study or how am I going to go to work – leaving my son in the street? I think that is the first thing I have to fight for [now], is to have a piece of land, a house, a decent place for my children. (Mari, FARC, B58).

For at least the last fifteen years, various scholars have documented the failures of DDR programs in various conflicts to address gender-based concerns.[17] As already noted, women are certainly not minor actors in Colombia's war, but the country's DDR programs are still largely designed for the default ex-combatant: young, male, and single with no children. In Colombia and elsewhere in Latin America, women ex-combatants have reportedly declined to participate in formal DDR programs, particularly when reintegration sites or camps were not deemed safe for them or their children.[18] Some women ex-guerrillas, including Lina and her friends, have stated that the stigma attached to being a known female ex-combatant was simply not worth the meager benefits offered by DDR programs.[19] Indeed, evidence indicates that women ex-combatants in Colombia disproportionately reintegrate without government support compared to men, suggesting that many either do not want to be in these programs or do not feel welcome, or both.[20]

---

[17] Lorena Aristizábal Farah, "Devenir Civil/Devenir Mujer: Una Mirada a Las Subjetividades de Mujeres Excombatientes En Proceso de Reinserción," in *Desafíos Para La Reintregración: Enfoques de Género, Edad y Etnia*, ed. Centro Nacional de Memoria Histórica (Bogotá: Imprenta Nacional, 2013), 179–215; Dietrich, "La Compañera Guerrilla as Construction of Politicised Femininity"; Juanita Esguerra Rezk, "Desarmando Las Manos y El Corazón: Transformaciones En Las Identidades de Género de Excombatientes (2004–2010)," in *Desafíos Para La Reintregración: Enfoques de Género, Edad y Etnia*, ed. Centro Nacional de Memoria Histórica (Bogotá: Imprenta Nacional, 2013), 116–77; Christiane Leliévre Aussel, Graciliana Moreno Echavarría, and Isabel Ortiz Pérez, *Haciendo Memoria Y Dejando Rastros: Encuentros Con Mujeres Excombatientes Del Nororiente de Colombia* (Bogota: Fundación Mujer y Futuro, 2004), http://bdigital .unal.edu.co/45755/1/9583369004.pdf; Londoño and Nieto, *Mujeres No Contadas*.
[18] Dietrich, "La Compañera Guerrilla as Construction of Politicised Femininity."
[19] Dietrich, "La Compañera Guerrilla as Construction of Politicised Femininity"; Gunhild Schwitalla and Luisa Maria Dietrich, "Demobilisation of Female Ex-combatants in Colombia," *Forced Migration Review* 27 (2007): 58–9.
[20] Anctil Avoine and Tillman, "Demobilized Women in Colombia."

Scholars have noted that the early demobilizations in Colombia in the 1990s were particularly problematic, as female participation in armed groups at this time was approximately 20–30 percent, but international discourse on gender in conflict had not yet fully emerged[21] and women's participation in armed conflict was only minimally recognized.[22] These early programs failed to recognize women's specific needs, such as sexual and reproductive healthcare, pre- or post-natal care, and menstrual hygiene products, nor did they provide proper legal, psycho-social, or health support for victims of gender-based violence.[23] DDR practitioners also had – and some continue to have – stereotypical assumptions around gender roles in society. For example, in the early demobilizations, couples were jointly registered for benefits deposited into a bank account in the man's name only.[24] This practice also ignored the high separation rates in ex-combatant populations that have resulted in women having disproportionate responsibility for children and the elderly, but often with only one income.[25] There is no additional money for children in the reintegration allowance, and the costs of school uniforms and supplies make it nearly impossible for many demobilized parents to send their children to school. One ARN representative told me that they used to provide supplemental support for each child, but the ARN determined that ex-combatants were having more children in order to get more money, so they rescinded this benefit.[26] (How they determined this was left unclear.) After speaking to ex-combatant women, I think another, and perhaps more likely, reason for the increased number of children is the prohibitive cost of contraceptives and difficulty in accessing reproductive healthcare services.

Overall, women have made up 7 percent of AUC demobilizations and 21–25 percent of guerrilla demobilizations.[27] While the importance of gender in DDR – largely conflated with addressing women's needs – was officially on Colombia's radar by at least 2008,[28] the ARN only began actively incorporating gender-based programming in 2013; this timing

---

[21] For example, the landmark UN Security Council Resolution 1325 on women in armed conflict was created in 2000.

[22] Dietrich, "La Compañera Guerrilla as Construction of Politicised Femininity."

[23] Dietrich, "La Compañera Guerrilla as Construction of Politicised Femininity."

[24] Dietrich, "La Compañera Guerrilla as Construction of Politicised Femininity."

[25] Dietrich, "La Compañera Guerrilla as Construction of Politicised Femininity."

[26] Author interview C14.

[27] ARN, "La Reintegración En Colombia – Cifras."

[28] DNP, "Política Nacional de Reintregación Social y Economíca Para Personas y Grupos Armados Ilegales" (Bogotá, 2008), https://colaboracion.dnp.gov.co/CDT/Conpes/Económicos/3554.pdf.

noncoincidentally corresponded with the start of peace talks and creation of the FARC's *Mujer Fariana* website.[29] Nonetheless, during my fieldwork several ARN officials insisted that the agency already had a good grasp of gendered needs and analysis in reintegration programming – stating that further research on this topic was not necessary. Yet, officials repeatedly conflated "gender" with "women" in these conversations and did not mention any gender-related issues beyond women's needs. Evidence also suggests that what is on paper at the agency is still not translating into practice, with traditional gender roles still emphasized in skills and job retraining.[30]

Indeed, like many programs worldwide on disengagement from violence, gender now appears as a key element in ARN documents, but in practice "women" are often treated as one homogenous category without considering intersecting identities such as age, race, class, and number of dependents. And gender considerations as they apply to men or LGBTQ+ individuals do not appear at all. The Covid-19 pandemic exacerbated these issues, as care-related duties resulting from the pandemic have affected women ex-combatants disproportionately more than men, in addition to increased restrictions around accessing sexual and reproductive health care and the risk of increased domestic violence as a result of lockdown measures.[31]

Researchers have repeatedly criticized DDR programs in Colombia for not taking women's unique needs into account or for paying lip service to gender policy without implementing it.[32] However, some scholars have noted that overemphasizing women's special needs as victims in post-conflict processes can contribute to their marginalization by taking away their agency.[33] That is, by treating women only as victims, they are not taken seriously as key players in the conflict and thus not adequately considered in peace negotiations and reintegration plans – especially not for lead roles.

Overall, the evidence of gender being taken seriously in Colombia's DDR programming is mixed at best, and there is no evidence that gender

---

[29] Alpert, "To Be a Guerrilla, and a Woman, in Colombia"; DNP, "Política Nacional de Reintregación Social y Economíca Para Personas y Grupos Armados Ilegales."
[30] Alpert, "To Be a Guerrilla, and a Woman, in Colombia."
[31] Guterres, "United Nations Verification Mission in Colombia: June 2020."
[32] Anctil Avoine and Tillman, "Demobilized Women in Colombia"; Dietrich, "La Compañera Guerrilla as Construction of Politicised Femininity."
[33] Fionnuala Ní Aoláin, Dina Francesca Haynes, and Naomi R Cahn, *On the Frontlines: Gender, War, and the Post-conflict Process* (New York and Oxford: Oxford University Press, 2011); E Hafner-Burton and M A Pollack, "Mainstreaming Gender in Global Governance," *European Journal of International Relations* 8, no. 3 (2002): 339–73; Dietrich, "La Compañera Guerrilla as Construction of Politicised Femininity."

concerns in the ARN incorporate any issues regarding harmful masculinities in terms of men's reintegration or any consideration at all of LGBTQ+ combatants. For example, of the 204 killings of former FARC members since the peace agreement, only four have been women.[34] Men face significant post-demobilization risks too, but their suffering is often disregarded. Indeed, there is widespread indifference to the deaths and disappearances of tens of thousands of men in Latin America, "because poor and Indigenous men are denied a place in the existing conceptual framework that determines who is worthy of sympathy."[35] Clearly, more attention is needed on the highly gendered risks that both men and women ex-combatants face once they are out of government protection.

THE INDIVIDUAL DEMOBILIZATION PROCESS

Throughout Colombia's later attempts at peace, the government was running an individual demobilization program for guerrilla and paramilitary combatants who wished to desert their groups, as a strategy to weaken rebel forces. While combatants had been demobilizing in small numbers since the 1990s, campaigns to actively encourage desertion began in earnest in 2007, when the government started running radio announcements – often narrated by ex-guerrillas themselves – that guerrilla combatants could surrender and receive amnesty and reintegration benefits.[36] These campaigns included radio programs that often included testimony from demobilized combatants, dropping leaflets from planes into the jungle, and, in 2010, sending little plastic lights down rivers with messages inside and decorating trees for Christmas along known guerrilla pathways.[37] While many guerrillas did not trust the government's messages – for valid reasons, given the proven collusion between politicians and paramilitaries – thousands of others did indeed turn themselves in during this time.[38] Between 2007 and 2010, the government states that 10,978 individual combatants deserted from various groups, mostly guerrillas.[39] But President Uribe was also

[34] Guterres, "United Nations Verification Mission in Colombia."
[35] Dolores Trevizo, "What Can Intersectional Approaches Reveal about Experiences of Violence?" (OpenGlobalRights, 2020).
[36] Henry Mance, "Colombia's Campaign to Win Rebel Minds," *BBC News*, January 23, 2008, http://news.bbc.co.uk/2/hi/americas/7194377.stm.
[37] Colombian Ministry of Defence, "Llevando La Navidad a La Selva Mindefensa Invita a La Desmovilización," 2010, www.mindefensa.gov.co/irj/go/km/docs/documents/News/NoticiaGrandeMDN/909f5a16-31ec-2d10-boa3-cb86efo98c23.xml.
[38] Colombian Ministry of Defence, "15 Años Transformando Historias."
[39] ARN, "La Reintegración En Colombia – Cifras."

running an intense US-backed military offensive (*Plan Patriota*) against the FARC in this same period, which was largely credited for significantly weakening guerrilla ranks.[40] It is thus unclear whether combatants were surrendering in this period because they were convinced by government propaganda, or simply because they were afraid to die, or both.

Of over 60,000 combatants that have officially demobilized and were eligible for the "reintegration" stream (i.e., excluding the collective FARC demobilization), over 24,000 were deserters.[41] Among these officially recognized deserters, approximately 90 percent surrender to the army,[42] after which they are directed to a division of the Ministry of Defense called the Group for Humanitarian Attention to the Demobilized (GAHD), which was set up in 2011. However, several respondents told me that they had spent months or even years in hiding before something triggered their official demobilization. Some said they lied to the military about how long ago they had deserted, fearing that the gap of months or years between desertion and official demobilization would disqualify them from receiving benefits. After handing in any weapons (if applicable), deserters have several interviews with military intelligence to confirm membership in the armed group, and then they enter one of two remaining safe houses (*Hogares de Paz*)[43] and must share intelligence with military officers over a series of interviews.[44] Receiving amnesty and demobilization benefits is contingent on sharing this intelligence; several deserters said they were warned that if they did not cooperate, they would go to prison.[45] Demobilized combatants from all groups stay in these GAHD compounds for two to three months, and while ex-combatants used to be gender segregated, the safe houses are now fully mixed, with many demobilized combatants housed with their spouses and children in an effort to replicate civilian life.[46] There is daycare and school on-site for these children, allowing both parents (where applicable) to take classes. The demobilized combatants are paid $8,000 Colombian pesos (COL$) per day (slightly less than US$3) and are encouraged to save this money while their living

---

[40] Douglas Porch and María José Rasmussen, "Demobilization of Paramilitaries in Colombia: Transformation or Transition?," *Studies in Conflict & Terrorism* 31, no. 6 (2008): 520–40.
[41] ARN, "La Reintegración En Colombia – Cifras."
[42] Author interview C01.
[43] There used to be many more of these houses, but due to the FARC peace agreement, the demand is lower and the government has closed all but two (interview C01).
[44] Interviews C01, C05.
[45] Interviews B38, B41, B55, B58, B59.
[46] Interviews C01, C02.

expenses are fully paid in the safe house.[47] However, many ex-combatants spent this small amount on mobile phone plans so that they could communicate with friends and family. Most deserters in this study said it was laughable to save anything out of COL$8,000 per day.

Inside these compounds, demobilized combatants are also supposed to have access to psychologists, and they receive classes in topics from basic literacy to how to send an email, open a bank account, and read a bus schedule.[48] However, several respondents told me that they had never once spoken to a psychologist and that only people with obvious psychological issues were referred to these services.

Once these individually demobilized combatants have finished their two to three months at a safe house, they receive a certificate stating that they have officially demobilized and are then released into the reintegration program, run by the ARN, where they can access anywhere from six months to six years of benefits – including a small monthly stipend – depending on what career and course of study they pursue; these decisions are made by the ex-combatant with recommendations and guidance from ARN staff and each ex-combatant's designated reintegration officers.[49] But in reality, this is where many ex-combatants drop out of the process, as these choices are highly constrained by a participant's existing skill set, security risks, literacy level, access to resources, programming constraints, and lack of childcare. Research suggests that single mothers have a particularly difficult time meeting the program requirements.[50] Some respondents indicated that a person's reintegration pathway depended heavily on individual reintegration officers and how supportive they were – or not. Participants also suggested that the supervisors in each of the two safe houses – who had very different approaches – had a high degree of influence on what a demobilized person chose to do upon leaving the safe house, including whether they returned to armed activity or not.[51] Participants also rarely receive any sort of protection once they have left the safe house. ARN staffers advise them to change their phone numbers regularly, and some are issued bulletproof vests in the case of credible threats, but most ex-combatants are not provided with any real form of security.

While the approach to reintegration benefits aims to be fair across the board by giving everyone the same standard benefits package, in reality

[47] Interviews C01, C02.
[48] Interviews C01, C02.
[49] Interviews C01, C02, C03.
[50] Mendez, "Militarized Gender Performativity."
[51] Interviews B17, B18, B63.

this approach significantly disadvantages parents – and single mothers in particular. For example, a single mother ex-combatant supporting two or three children, like Dayana, receives half as much as a married couple of two ex-combatants with no children. And a young man or woman with no dependents, like Michael, has a much greater ability to take advantage of the program's educational offerings compared to an ex-combatant with two or three small children to support. In addition, a person who joined an armed group at age ten and deserted after thirty years in the group, like Lina's husband, receives the exact same benefits as someone who joined as an adult and spent four months in the group. Yet these two people clearly have different losses and needs – not only in terms of psychological support but also in terms of learning general life skills and the years of education missed. One psychologist working in the safe houses agreed that high-ranking deserters needed a very different approach than rank-and-file combatants, but this is generally not possible within the constraints of the program.[52]

To remain eligible in the program, ex-combatants with children must demonstrate that they are financially supporting *all* of their children (as required by law), including ones not living with them, which is often a significant financial challenge given the lack of employment options and the fact that some ex-combatants have children in different areas of the country with multiple partners. Men, however, only need to support children who officially carry their last name. There is also financial assistance to obtain a house and property,[53] but the requirements to access these benefits are complex and difficult to understand, given that many ex-combatants only have basic literacy and numeracy skills. In addition, when reading over the legal documents, I realized that the conditions are nearly impossible to fulfill. In fact, some participants in this study claimed that the government had "promised them a house" and were angry that this never happened, when in reality the benefits around obtaining housing are extremely complicated. Others had no idea that housing benefits even existed. This confusion applied to education benefits as well, as most respondents told me that they could only receive education benefits up to a high school diploma – when the program officially offers access to technical training and higher education under certain conditions.

In addition, demobilized combatants are entitled to up to eight million pesos (approximately US$2,500) to start or acquire a business.[54] But

[52] Interview C01.
[53] Director General de la ARN, "Resolución 1356" (Bogotá: ARN, 2016).
[54] Resolutions 1391/2011 and 754/2013.

many ex-combatants were confused by this benefit, telling me that once they graduated from the program, they would receive this lump sum of money – which is not quite true. The process to obtain these funds is again fairly complex, and the majority of ex-combatants never go through it all. While this is a much larger sum than was given to the ex-AUC combatants (a fact noted with resentment by many ex-paramilitaries in this study), inflation must be considered, and the higher number was likely adjusted because the small sum given to AUC members was wholly insufficient to start a viable business. In fact, most ex-AUC respondents in this study told me stories of how they used this money, but their businesses failed:

[I]n the project that I started, they only covered 2,000,000 pesos [approx. US$550] and that, that required so much paperwork, a number of papers that were impossible for me … in the end I let it go, because I already saw it was impossible, so I said well, one day I will manage it on my own. (Mateo, ex-AUC, B76)

Indeed, most ex-combatants that I spoke to did not adequately understand the conditions for claiming these funds and several said they felt robbed because they "graduated" but never received this money. One ARN representative acknowledged that the majority of demobilized combatants never claimed their start-up funds because they failed to meet the detailed and complex requirements.[55]

As of December 2020, 48 percent of the ex-combatants that enrolled in the ARN reintegration program had completed the process and 10 percent were still in the process,[56] which suggests a very high dropout rate of 42 percent. But there is little to no data available for these ex-combatants who have dropped out. Separated by gender, 64 percent of women who entered reintegration finished the program, while only 46 percent of the men who entered have done so. While some research shows that women demobilize without government assistance disproportionately more than men do,[57] it is possible that there is a self-selection effect and that women who did enroll in the program were the ones most likely to complete it. Among the ex-combatants who are in the program or completed it, 70 percent are employed – but due to Colombia's large informal sector and the stigma that ex-combatants face (paired with low literacy and lack of education and/or training), only 26 percent are working in the formal sector.[58] The rest are in precarious, low-paying, informal jobs. Arguably,

[55] Interview C15.
[56] ARN, "Reincorporacion En Cifras."
[57] Anctil Avoine and Tillman, "Demobilized Women in Colombia."
[58] ARN, "La Reintegración En Colombia – Cifras."

these bleak employment prospects make reenlistment into armed groups or criminal organizations more likely – particularly for men like Andrés, who is under pressure to provide for a young family and constantly receiving offers to engage in lucrative criminal activity:

Of about 100 that left here [in the government safe house], 80 have gone back to crime ... Just now a friend of mine called. I said, "*Marica*, where are you?" He said, "I'm working in Bogotá. Did you get out of the [FARC dissident unit][59] down there?" And I said, "yeah, I had problems with ██████[60] and all that." That's what I told him. And he said: "Come on, they are paying three million pesos per fortnight to guard a *chongo*" – that is a drug crystallizer – "to return to arms and guard it." (Andrés, ex-FARC, B18)

Put into context, three million pesos is roughly equivalent to US$800, and the minimum *monthly* wage at this time was COP$737,717 (US$190).[61] For a rural, law-abiding Colombian, even one with a high school diploma as Andrés had, to earn three million pesos every two weeks is unfathomable. For years post-demobilization, Andrés could not find work, and when he did, it was informal, low-paid manual labor for far less than the official minimum wage. Indeed, in some paramilitary compounds, the men told me they would only make COL$20,000 (about US$5) for an entire day of cutting grass and firewood, earning them about US$120 per month if they could find work six days a week – which many could not.

The pull of illicit profits is very hard to resist.

THE COLLECTIVE DEMOBILIZATION PROCESS: AUC PARAMILITARIES

When I first met Nell, a rare female former member of the AUC, she was nothing like I had expected – although, looking back, I am not entirely sure what I expected. I had long wondered what women inside an organization known for its brutal sexual violence would say about their participation. Nell and the other two ex-AUC women that I met taught me a lot about resilience, economic desperation, looking the other way, and the mythology of "truth." Warm and with a frequent mischievous grin, Nell welcomed me into her home, cooked delicious meals, and told me – with much laughter – nearly unbelievable stories about travelers she had met coming

[59] Name of unit redacted to protect respondent's identity.
[60] Here he named a FARC dissident leader. Name redacted to protect respondent's identity.
[61] While that is the formal minimum wage, many low-skilled laborers earn far less than that, especially if they cannot obtain full-time hours. For detailed breakdowns, see: https://wageindicator.org/salary/living-wage/colombia-living-wages-2018-country-overview.

through this area. I say "nearly" unbelievable because this is Colombia. There is a reason the country is lauded as the birthplace of magical realism.

The AUC demobilization of nearly 30,000 members[62] was the Colombian government's first attempt to demobilize a massive number of combatants all at once, and it was also the first time there was a large amount of international support and funding for this process.[63] As such, it was indeed a "pilot" project from which the government, the international community, and the ex-combatant population have learned many lessons – though these lessons have not always materialized in programmatic changes. Many critics within and outside Colombia say it was not a peace process but an agreement between allies – especially as the links between Uribe's administration and the AUC became clearer.[64] Indeed, as subsequent chapters will show, many (if not most) AUC members that I spoke to saw the Colombian army as unquestionable allies and rarely as enemies. Or, in a few cases, they refused to talk about any links or operations with the military. As noted earlier, the overall legitimacy of these demobilizations has long been contested, and many emerging armed groups have ties to the supposedly demobilized paramilitaries who received government benefits.[65]

Before the demobilization process occurred, the AUC leadership had estimated that approximately 15,000 troops would demobilize, but this number nearly doubled by the time disarmament took place, causing critics to suggest that civilians were pretending to be AUC members to claim benefits.[66] But official troop counts often do not include people in support roles (especially women), sex workers sent to collect intelligence, urban militias, and informants. One ex-AUC respondent told me that he had been very surprised at how many women showed up at the demobilization site, because he had hardly seen any women in paramilitary combat units. But combat units are not the only components of an armed group.

Also, the high levels of stigma against AUC ex-combatants to this day, and the fact that many ex-paramilitaries continue to hide their AUC past, suggest that there would be a significant social cost to falsely claiming

---

[62] Nussio, "Learning from Shortcomings."
[63] García Duque and Martínez, "Cooperación Internacional, DDR y Los Retos de La Reincoporación."
[64] Nussio, "Learning from Shortcomings."
[65] Nussio, "Learning from Shortcomings"; Human Rights Watch, "Smoke and Mirrors"; Human Rights Watch, "Paramilitaries' Heirs"; Sontag, "Colombia's Paramilitaries and the U.S. War on Drugs."
[66] Nussio, "Learning from Shortcomings."

AUC status – especially for women.[67] Nonetheless, there is evidence that some nonparamilitaries were able to access DDR benefits due to lax eligibility criteria, and that many actual paramilitaries never demobilized.[68]

The general invisibility of women in the AUC meant that were no women involved in the AUC negotiations.[69] Lack of gender considerations or proper consultations with receiving communities also meant that for some women in areas with high levels of returning ex-paramilitaries, gender-based violence and overall insecurity went up; on the other hand, some communities reported more security as demobilized combatants took charge of community organizing.[70] Testimonies in this study suggest that many women within the AUC were subjected to highly exploitative conditions and systematized rape, and many were single mothers both when they joined and when they demobilized; however, there was little to nothing in the DDR program that addressed these special needs.[71] Indeed, both men and women ex-AUC members in this study derided the psycho-social support they received as "useless," or they lamented the fact that they did not receive more assistance to deal with their trauma.

The financial benefits package that demobilized paramilitaries received was similar to those that deserters later received in individual reintegration, but the amount of seed money they received was substantially less and reportedly handed out with far fewer conditions. For example, several of the paramilitaries in this study said the businesses they started failed quickly due a lack of proper training or business knowledge and insufficient capital. In addition, several told stories of being tricked by higher-ranking paramilitaries into handing over their funds for "collective" income-generating projects, only to have those commanders leave with all the money. Several participants, including Tobias, also complained to me that FARC ex-combatants were now getting far better benefits than they had received.

As part of the agreement, commanders and higher-ranking officers responsible for crimes against humanity served reduced prison sentences as part of the aforementioned Law 975, or the "Justice and Peace Law."[72] However, participant responses in this study suggest that many commanders lied about their rank or how many years they had spent in

---

[67] Interviews B82, B87, B99.
[68] Nussio, "Learning from Shortcomings."
[69] ARN, "La Reintegración En Colombia – Cifras."
[70] Elisa Tarnaala, "Legacies of Violence and the Unfinished Past: Women in Post-demobilization Colombia and Guatemala," *Peacebuilding* 7, no. 1 (2018): 1–15.
[71] Interviews B82, B87, B99.
[72] New York Times, "Colombia's Capitulation"; Nussio, "Learning from Shortcomings."

the group in order to avoid prison time. And because of the resurgence of AUC-connected armed groups under different names, many communities continue to use the term "paramilitaries" because they do not see the difference,[73] which makes reintegration for ex-paramilitaries who legitimately want to be law-abiding civilians very difficult:

They tell many tremendous stories [about us] ... even now, more terrible ... yes, imagine it. And to one [of us] they, how do I tell you, they *brand* you, is how we say it, you know? For being part of a demobilized group, they think the worst of you. They think the worst. Here, they asked me, "oh no, you're one of those. So, you haven't killed anyone?" And I said, "no! How could you think that?" Yes, they asked me that! My oldest daughter one day asked me that. (Clara, ex-AUC, B82)

While most ex-paramilitaries dispersed and went home after demobilization – or simply reemerged as different armed groups – some organized themselves and negotiated with the government to settle in collective farming communities. At least two of these communities where I conducted interviews were established on large properties that had been expropriated by the government from drug traffickers and then subdivided. The communities around these farms were largely unaware that the residents are former members of the AUC.[74] I conducted several interviews beside rundown mansions and old pools overgrown with weeds, or in the shadows of an enormous four-storey villa in disrepair, with the glass broken out of all the windows. It was surely a beautiful estate, long ago. But the irony that the government had expropriated land from drug traffickers, only to give it to ex-combatants from the AUC – a group transparent about its drug-trafficking income – was not lost on me, nor on them.

THE COLLECTIVE (AND ELITE) REINTEGRATION PROCESS: FARC

Well, we're not going to say that we are civilians, because on the day that the government truly says to us, "we've fulfilled [the peace accord]" ... then [we can say] we *were* guerrillas. Now I still say: "We *are* guerrillas" because for us they have not fulfilled anything.

Adrián, FARC (B44)

The peace negotiations with the FARC that began in 2012 led to a necessary review of existing mechanisms for reintegration. Critically, a key component

---

[73] Nussio, "Learning from Shortcomings."
[74] For this reason, and to respect the confidentiality of all participants, I have chosen not to disclose the locations of these communities. Interviews B76, B86, B87.

of the collective FARC reintegration was *political reintegration* – converting the armed group not only into law-abiding civilians but into political actors who were involved in government processes and decision-making.[75]

As noted earlier, the JEP is complex with highly technical elements, and some lower-ranking ex-combatants admitted to either being completely unaware of the JEP and other details on amnesty or of not understanding it properly.[76] Deserters remained unsure as to how or if the JEP applied to them as well. For example, during my first round of fieldwork interviews in February 2018, several ex-combatants in one of the GAHD safe houses became very agitated when police came to the compound and arrested one of their friends. They angrily confronted the colonel (the head of the military intelligence unit) in the middle of my conversation with him, because, in their view, they had immunity for their crimes and their friend had been unjustly arrested. I suddenly found myself in the middle of a heated shouting match between these ex-guerrilla men and the colonel about amnesty. The colonel had to repeatedly explain that they only had immunity for crimes committed in the context of the armed conflict. Their friend had been arrested for femicide, he said, allegedly committed *after* he demobilized. When they stormed off, the colonel apologized to me and explained that this was what he had to deal with daily: ex-combatants who did not understand their amnesty agreements. He shook his head and huffed out a big breath, shrugging his shoulders with his palms up, as if to say: "You see what I'm dealing with here?"

When I came back the next day, alone and without a military escort, I must have seemed more approachable (or at least more vulnerable) because several of these same men found me and demanded that I do something about their friend who had been unjustly arrested. But what could I possibly do? Unfortunately, the fact that I was unable to help them caused them to dismiss me entirely and refuse to talk to me – except for Junior.

There were many other issues with the JEP besides ex-combatant confusion. Voters on the "no" side of the peace accord argued that the JEP was far too lenient on the guerrillas for serious crimes such as drug trafficking and child recruitment.[77] While FARC commanders responsible for crimes against humanity are technically supposed to serve reduced sentences in prison – as some AUC leaders did – the peace deal with the FARC has caused much discontent in Colombian society because most

---

[75] Ugarriza and Quishpe, "Guerrilla Sin Armas."
[76] Interview B18.
[77] Schmidt and Tovar, "A 'Post-conflict' Colombia?"

of the top leaders (aside from Jesús Santrich, who was arrested but then released) have been allowed to run for office and take their seats in the Senate without serving any prison time.[78]

Further complicating matters, President Duque sent the JEP back to the legislature in March 2019, reopening a legal issue already decided by Congress, and receiving much international criticism for doing so.[79] Ex-guerrillas expressed heightened fears that this move undermined the peace accord, especially regarding the possibility that they could be arrested from within the protected reincorporation camps if the government reneged on portions of the agreement.[80] While this attempt to alter the JEP failed, Duque was reprimanded by both national and international judicial actors for not respecting judicial autonomy and for undermining the overall transitional justice process.

As noted earlier, compounding this sense of insecurity is the ongoing targeting of FARC members and social leaders.[81] This targeted violence – along with the historical memory of thousands of UP members being executed decades earlier – has made FARC loyalists extremely fearful for their safety, and most in this study said that they did not trust the government to sufficiently protect them. Indeed, at least seventeen former combatants have been killed while waiting for special protection measures that were supposed to be provided by the government, and women in particular are having trouble accessing adequate protection.[82]

The collective demobilization program originally housed the FARC ex-combatants in twenty-six ETCRs across the country, mostly in areas where the FARC traditionally had a strong presence. Each ex-combatant received COP$700,000 (approximately US$215) monthly, which at the time of the agreement was 90 percent of the current Colombian minimum wage. They also received a biweekly allotment of nonperishable food and rent-free housing, but any fresh items, medications, toiletries, diapers, and other supplies they had to purchase themselves. The higher monthly benefit and free housing and food – while still insufficient, given

---

[78] BBC, "Colombia Farc: Election Candidate Timochenko Taken to Hospital," *BBC News*, March 1, 2018, www.bbc.com/news/world-latin-america-43251435.

[79] El Tiempo, "Apoyos y Críticas a Decisión de Duque Sobre Ley Estatutaria de La JEP," *El Tiempo*, March 12, 2019, www.eltiempo.com/justicia/jep-colombia/apoyos-y-criticas-a-decision-de-duque-sobre-ley-estatutaria-de-la-jep-336988; The Economist, "Colombia's President Iván Duque Undermines a Peace Deal," *The Economist*, March 2019, www.economist.com/the-americas/2019/03/16/colombias-president-ivan-duque-undermines-a-peace-deal.

[80] The Economist, "Colombia's President Iván Duque Undermines a Peace Deal."

[81] Guterres, "United Nations Verification Mission in Colombia: December 2020."

[82] Guterres, "United Nations Verification Mission in Colombia: June 2020."

the poor housing conditions, overflowing septic fields, and limited access to healthcare – generated significant resentment from other groups of ex-combatants, especially deserters.

Like ex-combatants in the individual program, if collectively demobilized FARC combatants meet the conditions, they too are each eligible for eight million pesos (approximately US$2,500) of start-up funds for a small business. However, the FARC command structure has been pushing for collective projects, and most of the currently functioning collective projects have been funded through individual ex-combatants' benefit funds rather than the promised project funding from the government.[83] As of December 2021, 107 collective projects had been approved (though not all had received funding), but many of these face significant challenges in terms of market access and technical assistance.[84] With more ex-combatants moving away from ETCRs, at the time of writing fifty collective projects had been implemented outside these areas. In addition, because land tenure for many of the ETCRs is uncertain, it is not clear what will happen to the collective projects that have been established on rented land if the government does not extend or permanently secure tenure. During fieldwork for this project, it was also unclear whether the benefits, due to expire in August 2019, would be extended again – and this was causing much anxiety among ETCR residents. When the legal status of the ETCRs expired on August 15, 2019, the government announced that there would be a two-year "transition period" during which the provision of services, food, health care, and security would be extended.[85] However, the basic monthly allowance was initially only extended until December 2019. After the Covid-19 pandemic spread rapidly, the ARN issued a resolution to ensure that these benefits would continue until August 2020.[86] At the time of writing, it remained unclear how long the benefits would be extended for, leaving many ex-combatants in a highly precarious position – especially as lockdowns and other Covid-19 restrictions had devastated employment options; as of December 2021, the government had reiterated its commitment to ensuring reintegration benefits to all accredited former combatants.

---

[83] Antonio Guterres, "United Nations Verification Mission in Colombia: Report of the Secretary General, March 2019" (New York, 2019), https://doi.org/10.1017/S0020818300001107.

[84] Guterres, "United Nations Verification Mission in Colombia: December 2020."

[85] Antonio Guterres, "United Nations Verification Mission in Colombia: Report of the Secretary General, October 2019" (New York, 2019), www.securitycouncilreport.org/atf/cf/%7B65BFCF9B-6D27-4E9C-8CD3-CF6E4FF96FF9%7D/s_2019_780.pdf.

[86] Guterres, "United Nations Verification Mission in Colombia: June 2020."

The ETCRs are protected by two security perimeters – the outer perimeter is the Colombian military while the inner perimeter is operated by the national police. However, during this fieldwork, while I certainly saw these security perimeters in my repeated visits, I was stopped and questioned by the police only once when entering a camp and once while leaving a different one. Otherwise, my Colombian assistant and I passed in and out without question. I also observed many cars and motorcycles passing back and forth with no security checks. Indeed, many ex-combatants in this study did not feel that the security provided was keeping them safe in any substantive way, and I could see why. The one camp that had members of the Secretariat present had several armed bodyguards that immediately greeted any unknown people entering the camp (myself included, until they began to recognize me and wave me in). Many of these camps were also extremely isolated and far from urban centers, calling into question how "integrated" the ex-combatants really were with Colombian society. It was not a surprise to me that so many were leaving to seek work elsewhere. Many of these camps lacked proper access roads or adequate services to maintain profitable economic projects.[87] For example, in one ETCR that I visited in southern Colombia, access to the nearest real town was only possible if the river was low and ferry crossing was possible, as there was no bridge. If the river was too high, residents had to take a lengthy detour, putting children and other vulnerable individuals at great risk if they needed to access emergency medical services. They said this also made bringing agricultural goods to market very burdensome and expensive.

Thousands of ex-FARC members have since left the transition zones – with approximately 9,225 now living outside the ETCRs – largely due to disillusionment with government promises and the lack of economic opportunities.[88] While the ARN statistics claim that only 739 ex-FARC members are classified as "whereabouts unknown," UN reports suggest that this number is much larger.[89]

---

[87] Renata Segura, "Colombia Further Polarized by President's Action on Transitional Justice Law" (New York, 2019), https://theglobalobservatory.org/2019/04/colombia-polarized-president-action-transitional-justice-law/.

[88] ARN, "Reincorporacion En Cifras"; Vanda Felbab-Brown, "Death by Bad Implementation? The Duque Administration and Colombia's Peace Deal(S)," Brookings, 2018, www.brookings.edu/blog/order-from-chaos/2018/07/24/death-by-bad-implementation-the-duque-administration-and-colombias-peace-deals/; Antonio Guterres, "United Nations Verification Mission in Colombia: Report of the Secretary General, July 2018" (New York, 2018), https://doi.org/S/2010/579.

[89] ARN, "Reincorporacion En Cifras"; Guterres, "United Nations Verification Mission in Colombia: December 2019."

I also noticed drastic differences in the quality of the ETCRs depending on who was living there and where the ETCR was located. For example, in one ETCR in northern Colombia there were several top-level commanders, and in this camp the UN and ARN visited daily, multiple nongovernmental organizations (NGOs) came in to conduct activities with the ex-combatants, and several productive projects were running. However, in a different ETCR in central Colombia there were no high-level commanders left; there was no clear command structure or person in authority; and as a result there were few economic projects, poor living conditions, and an overall sense of idleness – along with heavy drinking by many of the younger men. In the first ETCR I visited, in southern Colombia, the space was very well organized due to a clear command structure, with several economic projects running, but the camp was a veritable ghost town because so many ex-combatants had left due to legitimate security concerns. For example, an armed gunman had managed to enter the camp and nonfatally shoot an ex-combatant living there only a month before I arrived. At the time of my visit, there were police officers stationed at the entry to this camp checking everyone who entered – which was not the case at the other ETCRs. In early 2019, overall maintenance on ETCR infrastructure had slowed even though two camps needed urgent improvements in order to prevent serious health risks to at least 400 ex-combatants.[90] Dayana told me that she was perpetually terrified that her toddler would wander off and fall into the open sewage pit.

TENSIONS BETWEEN COLLECTIVE AND INDIVIDUAL DEMOBILIZATION

In other words, they put us here [in the ETCRs] to waste time. Here, there are some comrades who are responsible for the reincorporation; we have the cooperative already set up, but they go to meeting after meeting and nothing ever gets agreed, and they wait … In this way [government officials] are using development strategies so that we will get bored and leave … And then, divided and alone, it's easier for them to fuck us.

Rafael, FARC, B46

Another area of tension in Colombia's DDR has been between the government's preference for and experience with individual demobilizations versus the FARC leadership's insistence on a collective process. These clashes arose during the Santos administration's negotiations with the

---

[90] Guterres, "United Nations Verification Mission in Colombia: March 2019."

FARC and increased with Duque's attempts to revise the peace accord, especially as funding for collective projects is an ongoing issue. Rather than ex-combatants dispersing and going home (or to another location) individually, the FARC guerrillas were initially housed collectively in the ETCRs with the aim of creating cooperative income-generating projects. However, as noted, the majority of collectively demobilized FARC members have since left the ETCRs, and the sustainability of these projects and lack of adequate training and infrastructure also remain as significant concerns. The UN has repeatedly cited housing for ex-combatants as an urgent concern.[91] Larger numbers of these FARC members are moving to major cities, including Bogotá, Villavicencio, Cali, and Medellín, further dismantling the collective strength and hierarchy of the group.[92] Compounding these tensions, during the peace negotiations some FARC members opted to enter the individual demobilization rather than the collective one for various reasons.

The additional difference between beneficiaries in these two streams (individual versus collective) is that the majority of people in the individual process are deserters from various groups – that is, they left the group because they wanted a different life and took great risks to escape. They are then intentionally housed with a mix of ex-combatants from other groups, to encourage them to release their guerrilla/fighter identity and transition to a civilian identity. All ranks are treated the same – again, in an attempt to transition to civilian life and to replace combatant identities.

But in the ETCRs that I visited, it was clear that military rank continued to matter significantly after demobilization. Reintegration experts that I talked to in Colombia also stated that ex-combatants in collective demobilization processes (i.e., those ordered to demobilize), whether guerrillas or paramilitaries, had a much harder time reintegrating than those who had willingly disarmed.[93] In addition, those in the collective process who have remained in the ETCRs tend to stay within their FARC networks, while deserters are forced to make new networks once they have left the group – which also affects their reintegration experiences. This same staff member noted that many ex-combatants in collective demobilization processes (i.e., AUC in 2003–2006 and FARC in 2016) did not want to disarm and only demobilized because they were ordered to – raising the risks of recidivism.[94]

---

[91] Guterres, "United Nations Verification Mission in Colombia: October 2019."

[92] Guterres, "United Nations Verification Mission in Colombia: October 2019."

[93] Author interviews Co1, Co3.

[94] Oliver Kaplan and Enzo Nussio, "Explaining Recidivism of Ex-combatants in Colombia," *Journal of Conflict Resolution* 62, no. 1 (2018): 64–93.

In addition, a staff member at the GAHD noted that some ex-FARC combatants have come to them and asked to leave the collective process and join the individual process instead.[95] But this attempt to switch streams has also gone the other way, with ex-FARC combatants who were in the individual program asking commanders in the ETCRs if they could join the collective process – with mixed results. Individual projects have also been approved at a much faster pace than collective ones: in the first half of 2020, for example, 415 individual projects were approved, while only ten collective projects were approved. And the ex-combatants that I spoke to were well aware of these inequities. These tensions indicate that, when studying demobilization and reintegration, it is crucial to distinguish between combatants who demobilized by choice and combatants who did so because they were following orders.

CONCLUSION

As this chapter demonstrates, over the last two decades in particular, Colombia has incorporated many changes and attempts at improvement in its approaches to DDR. But several major challenges remain. First, there continue to be tensions between the government's preference for (and experience with) individual reintegration and the FARC leaders' preference for collective reintegration – whether the lack of government funds for collective projects is a deliberate response to this tension is unclear. Several ex-combatants told me that the government's recalcitrance around land distribution is yet another deliberate political strategy to disperse and weaken the group. Some scholars have also argued that the "excessive" participation of international actors has impeded rather than empowered the rise of local leaders whose actions are critical to definitively end the violence.[96]

Second, DDR in Colombia still often pays lip service to gender without meaningful changes that directly address the specific challenges that women ex-combatants face – or the challenges that many men ex-combatants face when shifting to civilian life in a society where violent, armed men are often the ones with power and status. That is, "gender" in Colombia's DDR remains very limited to an "add women and stir" approach. As a result, gender is still entirely conflated with women in the reintegration process, and even then, there are significant gaps that

---

[95] Author interview C01.
[96] García Duque and Martínez, "Cooperación Internacional, DDR y Los Retos de La Reincoporación."

block women from fully participating in reintegration programs, especially in terms of the lack of childcare for single mothers. However, the fact that women complete the reintegration program at higher rates than men suggests there is something else impeding men's reintegration – or at least their completion of official programs – that is understudied and inadequately addressed. To truly challenge gender norms in Colombia is to go up against the influential conservative religious components of Colombian society – but that brings with it risks of being associated with, or at least sympathetic to, leftist guerrillas.

Third, confusion around what benefits ex-combatants are entitled to remains a problem, with many appearing to be unclear regarding what they need to do to access higher education options or capital to start businesses. This confusion extends to their psycho-social assistance benefits, with many ex-combatants only vaguely understanding that they were expected to use part of their monthly stipend for this, and with little knowledge on how to make this happen or how such assistance would actually help them. For the ones that were aware of this benefit, it was ludicrous that they would spend part of their inadequate monthly allowance on counseling when they could not even afford food, rent, or medication (including contraception). Because of this confusion, there is much ongoing resentment from ex-combatants toward the government. Some participants in this study entered the demobilization program after deserting because they had heard from friends that the benefits were good, while others felt disillusioned by the failure of those promises and had told other ex-combatants that it was not worth enrolling. Also, some reintegration officials expressed concern to me that the ELN would be watching the FARC reincorporation process quite closely, and if the government failed to deliver, then a peace agreement with the ELN seemed far less likely.

IV

Framing Victimhood

Of this war, and of which we are now victims ... we went from being victimizers to becoming victims. For those of us who were recruited as children, what are we?

Victims or perpetrators?

Johan, ex-FARC (B31)

I am perfectly capable of going before the government to say that I was from the FARC *and* that I am the victim. But that is not the case ... that is an irresponsibility of the media, because they don't see ... how is it "the people's army," or the "heroes" of the national army? For me, how is a national army going to be a hero, when this national army comes to rape the girls from my village?

Mafe, FARC (B29)

What does it mean to be a victim, and who or what draws the line between victim and perpetrator? In many cases, is there even a line at all? Most participants in this research struggled with these questions. No one wants to admit that they were (or still are) on the wrong side, especially in conflicts when there is no clear "right" side. Many ex-combatants in this study, including high-level commanders, insisted that they were the "real" victims in this conflict. But who then, I wondered, were the "fake" victims?

The first time I stepped into a FARC reincorporation camp, I was admittedly nervous and intimidated, and perhaps for good reason: four male guerrilla commanders grilled me for an hour in the sweltering Amazon heat about my motives, background, and interview questions before they would allow me to talk to anyone. A female guerrilla hovered in the background, her role unclear. It probably did not help that this was a highly remote camp that few foreigners had ever visited. But by the next evening, we were all drinking beer and laughing together as the sun went down, their dogs nuzzling into my hand so I would scratch their heads, their kids coming up shyly to touch my hair or ask why my eyes were blue. The more I spoke with former guerrillas and paramilitaries, and the more I heard the circumstances under which they made that life-altering decision to join the ranks and pick up a gun, the more I wondered: if facing the same circumstances, would I make different choices? Would my children? How far down that road do you have to go before you realize you have gone too far?

Among the ninety-nine former combatants that I interviewed, 37 percent had joined at age fifteen or younger – many of them were twelve or thirteen when they joined, some were as young as ten. For the FARC and ELN, these ages were not abnormal. At the time, my son was ten. It was both hard to imagine and easy to understand. Despite a ban on both real and toy guns in our house, he *loved* guns. It was not hard to see how a child that age could be drawn into a group like the FARC, especially if home was not a safe place or if school seemed useless. But what happens to young children who make this "choice" without understanding the long-term consequences, without understanding that it is impossible to take back? What happens when they become adults, and how do they make sense of these experiences?

The guerrillas who recruited these children insisted to me that they were protecting them, that they were providing a safe place from abusive families, and that even if they tried to send children back home, the children would refuse to go. And some participants who joined at young ages confirmed this, insisting that inside the FARC ranks was the safest place to be. Mafe was one of those ex-combatants.[1] A bright and charming individual, Mafe was one of the first loyalist FARC women who agreed to speak to me. In that first ETCR camp, women were quite wary of me, and it took time to build trust, but Mafe had no hesitation. She wanted to make sure that her story was heard. We spoke for over three hours and, when looking back at the transcript, I realized that I hardly asked her a single question.

Mafe grew up in a coca-growing family in southern Colombia in a poor, rural area. Her parents were both coca farmers, she told me, as that was the only crop that paid enough to keep their large family fed and healthy. She said that with other crops, it was too expensive

[1] Author interview B29.

and time-intensive to get them to market, and they would often spoil along the way. With coca, on the other hand, the buyers came to the farmers – there was no transport cost, no spoilage, no time lost. She said that because of coca, her parents were able to hire a teacher for their children's education, which she and her siblings otherwise would not have had.

But coca is not what she really wanted to talk about. Mafe told me how the police and military terrorized her community for her entire childhood, long before the FARC came into their lives. She told me how state fumigations would kill not only coca but everything else, poisoning the air and water and making the children sick. She told me that because the military had weapons and the community did not, the soldiers did whatever they wanted. The *campesinos* did not realize that they had rights against such violence, she said, until the guerrillas came into town:

Well, [then] FARC enters the community eager to contribute. To show us that the government, because all those abuses that it has been committing since, that it has not paid attention to the peasants. And what is the attention? Well, let's say we as peasants do not have, we do not have, or we *still* do not have access to roads. We do not have a good education, health. [There are] abuses, violations of human rights. We suffered as peasants because we lived in the fields and sowed coca crops. So, FARC at that time … see, they bring us together to the community and tell us, "you have some rights, you have a book called the political constitution." And to us at that time, because parents did not have that knowledge, one was therefore very child-like, no?

The FARC opened their eyes, she said, to the fact that they did not have to suffer this violence and that the state should not be treating its citizens this way. But the presence of the FARC also exposed their community to increased attacks from opposing forces. Mafe explained that she never officially "enlisted" in the FARC. It often did not work that way. She gave an example of how, if the FARC came into town and asked a civilian for a glass of water, and the paramilitaries heard about it, then that civilian would be accused by the paramilitaries of being a guerrilla collaborator. There were people, she said, military infiltrators, who kept lists. But when armed guerrillas came to the door, she said, *campesinos* could hardly refuse them a glass of water. As a result, many people were drawn into one side or the other whether they wanted to be or not:

So, they fought day and night, and many times we as *campesinos* were the ones who were affected by living there. See, us with my mother were fumigated three times from the ghost plane, fumigated with "lead" [bullets]. What my mother did was throw us on the floor and she lay on top of us, twice. I remember vividly that we went to the farm, because it was almost an hour and a half from the farm to where we lived, walking, and I was going with my seven-year-old brother. I was about eleven years old, and [the military] was with the FARC, facing each other, and then we were going our way, and the sky was cloudy. And when that plane came like this [motions with her hand, swooping down], it started to shoot bullets. And what we did was throw ourselves to the ground, throw ourselves to the ground and, and that was like that. And it made some things, some big holes, shredded with those same bullets. Twice, the third time, it came again, and we threw ourselves on the ground again with my brother and mother. And then my mother said, "my God, they don't even see us!" She said, "what are we? They're children!" That is, we had nothing to do with the war that the government had against FARC there.

With tears rolling down her cheeks, she said it was like a bad dream, cemented in her mind as her first traumatic memory of the war. But when the paramilitaries came into the area several years later, she said, it got much worse. When she was about seventeen, on May 12 (she recalled the *exact* date), they had spent the entire day getting ready for a festival to celebrate Mother's Day:

Then, around eleven at night, the paramilitaries arrived in the community and took us out of all the houses, children, the elderly, all of us, just like that, to the field, as they say. Because in the communities they always had their field in the middle and the little houses all around it. So, they took us out to the fields and with a list in hand and armed up to there, as much as could be. And then: "Such-and-such, step forward, such-and-such, step forward." And they would kill them right there. There were children, the elderly ... the government, in its eagerness to finish [off] the illegal armed groups, had infiltrated people to see who gave them a glass of water, or who spoke or not to the groups ... They took us out there with a list in hand, they were naming people and they were killing them. I remember that so vividly.

They had also brought in some women from "social life," that is, the ones who like to work like that with their body. And a boy had not paid one for the service, and that day the woman had already put him there on a list ... and they called that boy to the front, and four of them held him, and they blew off his member, alive, because he hadn't wanted to pay the girl. And then his mother arrived and ... she fainted, so I, I was then sixteen, seventeen years old ... and I felt the urge to go help that lady because she fell unconscious. So, I don't know, I momentarily, I forgot that we were in that, in that problem and that they had us like this. And I went to help the lady. When I went to help the lady, the armed man told me, "bitch! You son of a bitch, listen!" I don't know how many, so many very rude verbal words. "If you move a finger, you die." And I was a girl! A teenager of seventeen years old. All I did was stand up slowly, with the gun right here on my forehead and go back to where my parents were. But that's not all, because the man killed him anyway. The boy was killed, and it gave the mother such a shock that she died there too. So, I always say, and I ask the state the question, and I am *always* going to ask it in any space: how are they going to repair us psychologically? How?

*

Of all the various frames used by nonstate armed groups in Colombia, the frame of victimhood is particularly durable and credible – but it is also one of the most highly contested. Frames use labels, narratives, and identities to construct and reinforce meaning and – in situations of social movements or armed rebellion – these frames can help to recruit and to retain membership. However, when frames of rebel groups are contested by the government, opposing groups, or civilians, what determines which frame "wins," and what are the effects of that outcome? What do group members do when frame-makers lose credibility and/or when frame resonance breaks down?

As Krystalli notes, "[v]ictimhood does not merely describe an experience of harm; it is also a political status and identity that invites particular performances from the state, human rights actors, and conflict-affected individuals."[2] Indeed, in the last ten years in Colombia, victimhood itself has become highly politicized and often contested, creating a hierarchy of victims with far-reaching implications for lasting peace. For example, in 2008, a Victims' Rights Act was approved by the Colombian Senate but then encountered opposition from President Uribe's administration, who argued that victims of state forces should not be included, as this would morally equate the Colombian armed forces with illegal armed groups.[3] But discriminating among victims based on their victimizers is clearly problematic in terms of transitional justice and international law.

In 2011, a Victims' Law was formally put into place to recognize the rights and reparations due to victims, cited by some scholars as the "most ambitious reparations law in its history,"[4] and in 2014, the High Commissioner for Peace in Colombia declared an "era of the victims."[5]

---

[2] Roxani Krystalli, "'We Are Not Good Victims': Hierarchies of Suffering and the Politics of Victimhood in Colombia," PhD dissertation, Tufts University, 2019, ii.

[3] Dario Ghilarducci, "Víctimas y Memoria Histórica: Las Madres de Plaza de Mayo y El Movimiento de Víctimas de Crímenes de Estado En Colombia," *Análisis Político* 93 (May–August 2018): 189–207; Adam Isaacson, "Colombia's Victims' Rights Act," Latin America Working Group, 2008, www.lawg.org/colombias-victims-rights-act/; Giovanni Mora Lemus, "Memorias, Pluralidad, y Movimiento Social: La Experiencia Del MOV-ICE," MA dissertation, Universidad Javeriana, 2010.

[4] Nicole Summers, "Colombia's Victims' Law: Transitional Justice in a Time of Violent Conflict?," *Harvard Human Rights Journal* 25 (2012): 219–35.

[5] Krystalli, "'We Are Not Good Victims'."

Being officially recognized as a victim is, of course, critical, because that recognition influences who gets compensation and in what form, and who can participate in public policy forums.[6] And the four-year peace process with the FARC included several mechanisms through which officially recognized victims could participate in the proceedings.[7] But not all officially recognized victims receive reparations, and very few get to participate in public forums; in fact, only an estimated one million of the nine million officially recognized victims in Colombia have received reparations to date.[8] This lack of adequate reparations has undoubtedly heightened resentment against ex-combatants who receive monthly allowances from the state.

In this book, following Krystalli, I use "victim" not as a simple synonym to describe someone who has experienced harm, but as a "political status and category that different actors vie for, reject, wield, or contest."[9] And in my research, many ex-combatants like Dayana, Mafe, and Lina justifiably self-identified as victims but could not (and likely will not) ever be officially recognized by the state or the transitional justice process as victims. Indeed, the distinction between perpetrators and victims is often so reified in post-conflict situations that to be considered a "true" victim, one must be completely innocent, even though in most conflict situations this distinction is rarely so simple.[10] Research shows that the way victimhood is constructed and reproduced in transitional justice – often heavily reliant on this prerequisite of innocence – can be highly problematic for lasting peace in situations where victims may have also committed human rights abuses.[11] Even the way I have labeled this framing contest – *victims versus perpetrators* – is of course an oversimplification of the narrative battle taking place here. There are many layers of nuance in this discourse. However, simple frames are often the most effective to build a social movement, and as this and subsequent chapters will illustrate, many ex-combatants that I spoke with started with more nuanced understandings of their situation and over the course of their experience in armed groups were pushed further and further into stark,

[6] Isaacson, "Colombia's Victims' Rights Act"; Krystalli, "'We Are Not Good Victims'."
[7] Bouvier, "Gender and the Role of Women in Colombia's Peace Process"; Krystalli, "'We Are Not Good Victims'."
[8] Krystalli, "'We Are Not Good Victims'."
[9] Krystalli, "'We Are Not Good Victims'," 10.
[10] Kieran McEvoy and Kirsten McConnachie, "Victimology in Transitional Justice: Victimhood, Innocence and Hierarchy," ed. Susanne Karstedt and Stephan Parmentier, *European Journal of Criminology* 9, no. 5 (2012): 527–38.
[11] McEvoy and McConnachie, "Victimology in Transitional Justice."

combative binaries. After all, if everyone is a victim, who is to be held accountable?

Victimhood, then, is symbolic, hierarchical, political, and contested – it is a carefully constructed and strategically utilized frame. While claiming victimhood can have negative connotations in certain contexts (e.g., "playing the victim"), victimhood can also be a source of empowerment, resistance, and collective action. Indeed, "injustice frames" are one of the most common frames utilized by social movement leaders to inspire collective action.[12] Not only do the FARC and ELN use these injustice frames to justify taking up arms and using violence to challenge the government, but they also frequently invoked the narrative that they were only acting in self-defense due to this victimization, pointing to the government as the "real terrorist." However, this frame of victimhood was challenged by deserters, paramilitaries, and the government, in different ways.

In my research, the most common reason given to desert armed groups, for both men and women, was fear of violence, witnessing violence, or being a victim of violence from within their own group (including the fear of forced abortion): eighteen of the thirty-eight deserters, or 47 percent (five women, thirteen men) emphasized this as their main reason for leaving. Second, eleven of the twenty-four ex-paramilitaries (46 percent) said that they too wanted to desert – and some even tried and were recaptured – but most were too scared of what the group would do to their families; many of them also used language of victimhood to justify why they stayed in the group. These findings indicate that victimhood can work both ways – to either keep recruits in or push them out – depending on the components of the frame and who is creating it. It suggests that cost–benefit calculations, or at least the costs of group membership versus the costs of leaving, are very important in desertion decisions, but that these calculations depend on the structure, patterns of violence, and ideology of the group. Costs and benefits are often highly subjective. It is complex (and time consuming) to organize such experiences and make these individual calculations, which is why framing becomes such a useful heuristic – not only for analysis later, but also for those trying to make sense of confusing and traumatic experiences in the moment.

Once these frames become engrained as a shortcut to understand the world around them, it can be very difficult for ex-combatants to reframe their lives post-demobilization. It was clear in my interviews that most

[12] Benford and Snow, "Framing Processes and Social Movements."

ex-combatants I spoke to were highly influenced by the frames that they had learned in their armed groups, or they were conflicted and confused by the cognitive dissonance created by the framing contests between insurgent groups and the government.

THE GUERRILLA FRAME OF VICTIMHOOD

Well, I would say at this point that the FARC is the organization most persecuted by the state – by the Colombian government, and also by the United States.

Ricardo, FARC (B41)

In everything, in every army, those who stick their necks out, those who kill themselves are the poor, in every army, the poor. In the guerrilla, we were all poor, commanders, guerrillas, everything, everyone. And in the army, those who were sent to kill the guerrillas were the poor. Because generals who give orders, they are not going to go out and kill themselves with the poor. The one who goes is the lowliest soldier, the common soldier, among the poor, seeking the same small comforts, in the same economic situation.

Ernesto, FARC (B39)

There are three key components of the guerrilla frame of victimhood: the *campesino* identity, the gendered dimensions of victimhood, and the claim of acting in self-defense. While, as noted earlier, victimhood among civilians in Colombia is also highly contested and hierarchical, here I focus on the framing contest between the nonstate armed groups and the government as separate from – but still influenced by – the civilian debate on what makes a "good" victim.[13]

The *Campesino* Identity

But then, here in Colombia, the war forced weapons onto the *campesinos*. It was imposed on us, they imposed it on us, by the force of the bullet.

Vesino, FARC (B23)

One of the key determinants of frame resonance with constituents of a social movement is the "extent to which the frame taps into existing cultural values, beliefs, narratives, [and] folk wisdom."[14] This aspect of the guerrillas' frame construction is particularly clear in the history

---

[13] Krystalli, "'We Are Not Good Victims'."
[14] Benford and Snow, "Framing Processes and Social Movements," 624.

of *campesino* neglect and victimization by the state. While the war in Colombia may not technically fit the definition of an "ethnic conflict," there are strong racialized aspects to the ongoing armed violence. Armed conflict and disputes over territory have been particularly intense in regions with high levels of Indigenous and Afro-descendant populations, and both of these groups have often been recruited by armed actors disproportionately to their overall numbers in the population.[15] But the key divide in the conflict – based more on class and skin color than specific ethnicities – is that between urban dwellers, rich landowners, and rural *campesinos*. As this chapter shows, in Colombia this *campesino* identity is strongly linked not only to rural land but also to themes of victimhood, resistance, displacement, and persecution by the state.

As noted earlier, the Colombian conflict has affected rural areas to a much greater degree than urban centers, due to coca production, low presence of state forces and/or state infrastructure, guerrilla and paramilitary control of territory, and the protection of drug-trafficking routes, among other factors.[16] As a result, rural residents – predominantly *campesinos* like Lina and Mafe, Indigenous peoples like Dayana and her sister, and Afro-descendants like Clara and many of my other respondents – have been internally displaced at alarming rates, with well over seven million IDPs since 1985.[17] Of these, approximately 2.5 percent are Indigenous and 10.5 percent are Afro-descendant.[18] About 90 percent of displaced *campesinos* resettle in urban areas,[19] necessitating an abrupt change of livelihood options and an increased dependence on the state for services. *Campesinos* are generally not considered Indigenous or Afro-descendant, and they usually self-identify (or are categorized by

---

[15] Jonathan Watts, "Battle for the Mother Land: Indigenous People of Colombia Fighting for Their Lands," *The Guardian*, 2017, www.theguardian.com/environment/2017/oct/28/nasa-colombia-cauca-valley-battle-mother-land.

[16] Annette Idler, *Borderland Battles: Violence, Crime, and Governance at the Edges of Colombia's War* (New York: Oxford University Press, 2019); María Clemencia Ramírez, *Between the Guerrillas and the State: The Cocalero Movement, Citizenship, and Identity in the Colombian Amazon* (Durham, NC and London: Duke University Press, 2011).

[17] UNHCR, "UNHCR Fact Sheet: Colombia," 2017, http://reporting.unhcr.org/sites/default/files/UNHCR Colombia Factsheet – February 2017.pdf.

[18] UNHCR, "UNHCR Fact Sheet: Colombia"; while the 2005 census says that Afro-descendants make up 10 percent of Colombia's population, these numbers have been disputed by some Afro-descendant leaders, who argue that this number is far higher. Minority Rights, "Afro-Colombians," 2019, https://minorityrights.org/minorities/afro-colombians/.

[19] Sebastián Albuja and Marcela Ceballos, "Urban Displacement and Migration in Colombia," *Forced Migration Review* 34 (2010), www.fmreview.org/sites/fmr/files/FMRdownloads/en/urban-displacement/albuja-ceballos.pdf.

the state) as "mestizo" or mixed race.[20] However, even though the race lexicon separates *campesinos* from the distinct ethnicities of Indigenous and Afro-descendant populations, these farmers remain racialized in Colombia and face high levels of discrimination, often being viewed as "less than human" by the upper classes.[21] And, across Latin America, skin color rather than a specific ethnicity is often a determinant of ethnic inequality and discrimination: a "pigmentocracy" that places lighter-skinned people at the top of the ethnic hierarchy and darker-skinned people at the bottom.[22]

All of this discrimination, inequality, and racism creates the foundation from which the FARC and the ELN have been able to build their strong frame of victimhood. For most rural *campesinos*, insurgent or otherwise, their identity is inextricably linked to the state as a perpetrator of violence against them, which has enabled guerrilla leadership to frame the group as a *campesino* army ("army of the people") that has been forced to take up arms due to state actions. In this framing, the audience is not only made up of recruits and potential recruits, but also the Colombian (and in some cases international) public – as a way to explain and justify unpopular actions and refute the terrorist label placed on them by the state. Four of the FARC loyalists in this sample had grown up with parents who were members of the UP (the FARC political party in the 1980s) and had either witnessed their parents being assassinated or remembered constant displacement due to violent threats.[23] Indeed, most guerrilla respondents said that those who rule Colombia are rich oligarchs who do not care about the *campesinos*. Some civilian *campesinos* claimed that the war is a deliberate effort to get rid of them entirely, while others said that the state sees them as trash and not truly part of Colombian society, and thus has fully abandoned them.[24] Indeed, even after decades in cities, displaced *campesinos* continue to be excluded both politically and socio-economically.[25] Since the peace process, there

---

[20] Courtheyn, "De-indigenized but Not Defeated"; Angela J Lederach, "'The Campesino Was Born for the Campo': A Multispecies Approach to Territorial Peace in Colombia," *American Anthropologist* 119, no. 4 (2017): 589–602; López, "Contesting Double Displacement."

[21] Courtheyn, "De-indigenized but Not Defeated."

[22] Telles, *Pigmentocracies*.

[23] Interview numbers: B28, B36, B46, B58.

[24] Courtheyn, "De-indigenized but Not Defeated"; Ramírez, *Between the Guerrillas and the State*.

[25] López, "Contesting Double Displacement."

has also been considerable debate on whose experiences of victimization warrant the most attention, giving rise to a "hierarchy of suffering."[26]

In addition, while Indigenous and Afro-descendant populations can make legal or ethnic claims to land (even if not often successful), *campesinos* without a specific ethnic heritage cannot make these claims and thus, formulate political strategies around land based on the language of belonging. Mari explained to me that these disputes over land were why, in her view, "most" *campesinos* supported the FARC. As Mari's quote reflects at the beginning of this section, Uribe's "Democratic Security" policy that was supposed to win over the civilian population largely did the opposite for *campesinos* – what Mari saw was that when rural residents realized the state was investing in war and nothing else, they turned their support to the FARC, which was at least buying their coca and providing some form of security. Some loyalist FARC respondents also framed their *campesino* identity in terms of pride that they – despite victimization at the hands of the Colombian government and its military assistance from the United States – had been able to resist for decades:

Look how the organization FARC-EP was the only organization that voluntarily resisted and confronted the Colombian government, and not only the Colombian government, but also the government of the United States. Because it was not only here in Colombia but with all of their high-end technology, they fought us, men and women *campesinos*, many of whom did not know how to write nor read, but who had the capacity and the clarity to say: this is the only road we have left, to achieve change in this country one day. (Reina, FARC, B40)

This sense of pride was rooted directly in the narrative that *despite* the oppression and neglect they had experienced, they had been able to resist, and that the only reason they took up arms was because of the government's treatment of them. Indeed, the low levels of education of most respondents had led them to believe that they had few alternatives besides farming or fighting – which when combined with resentment of the government for not providing alternatives, created resonance around the collective injustice frame presented by FARC leadership.

For many rural residents of Colombia, the most significant role the state has played in their lives has been through its absence.[27] Alternatively, for some, the only state presence they had seen was in the form of male soldiers; that is, in many rural areas, particularly borderlands with high

---

[26] Krystalli, "'We Are Not Good Victims'."
[27] Londoño and Nieto, *Mujeres No Contadas*; Nieto-Valdivieso, "The Joy of the Militancy"; Ramírez, *Between the Guerrillas and the State.*

levels of drug trafficking, the government had a patriarchal and aggressive security presence, but nothing else – no social services, clinics, schools, or proper infrastructure.[28] For others, the state presence that was most influential in their lives was in the aerial fumigation of coca crops – fumigation that also killed any other crops, leaving *campesino* farmers destitute.[29] In contrast, the FARC was buying coca from those farmers and providing them with a reasonable income, especially compared to what farmers could earn from other crops. In these rural areas of Colombia where nonstate armed groups held (and often still hold) power, civilian relationships with the state have been complex and often violent, which only strengthens the victimhood frame's overall resonance.

While Indigenous and Afro-descendant respondents did not label themselves as *campesinos* – reflecting the ethnic dimension of this supposedly "nonethnic" identity – they often placed themselves in solidarity with the *campesinos* in terms of facing the same poverty and government neglect. Similarly, some *campesino* respondents said that they had always identified strongly with Indigenous communities, while many emphasized that everyone was equal in the FARC and that skin color or ethnicity did not matter. In fact, some *campesino* respondents seemed confused by my ethnicity question and were not sure how to answer. Notably, Indigenous and Afro-descendant respondents did not have this hesitation. When I asked about racism, most respondents (from all three of the armed groups) agreed that Colombian society was very racist against Afro-descendants, but the answers were more diverse about discrimination against Indigenous peoples. Some Indigenous respondents did not feel that there was necessarily racism against them in Colombian society, stating that the discrimination for being an ex-combatant and/or for being poor was far worse. But when asked, most Indigenous and Afro-descendant respondents agreed that racism was much worse in Colombian society than within FARC, ELN, and AUC ranks – where they insisted it did not exist. But "racism" was sometimes used by respondents to mean any kind of discrimination based on identity, and several respondents spoke of facing compounded discrimination due to gender, race, and class:

You mean, in the life from there [in the armed group] compared to coming here, is there racism? Oh, of course! Racism not just for your color or race, but just for the fact that you are poor. Those in power discriminate against us for being poor, for the fact that we are poor, and no more … now imagine if I'm Indigenous

[28] Idler, *Borderland Battles*.
[29] Ramírez, *Between the Guerrillas and the State*.

and I am poor, well, I face a double discrimination, just for being Indigenous and poor … and for being a woman. And for being a woman. So now: for being Indigenous, for being a woman, for being poor, and for having belonged to the FARC. (Paula, FARC, B24)

As most of the respondents in the ETCRs pointed to their *campesino* backgrounds and/or living amid poverty and unpredictable violence as their main reasons for taking up arms, a shared sense of being simultaneously abandoned and exploited by the state became a strong and cohesive force. As Mafe articulated well, it was this collective victimhood that motivated them: "Then FARC enters with this work, no? … to wake up the *campesino* from that [ignorance], that we had equal rights like any citizen living in Bogotá, in the big cities, because the government has never been interested in the development of the *campesino*" (Mafe, FARC, B29). What the loyalists left out, of course, were the millions of *campesinos* who never took up arms and were victims of FARC violence. They also omitted the fact that when some *campesino* farmers tried to switch away from growing coca, they were forced at gunpoint to continue.[30] The FARC may have declared themselves representative of *campesinos*, but millions of *campesinos* would surely refute this. Many Indigenous communities have also long contested the FARC's claims of representing Indigenous concerns

Gendered Victimhood

That is why I tell you now, if I had not come to this organization, I would be on whatever ranch, I would be under whatever conditions, and under a man that mistreated me. However, now I am not. I have been fortunate.

Mari, FARC (B58)

Well, why do you think we are still here? Because we *like* being raped? … The people who believe this tale that we are raped and mistreated in the FARC, no, it's not true.

Paula, FARC (B24)

War is never gender neutral, even though many war scholars might portray it that way. Men's and women's experiences of armed conflict and the types of violence they face are often vastly different.[31] In Colombia,

---

[30] Fattal, *Guerrilla Marketing*.
[31] R Charli Carpenter, "Recognizing Gender-Based Violence Against Civilian Men and Boys in Conflict Situations," *Security Dialogue* 37, no. 1 (2006): 83–103.

the war has been gendered even further by the rhetoric and actions of the armed groups and the state. Because the leftist guerrillas adopted a discourse of gender equality, and then actively recruited women in part to boost their credibility of fighting against the country's dominant *machismo*, those defending the status quo (i.e., the government and the paramilitaries) stood against those values and thus protected entrenched gender norms. And while Colombian feminists continue working to improve gender equality, and the Colombian state has very robust laws about women's rights, rural areas in particular often still ascribe to very traditional gender norms – which may be why many grassroots feminist movements are emerging precisely from these areas.[32] Indeed, for many campesino communities, this *machismo* is highly prevalent and the reality for women in terms of gender inequality is much more challenging than in urban centers, where women attend university in high numbers, hold key government positions, and run for office, among other professions.[33] Within their victimhood frame, then, the guerrillas utilize a language of gender equality and a mission of fighting harmful gender norms to create resonance – particularly among its women members. This gendered element of the frame also specifically affects and is affected by how the victimhood frame is contested by the government.

Loyalist men in the FARC, for example, often described their victimhood in terms of the loss of land and/or inability to obtain land, or in terms of the general government neglect of rural areas. Men in the ETCRs were especially frustrated with not having land that they could farm, frequently expressing the sentiment that "a *campesino* without land is nothing." There was a functioning farming collective at one ETCR, but it could only provide enough work for a few men in the fields, and a few women who ran the shop and kitchen – about twenty-five people in total worked there. One man recalled a play that the guerrillas would put on during the FARC's "cultural hour" (before demobilization) called "Juan without Land," which depicted a male *campesino* that "invaded land," presumably belonging to elites, to work and provide for his family.[34] This is a key example of how frames are established through stories, performances, slogans, and shared narratives. Another man explained why getting land from the government was more important than any other part

---

[32] Yira Carmiña Lazala Silva Hernandez, "From Home Gardens to the Palais Des Nations: Translocal Action for Rural Women's Human Right to Land and Territory in Nariño-Colombia" (Graduate Institute of International and Development Studies, 2020).

[33] Ramírez, *Between the Guerrillas and the State.*

[34] Interview B59.

of the peace deal: "I was a *campesino*, I've worked the land since I was little ... we *campesinos*, we don't need riches, but we need to be able to work the land, every day."[35]

Indeed, when I asked ex-combatants in the ETCRs about future jobs and aspirations, almost all of them expressed a desire to stay in the country, but men in particular emphasized that they needed to farm, saying that urban life was far too stressful and strange for them:

> I, as a *campesino*, never thought of leaving the countryside. The city is another world for us, the *campesino*. And in the city, one is exposed daily to near death, because you do not know if you go out and ... and a cycle, a motorcycle, a taxi, a truck will run you over, or someone will simply come out with a knife [and say]: "Well, give me what you have." (Vesino, FARC, B23)

Thus, the *campesino* identity for men in particular was formulated around this sense of being rural farmers who were resilient and hard-working, victimized by the state, and simply could not function in urban life. (It was interesting to me that these former guerrillas were afraid of being attacked in cities without recognizing that people in cities might be afraid of *them*.) This identity was clearly informed by gender norms of men as providers and protectors. Indeed, many men in the ETCRs did not feel like there were any other options for them aside from working the land as small-scale farmers, saying that the land was the main thing they had been fighting for all these years. Now that the fighting was over, and they still did not have land, respondents felt resentful, and a few lower-ranking guerrilla men felt that their educated and well-connected leaders had been prepared for politics and (urban) civilian life, whereas they had had no preparation at all. Elite and collective reintegration are indeed two very different things.

The other strong component of male guerrilla victimhood that built resonance around the victimhood frame was the recounting of the "false positives" scandal. As noted in previous chapters, the Colombian military (and, to a lesser extent, the national police) was responsible for thousands of civilian extrajudicial executions between 2002 and 2010, where the victims were dressed up in military fatigues and counted as guerrilla "battle deaths" – and these "false positives" were overwhelmingly boys and men.[36] Even the widely adopted euphemism of "false positives" – as opposed to calling the deaths what they were: extrajudicial executions of civilians – was seen by respondents as a government attempt to erase the

---

[35] Interview B23.
[36] Rojas Bolaños and Benavides, *Ejecuciones Extrajudiciales En Colombia, 2002–2010*.

strategic violence of these crimes. Several respondents pointed to this scandal as evidence that the military was systemically eliminating *campesinos*, and particularly men, whether they were actually guerrillas or not:

This is the bourgeois army: they get paid to kill us; to kill *campesinos*. Because of that they killed civilians, they passed them off ... as guerrillas, they put camouflage on them. And this is how it is: the government asks for results, and [soldiers] don't give results, they don't kill a guerrilla, they don't kill anyone. They kill a civilian and they say he's a guerrilla. (Adrián, FARC, B44).

Several deserters, including Andrés, also mentioned the "false positives" scandal as evidence of the government's ongoing persecution of *campesinos*: "For example, in the Álvaro Uribe government, all the 'false positives.' They found boys, and just like that, they took them and bang – they killed them. Moreover, they took *campesinos* and shot them in the back and then said they were guerrillas killed in combat" (Andrés, ex-FARC, B18). Indeed, this legitimate narrative of victimization where the government was outright executing *campesino* men and boys – and thus forcing them to take up arms as their only option for survival – was repeated in many interviews and informal conversations:

All the minors at that time – because I was a child too – they put us there to starve, under an orange bush, and the others, well, they took them over there. We heard the screams, from where we were, we heard the screams ... they killed seventeen. There they killed two brothers of mine ... and they killed my dad and they killed one of my grandfathers.

[Me: The army?]

Yes, the army. And that lasted ... we lived with that fear for about a month. And then the guerrillas began to appear more frequently. They began, the FARC, began to come there, to appear more frequently, to talk to us, to ask what we thought [of the situation]. To look at what they were, what the army was, what the police were.

(Philippe, FARC, B27)

Women FARC loyalists, however, expressed a different version of *campesino* victimhood in relation to state forces than the men, largely due to their experiences of gender-based violence and sexual assault perpetrated by the military and paramilitary forces. These experiences of gendered victimhood gave rise to the "insurgent feminism" that many FARC women have since claimed, which I discuss further in Chapter VI. The choice to use "insurgent feminism" encapsulates the combative/insurgent stance of wanting to change society (and/or overthrow the government) combined with the primacy of women's rights and gender equality, largely inspired by the systemic discrimination and victimization that the women have experienced. Thus, while the insurgent feminist identity primarily reinforces the revolution frame (discussed in Chapter V), it is also important in building resonance in the victimhood frame. For women guerrillas, the valid fear of being raped by military or paramilitary groups was a strong motivator to join the FARC or the ELN, which in general did not use sexual assault against civilians as a tactic.[37] Indeed, many guerrilla respondents (men and women) noted proudly that their large numbers of women showed that they were clearly different from what they saw as ruthless paramilitaries and a corrupt military. One woman explained how this fear of sexual violence from other armed groups, combined with a lack of alternative options, drove her to join the FARC at age twelve:

I studied for six months, four months, in a school and I left and never got the diploma. So, for me that was a setback. And second, with all those massacres that people were doing, the paramilitaries, I was very afraid of that, and more so because I was a woman. Because, well, they also tortured the men, but they did worse things to the women. (Valen, FARC, B52)

Like the men, this violence from the state and paramilitaries was often given by women respondents as a reason for taking up arms, but the type of victimhood was different. Men emphasized the lack of land and the state murders of boys and men, while women emphasized sexual violence and the fear and insecurity that resulted from losing men in their communities.

Many FARC women (including deserters) in this study were also frustrated about the insistence of the government and Colombian media to portray them as victims of their own group, particularly around themes of sexual violence. (Notably, ELN deserters were less reticent to describe themselves as victims of their commanders and comrades.) Many of these women strongly contested this government frame because it did not resonate with their own experiences, and because they saw the frame-makers (i.e., politicians and the mainstream media) as having no credibility. The women spoke at length about how women were raped, abused, and murdered all over Colombia with total impunity, using this to illustrate that

---

[37] Interviews C10, C13; Grupo de Memoria Histórica, "Basta Ya! Colombia." Previous chapters have outlined the prevalence of gender-based violence in Colombia, and a lawyer with the Colombian Victim's Unit confirmed that most registered cases of sexual violence in the armed conflict had been perpetrated by the paramilitaries (C13). Some reports suggest, however, that sexual violence perpetrated by guerrillas was prevalent but much more hidden. See: Grupo de Memoria Histórica, "Basta Ya! Colombia."

the government did not care about women at all, and to explain why they needed insurgent feminism. Most of these loyalist women said that they felt safer inside the guerrilla organization than they did as civilians:

In a certain way there was trust and that respect between the guerrillas, but do we already have that here [in civilian life]? No. First, because of this bad opinion of all women and second, because there is no respect, yes? ... Meanwhile there [in the guerrilla] it was different, there it was, many times there were fifty men and four women and well, you were never scared of anything because you knew that inside the organization there was respect. But already one here – and there were no vices [there], there wasn't anything – and a woman here, for example, goes out in the middle of ten or five men, knowing that there is lots of [social] decay, that the one who doesn't smoke marijuana is a rapist, or [wondering] which one is a rapist like that, you know? Yes, you have bad thoughts. (Reina, FARC, B40)

Some women loyalists felt that, due to government neglect, the FARC was the only organization in Colombia doing anything to help women in need. Like the men, the women loyalists also expressed fears of going into the city because of violence, but the women's fears were more specific to gender-based violence and rape, whereas the men were more likely to talk about general crime and lawlessness.

Several women in the ETCRs also mentioned that they felt less safe without their weapons because they had nothing to defend themselves. This was linked to the repeated belief among both men and women FARC loyalists that women guerrillas could not be raped or otherwise sexually abused because they were armed. But this argument also implies – perhaps unintentionally – that without their weapons, it was indeed possible that women guerrillas could be raped by comrades. While a small number of loyalists agreed that mistreatment sometimes happened in the FARC as a large organization, it always happened "in other units" and never their own. The vast majority of FARC loyalists, men and women, were adamant that the idea of any armed woman guerrilla being raped or otherwise abused by a comrade was a lie meant to discredit their true victimhood claims. Despite evidence indicating that many FARC women were indeed victims of their own group, the resonance of the FARC's victimhood frame was so strong for many loyalists that they held to it despite serious challenges to its validity. That is, this insistence that stories of abuse were all lies was a form of forceful reduction to address the cognitive dissonance that such stories created. This framing became so engrained that it left no room for the possibility that some combatants (both men and women) were indeed victims of abuse by FARC members. And this extended denial affected both reintegration and the process of truth and reconciliation, where different groups of ex-combatants continued to resent each other long after they had all disarmed.

Within this gendered victimhood there was also a hierarchy of victims, with FARC women presenting themselves as victimized by the state but enlightened by the FARC, and portraying *campesino* civilian women as the most victimized of all. In fact, FARC loyalist women often said they were proud of their *campesino* heritage and felt responsible for the well-being and education of civilian *campesino* women, who they saw as even greater victims of the state than themselves. For example, FARC loyalist women often referred to civilian *campesino* women as submissive, traditional, ignorant, and/or needing their help. For FARC women, the *campesino* identity was inextricably linked to gendered hierarchies of power, where civilian *campesino* men dominated and were often labeled as abusers of their women. This was a theme that Mari became emotional about, her tough demeanor softening a bit:

It is a difficult thing to see women in those ... And there are many, many! In the countryside most of the *campesino* women live in that life that they have no freedom, that they cannot express themselves, where they go to a Community Action Meeting, to a community meeting, and they ask her a question and she first looks at the husband to see if she can talk, and then with a gesture [the husband] tells her if she can or cannot ... We were forced to go to war, because we did not have the conditions to live with dignity in this country the way a Colombian woman deserves. The Colombian people are victims, the Colombian people. The women that are abused, that are mistreated, by their own partners, they are victims due to their own state that has not been capable of organizing, to influence, in order for women to get ahead ... and this is the job of the state. The women, yes, they are victims, they are mistreated, they are abused, and no one says anything.

In addition, many of these women expressed gratitude that the FARC had given them opportunities outside traditional patriarchal structures and said that without the FARC, they would be trapped in abusive relationships just like other *campesino* women. These depictions somewhat inadvertently rely on stereotypes of civilian *campesinos* as uneducated, lawless, and backward – with the civilian *campesino* men depicted as "barbaric" and violent (unlike *campesino* guerrilla men) and the civilian *campesino* women as ignorant and submissive (unlike *campesino* guerrilla women). Ironically, these are many of the very same stereotypes that the government has used to marginalize *campesinos* and justify armed incursions and land grabs in rural areas.

Indeed, loyalist women refuted any suggestion of rape or exploitation within the ranks by comparing themselves against civilian women, particularly *campesino* women, whom they saw as mistreated and systemically victimized by men. This perception was, in large part, informed by their own civilian experiences of violence. Though not all spoke openly about this, Mari held little back:

When you have a weapon in your hand, the single fact of having a weapon, for me, gives me a lot ... how do you say, it puts me in another position. A woman in normal life, they grab her in the road, unarmed, without training and without anything, and they will rape her. They will grab her, and they will return her [like] nothing. Here, no.

This positioning against the vulnerable, victimized, less educated "other" (i.e., *campesino* women) was important for the loyalist women to prove that they were more enlightened and that claims of mistreatment in the ranks were false. The women loyalists could not allow the possibility that some women were facing the same gender-based violence inside the ranks that they were fighting against outside the ranks. To accept this, even if maintaining that abuses were exceptions and not systemic, would acknowledge some truth to the government's counter-frame and would thus weaken the entire premise of insurgent feminism and, in turn, of the victimhood frame.

As a result, the respondents in the ETCRs (both men and women) placed a lot of emphasis on infiltrators and deserters as the source of what they felt were false stories of abuse (discussed further in Chapter V). This again is where a strong frame helps to organize confusing or contradictory events into a narrative that people can accept and that motivates action. Framing helps to reduce cognitive dissonance by organizing these stories into an experience that fits expectations. That is, the claim that women were abused within FARC ranks did not fit into the FARC's framing that they were a victimized army of the people fighting for human rights. An effective way for leaders and their followers to reduce this cognitive dissonance and retain frame credibility was simply to dismiss claims of gender-based violence and harassment as outright lies, and to claim that these women were never really FARC women at all.

Taking gender into consideration sharpens our understanding of these discursive contests while shedding light on an important hierarchy of victims: while all *campesinos* are encompassed in the FARC's utilization of the victimhood frame due to the neglect and persecution of the state, women *campesinos* are doubly victimized in this frame because of the FARC women's emphasis that these women are abused by their own partners. This victimhood framing is particularly effective in convincing FARC combatants that they have nowhere else to go, because within the

ranks is the only place where they will be safe. From the women guerrillas' perspective, the perpetrators are not only the state and the paramilitaries, but also *campesino* men and women infiltrators. And if they dare
to leave, they too will be accused of being infiltrators and lying traitors.
Where, then, are women guerrillas safe if they demobilize? One loyalist
woman, who said that she "retired" from the FARC when she became
pregnant[38] (but then returned to an ETCR after the peace agreement),
clearly explained this rationale during a discussion of why there were
conflicting accounts of abuse in the ranks:

> Well, I don't know, one ... one thinks, the women chose this life because of how
> happy they are ... But, nevertheless, they told sad stories, but they still said no,
> that they would not leave. Then one would say, why? That is, if there is so much
> suffering [in the group], why don't they leave? Even I once asked this question
> of a former female guerrilla, and she told me, "do you not see what happens? If
> one leaves, suddenly the army takes her, they put her in jail ... . Even if we don't
> leave in that way, even if we leave without anyone noticing, they can still kill us,
> the same guerrillas." So, the women would say that they had chosen that life, so
> they had to deal with it and finish it.
> *[Me: So, many women stayed because they were afraid?]*
> Yes.
> (Tiann, FARC, B37)

This aspect of the victimhood frame is a powerful but often overlooked
retention tool for women combatants in particular: if they are convinced
and can in turn convince other women that the safest place for them is inside
the group – and that men outside the group are mostly thugs and rapists
just waiting to attack or arrest them (which, again, is a hierarchical framing
of different types of masculinity) – why would they leave? As one loyalist
woman said: "No, I never thought of leaving, because where would I go?"[39]
Indeed, once they disarm, these insurgent women face an especially problematic public framing. They are, as Gowrinathan articulates, "neither the
good victim to be saved nor the peaceful political agent to be supported."[40]

The "Original *Autodefensas*"

Contributing to the strong resonance of the victimhood frame among
guerrilla loyalists was the functionality of this frame in justifying the use

---

[38] While this seems to have been very rare, two respondents in this study claim to have
"retired" with FARC permission.
[39] Author interview B53.
[40] Gowrinathan, *Radicalizing Her*, 29.

of violence. The FARC victimhood frame and related *campesino* identity helped guerrilla loyalist members (and many deserters too) to justify their armed violence as self-defense, as something the government forced them to do, and something they were doing on behalf of all *campesinos*: "We had armed ourselves because there was an injustice against *campesinos*, that the people wanted to take away their lands, [remove] the *campesinos*, to build their cities, to build their fifth houses, their mansions. And the *campesinos* are the ones who cultivated the land" (Rob, ex-FARC, B01). This idea of self-defense against both the government and the paramilitaries is not only important in framing themselves as victims – it also reinforces the false binary of victims versus perpetrators. And the guerrillas used this frame to discredit paramilitary claims of self-defense:

I am going to explain this situation to you: the FARC, before taking up arms, always had the symbol and the will to have peace, because they were organized *campesinos*, right? And that, that was the root of collecting some small weapons, but to create a few self-defense groups, not to hurt anyone. Only for that, that is why they call it that – "to defend oneself" ... Just to watch over the *campesinos*, for the *campesino* movement of the region, against the thieves, the rustlers, the ones that caused harm, or the same *pájaros*[41] at that time. (Elias, FARC, B59)

As this quote indicates, the guerrillas often used *pájaros* or *paracos* to refer to the paramilitaries instead of the paramilitary-preferred term *autodefensas*, as that is what the original guerrillas also called themselves before they consolidated and became the FARC.[42] Indeed, the guerrillas' victimhood frame is reinforced by the narrative of being the "original" self-defense forces, as opposed to the paramilitaries who, in the guerrilla view, exploited this claim to self-defense to legitimize their violence and involvement in the drug trade. This idea of acting only in self-defense, defending themselves and *campesinos* more generally, is integral to the guerrillas' carefully constructed frame that depicts an honest, hard-working army of laborers – and certainly *not* drug traffickers – that are only fighting back because they are victims of the state.

In many conversations with FARC ex-combatants in the reincorporation zones, both during formal interviews and informally, ex-combatants described themselves as protectors of – and role models for – "the people." And the FARC went to great lengths to reinforce this (often false) narrative of protection. For example, over beer one evening, Andrés told

---

[41] *Pájaro* translates as "bird" but can also be slang for "penis" in some contexts – it is used commonly to refer to the paramilitaries.

[42] Michael LaRosa and Germán Mejía P, *Colombia: A Concise Contemporary History* (Lanham: Rowman & Littlefield Publishers, 2012); Livingstone, *Inside Colombia*.

me how he had once been ordered to kill two civilians at night, and then his front commander (who had ordered the murders) came into town the next day blaming the paramilitaries for the deaths, promising to protect the community from then on. He shook his head, chuckling but also looking down at his feet, seemingly both ashamed and astounded by what he had done. He often laughed when telling me about awful things that were not remotely funny. This seemed to be a common coping mechanism among men that I interviewed.

The FARC loyalists frequently repeated narratives of being forced to take up arms to protect the *campesino* population, and often as being the "real" government in areas essentially abandoned by the state. And the FARC did function like a pseudo-government, not only organizing economic and political life and taxing residents in areas under their control, but even resolving personal conflicts, settling disputes between neighbors, and establishing codes of conduct for residents.[43] In fact, the FARC's depiction of the Colombian state as having failed their citizens and of being the "real terrorist" – including state support of the paramilitaries – is critical to the FARC's victimhood frame and claims of self-defense: "The origin of the causes, of those struggles, the state could be more remorseful, because it could have solved the problems of these farmers, and not forced us to take up arms and become a powerful army against the state. Because the whole time, we were resisting [the state]" (Rafael, FARC, B46). In addition, these FARC loyalists saw themselves not only as victims but also as the clear "good guys," positioning themselves as reluctant self-defense forces that were protecting others against aggressive, violent actors operating in Colombia.

CONCLUSION

The victimhood frame – with its *campesino* identity, challenges to harmful gender norms, and self-defense components – was clearly a strong cohesive factor for loyalist respondents. Framing themselves as poor *campesinos* rising up against a corrupt and wealthy oligarchy is an important origin story with a high level of resonance for both the FARC and the ELN. The lack of specific ethnicity in the *campesino* identity has also allowed the group to draw Indigenous and Afro-descendant members into their cause, with claims of fighting for Indigenous land rights and for the rights of the poor in general.

[43] Ugarriza and Quishpe, "Guerrilla Sin Armas."

Despite serious challenges to frame credibility (i.e., women guerrillas voicing accusations of abuse), loyalist respondents found ways to explain or reject these challenges in order to reduce cognitive dissonance and maintain the frame. Social identity theory predicts that if people are in a low-status group they will try to leave; however, if they cannot leave, these low-status people will participate in collective action to raise the group's status – especially if they believe that their low status is illegitimate.[44] In addition to having high consistency and empirical credibility, the *campesino* victimhood frame is also essential to these combatants' beliefs and values (i.e., salience) and resonates with their daily lives and cultural narratives. They are committed to protecting their social group and improving their collective lives. The victimhood frame is thus reinforced by the sense that *campesino* poverty and loss of land is due to the illegitimate and repressive actions of the government and the paramilitaries.

The strategically gendered aspects of the frame are also highly effective in the recruitment and retention of women combatants without threatening the recruitment and retention of combatant men. The overall guerrilla victimhood frame is thus very durable, adopted by loyalists and deserters alike and brought forward into post-demobilization life. But this does not mean that the frame is not contested.

---

[44] Van Stekelenburg and Klandermans, "The Social Psychology of Protest."

V

Contesting the Victimhood Frame

Many of [the guerrilla women] don't have clarity ... they are recruited as children, they are submitted to sexual activity, and later they are trained physically, as combatants. But logically, they cannot stand this training, they cannot handle it, and once they realize what the guerrilla is like inside, that it is not easy, they are shot, or disappeared ... in some [guerrilla] fronts, relationships are allowed but in others the girls are rotated, they are a sexual object for whoever wants them.

GAHD military official (Co5)

"I don't even want to be here," Dayana said to me softly, looking around nervously to make sure no one was close enough to overhear us. She waved a hand around us with a frown. "I left to get my kids away from all this." By "all this," she meant the FARC loyalists – the diehards who were still loyal to the group's leadership and fighting against the government with each breath, albeit without weapons. The loyalists that she had tried to escape.

We were sitting on two plastic chairs in the meeting hall of a FARC reintegration camp – one of the ETCRs mentioned earlier – in central Colombia. Steep hills with coffee plants sloped upwards all around us. Dayana's two children were playing on the concrete floor, the older one repeatedly hacking out an alarming, wet cough. She told me later that all the children were coughing. A few buildings over was the temporary housing that she was sharing with a relative, that relative's husband, and another ex-combatant of the FARC. I had eaten lunch with them the day before, holding one of the children in my lap, feeling the bony ribs of his back heave against my torso when he coughed. Chickens wandered in and out, and I could hear the hogs in a pen nearby, snorting and squealing.

Dayana was a rarity in these camps, as she had deserted the FARC years ago, when she became pregnant and did not want another abortion. She said that the contraception provided in the ranks never worked for her, and she had already had four abortions by the time she fled. She said she simply could not tolerate the thought of having another one. So, one day, she left without permission. She was a rarity not because of the abortions nor because she deserted, but because, as other FARC members in this camp had made very clear, deserters were *not* welcome here in the ETCRs. However, unlike many other guerrilla deserters, Dayana had never surrendered to the military or entered a government demobilization and reintegration program. When she fled, she had no intention of cooperating with the Colombian government or asking them for protection. Instead, she went home to have her baby and find work near her parents' farm. She was one of many undocumented ex-combatants who had deserted but had never registered with the government – and information on this hidden population is scarce.

According to FARC statutes, leaving the group without permission was punishable by death, and word soon came to Dayana's community that FARC commanders were looking for her. To prevent anything from happening to her family, she went to them:

I spoke with the wife of ▇▇▇▇▇▇ ... she was the one who recruited me, and I went to fix my situation because I heard that they were looking for me, to fuck me, because I had given information to the army. So, I went and spoke to her directly, and I told her that never happened, that I was working, that I was dedicated to working, studying, doing things that would benefit my life ... I said to her, "I'm not doing anything. I don't understand why you're looking for me. For what? I don't understand."

To convince the FARC not to kill her, Dayana's stepfather gathered one hundred signatures from the community, attesting to the fact that she had been working and living there since deserting and had never surrendered or spoken to the army: "Those same guerrillas were going to kill me," she said, waving around her. She shrugged. "Yes, okay, I deserted. But my stepfather wrote this letter where he said: 'She deserted but she didn't do anything bad. She is working, she is studying.'"

Why, then, had she come back? I asked her. Why come back to a group that had threatened to kill her, had forced her to have abortions, and that she clearly no longer believed in? She said her sister had convinced her to come to the ETCR, because she would qualify for reintegration benefits to help provide for her children. But she confessed quietly that she planned to leave soon, because she couldn't stand the revolutionary rhetoric and all the anger that loyalists had toward the government.

She said that she had seen what the group really was, and that her sister – a staunch female loyalist – had been brainwashed. (When I talked to the sister later, she said without prompting that Dayana was the one who had been brainwashed, though it was unclear by whom.) Months later, Dayana texted me to let me know she had gone back to Bogotá.

"There are things people don't talk about," Dayana said, tears filling her eyes. We sat in silence for a while, and I waited, giving her space. I told her we could stop, that she didn't need to tell me more. But she stayed on her seat, looking at the floor.

Then, slowly, the story came out. She had been recruited at age fourteen, after growing up in an abusive family. As a child she had been raped and repeatedly molested by stepbrothers, and her mother had done nothing. She confessed that she had never felt loved. When the opportunity to join the FARC came along, she jumped at the chance to escape, and she soon attached herself to a commander that, to her, felt like the protective father she never had. But this much older commander later asked her to "move in" with him; not knowing what he meant, but desperately wanting his approval and protection, she agreed. When she realized that this man she saw as a father actually wanted her as a sexual partner, Dayana did not feel like she could say no. He was, after all, protecting her from everything else – dangerous missions, other men, her family back home. But that relationship quickly became abusive and she felt trapped – back in the situation she had tried to escape, with nothing she could do or say:

But those who were commanders were not sanctioned. Never … nothing happened, that is, nothing corrective for this, we say, for a female comrade that was subjected to that [abuse] by the other. There was nothing corrective, yes? … because he was a commander … We say every six months there is an assembly … where one can speak up [about mistreatment]. And I was one of the ones who spoke up: "Okay, comrade, what happened is this and this; there is a lot of mistreatment against this woman, there is … " "That's a lie! That, I don't know what." And so they cover each other's backs. And she stood there like a single little bird who could not do anything. And … if someone said to them what I am telling you clearly, they would mark that person as an infiltrator. So, you could not, that is, you shut up. If one said, "look, comrade, this is happening." "You are an infiltrator!" And then they would start to come after you. I saw four girls killed for that … And they branded them as infiltrators and shut them up. I saw them, I saw … and then it is your turn to keep quiet. I learned from the first one, who always spoke up. And they shot her. They *shot* her. And so, these are things that stay hidden there, you see? So that no one is aware of anything.

*

While durable and credible to their primary target audience (i.e., guerrilla recruits), the FARC and ELN framing of themselves as victims of the government and the state-supported paramilitaries certainly does not go unchallenged. Multiple Colombian governments have systematically contested the credibility of the guerrillas' victimhood frame, particularly in regard to the *campesino* and gendered components. In addition, while some deserters fully adopted the guerrillas' victimhood frame, others challenged it by claiming an identity as rule-breakers who would not be victimized or stay silent – or by accepting the government's version of events that they truly were victims of the FARC. The government, after all, would only allow ex-combatants to be certain types of victims: victims of their own comrades, but not victims of the state. Some guerrilla deserters also claimed to be the "real victims" after the peace agreement because, they felt, everyone had forgotten about them – again, invoking a certain hierarchy of victimhood. Finally, paramilitaries co-opted the self-defense component of the victim frame, repeatedly portraying the guerrillas as the real perpetrators and themselves as the real defenders of the people.

GOVERNMENT CONTESTATIONS: "HER SPANISH IS BETTER THAN YOURS"

When I first arrived in Colombia in February 2018 to conduct research at the GAHD safe houses, with permission from the Ministry of Defense, I had to meet with several professionals working in demobilization, as well as with the colonel who oversaw this aspect of military operations, before conducting interviews. It was clearly important to these government representatives that I hear their perspectives and their assessment of the population and their program before I spoke to the ex-combatants themselves. In other words, they wanted to set the frame. At one of these meetings, I was handed a Ministry of Defense newsletter, formatted like a newspaper, with a headline celebrating fifteen years of demobilization (Figure 6).

It was full of heartwarming stories and photographs of "successful" demobilization and reintegration. They were eager for me to take these stories back to Canada, to show other countries how successful they had been in demobilizing the ex-combatant population. Other countries would want to learn from them, they said. It was the first instance of these discursive battles that I would witness firsthand. But not long after, I witnessed another much subtler one: when introducing me to a group of ex-combatants at a GAHD safe house, a psychologist publicly joked that I spoke better Spanish than they did. Some ex-combatants laughed uncomfortably while I emphatically denied this, but I could tell by the

FIGURE 6 Photo of *Laz Fuerzas* newspaper, given to author by the Ministry of Defense.
Photo credit: author.

looks on their faces that others did not find his comment funny at all. It was yet another reminder from government officials that they, as ex-combatants and *campesinos*, were considered uneducated and inferior.

As part of the Colombian state's decades-long fight against the guer-rillas, *campesinos* have not only been dehumanized but also became engulfed by the categorization of "internal enemies" that were legitimate targets: guerrillas, political dissidents, union members, social leaders, radical intellectuals, and *campesino* movements.[1] But the limited amount of scholarship on discrimination against *campesinos* and on the racializa-tion of theoretically "nonethnic" groups suggests that the lack of a spe-cific ethnic identity precludes racism and racist violence.[2] In Colombia, however, this is clearly not the case. Understanding the underpinnings of the government's counter-frame to the guerrillas' *campesino* victimhood

[1] Courtheyn, "De-indigenized but Not Defeated."
[2] Courtheyn, "De-indigenized but Not Defeated."

is key to understanding why this counter-frame does not resonate with so many ex-combatants – and why it is problematic to sustainable peace.

From a historical perspective, Latin American elites in the late nineteenth to early twentieth centuries became concerned that their large nonwhite populations would "imperil national development" and relegate their countries to second-class status on the global stage.[3] However, by the 1930s, having fallen short of their goals to attract European immigrants, elites and leading thinkers introduced the nation-building theory of *mestizaje* (cultural/racial mixture), which, they claimed, signaled racial harmony and placed them as "morally superior to a racially segregated United States."[4] These *mestizaje* ideologies presented racial mixture as essential to Latin American nations, with elites creating false visions of their nations as homogenous, with *mestizo* identities replacing previous ethno-racial identities.[5] Colombia explicitly embraced the *mestizaje* vision as a tool to move the population toward whiteness, simultaneously solidifying the exclusion of Indigenous and Afro-descendant populations while hiding systemic discrimination and violence against mixed-race populations.[6] Thus, while I use the term "militarized masculinities" throughout this book, it is inaccurate to describe Colombia's society writ large as "militari*zed*," which implies the encroachment of military institutions onto civilian politics and an previously peaceful society. Rather, decades of structural violence against racialized populations in Colombia is better reflected by Alison Howell's concept of martial politics, defined as "producing White social and economic order through war-like relations with Indigenous, racialized, disabled, poor and other communities."[7] This definition acknowledges the indivisibility of national and social security in Colombia and challenges the "post-conflict" label.

For *campesinos* who cannot claim a specific ethnic identity, their cultural identity is tied to land far more than to skin color or ethnic composition.[8] Colombians *campesinos* have long demanded territory and resisted

---

[3] Telles, *Pigmentocracies*, 17.

[4] Telles, *Pigmentocracies*, 19.

[5] Telles, *Pigmentocracies*.

[6] Courtheyn, "De-indigenized but Not Defeated"; Peter Wade, *Blackness and Race Mixture: The Dynamics of Racial Identity in Colombia* (Baltimore: Johns Hopkins University Press, 1993).

[7] Alison Howell, "Forget 'Militarization': Race, Disability and the 'Martial Politics' of the Police and of the University," *International Feminist Journal of Politics* 20, no. 2 (2018): 117–36.

[8] Courtheyn, "De-indigenized but Not Defeated."

extractive projects – often alongside Indigenous and Afro-descendant populations – placing them in direct conflict with the state's neoliberal megaprojects that are often set up in the name of economic development.[9] As a result, *campesinos* have caused many problems for Colombia's elitist government as a poor, racialized segment of the population that has fought against mining projects and petroleum extraction, has put a strain on urban centers with mass internal displacement and informal shanty towns at city margins, and has made up the vast majority of rebel group members.

The combination of these elements has put all *campesinos* in danger, as the state has deliberately framed them not only as poor, ignorant, second-class troublemakers, but also as guerrilla sympathizers, combatants, and/or drug producers – and thus legitimate targets.[10] Also, a form of environmental determinism means that many *campesinos* have been classified by the state and elites as "barbaric," "backward," and often "lawless" simply based on where they are located, despite the fact that the conditions in which they live are often due to state neglect and/or aggressive fumigations and military violence.[11] In fact, these areas of high violence and low infrastructure – such as Putumayo, Urabá, Chocó, and other primarily rural departments – have often been labeled by the state as "empty," "savage," or the "land of nobody," signaling a colonialist understanding that without private property and state institutions, there is simply "no one there."[12] Here, the strategic framing of *campesinos* and the land on which they live directly affects the policy options available. Thus, the government actions that the guerrillas point to as causing their victimhood – exploitation by multinational extractive industries, coca fumigation, neglect, lack of infrastructure – can all be justified or at least explained away by the government if "no one" lives in these areas. Compounding this issue is that the vast majority of displaced rural Colombians settle in urban areas and often "auto-construct" neighborhoods on the mountainous peripheries of major cities, which the state sees as a nuisance and elites label as neighborhoods of "invasion" and "contamination."[13]

[9] Courtheyn, "De-indigenized but Not Defeated"; Liliana Mesias Garcia, "Relatos y Contrarrelatos de Los Actores Subalternos: El Campesino Organizado En La Construccion de Narrativas Democraticas En Colombia," *Cuadernos de Desarrollo Rural*, 2009, 139.
[10] Ramírez, *Between the Guerrillas and the State*.
[11] Courtheyn, "De-indigenized but Not Defeated"; Ramírez, *Between the Guerrillas and the State*; Wade, *Blackness and Race Mixture*.
[12] Courtheyn, "De-indigenized but Not Defeated"; Idler, *Borderland Battles*; Ramírez, *Between the Guerrillas and the State*.
[13] López, "Contesting Double Displacement"; Mary Roldán, *Blood and Fire: La Violencia in Antioquia, Colombia, 1946–1953* (Durham, NC: Duke University Press, 2002).

Conversely, *all* of the armed actors in Colombia – including the state military and allied paramilitary forces – have at some point justified their actions through the narrative of defending the civilian *campesino* population. In addition, most soldiers come from *campesino* backgrounds, as do most paramilitary and guerrilla members. Military service is mandatory for men in Colombia upon reaching age eighteen: those with a high school diploma only have to serve one year, while those without one have to serve 18–24 months. Once men complete this service, they are issued a military card (*libreta militar*), which they need to own property, graduate from university, receive professional contracts, or run for office.[14] This process entrenches notions of militarized masculinity, where young men – and especially poor ones – rely on military experience in order to prove that they are "real men."[15] As Eichler notes: "Put simply, militarized masculinity refers to the idea that real men are soldiers and real soldiers are men."[16] In fact, some guerrilla ex-combatants told me – with no shortage of confusion and wonder – that they unexpectedly received these military cards after they demobilized, even though they had never spent time in the military (and in fact had fought against the military). But without one of these cards, they were barred from participating in a significant portion of Colombian life. The demilitarization of masculinities, then, is impossible when young men rely on military service to participate fully in civilian life.

In fact, these cards are so essential for men to thrive in Colombian society that members of the Colombian elite often buy them – a process so common it is frequently assumed to be legal when it is not.[17] Wealthy Colombian men do not need military experience to prove their value to society, but poor ones certainly do. The result is a system where the vast majority of soldiers are from *campesino* and racialized communities, fighting at the behest of urban elites against (or alongside) the same *campesino* and racialized communities that make up guerrilla factions and paramilitary groups. Civilian *campesinos* who do not belong to any of these groups are then caught in the construction of being both "victims" in need of protection used to justify armed incursions and "enemies" due to suspected ties with any of the competing armed groups. But how *campesinos* are framed depends on the

[14] Luke Finn, "Military Recruitment Breeds Inequality for Colombia's Teenage Boys," NACLA, 2014, https://nacla.org/blog/2014/2/11/military-recruitment-breeds-inequality-colombias-teenage-boys.

[15] Maya Eichler, "Militarized Masculinities in International Relations," *The Brown Journal of World Affairs* 21, no. 1 (2014): 81–93.

[16] Eichler, "Militarized Masculinities in International Relations," 90.

[17] Finn, "Military Recruitment Breeds Inequality for Colombia's Teenage Boys."

military objectives and territorial situation of each group, and rarely on the actions of the *campesinos* themselves. As with ex-combatants, the government wants *campesinos* to be specific kinds of victims.

And, around all of this, there is the frame of a "humanitarian counter-insurgency" constructed around the supposed benevolence that the military extends to ex-combatants.[18] Indeed, one commanding officer told me proudly that while it was a significant challenge to train soldiers to help ex-guerrillas instead of killing them, the program worked, and the ex-guerrillas were very grateful. But were they?

The government has also gone to great lengths to contest the guerrillas' portrayals of women as the victims of the government, instead portraying women guerrillas as victims of their own group – but only as very specific types of victims. In both international and national rhetoric, women have been repeatedly portrayed as the main victims of Colombia's conflict – but importantly, these narratives show women as victims of the nonstate armed groups and the conflict in general, not specifically as victims of the state. In addition, studies on child soldiers have drawn special attention to the plight of young girls, often emphasizing their vulnerable status as victims of sexual abuse.[19] Indeed, humanitarian rhetoric worldwide has long emphasized the plight of "women and children" in order to get civilian needs in war onto the international agenda – another key aspect of resonance for the women-as-victims framing on both sides. But at the same time this practice infantilizes women by conflating them with children while also disregarding brutal violence against civilian men and teenage boys.[20] As noted earlier, while international resolutions on women in armed conflicts[21] – especially regarding rape as a weapon of war – were a significant step in acknowledging women's and girls' unique experiences in war, the dominant narrative entrenched misconceptions that all (or most) women in conflict environments are rape victims.[22] Compounding this imagery is the misconception that victims of violence – particularly female victims – have no agency, even though this is often untrue.[23]

[18] Fattal, *Guerrilla Marketing*.
[19] Denov, "Girl Soldiers and Human Rights"; Human Rights Watch, "'You'll Learn Not to Cry'"; McKay and Mazurana, *Where Are the Girls?*
[20] Carpenter, "'Women, Children and Other Vulnerable Groups'."
[21] See UNSC resolutions on Women, Peace and Security, available at: www.securitycouncil report.org/un-documents/women-peace-and-security/
[22] Ní Aoláin, Haynes, and Cahn, *On the Frontlines*.
[23] Chris Coulter, "Female Fighters in the Sierra Leone War: Challenging the Assumptions?" *Feminist Review* 88, no. 88 (2008): 54–73; Ní Aoláin, Haynes, and Cahn, *On the Frontlines*.

While in some circumstances this victim categorization makes it easy for armed groups to purposefully exploit gender stereotypes of victimhood to allow women insurgents and gang members to go undetected,[24] in Colombia the government has been particularly strategic in using gendered narratives to discredit the FARC and the ELN, and to contest the guerrillas' victimhood frame. For example, women ex-combatant testimonies of forced abortions and sexual abuse in the guerrilla ranks are prolific in the Colombian media and have also been issued in statements from the Colombian military and on radio programs encouraging desertion.[25] I was told these stories repeatedly in conversations with government officials, more than any other narrative. Indeed, stories of abuse against women and girls were much more widespread than stories of violence against men and boys, making them particularly powerful in damaging the FARC's proclamations of being an egalitarian organization that fights for women's rights. Male guerrillas, it seems, were not allowed to be victims. In some interviews with military and ARN staff, the gender equality in the guerrillas was described as a specific reintegration "challenge" – not as a challenge that the DDR program must address but a challenge for the guerrilla women in terms of adapting to existing (status quo) social norms:

All of this [demobilization and reintegration] is more difficult for women. Because women in the guerrilla structure, the treatment is equal for the men and women. If the man can carry something of [a certain] weight, they say to the women, do it. So, when they come to the safe houses, they say: "Men and women are equal." But society says: "No, you can't do this because you're a woman." So, there's a change ... in the group you were treated equal, [but now] they say, a woman can't study to become a mechanic, and so this creates a crisis of conflict in the woman. (GAHD psychologist, C01)

In addition, some stories from former guerrilla members and kidnap victims have portrayed FARC women as unpaid prostitutes who are obligated to have sex with their male comrades as a "revolutionary duty."[26] One military respondent also told me that many young recruits in rural areas, especially girls and young women, were enticed by promises of money, drugs, and technology. He did not address why these young people were so vulnerable to recruitment in the first place, though he did say

[24] Schmidt, "Duped."
[25] Interview C01; Maureen Orth, "She Was Colombia's Most-Feared Female Revolutionary: Can She Help It Find Peace?," *Vanity Fair*, August 2018, www.vanityfair.com/news/2018/08/colombia-civil-war-farc-female-revolutionary.
[26] Author interviews B31, B63.

this: "I don't want to victimize the [ex-combatant] population, but lots of this population were victims before they converted into predators."[27] In the context of this conversation, however, he meant that they were victims of the guerrillas' predatory recruitment tactics, not victims of state neglect or violence. What interested me here was the idea that these young people "converted into predators." Did he mean that they were no longer victims? That their prior victimization had somehow been erased, and that upon becoming perpetrators they could no longer be victimized?

Several government officials also told me in meetings that the guerrillas had no birth control in the ranks, and that is why there were so many abortions. But interviews with both deserter and loyalist women indicate that this is categorically untrue. Government officials also emphasized the FARC's use of forced contraception, without acknowledging that most guerrilla women *wanted* contraception. While there certainly were abortions in the ranks, all ex-combatants in this study stated that women in both the ELN and FARC had regular access to birth control – both pills and injections. And while this was indeed mandatory, many of the guerrilla women I spoke to were incredibly careful about their contraception protocols, because they did not want to be pregnant while in the ranks. But the government's insistence on portraying women guerrillas as uneducated victims that either (1) had no control over their own bodies or (2) willingly aborted or abandoned their babies, was very effective in further demonizing both the FARC and ELN in the eyes of the public. This strategy also aligns with portrayals of *campesinos* in general as barbaric and ignorant.

The forced abortion narrative, of course, resonates with the majority Catholic population and not only portrays women guerrillas as victims of the FARC, but positions the state as the savior for these victims – a strong challenge to the guerrilla victimhood frame. This savior positioning serves a double purpose in that it masks the state's role in victimizing and displacing rural women, disregards the abject poverty that prevents many *campesino* women from accessing reliable birth control and/or family planning education, and ignores the sexual violence against women perpetrated by government forces and state-sponsored paramilitaries.

While the government actively tries to encourage combatants to desert, the effect of this counter-frame is the creation of an environment in which women know they will be both pitied and vilified if they demobilize. Arguably, it is damaging long-term reintegration and sustainable

---

[27] Author interview C01.

peace to reach out and help with one hand while viciously maligning ex-combatants with the other.

For the self-defense component of the guerrilla frame, the government has tried to counter this claim in several ways. First, by allowing the AUC to move into guerrilla territory and take control of other areas of Colombia, and then supporting AUC operations against the guerrillas, the government tacitly accepted the paramilitary co-optation of the *autodefensa* (self-defense) label. Second, by portraying the FARC and the ELN as criminals, terrorists, and attackers of their own women (especially in the case of the FARC), the government not only set up the expected narrative of the guerrillas as the main perpetrators, but also created the frame that they are perpetrators not only against Colombian society but also against their own recruits. At the same time, the military was running campaigns encouraging guerrillas to demobilize and promising protection. Again, offering help with one hand and cracking down with the other.

DESERTER CONTESTATIONS: "I BOUGHT DRUGS FROM THOSE GUYS ALL THE TIME"

> Many [young people] join because they feel cornered in a problem or because of parents, but ... [they] cannot think that or even that it's a game. Because he told me I can do it, that it's easy. But being there is very difficult, because getting in is easy. It is like someone who goes to jail ... entering is easy, but exit is very difficult.
>
> Val, ex-ELN (B07)

Some deserters, like Lina and her husband (and later Michael), had tried to claim benefits through the Colombian Victims' Unit – in this specific case because Johan had joined the FARC as a child and Lina said she had been tricked into joining.[28] Both considered themselves to be, above all else, victims of the armed conflict. But this narrative was quite different from the FARC's organizational victimhood frame. This counter-frame from deserters was not meant to recruit or retain followers, nor to contest a government propaganda war – it had formed organically to contest the organizational frame(s) that they had escaped. In fact, Johan and Lina went to great lengths over many conversations with me to discredit the FARC's victimhood narrative. But who, exactly, was the audience for this frame? Was it even a frame without an audience?

---

[28] Author interviews B31, B63.

The story that Lina and her husband told me over the course of several months was so complex and fantastical that it nearly defied belief – but again, this is Colombia. By this point, I had heard dozens of unbelievable stories. Lina had been a hairdresser in her early twenties when a woman offered her a hairdressing job in southern Colombia. Lina accepted, desperately in need of better pay, and left her six-month-old baby with her mother. But the woman who hired her disappeared after only five days (this, too, is unfortunately common in Colombia). Armed men then showed up at the salon and told Lina that she worked for them now. She would be doing intelligence work for them, they told her. But she quickly realized they wanted more than intelligence; they also expected her to be available sexually. She said she was drugged and beaten regularly. She assumed, based on their treatment of her and what she knew about the guerrillas, that they were AUC paramilitaries.

Later, she worked as a buyer, purchasing coca from *campesino* farmers and then passing it to the group's financiers for processing and export. For years, she worked for the group, storing supplies, collecting intelligence, and collecting coca, too terrified to escape, even when she was pressured to have sex with men in order to obtain information. But one of the financiers, Johan, who came around regularly, was very nice to her and the two of them started talking more often. He had been in the ranks for well over a decade, she learned, but had become disillusioned long ago. (When I asked Johan later when he first thought of leaving the FARC, he told me that he wanted to leave since the day he was recruited as a ten-year-old child.) When word came that the paramilitaries were demobilizing, Lina left her shop to watch AUC combatants getting into trucks to the demobilization zone, ready to be ushered into the line. But then something strange happened:

Look, it was a day and a half that troops, AUC, left, and a few days after they left, the FARC arrived, already in uniform, to the town. That's when I said [to the men I worked with]: "Hang on a second, what is happening?" And they tell me, "no, honey, we are always going to be here and from here we receive FARC and we receive AUC, depending on who comes to give us the order. [But] it is the same order."

What she was trying to explain was that the famous rivalry between the AUC and the FARC was not what it seemed. The two groups often had working arrangements, transfers of power, and business partnerships. She and her husband Johan, the financier, explained it like this: the AUC, ELN, FARC, police, and the military were just different branches of the drug trade, like different government departments. Sometimes the departments disagreed on the best way to do things, but often they worked together. And Johan and Lina were not the only guerrillas who told me this; in fact, several FARC militia respondents told me that they interacted frequently with members of the AUC as part of their drug-trafficking operations. Andrés even helped me make the initial connection to the paramilitary compounds where I conducted interviews, and he greeted the ex-AUC commander there like they were old friends. I asked him about this later, and he laughed. "Remember I told you how I was a financier?" he said. "Yeah, I bought drugs from those guys all the time." It was a surreal experience that put the credibility of everyone's competing frames into question. How much did the militia members know about the financial underpinnings of their group, and their collaboration with so-called enemies, that rank-and-file guerrillas in the mountains simply did not know?

I asked Johan this question later, and he, too, laughed. Then he shrugged and said: "People see what they want to see."

Johan had been recruited at the age of ten and worked his way up the ranks, so by the time he met Lina, he had already spent over fifteen years in the FARC. By then, in his late-twenties, he was disillusioned by his involvement in the drug trade and how often he did business with the AUC – their supposed rivals. When Lina became pregnant, the two of them were not married yet, and she had no idea who the father of her baby was. Facing a mandatory abortion, Lina became desperate to flee the group and Johan, having fallen in love with her, made a plan. The two of them escaped together and went into hiding, and Johan accepted the baby as his own. At this point, they did not know about the government's demobilization and safe houses. They only knew to run. But the FARC does not simply let people go, especially not commanders like Johan. They began to receive terrifying threats and were constantly on the move.

Two years later, they told me, someone from the FARC tracked them down and kidnapped their two-year-old daughter from a state-run daycare in order to coerce Johan to run drugs again. Almost mad with grief and desperation, the couple traveled from city to city, searching for their daughter. One day, Lina ran into a woman that had also worked intelligence for the FARC, and the woman admitted to knowing about the kidnapping. But it was not until Lina and her husband repeatedly threatened this woman that she finally gave up the girl's location. By this time, their daughter had been held by the FARC for six months. I could hardly imagine the extent of Lina's grief and panic. When they finally found the child, the man holding her said he would only release the girl upon orders from the police captain, who was apparently complicit in the abduction. But the police did not agree readily; they claimed that the girl had been abandoned, that the child's mother had been killed by her husband, who was now in jail, and that the girl was considered an orphan and thus a ward of the state. This was all a lie spun by the FARC, according to Lina, and is also what the kidnappers had told Lina's three-year-old daughter.

When they were able to produce identification and paperwork showing that the girl was indeed theirs and that Lina was not, in fact, dead, the couple took their daughter and fled once again. They told me that their young daughter soon began saying troubling things that indicated sexual abuse during her captivity. For years, they fled from city to city. When they finally came to Bogotá to register themselves in the nearest branch of the Victim's Unit, called the Local Center for Victim Attention, they had to undergo a psychological evaluation to verify that they were truly victims. At that time, the psychologists also noted that the daughter was showing signs of sexual abuse and suspected Lina's husband. Then, according to Lina, they accused both parents of being drug addicts:

And the truth is that only one session was held with the psychologists at my house, and I did not like it, they told me not to name God, to get God out of this, that God had nothing to do with it. Two days later my husband received threats again, and we started calling them, he went to them, to the psychologists and they arrived with two ambulances. They put us into the ambulances and took us to the hospital saying that I had taken poison, had given it to them, to my husband and the girl, that I was crazy, arguing that he was a drug addict and that we were both not fit to have the girl.[29]

It was obviously impossible to verify all the details of this story, especially as there is no documentation of the kidnapping, and I was not able to speak to the psychologists involved. I did confirm that both Lina and her husband were approved to receive benefits from the Victim's Unit and did so for years. I do not know why the psychologists thought they were drug addicts. However, Lina did tell me that one of the ways the group would keep militia women from running away was to get them hooked on drugs. At this point in the story, Lina just shook her head in disbelief. She often did that when telling me about her life: shook her head, raised her eyebrows, and watched my face for a reaction. She said that no one ever bothered investigating the kidnapping of their daughter. No one

---

[29] Author interview B63.

bothered to assess or treat their level of trauma from that event. And no one would take the ongoing threats they were receiving seriously. Then, when it was finally clear that their daughter had indeed been sexually abused, the blame was immediately directed at the parents. While they said they were eventually cleared of the accusations, the investigation revealed that they were former combatants, and they were forced to leave the Victim's Unit program and enroll in the military's demobilization program. When they hesitated to comply – not wanting to be officially recognized as ex-combatants – the military threatened to charge them with sedition, terrorism, and murder.

The official military transcript from Johan's demobilization interview, however, tells a markedly different story. In that interview, the officer unsurprisingly recorded that Johan's demobilization had been "voluntary." And later in the transcript, Johan tells the military officer that only eight hours had lapsed from the time he escaped the FARC to the time he surrendered to the military, when in reality it had been several years. And while Lina and Johan showed me multiple certificates and official paperwork verifying their time in the Victim's Unit, nothing at all is recorded in the transcript about Johan and Lina's time in that program, nor of the benefits that they received there.

*

When I spoke to guerrilla loyalists, most assured me of their benevolence toward deserters, and that it was not a big deal if someone wanted to leave the group. Deserters, however, told a very different story. It *was* a big deal – it was, in fact, one of the worst things a combatant could do, and the official punishment for desertion was death. But many of the respondents who joined as children did not understand that membership was for life when they signed up. They had no idea that they could not go home again if they changed their minds. Even if the recruiter had told them that outright, many were too young to fully understand it.

As Dayana's story at the beginning of this chapter illustrates, many deserters actually adopted two competing victimhood frames – that of being victims of the government and that of being victims of their own group. After listening to nearly forty deserters' stories – all of them unique in some ways and remarkably similar in others – I noticed patterns that have largely been understudied and often obscured by reintegration statistics. It was clear that a person's age at recruitment affected later desertion decisions and reintegration experiences – especially when the person was too young when joining to understand that leaving was not an option. Ex-combatants who joined at ten and eleven years old and then spent twenty to thirty years in arms simply cannot be expected to navigate the world in the same way as those who joined as adults, and yet they were – and are. There were also marked differences in alternative options between urban and rural armed group members, as members of urban militias were not secluded in the jungle and generally had more life and literacy skills upon demobilization. In addition, while the gendered aspects of DDR and related decisions have received growing research attention, scholarly literature on desertion often homogenizes all ex-combatants from the same group, and many studies on disengagement and reintegration do not disaggregate by gender, race, and age, let alone by urban and rural. This failure to disaggregate a very diverse population obscures important details about desertion decisions and does not adequately explore how ex-combatants organize and justify their experiences as they transition to civilian life.

Overall, while men and women guerrilla deserters framed their victimhood in relation to state neglect, they did not use the *campesino* identifier to the same extent as loyalists. It is difficult to determine whether this is because they never bought into the *campesino* victimhood frame in the first place, or because they changed their interpretation of the frame *after* desertion to make sense of their life choices. Because the vast majority of deserters relocate to urban centers – for employment as well as safety and anonymity – it may simply be impractical or even dangerous to cling to a *campesino* identity that is so strongly attached to rural life and is stigmatized in the city. These deserters expressed a desire to blend into the urban population, and most did not want to be associated with anything that could mark them as former guerrillas. Indeed, some deserters spoke of the *campesino* identity itself as dangerous, due to the conflation of *campesinos* with guerrillas that was amplified by the government's framing of the conflict.

Like the paramilitaries, guerrilla deserters also complained consistently that the FARC loyalists were getting better benefits than they were. In addition, in some informal conversations, both ARN staffers and ex-combatants expressed frustration that the DDR model was set up to reinforce a sense of victimhood and dependency on the government. A notable difference, though, was that when the loyalists expressed these frustrations, they often followed up with complaints that the government was not providing enough help – or that the commanders were far more prepared for the transition to civilian life than the rank-and-file.

In contrast, when the deserters talked about these concerns, many of them immediately expressed a resolve to figure it out. For example, one deserter from the FARC said:

It's not easy to return to civilian life when for a while you were over there [in the armed group], well, there are many things you don't know. For example, I've never been in a city so big. I don't know [this city]. And ... everything is already very different. Well, the liberty is beautiful, but ... you have to learn how to live. (Claudia, ex-FARC, B14)

When I spoke to Junior, he was about to leave the safe house, and despite all of his bravado earlier in our conversation, when I asked him how he felt about leaving, he admitted to being scared:

It feels strange. It feels different and strange and scary ... it's a different life. It's another world. I've never paid rent, I've never paid ... I've never paid for electricity, I've never paid for water, I've never had to buy my own clothes, right? I've never had to take care of myself, because the guerrillas take care of you. Now I have to work, I have to study ... because the ARN says you have to study, so I have to work, study, pay rent, pay for electricity, pay for water ... and I have a daughter, I have to take care of my daughter. Well, it's frustrating, I am frustrated, but I have to do it ... we have to face it and push forward.

But the Colombian reintegration programs do not account for the vast differences and reintegration needs of someone who joined at age eleven, such as Junior, and someone who joined at age twenty-five or thirty. They only consider age-based needs if the person is still a minor at the time of demobilization.

Another interesting variation on the victimhood frame was a stratification between urban militia and rural guerrillas. Some rural guerrillas, for example, did not consider militia members to be "real" guerrillas. As Michael said: "The people who complain about the food here [in the safe house], about whatever, those people weren't really guerrillas ... because the people who were *real* guerrillas suffered a lot."[30] This view again reinforces the idea of a hierarchy of victimhood: like the paramilitaries, some deserters maintained that they were the "real victims" of the conflict because, since the peace process, everyone was paying attention to the guerrillas in the ETCRs and had forgotten all about the deserters.

Conversely, some militia members sometimes portrayed themselves as more educated and more sophisticated than their rural counterparts – equating the term *campesino* with illiteracy:

---

[30] Author interview B08.

I do come from *campesino* parents, but I was a very urban child ... [in the] FARC, most of my comrades were *campesinos*, by that I mean, many were illiterate. And coming here to this city, of course, for me, that was all very new, but we all had opportunities. It is understandable that there are great differences [in experiences] because not all the guerrillas were guerrilla fighters. There was a large component of [urban] collaborators and militia, and that has been a significant issue in demobilization. (Caleb, ex-FARC, B68)

Indeed, having connections in the city (i.e., networks with law-abiding citizens), and at the very least having the ability to read and write, to understand the demobilization process and its benefits, and especially to understand the forms that one is signing, all appear to be critical aspects of deciding whether to desert an armed group or not, and they seem to affect ex-combatants' sense of victimhood as well. That is, combatants who identified as "country folk," and/or as farmers who could not possibly function in the city, appeared to have more inhibitions about deserting, and certainly a greater sense of victimhood and lack of options, than those with urban connections who could feasibly obtain a job in the city or at least have networks available to help them. While many guerrilla loyalists expressed gratitude that the FARC had taught them to read and write, the literacy of many of these respondents was rudimentary at best – which I observed when they had difficulty writing down phone numbers, for example, or when they asked me to send voice messages rather than written messages on WhatsApp. With FARC militia deserters, this problem was rare, and in fact many of them were proud of their prior education and their ability (whether old or recently acquired) to use computers or work with numbers.

In fact, some deserters distinctly did *not* want to be labeled as *campesinos* or victims for this very reason – a direct rejection of the victimhood frame. These respondents were resentful of the ARN's apparent assumption that they were all ignorant *campesinos* who knew nothing, especially the ones who had some secondary education before they joined an armed group. Militia deserters were more likely to tell me about their education and to be proud of their role in certain illegal operations that required a higher level of knowledge and ability than the average *campesino*.

Andrés explained to me that he had already earned his high school diploma before joining the FARC, but because he could not produce the certificate, the ARN had him taking the same basic classes as everyone else – a source of significant resentment for him.

Notably, in contrast to the loyalist FARC members who emphasized the importance of rule following and the chain of command, some deserters identified themselves as rebels, as independent thinkers, as people who refused to blindly obey, while often labeling the loyalist guerrilla members as submissive people who did not think for themselves. This sense of a "rebel" identity, of being someone who did not submit, was an important factor in some deserters' decisions to abandon their groups, especially when paired with experiencing or witnessing mistreatment, or fearing threats of harm from within the group – that is, a combination of identity factors and cost–benefit calculations. And this affected how they interpreted post-demobilization experiences. For example, Lina expressed dismay at how they were treated in the safe houses, because it was exactly what she had been trying to escape:

I did not like it [at the safe house], that treatment, in the sense of shouting. I thought that, well, that's why many of us deserted, right? Because of the treatment, in the way they talked to us, we had to submit to someone else's orders, whether we liked it or not. And if I am going to demobilize and if I make that decision, it is because I am sick of this regime.

She also told me that women who remained in the FARC were actually more submissive than civilian women – a direct contrast to the loyalist depiction of the feminist insurgents as superior to submissive, abused civilian *campesino* women:

I have always said that those that are, those that were in the, on the mountain, the [base-rank] female guerrillas submitted, always submitted. Submissive, submissive. That's why [gender equality] is a lie. All I can say is that to survive there and to have a little bit of, of respect … we had to screw them, as they say vulgarly, to fall in love with the highest ranks, that is one way to survive in there.

However, even though some deserter women portrayed themselves as more enlightened than the FARC loyalist women, and other deserters said that they had learned a lot and did not regret their guerrilla experiences, several women deserters talked about mistreatment from their own commanders. As noted earlier, this has been perhaps the biggest challenge to the FARC's victimhood frame, as the government has utilized these stories repeatedly. These stories are specifically damaging to the credibility of the guerrilla frame, which has the effect of decreasing overall resonance. It is thus quite clear why so many loyalists said that the women who told stories of abuse and exploitation were infiltrators.

Comparing the testimonies of loyalists and deserters, there was a significant amount of disagreement over the mistreatment of women, which is examined further in Chapter VI. Some deserters, for example, told me that they never saw any abuse of women and they were treated well. It was also clear that guerrilla rules functioned quite differently for militia members compared to traditional guerrilla units.

In summary, while many deserters still utilized the victimhood frame in terms of being victims of the government, they presented two main contestations. First, some deserters did not want to be portrayed or labeled as victims and in fact were eager to portray themselves as educated and capable. Second, other deserters, and especially the women, utilized the government framing that they were victims of the FARC, while retaining the guerrilla frame that they were victims of government. This appeared to be a strategic use of frames and their narratives depending on the situation at hand, which was more about convenience than about the resonance, credibility, or salience of the frame. That is, framing can help people understand their complex experiences, but it can also be adapted strategically to justify behavior, garner sympathy, or win support.

PARAMILITARY CONTESTATIONS: "LOSE YOUR GUN, LOSE YOUR LIFE"

While many of the paramilitary respondents utilized a form of the victimhood frame – especially in regard to being victims of government neglect – they presented a very particular challenge to the guerrillas' narrative of self-defense. While only a few described themselves as *campesinos*, almost all of them pointed to poverty and a lack of work for the main reason they joined the group. Many of them were self-conscious of their low literacy abilities, and several told stories of being tricked by the government to sign paperwork that they did not understand, and/or having commanders trick them out of their reintegration money. From my very first paramilitary interview in this study, victimhood stood out as a prominent – and sometimes surprising – theme.

In one of my many conversations with Nell, she explained to me that she used to sell clothing by traveling across several Colombian departments. But her life changed when the guerrillas took everything from her, and the paramilitaries then accused her of working for the guerrillas because she had been seen with them. As with Mafe, this is what happens to many civilians trapped between warring armed groups – they get pulled in even when they do not want to be. Or at least, this is the story they tell later. It is often hard to know the difference. When the AUC threatened her as a guerrilla collaborator, she offered to work for them to prove that she was not a guerrilla, and after that, she said, there was no going back. She explained, her palms up in a gesture of surrender or hopelessness, that she had no choice: "I had no education, I had nothing, and the one thing I had was taken. And one has to look at what you can get, what you can do to raise your children. You cannot leave them to starve to death."[31] Indeed, many former paramilitaries had similar stories: economic desperation, offers of well-paying work, threats of violence from the other side, a will to survive. And a refusal to express any regrets.

Like the FARC loyalists, the ex-paramilitaries in this sample were very particular about language. In one interaction, while explaining my study to a former AUC commander, I used the word *paramilitar*, as that was the word everyone in Colombia had used with me up until that point. I was immediately and forcefully reprimanded by this commander that they were *not* former paramilitaries – they were *autodefensas* ("self-defense forces"). He said he hated the word paramilitary, because in his mind it meant they worked for the military ("para" in Spanish means "for," so he understood the word to mean "for the military"). He was very clear that while they worked *with* the military, they never worked *for* the military.[32]

As with the guerrillas, this insistence on being *autodefensas* implies being nonaggressive and not liable. And if those *autodefensas* are also acting in the defense of others, then they are protectors and heroes. Indeed, this self-defense/protector narrative is one that many ex-paramilitaries adopted for themselves, directly challenging guerrilla claims of being self-defense forces and victims of paramilitary violence. But this was not just a collection of individual narratives; this was a strategic frame that ACCU and then AUC leaders had adopted from the outset. Rather than fighting for a political cause – as many paramilitary respondents admitted that the AUC had no cause except drug trafficking – the ideological frame that the paramilitary leadership had adopted was that of protecting the *campesinos* (and themselves) from the guerrillas because the state could not do it.[33] They said they had to step in to fight against the guerrillas because the government was absent and that they were forced to arm themselves for protection – the exact same reasoning given by FARC members for taking up arms and a direct contestation of the FARC victimhood frame.

Some, of course, admitted that they only joined the AUC because the group paid well (though this was not always true), but even this they

[31] Author interview B87.
[32] Author interview B81.
[33] Romero, *Paramilitares y Autodefensas*.

framed as the noble action – or at least justifiable – of providing for their families. One respondent said that he knew that the group was bad before he joined, but he needed the money, while another former commander said: "I can't think of peace when my child is going hungry."[34] Several told me that they realized they had made a mistake after they enlisted but that they needed a job. Another paramilitary respondent described himself as someone "fighting for his salary" in order to provide for his three children – thus the fight was justifiable.[35] Nell said that she knew if she ever left the group, life would be even worse. Then she said, with a shrug: "My children never went hungry, and I was never involved in any violence."[36] Of course, like the FARC loyalists, she *was* involved in violence. They all were, even if they did not want to be, even if they did not directly harm anyone. Her supportive work, behind the scenes or not, sustained the very violence that she claimed to abhor. She took the money, knowing full well how it was produced. And if she received years of demobilization benefits, could she really claim that she was not involved?

But this is the issue with the lauded "innocent victim" in transitional justice processes. In complex and prolonged armed conflicts, the idea of victims and perpetrators is not a binary – it is a complex and fuzzy spectrum.

Some male respondents also felt that being in the AUC was essentially the same as their military experience – and the fact that they often worked with the military gave their roles legitimacy. Even when they acknowledged being paid mercenaries, some ex-paramilitaries exhibited a sense of pride that they had defended Colombia from the guerrillas. Like the guerrillas, this self-defense narrative was a key component in the paramilitary's counter-frame as it positioned all other armed actors as worse and more violent than they were. Several of the AUC respondents pointed out that the FARC guerrillas were not holding up their end of the peace deal, or that guerrillas in general were still kidnapping and killing people – with little acknowledgment (at first) that their former comrades were doing the same. One ex-combatant said that, unlike the guerrillas, it was a lie that the AUC ever kidnapped people,[37] even though another respondent had already told me how he had been trained to use

---

[34] Author interview B81.
[35] Author interview B78.
[36] Author interview B87.
[37] Author interview B86.

kidnappings to finance the group.[38] Another said that the main thing the commanders taught him were "human values" and how to respect people,[39] which, admittedly, struck me as odd given the documented and widespread egregious human rights violations perpetrated by his group. One ex-AUC member told me that his commanders always told them that their fight "was about defending the poor, to give a person what he deserved. So, the *autodefensas*, many times, fought a lot for, for the *campesino*. And so, it was not how, how for example the guerrillas come and go, and ... don't return [to the community]."[40] Another respondent explained that they were fighting at the behest of ranchers and *campesinos* to get rid of the guerrillas:

The reason for our fight was to get rid of the guerrillas ... the Colombian guerrillas, because at that time there were a lot of guerrillas, and the guerrillas were ripping off the ranchers, and they took land from the *campesinos*. For example, our department was very rich in livestock, and farmers complained a lot and paid a lot, a lot of money to get rid of the guerrillas. (Gello, ex-AUC, B80)

Several respondents also pointed out that AUC commanders did not like recruiting minors or women "like the guerrillas did"; they only wanted male adult recruits with military experience. This seemed important for them to emphasize, showing that they were (1) not so desperate for recruits that they would settle for women and children, and (2) not "radical" in that they would disrupt gender norms and put women on the front lines. In fact, one respondent openly expressed dismay that any women wanted to join the AUC, saying that women could find jobs easier than men could and thus did not need to join armed groups. He had threatened to quit if any women were promoted to a command position, and he later told me that women should not get equal pay for the same jobs because they could not do an equal amount of work.[41] He spent a great deal of time telling me (a woman) how women are weak, cause problems, and that if they were mistreated in the group they were "looking for it." He also told me that he "wanted everything to be correct" in terms of what types of work men and women were given. I could not help but wonder what he thought of me, traveling solo across Colombia, having left my children behind with my husband for a few months to do this fieldwork. But I never asked.

---

[38] Author interview B78.
[39] Author interview B89.
[40] Author interview B76.
[41] Author interview B81.

Now that both groups had disarmed, there was also notable resentment that the collectively demobilized FARC combatants were getting better benefits than the AUC had received – with some complaining that the FARC was capitalizing on the lessons learned from the government's DDR experiment with the paramilitaries. Indeed, this theme of being a "pilot project" – suffering the mistakes from which thousands of other ex-combatants benefited – was common and reinforced the sense of victimhood from AUC respondents. One respondent – who had been sentenced to five years in prison but only served two and half – asked me how it was possible that no FARC leaders went to jail but many AUC leaders did.[42] And, in fact, an ARN representative confirmed that the FARC had learned from the AUC process and in their negotiations demanded guarantees that certain juridical changes that happened during the AUC reintegration – which threatened more ex-combatants with jail time and essentially caused mass recidivism – would not happen to them.[43] This outrage that no top FARC commanders had gone to jail (with the exception of Santrich) was consistent throughout the paramilitary interviews. Like the deserters, AUC respondents claimed that they were the "true victims" because the government did not know what they were doing with the first iteration of collective DDR, and now everyone had forgotten about them:

So, we feel like, like we were abandoned by the state, and it makes one feel like, like bad from this because the [AUC] bosses, bosses, bosses left with money and are in the United States and we are left here, tossed aside. So, for me, for me I feel uncomfortable with the government, do you understand? (Pedro, ex-AUC, B77)

Indeed, several ex-paramilitaries discussed the profound sense of physical and economic insecurity when they demobilized. As one said to me, they had been trained that "if you lose your gun, you lose your life."[44] And then, with little to no warning, they were asked to hand over all their weapons. Indeed, many of these respondents told me that they had no idea a demobilization was being negotiated until trucks showed up to bring them to the demobilization centers. This sudden and nonvoluntary loss of arms left them feeling extremely vulnerable to retaliatory attacks. And, in addition to feeling abandoned by the state, several former AUC combatants felt abandoned and exploited by higher-ranking paramilitary members. Often, these respondents would start out with a lot of bravado

42 Author interview B95.
43 Author interview C15.
44 Author interview B95.

and then open up later in the conversation, admitting to being tricked or feeling regretful. For example, one respondent first proudly said he was fighting for his salary and then later said he regretted that he had hurt so many people.[45] And the respondent who initially declared that the country would have been worse without the AUC, told me twenty minutes later: "[F]irst, one is ignorant, you don't know. You think you are doing something for the country, and you are not doing it for the country, you are doing it for another. You are doing it for the commander. You aren't doing anything for the country there" (Pedro, ex-AUC, B77). This sense of exploitation was intensified by a frequently expressed fear that someone was always trying to trick them. In informal conversations over meals and coffee (when I was not recording audio), the respondents were often more candid, and several told stories of how government officials had come into their compound pretending to be other people and had on occasion brought complicated papers for them to sign, sometimes tricking them into forfeiting certain benefits. Stories of being tricked out of their money was repeated, in different forms, by several different ex-paramilitary respondents. Some also spoke about journalists or state officials who had misrepresented themselves in order to get information from them. And there is indeed evidence for this: the military has run various intelligence collection missions among the civilian population pretending to be anything from marketing researchers for cell phone companies to public health officers conducting surveys.[46] The ex-paramilitaries knew they had fallen for this several times and were, as a result, very wary of outsiders. The only reason I got anywhere near their compounds is because of snowball sampling methods: a former FARC militia member with whom I had built trust vouched for me, and then the first group of former paramilitaries vouched for me to the next group. Nell later told me that ten years ago, if I had walked onto their farming compound like I did on the day I met her, I would have been shot on sight.

Nell and her husband also told me several stories of how the drug traffickers whose land had been expropriated by the government and given to the ex-paramilitaries were repeatedly threatening them to get their land back. The government had essentially ignored the ex-combatants' claims of being in danger due to government action. (Later, a former guerrilla who worked with the local government told me that this land was never "given" to the ex-paramilitaries but was actually taken by force – which

---

[45] Author interview B78.
[46] Fattal, *Guerrilla Marketing*.

may be why the government ignored their claims of being in danger.) Nell even told me to be very careful when I was coming to and from the rural compound, as they were not sure who would be watching the road; they told me to always leave before dark. Nell then told me a story of how drug traffickers had once come and tied her up, trashing their house and threatening her, leaving her there for her husband to find. And yet, she and her husband refused to leave – because where else would they go? They claimed to have nothing except the little corner store that Nell ran and her husband's mechanics business. But I got the impression that they had reached some sort of business arrangement with the drug traffickers, based on the new truck and flat screen television they owned, as well as comments from other respondents about the active drug-trafficking operations in that area. No one said this outright, of course. Few of the ex-paramilitaries said anything outright. But they implied many things with jokes and sarcasm, winks, shrugs, and nods.

While this makes some information nearly impossible to verify, there is no disputing that the ex-paramilitaries in this sample felt abused and exploited by a government that they felt they had tried to help. In addition, while there was only one successful AUC deserter in my research, there were many "would-be" deserters. Rebel cohesion theories predict that economically motivated recruits should be the most likely to desert,[47] but this study and other data from Colombia indicate the opposite: desertion flows went primarily one way, from the guerrillas to the paramilitaries, and rarely the reverse.[48] Nearly half of the paramilitary respondents in this study said that they had wanted to desert the group but were too scared to do so. Others said they had asked to leave but the commanders had refused. One had tried to escape twice but had been caught both times and brought back. The one who did successfully escape said he left because the group had promised to pay a salary and did not, and then the group had started to kill his friends, so he felt he was next.[49] But he did not demobilize to the army; instead, he fled to the FARC for protection.

In fact, nearly all the ex-paramilitary respondents agreed that most people in the AUC did not dare desert because of the consequences. I wondered if that also had to do with the collaboration between the AUC and the military – after all, how could AUC deserters really be safe if they

---

[47] Oppenheim et al., "True Believers, Deserters, and Traitors"; Kalyvas, *The Logic of Violence in Civil War*; Jeremy M Weinstein, *Inside Rebellion: The Politics of Insurgent Violence* (Cambridge and New York: Cambridge University Press, 2007).
[48] Gutiérrez Sanín, "The FARC's Militaristic Blueprint."
[49] Author interview B73.

surrendered to the military? Surely the AUC could get to them easily in that case. Indeed, their reasoning was the reverse of what many guerrilla deserters said. In the AUC case, threats of harm from within the group served to keep people *in* the ranks, not to drive them out – and this reinforced, in the lower ranks at least, an overall sense of helplessness. One man, who became a father at age fourteen, explained to me that he simply had no other options:

It was all very hard, it was very hard because I never wanted to be in the army, because ... because I was a very young father, and I thought about leaving [the AUC] and then my children, what, go hungry? No. So in the beginning it is very hard, very hard because you stay up late almost every night, sometimes hungry, cold, wet. All night you are in danger, at any moment while you are sleeping there, someone might throw in a grenade and you're in that, and it's hard ... but you adapt. (Rio, ex-AUC, B95)

Some said that they had no friends, that they could not trust anyone, or that they had lost all their friends as a result of their membership in the group. In fact, the ex-paramilitaries talked significantly more about trauma than the ex-guerrillas did, even when including guerrilla deserters. These stories of trauma were often related to the rules of the organization and related punishments. And while this fear and trauma suggest that the costs of membership were very high and should inspire desertion, fear seems to have had the opposite effect. Guerrilla loyalists spoke of the importance of rules, and guerrilla deserters often talked about rebelling against the rules, but most ex-AUC respondents spoke about the rules with fear: the rules were a reason to stay in the group, even if you did not agree with them, because violating the rules was far too dangerous. While the paramilitary leadership had created a convincing frame around filling the security void left by the government, they also established a highly credible threat to prevent recruits from leaving. The one successful AUC deserter I spoke to explained how the rules were quite different in the paramilitaries, compared to his subsequent experience in the FARC:

Because they [the FARC] respected the lives of others. If you did not commit a mistake that you could not escape from, they [the FARC] drew your attention to it, they did not kill you, but the paras did. The paras, if you did something one time they would kill you, they would not draw your attention to it. And there [in the FARC] they drew your attention, they sanctioned you, like: "Well, we are going to sanction you because you did this wrong." Do you understand me? (Diego, ex-FARC/ex-AUC, B73)

Another respondent, who had gone the other way (from the FARC to the AUC), agreed and said the FARC was like a family. He expressed profound and tearful regret that he had ever left the FARC and was unable to shake the sense that he had betrayed his guerrilla friends.[50] This interview stayed with me, and it made me once again rethink my preconceived notions of who AUC members were.

Indeed, many AUC respondents became quite emotional, often telling stories of brutal punishments (without my asking for them). One of the women respondents – who was a single mother of three children – said that she had gone for six months without a salary, so she had finally gone home to seek other work. But when the woman and her friends went back because they still needed work, all of their former commanders had been killed – apparently on orders from the high command (*estado mayor*) because those commanders had been withholding salaries.[51] There were many such stories of in-group violence. One man said that the AUC treated people like animals, but they could never say anything or show any emotion at all, for risk of being punished: "I could never cry for the death of a friend."[52] Another participant did not want to return to the past as it was simply too awful. He recalled being sent to kill his own friends and said, in tears: "Now I have no friends."[53] When I asked why he did not leave rather than kill his own friends, he said that he "had to get something" out of the experience, that he could not possibly return to his family empty-handed. This rationale for staying in the ranks was shared by several other respondents. The costs of membership were high, but for many respondents in this study, the costs of leaving were much higher. Some of these combatants had committed crimes and acts of violence that they deeply regretted, but they also saw these as significant and sunk investments for which they had to get something back, or it would all be for nothing – despite deep dissatisfaction with the group.

When I got home from this set of interviews, I stared at the ceiling of my Bogotá apartment for a very long time. Stories of war and trauma are often hard to process, but this set of interviews had been different. The AUC arguably has the worst reputation in all of Colombia in terms of raw violence: this is the group that ripped fetuses from pregnant women and gang raped young girls; this is the group that played soccer with the heads of their victims and threw people into alligator ponds to be eaten alive; this is the group that enforced gendered dress codes and coldly executed homeless children, prostitutes, and LGBTQ+ people in "social

---

[50] Author interview B91.
[51] Author interview B99.
[52] Author interview B90.
[53] Author interview B94.

cleansing" raids. As a feminist and human rights scholar, I was troubled that I found myself deeply empathizing with members of this group. But this is the thing about really listening to people: this is when all the shades of gray filter in, and we begin to doubt the credibility of frames we have long accepted. While there is no disputing the violence and human rights violations committed by the AUC as a whole, if we fail to empathize at all with perpetrators of such violence, if we fail to listen to their reasons why, we will fail to understand the complexity of their decisions, dilemmas, and regrets around that participation.[54] And we will fail to prevent it from happening again.

Overall, the victimhood counter-frame was extremely durable among the paramilitary population in this sample, and it was still informing their choices and world views nearly fifteen years post-demobilization. While the AUC respondents did not speak much of their own identity as *campesinos* during the conflict (rather, they positioned themselves as defending *campesinos*), some spoke of wanting to be regular *campesinos* in their demobilized life, and how that was very challenging because of stigma:

Because we were no longer patrolling and we were going to be people, for example, *campesinos*, civilians; we no longer had to be hidden there ... We were going to be different people, without conflicts, without anything. But people refused [to let us]. Many people rejected us ... for being paramilitaries. (Gello, ex-AUC, B80)

The concept of self-defense forces was perhaps even more critical to the paramilitaries compared to the guerrillas: self-defense was not part of AUC ideology, it was their entire ideology. And it allowed the paramilitaries to justify membership in a group known for its brutality against civilians – by claiming that they were forced to do so in order to help others. But their post-demobilization experiences of stigma and discrimination due to their membership in the AUC illustrate the challenges of constructing an identity within a frame contested by so many different actors.

CONCLUSION

This chapter indicates that the combined influence of identity, networks, and cost–benefit calculations are important in desertion decisions – and the perception of these variables is inevitably affected by framing

---

[54] Anastasia Shesterinina, "Ethics, Empathy, and Fear in Research on Violent Conflict," *Journal of Peace Research* 56, no. 2 (2019): 190–202.

contests. Overall, while the victimhood frame was strong in encouraging cohesion through a shared identity within the guerrilla ranks, and especially within the FARC, it was not a strong enough frame on its own to prevent desertion. The FARC and ELN may portray the government as the "real terrorist" – with sufficient evidence to support their claims – but this frame will not resonate with civilians who have borne the brunt of guerrilla violence (because the frame does not match their lived experience), or those in the cities that have seen hardly any armed conflict at all (because the frame is not essential to them). The government also has sufficient evidence for its perpetrator framing of the guerrillas, but evidence (i.e., empirical credibility of the frame) is not the sole factor in determining who adopts which frame and how they use it. Indeed, as noted earlier, empirical credibility is only one aspect of frame resonance; credibility also depends on frame consistency as well as the reputation and credibility of the frame-makers. And this chapter shows that both the guerrillas and the government have lost their credibility in various ways.

How, then, does the victimhood frame – or its counter-frame – affect decisions to disengage and the experiences that follow? First, combatants who were most strongly tied to the collective *campesino* identity as a component of this victimhood appear less likely to entertain the thought of deserting, much less to actually do it. While there is evidence to suggest that some deserters downplayed their *campesino* identity after demobilization in order to survive in the city, overall, deserters seemed to have far less attachment to this identity, even when talking about their childhoods. It is, of course, difficult to tell with retrospective accounts if that lack of attachment to the *campesino* identity occurred before desertion, or if it was an adaptation to the demands of post-demobilization life.

For many combatants, a willingness to take the risk and leave the group was clearly influenced by perceived alternatives: combatants who saw themselves as uneducated victims, as farmers who could not possibly function in the city, seemed most likely to have inhibitions about deserting compared to those that had urban connections and could feasibly obtain a job in the city, especially if that job required good literacy skills.

As noted earlier, the most common reason that deserters gave for leaving their group was threats or perceived threats from their own comrades – including the threat of forced abortion. The cost–benefit calculation matters, but it is deeply affected by perceptions of reality and threat. Recalling that frame resonance depends on the credibility and salience of the frame, it appears that with a serious enough threat to the frame's validity (i.e., realizing that the FARC could not always protect them), the frame may begin to lose salience; that is, it may no longer be essential to these deserters and/or it may no longer resonate with their lived experiences. If threats to their safety are large enough, combatants may start to accept the government frame that they are, in fact, victims of their own group and that they need to leave. And when the risk to one's life was big enough, some combatants deserted seemingly without any calculation of these alternatives and then found themselves at a loss in terms of what to do next. In fact, some respondents in this situation ended up so panicked about what to do that they immediately joined another armed group for protection. Desertion is not always a planned-out process.

Clearly, there is significant tension within the guerrilla victimhood frame. Many deserters had at some point accepted a shift in framing from being victims of the government to being victims of their group. However, utilizing the government frame to justify choices does not require fully abandoning the guerrilla frame, and many ex-combatants used them both strategically. That is, deserters may leave the group and adopt the government framing for protection and survival, but most of them still organized their experiences within the frame that their entire trajectory in the armed group had happened because they were victims of the state.

Overall, among the ex-combatant population, the frame of victimhood was much more dominant than the government's counter-frame, even among deserters and former paramilitaries. This frame appears to have high resonance even when the frame-makers lose credibility (i.e., when recruits realize that their ideological leaders are also trafficking drugs), or when the frame loses some salience in terms of connection to lived experiences (i.e., when recruits are victimized by their own comrades). Arguably, this enduring resonance is due to the fact that the victimhood frame is strongly connected to cultural narratives of *campesinos* and historical neglect of the state in rural areas.

In addition, this victimhood framing was repeatedly paired with – or resisted by – a narrative of agency and resilience. That is, the guerrillas were victims, but they rose up against their oppressors. Deserters were victims, and reintegration was hard, but they were making the best of their new lives. Paramilitaries were victims but they bravely took up arms to defend themselves and their communities. While there are, of course, issues of empirical credibility with each of these narratives, the overall framing of victimhood had a strong cohesive effect of making each group feel proud of their collective resistance.

VI

Framing a Revolution

And in any case, the FARC [grew] because of its political activity, because of its political program, because of its struggle to align with the masses, by bringing the political message to the population that the struggle is to reform state structures that are not working well. [Our fight] is to provide guarantees to the poor, to the workers, to the students, to the Indigenous, that is the political discourse that ... allows us then to grow, to become stronger.

Pablo, FARC Secretariat member (B47)

So, we first have to arm the brain, the head, the thoughts and everything towards where we are going. And there, yes, we use weapons when we need them. Of course, weapons are a mere continuation of politics by other means, according to Clausewitz, no? One of the war classics. But this signifies that in the context of the fight, in the context of the war, the fundamental ideology is much more important than the weapons.

Rafael, FARC (B46)

I spoke with two members of the FARC Secretariat during my fieldwork, which was entirely unexpected and provided several impromptu master classes in framing. While I only secured a formal interview with one of them, I spent hours with both, eating meals and drinking coffee, observing political meetings, talking to their wives and children, and watching the comings and goings of their armored, tinted out trucks. They were hospitable, polite, and eager to tell their side of things. At times, it was hard to square these personable and intelligent men – often scooping up their toddlers with laughter – with the violence and human rights violations they have been involved in. My conversations with these commanders were fascinating – a once-in-a-lifetime experience to get the revolutionary tract straight from the mouths of true ideologues. They spun a compelling story, but as is often the case, it was only half the story – less than half, probably. And right before I left, one of them kissed my cheek and warned me softly: "If you publish anything bad about us, we'll know it's a lie." We both laughed, but I walked away understanding the threat.

Colombia's guerrillas have long clashed with the Colombian government about how their revolution is framed – a version of the classic "freedom fighter" versus "terrorist" debate. While the victimhood frame and associated contests discussed in the preceding chapters are clearly important to recruit and retain members, the revolution frame is the one most vehemently contested by the government and plays a powerful role in both rebel group cohesion and the stigmatization of ex-combatants after they disarm. But I do not want to falsely portray this as purely a right versus left ideological competition, or even as a "government versus rebels" competition. Many ex-combatants in this study did not fully understand their group's ideology, especially respondents from the ELN. Rather, the contest I examine here is about the narratives, labels, and identities constructed around what it means to wage a revolution, and what it means to fight against one. Indeed, the government – with significant assistance from the Colombian media – has run a long campaign of portraying the FARC and the ELN as criminals and drug lords, denying the very existence of an armed conflict. The effect of this contest has entrenched each side in overly simplistic narratives: the FARC and ELN accusing the state of waging a dirty propaganda war against them, and the government asserting that the frame of revolution is simply a smokescreen to cover up illicit activities. As the most resonant frames are salient when they are built on partial truths, these narratives have become highly resonant with their target audiences.

The Colombian government's labeling of the guerrillas – particularly the FARC – as narco-guerrillas, and then later as narco-terrorists, has been a deliberate and strategic effort to discredit a group that survived for over fifty years partly due to legitimate grievances that generated a large amount of *campesino* support.[1] As Chapter VII illustrates, this framing was integral to Uribe's insistence that the country was not in a state of civil war. While a great deal of the guerrillas' support was due to government neglect of *campesino* areas, the government framing of the group as narco-terrorists attempted to place the guerrillas at the level of criminals and drug traffickers, erasing any legitimate grievances they had and by extension criminalizing

---

[1] Courtheyn, "De-indigenized but Not Defeated"; Idler, *Borderland Battles*; Ramírez, *Between the Guerrillas and the State*.

the *campesinos* who supported them or lived in areas under guerrilla control.[2] Of course, most of the FARC loyalists in this project were emphatic that they were not terrorists; convincing me of this and explaining the government's "dirty war" – and asking me to share this with the world – was important to them. Paramilitaries also unsurprisingly rejected the terrorist label or any version of history suggesting that they were ruthless or inherently violent people. Respondents in all ex-combatant categories saw themselves as fighters and, more specifically, as revolutionaries for justice and/or defenders of the people. All the fighters understood that they were in a war; it was only the government insisting that they were not.

In addition, while the frame of revolution implies major societal change and redistribution of power, the "fighter" identity inside this frame is not necessarily tied to violence or even to revolution – and that is critical to understanding how organizational framing affects personal decisions. Disarming as a group, or deserting as an individual, does not automatically remove one's sense of being a fighter. Many of these women are often hesitant to settle in cities, as urban life is foreign and intimidating, and stigma against them is high. Dropping the fighter identity has also been problematic for paramilitaries, many of whom saw themselves as fighting to help the government, only to find themselves in a revisionist version of history that erased government involvement and placed them into the narco-criminal-terrorist frame as well.

This chapter and Chapter VII explore the contest between the guerrillas' revolution frame – where the government is framed as the "real terrorist" – and the government's frame of the guerrillas as narco-terrorists, into which the government later subsumes the paramilitaries. In turn, the paramilitaries contest both of these frames by asserting themselves as self-defense forces and protectors of the people. This chapter discusses the utility and primacy of the revolution frame for the guerrillas, including their identity as fighters, and a more recent emphasis on the FARC's insurgent feminism, including how this unique brand of feminism simultaneously challenges and reinforces Colombia's militarized masculinities.

THE GUERRILLA FRAMING OF THE REVOLUTION

While eating lunch with one of the FARC Secretariat leaders, it was clear he had aged out of this fight. He moved slowly and napped often. But

---

[2] Ramírez, *Between the Guerrillas and the State*; Ricardo Vargas, "Colombia y El Area Andina: Los Vacíos de La Guerra.," *Controversía* 169 (1996): 53–72.

that was not surprising: at the time of this research, the Secretariat members were mostly in their sixties and seventies, an aging vanguard that had seen their troops decimated by Uribe's "Democratic Security" offensive. And while they all insisted that the peace accord was a victory, it was hard to see that when staying in the impoverished FARC camps, where access to fresh food and medical care was a constant struggle and income-generating opportunities were sparse. I could not help but wonder, as many others have, if this peace accord was a desperate attempt to staunch the blood flow that Uribe had started. Because what had they really won in the end? A few political seats, yes, and a written agreement on land reform and other changes. But the government was still being run by the same elite families, the chasm between rich and poor was as wide as ever, and the cocaine trade was thriving. While a third of the promised three million hectares has been added to the Land Fund to grant land to *campesinos*, the majority of these plots are currently occupied – at the time of writing, very limited formal land reallocation had taken place,[3] and violence in some areas was worse than before the peace accord.[4] Rank-and-file guerrillas were struggling in the same *campesino* existence that drove them to arms in the first place. Women had only marginal leadership roles in FARC collective economic projects.[5] As I looked around, watching kids playing in the dirt and women cooking under the punishing heat of "temporary" plastic roofing, seeing the men drinking beer after beer, I wondered: where was the revolution now?

As with any rebellion or social uprising, leaders must frame their movement to get and keep recruits: as a cause, as a fight for justice, for redistribution of resources, or in some cases as a purely income-generating endeavor. Indeed, to construct any sort of collective action frame is to suggest that there is a real opportunity to affect social change.[6] In Colombia, the FARC and ELN framing of a legitimate fight for justice is particularly crucial when placed against the government's counter-frame of the guerrillas as nothing but drug traffickers. With the FARC in particular, I identify three key components of the revolution frame: (1) the fighter identity, (2) militarized masculinities, and (3) insurgent feminism. This chapter explores the construction, meaning, and impact of these three components in terms of group cohesion, disengagement decisions, and transitions to civilian life.

---

[3] Guterres, "United Nations Verification Mission in Colombia: December 2020."
[4] Daniels, "Peace Is War as Armed Groups Roil Colombia's Lawless Border Region"; Watts, "Battle for the Mother Land."
[5] Guterres, "United Nations Verification Mission in Colombia: December 2020."
[6] Benford and Snow, "Framing Processes and Social Movements."

While the ELN leadership also uses these components, responses in this study suggest that the group's indoctrination and propaganda strategy is less centralized and less successful overall. That is, while some ELN respondents (like Junior) could articulate a revolution frame, many admitted that they had no idea why they were fighting. Such an admission was almost nonexistent among FARC respondents, including deserters, suggesting several factors: (1) the FARC indoctrination strategy was generally more successful and their framing more resonant than that of the ELN, and (2) many recruits attracted to the FARC likely had a strong ideology of their own before joining, compared to ELN recruits.

Fighters for Justice against the "Real" Terrorists

While Pablo stuck mostly to FARC ideology in our interview and was initially quite wary of me, he became more candid when talking about his childhood. He told me he grew up in a "guerrilla corridor" in the 1960s, and as he grew older, he noticed that the guerrillas were helping the *campesinos* to find food, organize their communities, learn how to defend themselves, and so on. Soon after, he said, violent persecutions began, with people branded as communists, liberals, or "enemies" who had to be killed for one reason or another. He remembered a childhood running from one place to the next, watching parents leave in the middle of the night with children in their arms. He recalled how no one was spared – pregnant women, the elderly, adults, children. Everyone was killed. At one point, he said, he realized that the state was never going to help them and that it was, in fact, complicit in the violence. Finally, at age twenty-five and after more than a decade of running, he decided that there was nothing to do but to fight back. This is what he remembered – or, at least, this is what he chose to tell me – his eyes distant as he sipped hot soup at the table across from me.

Sick of always running, Pablo and many of his comrades decided to stop being victims and start fighting back – but it soon became more than just self-defense. It became about revolution, about overthrowing a corrupt system. The fighter identity was a key part of that frame. Identity construction is, after all, an inherent part of the framing process, in part because it facilitates alignment between personal and collective identities and suggests specific relationships and lines of action.[7] While scholars have certainly shown that ideology matters to rebel group cohesion,[8] what is

---

[7] Benford and Snow, "Framing Processes and Social Movements."
[8] Gutiérrez Sanín and Wood, "Ideology in Civil War."

just as critical is how leaders "sell" the ideology to their members and how leaders and members together carefully construct identities within this ideology that build group cohesion. For this purpose, simple frames are most effective. Indeed, many ex-combatants that I interviewed had only a very rudimentary idea of the Marxist ideology claimed by both the FARC and ELN – though this lack of knowledge was more pronounced with ELN respondents. What was more important than granular ideological details for most of the respondents was the sense that their fight mattered – and by extension, that *they* mattered. Indeed, for many ex-combatants in this sample, the importance of "being someone" was a clear pattern, and many former insurgents got this sense of importance from being a fighter – and for men, especially one of higher rank. In addition, this fighter identity was not something that combatants dropped after demobilization, not even among deserters. Many ex-guerrillas saw themselves as fighters against government tyranny even before they joined their groups. One can, of course, be a political fighter without being violent, and without ascribing to the ideology of an armed group. However, for many *campesinos* caught in the martial politics of Colombia, this was a difficult separation to make, especially if they were designated as legitimate military targets simply for being political at all. As this chapter shows, the fighter identity constructed within the revolution frame remains highly durable across all respondent categories, even though the revolution frame itself has been subject to many intramovement disputes and faced an overall decline of resonance amid the daily challenges of post-demobilization civilian life.

Reflected by the FARC's rebranding of its original acronym after signing the peace accord – from the "Revolutionary Armed Forces of Colombia" to the "Common Alternative Revolutionary Force" – many ex-combatants in the reincorporation camps still saw themselves as revolutionaries. In fact, most loyalists insisted that they had not demobilized at all, which they considered to be a disbanding of the group:

With the FARC, [the government] was only interested in disarming us and then that's it. They thought that war was only waged with weapons, but no sir. War is not only made with weapons. If they take our weapons, the war and the conflict do not end. It is false, that war is only waged with weapons. (Mafe, FARC, B29)

Most of these individuals had not dropped their sense of being fighters just because they had disarmed. Similarly, not all deserters demobilize because they have renounced their group or its goals – in fact, participants here suggested that many do not. The majority of these respondents articulated that they still had something to fight for, and against.

Most agreed that, above all, the government was the greatest enemy, liar, and manipulator in this conflict. And most of them, including paramilitaries, saw themselves as continuing to fight against injustice.

Indeed, less than a year after I met Pablo, three top FARC commanders publicly echoed this sentiment about the government's failure to fulfill the peace deal and announced their return to arms.[9] In fact, many ex-combatants emphasized to me that the government was still fighting a dirty war against them, and that the arrest of Jesús Santrich (a Secretariat commander and key negotiator of the peace accord) on drug-trafficking charges soon after the peace deal created significant insecurity within FARC ranks that President Duque would not honor the JEP. They worried that they could all be subject to arrests or threats of extradition:

> We don't have any security ... we don't have any of that, none of that. I mean that we don't, no, nobody is safe in that tomorrow, or later, I could have a warrant and go to jail. Because it has already happened with comrades ... [for example], the Santrich case: Jesús Santrich was one of those who was in the peace process, who was insisting on the peace process, the one, one of the people who was convinced of the peace process ... He was convinced that with peace many things could be achieved, and what the government did with Santrich was a set-up, and [now] Santrich is imprisoned. (Ana, FARC, B50)

The repeated insistence that Santrich's arrest was a set-up – and that Santrich himself continued to be a noble fighter and *not* a drug trafficker – reinforced and was reinforced by the revolutionary frame of guerrillas as fighters against government injustice. In fact, Mari spent a great deal of time proudly describing her arrest, imprisonment, and escape, portraying herself as the loyal, unwavering prisoner of conscience held by a manipulative state.

Here is where I need to go back, to the start of Mari's story, to illustrate how organizational frames work at an individual level – and especially how pre-existing personal frames can reinforce and be reinforced by organizational ones. Guerrilla recruits are, of course, not blank slates before joining. While the FARC had especially effective indoctrination techniques, the pre-existing personal traumas, experiences, and beliefs of recruits had an enormous impact on their commitment to the group and on the degree to which organizational frames resonated with them.

Mari joined the FARC when she was fourteen years old and had spent nearly twenty-seven years as part of the group. She initially told me that her life had been "normal" before joining, but I pushed her a bit on

---

[9] EFE, "El Ex Número Dos de Las FARC, Iván Márquez, Anuncia Que Retoma Las Armas."

this. What was "normal" to her, I asked, if joining an armed insurgency at fourteen seemed like a good option? She slowly began to elaborate: at that time, the paramilitaries and drug cartels had begun to murder members of the UP. And her parents were both members of the UP. Her childhood was not "normal" at all – not even by Colombian *campesino* standards. She grew up with two parents who were members of the FARC political party and were on the run because their colleagues were being assassinated. She had a strong formative education not only in Marxism but also in persecution and violence. Her parents were poor subsistence farmers, with few income options, until the FARC came and organized their community. She told me that the FARC built a school, brought in electricity, and created a "Community Action Board" that was made up entirely by UP members. Since the government had never done anything in that community – except when the military attacked them for being FARC supporters, according to Mari – the people began to respect and trust the FARC as their de facto government. A frame was being created here, not only within the organization, but in the community and directly in Mari's young life: the FARC was the only group helping them, the FARC had a legitimate revolution, the FARC would use Marxism to rectify oppression and inequality.

Eventually, military and/or paramilitary attacks became more frequent in their area. She said she stopped studying because "you went to school and found a dead *campesino* [there], and then you would be filled with fear." Everyone felt unsafe. Then she said, holding my gaze fiercely: "I did not join because the FARC invited me, or because they forced me, or because I wanted to. I joined the FARC out of fear … because who was going to take me? I had to take care of myself." Her mother had died in childbirth by that point, and although her father did not want her to go, he did not stop her. She admitted that she did not fully understand the magnitude of the war back then, but she knew that someone would eventually come to assassinate her father, and she did not want to be there when it happened: "Sometimes I would say [to myself], 'I want to go far away. When that day comes that they arrive to assassinate my father, I don't want to be here.'"

Like many child recruits, Mari joined because she was terrified. And just as she feared, her father was later assassinated. She admitted she had no idea that guerrilla life would be so hard, but because she was good at following rules, she adapted quickly. Mari told me that she never once thought of leaving, and that no one ever discussed desertion with her. I do not doubt the latter – Mari is a formidable woman and a committed loyalist. No one would dare discuss desertion with her, as she would undoubtedly report it. But I wondered – did she really *never* think of leaving, even when she was fourteen or fifteen? Or was it just that clear to her, as a teenage girl with no parents and no home, that leaving was not an option?

Group rules and norms came up frequently in interviews with both loyalists and deserters of all three groups. Loyalists like Mari spoke about the importance of rules and how deserters often incorrectly viewed sanctions as "mistreatment," when sanctions were simply a fair consequence of breaking the rules. Indeed, sometimes I would ask participants if they were ever punished and they said no, but then I would ask if they were ever sanctioned, and they would laugh and say: "All the time!" The idea of being a rule follower and always respecting the chain of command was deeply ingrained in loyalist respondents – as opposed to many deserters who insisted on being rule-breakers and independent thinkers, and sometimes criticized FARC or ELN ideology as hypocritical. Many loyalists had internalized a rule-following mentality from a young age, even before joining the FARC, saying that they had no trouble following rules in the organization because they had already learned this at home.

Another critical component in the construction of the fighter identity, especially in the FARC, was separation from the civilian population. Wearing uniforms, living in camps, a strict daily routine, being discouraged (and in some cases prohibited) from romantic relationships with civilians – all of these aspects fostered a very specific fighter identity to help maintain cohesion.[10] The separation from civilians also kept some rank-and-file guerrillas siloed from criminal activities that happened largely in the cities – which explains why militia members seemed to know a lot more about FARC involvement in the drug trade. This is not to say that base-level guerrillas *en el monte* ("on the mountain")[11] were unaware of the FARC's involvement in cocaine production and drug trafficking, but very few talked openly about it. Those activities, after all, present a significant challenge to the revolution frame. For base-level

[10] Gutiérrez Sanín, "The FARC's Militaristic Blueprint."

[11] This phrase "en el monte" (on the mountain) or "al monte" (to the mountain) referred to being in or returning to the jungle or mountains, or general rural areas with the guerrillas, regardless of the presence of actual mountains. It was also used to distinguish themselves from guerrilla militia members, who were operatives in towns and cities, and – some felt – not "real" guerrillas (though certainly not all ex-combatants felt this way). Thus, most guerrilla ex-combatants referred to their time in the group as time "en el monte," whereas some militia members would specify that they had never gone "al monte."

guerrillas in certain units, especially ones that rarely traveled (e.g., the protection units for Secretariat members), it is conceivable that they would not have witnessed or been informed of income-generating criminal activities performed for the FARC.

Reducing cognitive dissonance by willfully ignoring certain activities, or by keeping certain troops siloed from criminal activities, can be an effective way for leaders to maintain cohesion and strengthen the salience, resonance, and credibility of the frame for their followers.

Keeping rank-and-file guerrilla fighters separate from civilians also controlled the networks that fighters had, especially as recruits were discouraged (and sometimes forbidden) from contacting their family members. In addition, being known as a committed rule follower affected one's social network within the group. That is, most of the loyalist respondents who were proud of their adherence to rules and norms also reported that they had never heard anyone talking about wanting to desert. Mari laughed at this question, saying: "No one would ever say that to me. They know who I am." Around someone like Mari, a committed revolutionary who has signaled this clearly to the group, no one talked about wanting to desert – it was something people did on their own, in secret, because the risks were so great. Mari's identity thus affected who was in her network of confidantes, and this social network – which never, ever discussed desertion – reinforced the framing of committed revolution by reducing any cognitive dissonance that might have been caused by discussions of desertion.

But testimonies of deserters challenge the view that no one talked about desertion, as many reported leaving in pairs or in groups of three, or one would leave and the other would follow a few days or weeks later. Desertion *was* something that combatants talked about and planned with each other, but only in certain social groups. Thus, while networks may influence desertion, a person's public level of commitment to the revolution frame clearly influenced who was in their networks and what type of information was shared.

Many ex-combatants also talked about wanting to "be someone" – and being a fighter had given them exactly that. In fact, for men in particular, an important aspect of the fighter identity was the issue of rank. Junior was having a particularly hard time with this when I met him. He was suspicious and wary of me at first. But by the end of my third day at the safe house, his curiosity won out and he decided to talk to me. Junior was twenty-five and a mid-level commander of the ELN at this time – already a fourteen-year veteran, he joined the group when he was only eleven. His entire family, he told me, was in the ELN: mother, father, siblings, aunts, uncles. Everyone. "We were twelve," he told me, then sighed. "But now eleven." For him, deserting had meant losing his entire family. He had not wanted to demobilize; he had only done so because he had entrusted a large sum of money to a subordinate, who then deserted with all the money. Knowing he would face a harsh punishment for this mistake, Junior fled. When I asked him what he had learned in the ranks, he said: "Not to trust anyone." Now there was a price on Junior's head, placed there by his own father, a top ELN commander. Yet, Junior was desperately sad about leaving – he liked being a guerrilla.

Indeed, another sign of frame tension among loyalists guerrillas was the intense nostalgia that many respondents had for their guerrilla life "on the mountain." Arguably, this was not an internal resonance dispute or even a frame dispute. Instead, it was a simple loss of frame salience: the revolution frame was becoming harder and harder to connect to their daily lives in the face of civilian challenges, such as buying food, clothing, and medicine amid the hard reality of continued poverty and government neglect. A key component of being a fighter for lower-ranking respondents was that they felt safer inside the group than outside of it, while others said that life seemed easier "on the mountain" compared to civilian life, because as rank-and-file guerrillas, they never had to worry about basic necessities:

> Yes, it was a very abrupt change because ... first we entered the FARC very young and we never had independence or knew how to become independent, and we got to the organization and there too they gave us everything, and we did nothing but comply and we had everything that we needed there. But when they released us [after the peace agreement], it was like, "uuff!" It was like someone slapped you and you said, "oh, son of a mother!"[12] Civilian life is hard. One always says that, that, it is better [in civilian life], you see, but in this case, personally, I say that we maintained ... life was better on the mountain than, than right now. Of course, one has like, like more freedom, but one has far, far fewer resources. (Reina, FARC, B40)

For many of the rank-and-file, then, the revolution had not succeeded at all. They were right back in the subsistence poverty that they had been in before, still facing the structural violence of the state's martial politics that long preexisted the war.

Respondents from all groups also mourned the loss of purpose that they felt after demobilizing – regardless of whether they decided to desert

---

[12] The slang expression used here is unique to Colombia: *juemadre* (roughly, "son of a mother"), used as a softer version of *jueputa* or *hijo de puta* ("son of a bitch").

or had been ordered to disarm. For many of the loyalists, adjusting to the idea of being responsible for themselves, and finding a new identity as self-sufficient civilians who could not rely on commanders to provide decisions and supplies and orders, was very difficult:

[There] the commander solved everything, right? ... You got used to it. Everything always got there, right? And here you already find yourself with a different picture, right? That one practically has to depend on oneself, because here that basic rent that they give us is very little. You know that it is not enough to buy one what one needs daily, much less for medications if you are sick. In my case, because I arrived here ill, most of that income has been to buy drugs [medicine]. Buy drugs and buy drugs, right? (Roberto, FARC, B25).

Those of lower ranks were also more likely to complain about the challenges of managing and acquiring daily necessities; those at higher levels of command already had experience obtaining supplies for their subordinates and knew how to manage budgets and other logistics. Also, militia members who had remained at home while working for the guerrillas were much less likely to complain about these things – as they were the people responsible for acquiring most goods (at the behest of commanders) in the first place, while also managing their own household budgets. Several FARC ex-combatants also pointed out the discrepancy between the ability of high commanders to disengage from armed violence and become political leaders, and the inability of rank-and-file guerrillas or lower-level commanders to reframe their lives:

The commanders were immediately prepared to arrive and be part of the political leaders in Congress, in whatever political [party], NGO, or political rank in the structure of the government. But the base guerrillas are not prepared, so it is very hard, very hard because, because when one is not prepared and one needs medicine or to be treated in the hospital it is already ... in the organization when one was sick, they treated you right away or they operated immediately and there was no red tape, paperwork, that's how it happened. Because of this, many people do not have a mentality, a goal, a project to follow. (Jaime, FARC, B36)

This lack of purpose – related to a pressing lack of economic options for all but the top-level commanders – was cited by respondents as a key factor influencing large numbers of loyalists to leave the ETCRs. FARC political leaders have tried to transform their revolutionary frame from armed insurgency to politics, but for many FARC ex-combatants who were not directly involved in political positions, this frame no longer resonated. In fact, those still in the ETCRs reported that disillusionment with the peace process had caused many ex-combatants to drop out of or avoid any reintegration program altogether – and this, arguably, is not only a failure of the DDR process but is also a failure of frame transformation from armed conflict to political conflict.

While one ARN representative assured me that the agency is still in contact with everyone who had left the ETCRs, another representative from the same agency declined to answer when I asked her to verify that claim. Indeed, multiple UN reports have stated that there is little knowledge as to where many ex-combatants have gone after leaving the ETCRs.[13] And while having ex-combatants abandon the process may initially be cheaper for the government if those people fully drop out of the DDR program, it only reinforces what many ex-combatants already think about the complacency of the state toward their needs. And it increases the risk that ex-combatants will return to arms and/or engage in criminal activity:

> Well, what I have to say that the world does not know: we are here in a fight, dealing with all the difficulties that exist in these transition zones, that is, not only in this one but in all of them, to the national level. We remain here, all the time, with the expectation of this commitment we made to leave our weapons and not pick them up again. Because we are here with many difficulties, with many. Here [we have], like I have said for a while now: insecurity. (Ricardo, FARC, B26)

"The Fight Was Only for Machos": Militarized Masculinities

As noted earlier, there are two predominant traditions of gender norms in Colombia: *machismo* (emphasizing the masculine warrior/protector/provider) and *marianismo* (emphasizing feminine fertility, domesticity, and self-sacrifice).[14] Particularly important when looking at armed groups is understanding that *machismo* can be used to structure power relationships between men, not just between men and women.[15] And, in the FARC in particular, *machismo* structures some relationships between women as well. With martial politics, violence is unavoidably intertwined with gendered and racialized hierarchies,[16] which has particular implications for demobilization and predictions for reintegration.[17] When masculinity is militarized (i.e., when what it means to be a man is closely

---

[13] Guterres, "United Nations Verification Mission in Colombia: March 2019"; Antonio Guterres, "United Nations Verification Mission in Colombia: Report of the Secretary General, December 2018" (New York, 2018), https://colombia.unmissions.org/sites/default/files/n1845592.pdf; Antonio Guterres, "United Nations Verification Mission in Colombia: Report of the Secretary General, September 2018" (New York, 2018).

[14] Chant and Craske, *Gender in Latin America.*

[15] Chant and Craske, *Gender in Latin America.*

[16] Howell, "Forget 'Militarization'."

[17] Theidon, "Reconstructing Masculinities."

tied to military service), militarism and masculinism serve to reinforce each other.[18] I use the term "militarized masculinities" frequently here, but as noted in earlier chapters, I do not mean it as the encroachment of militarized institutions onto a previously peaceful and liberal society. Masculinity in Colombia is literally militarized by linking men's civilian status directly to the possession of a military service card. But decades of martial politics in Colombia have made the militarization of men and subjugation of women inevitable and indivisible from civilian life. When FARC loyalists argue that they have not demobilized but have simply laid down their arms, they reflect an understanding that war and peace are not binary but are instead part of a complex political spectrum.

Enloe argues that militaries must control images of women to emphasize traditional narratives of masculinity such as physical strength and bravado that encourage young men to sign up.[19] In contrast, feminization of the enemy is a key factor in militarized masculinities, where the enemy is portrayed as something to be conquered, penetrated, and ruled over, and the use of feminine terms is commonly derogatory.[20] Indeed, feminist scholars note that gendered dichotomies help to legitimize military force as well as unequal gender relations.[21] While this feminization of the enemy was more prominent in the AUC, which rarely recruited women into front-line roles, it was also evident when FARC loyalists discussed infiltrators and informants. Not only were women the subject of many derogatory discussions about deserters, but I also heard many jokes between male guerrillas accusing each other of being gay. The term *marica* (meaning "sissy," but also used as a slur for gay men) was common among male respondents as slang for men they did not like, or as a confrontational challenge. It was also used among male friends when mocking each other.

The adoption of an army-like organization in the early 1980s had profound implications for the gendered nature of the FARC. Until this point, there were very few women in combat roles in the group.[22] When the FARC made the explicit decision to adopt an army-like structure, they created a hierarchy that mirrored the army's ranking system[23] – and with

---

[18] Eichler, "Militarized Masculinities in International Relations."
[19] Enloe, *Maneuvers*.
[20] Goldstein, *War and Gender*.
[21] Eichler, "Militarized Masculinities in International Relations."
[22] Francisco Gutiérrez Sanín and Francy Carranza Franco, "Organizing Women for Combat: The Experience of the FARC in the Colombian War," *Journal of Agrarian Change* 17, no. 4 (2017): 770–8.
[23] Gutiérrez Sanín, "The FARC's Militaristic Blueprint."

that, they reinforced promotion practices that rewarded values related to *machismo*. Like most armies and army-like structures, these militarized masculinities became essential for holding the group together.[24]

For example, male and female respondents in this research told many stories of women infiltrators and women traitors, even as they lauded the women in their group for being dedicated to the cause. Many respondents said that all of the armed groups, including the state military, used women as infiltrators and informants, which created an effect in which all sides appeared somewhat wary of women members. This narrative at times reinforced militarized masculinities that devalue the feminine, and the fear of duplicitous women generated some particularly wild stories:

> We also have an enemy, and the enemy sent many, many people. They sent them to work, to enroll in the FARC and whatever, and suddenly they come with some mission that, that, well, their mission was to be that, to cause damage there in the organization ... to infiltrate there ... to do a job, well, to collect information at least, sometimes, the majority of the time it happened ... one time we had an experience where they [the army] sent one hundred women to Caquetá ... with AIDS, infected with AIDS, to infiltrate the organization and infect the entire guerrilla with AIDS. So, in this, in this, in this dynamic many people came to cause harm. (Ana, FARC, B50)

These types of stories were rampant in the FARC ETCRs, which – intentionally or not – reinforced an image of women as untrustworthy. These stories were also used to counter the state framing of FARC women; that is, these stories of falsified abuse discredited women deserters as never having been true FARC women at all. Indeed, when I asked Pablo (the Secretariat member) about deserters' testimonies that women members had been abused, he scoffed and told me the army had sent countless young girls into the FARC as spies:

> Then [the girls] got there and at once the psychological work and everything started. They are the ones that have been talking about how the guerrillas mistreated them, that they raped them, that they entered as a girl. And it turns out that those fourteen-, fifteen-year-old girls were sent by the army, who previously trained them in battalions and corrupted them, prostituted them, and they were sent to the guerrillas to generate internal decay, to sleep with one, with another, with everyone, to steal, to harm, to cut tarps, things like that, to do damage, to waste ammunition, to let go of shots while on guard or on-site, things like that.

While this story might seem unlikely, it is not impossible: several ex-AUC members told me that their group had sent "many women" to infiltrate

---

[24] Goldstein, *War and Gender*; Theidon, "Reconstructing Masculinities."

the FARC over the years. And since FARC members often equated para-militaries with the military – and the military used the AUC to do things it could not do – these rumors were just feasible enough to get traction in FARC camps. As a result, when there was evidence of betrayal, women were often suspected first. Indeed, some FARC loyalists told me that men deserted when their women convinced them to, which was why couples were split up and sent to different fronts if their relationships became too serious.

As noted in previous chapters, accusations of women infiltrators effectively suppressed stories of sexual abuse or harassment in the ranks by discrediting anyone who told such stories – a systematic silencing of anyone who dared speak out. While militarized masculinities seem to play against guerrilla claims of gender equality, they are entrenched in the martial politics of Colombia and were in fact a central factor organizing the experiences of guerrilla combatants. And in the FARC, these values set bounds around the women's insurgent feminism, creating a "guerrilla glass ceiling" that maintained patriarchal gender norms of men in leadership roles and women as subordinates, while somewhat ironically celebrating women as central to the guerrilla cause.

Other scholars have written about the importance of the FARC's adoption of a "militaristic blueprint" as key to its battle successes and control over large swaths of territory and people, and some have argued that it was only when the FARC adopted this army-like structure that it began to recruit large numbers of women.[25] Missing from this discussion is the importance of highly gendered identities in militaristic control, and the fact that both men and women often adopt militarized masculinities in order to be taken seriously and especially to be promoted in army-like structures.[26] Indeed, both the FARC and the ELN used the language of women's rights while relying on these militarized and sometimes misogynistic gender norms in order to keep troops in check and to achieve operational goals.

While the women FARC loyalists spoke of gender equality at length, many had essentially adopted masculine traits in order to survive and thrive in the group – something that women in state militaries have also done.[27] Indeed, several of the women told me that there were "no

[25] Gutiérrez Sanín, "The FARC's Militaristic Blueprint"; Gutiérrez Sanín and Carranza Franco, "Organizing Women for Combat."
[26] King, "The Female Combat Soldier."
[27] King, "The Female Combat Soldier."

women" in the FARC, because they were all treated like men: "[The fight] wasn't, how do you say, it wasn't for many, only for machos. It wasn't for many, only for machos, because they [female recruits] were going to face regulations, a regimen, what is it called? A regimen. Because there were strict rules, strict, strict" (Laidy, FARC, B34). That women would want to be seen as men did not surprise me, as Junior had already complained at length about how women were a hassle and expensive: "They need so much stuff! Shampoo, conditioner, bras, lotions, sanitary pads, everything! Men need a bar of soap, a razor, underwear, and that's it." For women who could do what men did and be treated like men in the ranks – that is, to be an asset rather than a burden – was a source of pride.

What was left unsaid was that they were not equal as *women* – they were only equal if they could be as similar to men as possible. And when it came to promotions, they were not equal at all: as shown earlier, while 19 percent of the women in this sample had reached a command level of any kind, 42 percent of the men had done so. In addition, only 3 percent of the women respondents had reached a rank beyond squad commander (the lowest level of command, in charge of twelve combatants), while 21 percent of men had done so. And the women who had gone past squad commander had only reached the next level (commanding twenty-six combatants), while men in this sample occupied all available ranks, from squad commander all the way up to the Secretariat. In-depth discussions on rank and promotion with respondents indicated that these proportions were not an anomaly of the sample, but rather represented a fairly standard pattern in guerrilla ranks where women were simply not promoted. Of course, this makes sense if women were trusted less and masculine traits were valued more. Despite proclamations of gender equality and insurgent feminism, women simply did not reach high FARC or ELN ranks in any substantive way.

This line of questioning about women commanders in the FARC made some loyalist respondents visibly uncomfortable, particularly men. These respondents seemed well aware that the lack of women in command positions clashed with their claims of gender equality. In a telling illustration of this justification, men and even several women loyalists claimed that most women did not *want* to be commanders, while pointing to new leadership positions that women had taken up since the peace process – such as the newly formed FARC gender commission and the female FARC senator who led it (Victoria Sandino, aka Judith Simanca Herrera). Some also argued that women were taking more of a leadership role now that the group had disarmed. This was directly observable in some cases: women were in charge of the FARC ecotourism project in one of the ETCRs, in charge of communication projects in another, and in one camp, FARC women leaders convened a large meeting on women's rights with women community members from the area. Several women in one ETCR pointed to the man leading their sewing collective as a sign of shifting gender norms; however, he was the only man in the sewing collective and was the manager – which hardly seemed like a shifting of gender norms to me. Notably, I observed several political meetings between commanders and community leaders that were entirely men. Also, all of the gatekeepers in positions of authority (e.g., people who gave me permission to enter the camps) were men, with only one exception – and in that case it was because nearly all the male commanders had left that particular camp. When it came to hospitality issues (e.g., meals, beds, access to bathrooms/showers, etc.), I was always referred to women.

However, some men pointed to women's involvement in battle – even if they were not commanders – as being a very important motivator for men. One man said, "there is no revolution in the world that can succeed without the participation of women,"[28] while another said that if he felt scared but saw a woman ready to fight, it helped: "Why? Because one looks at an armed female comrade, equipped to confront the same situation that you suddenly have to face at a certain moment, that is very beautiful. And that fills you with motivation, with reasons [to fight], right?" (Roberto, FARC, B25). However, those brave women were bound within the confines of the group's masculine dominance, so as not to threaten established hierarchies of power. For example, when I asked why there had never been any women in the Central Command or Secretariat of the FARC, most men again pointed to the woman FARC senator (Sandino) as evidence that women could rise to the top levels. This, however, further illustrates the dominance of the FARC's militarized masculinity: women were only able to rise to top levels once the group reinvented itself as a civilian organization. Even Sandino herself argued that in the early days of the organization, women FARC members marginalized themselves by getting pregnant, choosing motherhood over leadership and decision-making roles.[29] Although contraception quickly became mandatory in FARC ranks, there was little acknowledgment that men were also responsible for unwanted pregnancies; women bore the

---

[28] Author interview B21.
[29] Orth, "She Was Colombia's Most-Feared Female Revolutionary."

entire burden of forbidden pregnancies if their contraception failed. For example, one loyalist respondent told me how she had been sanctioned with extra chores for getting pregnant and seemed surprised when I asked if her partner had also been punished; unsurprisingly, he had not.[30]

In addition, the men's concept of equality was similar to many of the loyalist women in that it was fairly limited to equal duties. For example, many men pointed to the fact that men and women all had the same tasks (i.e., everyone had to march, cook, collect firewood, do laundry, etc.), and while they insisted that women had the same opportunities to advance in the ranks, the evidence suggests otherwise. Several men explained that there were many female guerrillas who simply did not have the "capacity" to be commanders. Consider this explanation from Pablo, who was visibly uncomfortable when I asked him why there had never been even one woman in the Secretariat:

Almost, almost, usually, in all irregular armies, where that [few women at the top] has happened, that phenomenon has been a problem of *machismo*. It has not been a problem of revenge, of discrimination, but because the guerrilla struggle has been very hard, very hard, because the first thing that has to be done, the first thing to bear is a large backpack here on the back, a large backpack with books, with food, with medicine, with clothes, with the tent for shelter, water, that is to say, with your entire house on your back ... And for that then you had to be in very good physical condition. Although that said, there were even women who were stronger to carry the backpacks than we were, to carry the rifle also, than many men, much stronger. But ... in our case undoubtedly there was not, there was not like a, like a generation of women who could last as long as we managed to endure, for many reasons, for many reasons. Sometimes their appearance, their physical conditions were deteriorating faster due to the same circumstances of war, of the hard way of life ... And then that also meant that they had to leave ... to leave them with the lightest jobs, in the lightest tasks of everyday life, such as communications, medicine, the relationship with the civilian population.[31]

Many women loyalists internalized these explanations. Two loyalists told me separately how, even if women were nominated for a promotion, they would often decline and recommend someone else (usually a man) that they thought was more competent. One woman blamed the women themselves for their inability to promote:

No, because what happened was that a woman focuses more, I mean, she finds her companion and she focuses more on staying by his side ... meanwhile, for one to get ahead there you have to be detached from someone. You have to be

---

[30] Author interview B51.
[31] Author interview B47.

focused on the fight that we have. So, the women they put, some of them, not because it's an obligation but ... to keep her husband's clothes clean, to have everything ready only for her companion. Meanwhile if one wants to be someone you have to spend your time studying. I mean, to demonstrate that you are capable and that you are not only ... that if I am going to be a boss and then they give me troops, but because of always waiting on my husband I am going to neglect the troops. So, yes, the bosses see that in a woman and then they hardly give them a chance to be part of the big picture. But there are some outstanding women in the fight. (Paula, FARC, B24)

Other FARC loyalists reiterated versions of this opinion – that women were not commanders because they did not want to be or because they were not capable. A few men said that women were simply afraid to be commanders or afraid of responsibility in general, and some (though certainly not all) women loyalists agreed with this. The dominant loyalist framing justified the overwhelming dominance of men at higher ranks. And this narrative allowed the women to be "insurgent feminists" in a way that did not disrupt the militarized masculinities of the group.

However, there were two notable deviations of this opinion from older loyalist women who had served forty-three and thirty years, respectively, in the FARC. These women were both highly critical of the FARC's claims of gender equality, while still being committed to equal rights and to the group overall. One of these women argued that the way that members of the Central Command were chosen was inherently discriminatory against women. She said that even though they all had to vote on promotions, the guerrillas came out of a very *machista* society and even the women were *machista*. That is, when voting, masculine-associated qualities like aggression, battle success, and dominance were valued over qualities considered feminine, like cooperation, caregiving, and empathy.[32] In addition, she said, if a woman had had romantic relationships with four or five men, that was the first concern raised, whereas promiscuity was not an issue for male candidates. This focus on women's promiscuity is undoubtedly linked to fears of women infiltrators sent into the group to cause "decay" and chaos. As someone dedicated to the goals of the organization, who had always wanted to be in the Secretariat, she found the overall gender discrimination very frustrating:

Because of this [discrimination] there was never one woman in the Central Command, and I criticized them harshly for this. Because how is it possible, that there was not one woman? And there were women capable of going to combat, women capable of completing many, many missions, including many male comrades that

[32] Author interview B51.

were in the Central Command who were not capable of completing them. Not everyone in the Central Command went to combat and there were women who went. We began from zero. But if only they didn't see [the men] in favor of a woman in the Central Command ... and what a shame for them because now here I am, I am still making this criticism. (Rosa, FARC, B51)

The other female FARC veteran was less directly critical of the group's promotion policies, but she felt that the requirements for women to move up in the ranks were unclear and inconsistent. She struggled to explain why she did not advance in the ranks despite wanting to, but after a long silence she shrugged and said she was just not capable.[33]

The presence of women was embraced by FARC men and women as one of the qualities that set them apart from the paramilitaries and the army. While men still retained dominance over the group, allowing women to be present and to have some leadership roles that were not military commands (usually in communications, logistics, and community relations) permitted the men to reinvent a form of militarized masculinity that tolerated women in traditionally men's roles and, in some areas at least, championed women's rights. But perhaps more importantly, the high numbers of women allowed them to claim moral superiority over the state military and paramilitary forces frequently associated with misogynist violence – while keeping their own male-dominated structure firmly intact.

However, despite these claims of superiority over other military organizations, women's bodies were still highly controlled by male commanders: women were forbidden from having relationships with civilian men, relationships were highly controlled, and many were forced to have abortions.[34] Several loyalist men in this study pointed out that without women in the group, FARC men would be forced to seek romantic and/or sexual relationships in the civilian population, which would threaten the group's overall security and control of information.[35] Women, then, helped to make FARC a completely self-contained unit that did not need to interact with the civilian population.[36] But when the FARC realized that couples had a tendency to desert together, it began to physically separate partners by sending them to different fronts or to mobile units[37] – a practice that several of my

---

[33] Author interview B61.
[34] Gutiérrez Sanín and Carranza Franco, "Organizing Women for Combat."
[35] Gutiérrez Sanín and Carranza Franco, "Organizing Women for Combat."
[36] Gutiérrez Sanín and Carranza Franco, "Organizing Women for Combat."
[37] Gutiérrez Sanín and Carranza Franco, "Organizing Women for Combat."

loyalist respondents discussed as making monogamous relationships impossible while simultaneously punishing women for promiscuity. Separation and divorce rates are very high in the ex-combatant population.[38] In my sample, the only respondents who had had long-term romantic relationships were either couples that had deserted together or couples where the man was a commander. The only woman in this sample who had been permitted to keep her baby while in the ranks was Pablo's wife. While she said this exception was because the baby had been born in 2012 when peace talks had already started, other women guerrillas in this sample had been pregnant between 2012 and 2016 and had certainly not been permitted to keep their babies.

While several women guerrilla deserters agreed with the loyalists that they had never seen nor experienced sexual violence in the guerrilla ranks, it became clearer in these conversations that what I would categorize as sexual violence, or at least sexual exploitation, was not necessarily seen that way by the guerrillas. Two loyalist women told me that any FARC women who were abused had low self-esteem or were masochists who wanted to be mistreated.[39] I was also warned not to misinterpret consensual relationships between older men and younger women as abuse: "So, be careful: if one is thirty years old, if one is thirty years old and you get a girl of fifteen years in the guerrilla, of sixteen years, to you they are going to say … they are going to say to you that this is rape. But for the guerrillas, that was the age of majority" (Adrián, FARC, B44). While the loyalist men often discussed how critical women were to the cause, some also directly mentioned the importance of having women for sexual partnership in the ranks:

Women are important everywhere and much more so in that type of army. Because they gave us talks about that, because they told us: "How would it be to have an army here, of pure men, in this jungle?" Right? Will one endure for twenty, thirty years, forty years? I do not believe so; I do not believe. Or one would transgress, because in our rules there were policies that one could not mess with a civilian. So, then what? If there were no women there, then the men would break the rules and then they were going to be sanctioned. But no, it was beautiful because a lot of women entered the organization, and they still played the normal role that any man played. (Manuel, FARC, B32)

I mulled this over later, when reading through the transcripts. *They gave us talks about that.* I wish now that I had asked him to elaborate. Did

---

[38] Author interview C01.
[39] Author interviews B34, B51.

that mean what I had instinctively inferred? That men initially resisted
the presence of women until commanders explained that this would
mean regular access to sex? I wondered if women recruits knew that this
is how their recruitment into the ranks was initially framed to the men.
This initial framing inevitably affected how women were treated in the
ranks – especially by more senior members who still remembered this
framing. And this was not mere conjecture on my part. In earlier interviews, several deserters made it clear that the guerrillas' ideals of gender
equality (and what counted as exploitation) were highly constrained:

> Yes, I have heard these stories [of abuse] on television and I still ... no, that is, I
> say no, because it's that I had ... or in other units, in other units possibly. But in
> the unit I was in, in my company, that never happened. Never there. For example,
> I don't deny this: I was with the commander for a better life, to win points, but
> voluntarily. That is, no one obliged me there, like "you have to sleep with me."
> No. It's what *you* want. That [was] simply to improve my life in the guerrilla.
> (Keli, ex-FARC, B11)

In fact, this claim that being romantically involved with a commander brought benefits was a source of much disagreement between
respondents – it was clearly damaging to the revolution frame as a
whole and specifically to insurgent feminism. Those who admitted they
received benefits for partnering with male commanders were illustrating a form of sexual exploitation and social stratification based on
rank and gender roles, even if they did not mean to. Most loyalists
staunchly denied such beneficial treatment was possible, as everyone
was equal and preferential treatment was against the rules – but a few
acknowledged that it did happen occasionally, and I witnessed it playing out in the ETCRs.

Other testimony illustrates that this preferential treatment was not
random or rare: several female deserters from both the FARC and ELN
explained (often with resentment) that the wives or partners of commanders consistently received more benefits than other women, further
illustrating the incentives to partner with higher-ranking men: "The
wives of the commanders are not normal guerrillas. They can do whatever they want, get good food, they don't have to carry bags – nothing."[40] As one FARC woman put it: "Everything is equal, but there is also
discrimination."[41] The reported benefits ranged from better brands of
shampoo to being exempt from battles, guard duty, intelligence, or other

---

[40] Author interview B03.
[41] Author interview B02.

dangerous tasks.[42] The female FARC deserter who admitted being with a commander to "earn points" explained:

To live well in the guerrillas, we women often "hook" a commander. Or we are, that is, we are looking for a commander, like that of a squadron, and that [helps] women live well. Because there, a woman's life with a commander is super. That is, it is the best there can be. It is the best life. So sometimes we women would arrive and "make eyes" at a commander, to be able to live well: have amenities, permissions. (Keli, ex-FARC, B11)

Lina's husband went so far as to claim that the only way a woman in the group could avoid being sexually pressured or prostituted out for intelligence purposes (which he claimed was common in the militias) was to attach herself to a commander, where she would be protected.[43] Lina agreed, saying that this exact scenario is what happened to her.[44] Thus, multiple respondents painted this picture of women competing for commanders' attention in order to improve their security and quality of life – implying that male commanders clearly had their choice of women. In fact, a few lower-ranking men mentioned with some resentment that the female guerrillas were only interested in commanders. Clearly, there were rewards for both men and women combatants when they stayed within the bounds of this patriarchal hierarchy.

Despite its feminist discourse and policies that seemingly empowered women, the FARC still reflected and reinforced problematic gender norms in Colombian society – especially militarized masculinities. Linking militarism to manliness and controlling FARC women, including control over their bodies and relationships, and rewarding them when they were romantically attached to high-ranking officers, were key factors in maintaining cohesion in the group's militaristic structure. But this male control over women threatens the credibility of the Marxist, socialist goals of the group and their purported revolutionary goals of gender equality. Other scholars have noted that various guerrilla groups in Colombia have "muted" gender in order to give primacy to class struggles, but in the FARC there was an obvious tension in the reinforcement of hegemonic masculinity on an operational level while ideologically emphasizing the women's fight for equality. The FARC did not mute gender; in fact, their frame emphasized gender equality as a primary ideological battleground, even when their actions indicated otherwise.

---

[42] Author interviews B04, B11, B21, B60, B63 B04, B11, B21, B60, B63.
[43] Author interview B31.
[44] Author interview B63.

Insurgent Feminism and the Guerrilla Glass Ceiling

If the guerrillas relied on militant masculinities for troop cohesion and clearly valued a patriarchal chain of command, then what is the role of the FARC's insurgent feminism in the revolution frame? How do women assert their insurgent feminist identity while negotiating militant masculinities? And does this clash of gendered narratives have any influence on combatants' decisions to leave the ranks and their transition to civilian life?

As noted earlier, it is not entirely clear when the term "insurgent feminism" was adopted. One FARC deserter who left in 2005 said that during his time in the group (mostly in the 1990s) no one used the term "feminism."[45] Indeed, the concept of insurgent feminism appears to be a relatively new invention corresponding with the creation of the *Mujer Fariana* website shortly after peace talks started (2012–13) – not even my FARC respondents were entirely sure of the term's origins. In any case, the FARC loyalist women carefully distanced themselves from what they called "true" feminism. This may, in part, be because women who deliberately take up violence as a form of resistance run directly counter to the anti-war, nonviolent stance of traditional feminism. But these women saw violent resistance as the only route to access power. For many of these women, "peaceful resistance [was] a death sentence."[46] The guerrillas' adoption of "insurgent" feminism was underpinned by the female fighters demanding to be seen as capable political actors:[47]

So that has been a lifelong struggle, to put us on equal terms with men, and we as guerrillas of the FARC never wanted to be part of true feminism, because what is called feminism is the struggle to do everything apart from men, that is, a fight against men, and that is not the case [for us]. It has to be a fight for equal rights, that both men are exploited, and we are exploited, men are discriminated against as we are. So that is why our struggle has always been for equal rights; that if he is able to go to combat, I am also able to go to combat, if he is able to carry a rifle, why would I not be able to carry a rifle? (Rosa, FARC, B51)

The FARC started recruiting significant numbers of women when the organization shifted from a *campesino* self-defense group into a "people's army" in 1982, and some scholars argue that the "feminization" of the FARC that occurred through mass recruitment of women was necessary to implement this people's army project.[48] Before this shift, the

45 Author interview B68.
46 Gowrinathan, *Radicalizing Her*, 58.
47 Gowrinathan, *Radicalizing Her*.
48 Gutiérrez Sanín and Carranza Franco, "Organizing Women for Combat."

guerrillas had largely been a male fighting force, and Manuel Marulanda (aka "Tirofijo"), the FARC's main leader at the time, had spoken against recruiting women, arguing that women did not have the capacity or resilience to participate in war.[49] This statement, of course, ignored that Colombian women were already participating in the war, whether they wanted to or not. Some researchers have argued that the FARC simply could not have reached its peak size with an all-male force, implying that the recruitment of women was primarily a numbers issue.[50] But organizational demands alone are unsatisfactory explanations when other significant nonstate armed groups in Colombia, such as the AUC, did not recruit large numbers of women combatants. Marulanda later said, in a reversal of his earlier views, that their expansion of recruitment demographics was a deliberate decision so that "many men, women, students and campesinos see in the FARC an organization that represents their class interests and that will contribute to finding solutions to their serious problems."[51] At this time the FARC also began to massively recruit minors.[52] The explanation that recruitment shifts were about representing multiple interests, whether true or not, helped to strengthen the revolution frame, especially as the leadership could not admit that the FARC had a serious cohesion problem.[53] What few of these analysts seem to be asking, though, is why the FARC was able to recruit so many women so easily and quickly.

More recently, the head of the FARC's national commission on women and gender explained "insurgent feminism" after the peace accord was finalized: "We realized that to construct a feminism that represented us, we had to form our own theory. Our feminism is called insurgent because we changed the type of fight, but we did not renounce the fight to transform society. We are continuing our insurrection but without weapons."[54] The choice to use "insurgent feminism" encapsulates the insurgent stance of wanting to change society (and/or overthrow the government) combined with the primacy of women's rights and gender equality. This maps

[49] Manuel Marulanda, *Resistencia de Un Pueblo En Armas*, Vol. 1 (Havana: Ocean Sur, 2015).

[50] Gutiérrez Sanín and Carranza Franco, "Organizing Women for Combat."

[51] C. Arango, *Farc Veinte Años de Marquetalia a La Uribe* (Bogotá: Aurora, 1984), 105.

[52] Gutiérrez Sanín and Carranza Franco, "Organizing Women for Combat."

[53] Gutiérrez Sanín, "The FARC's Militaristic Blueprint."

[54] Alejandra Hayon, "Feminismo Insurgente: Cómo Las Exguerrilleras de Las FARC Piensan Su Rol En La Sociedad," *Latinoamérica piensa*, 2019, https://latinoamericapiensa .com/feminismo-insurgente-como-las-exguerrilleras-de-las-farc-piensan-su-rol-en-la-sociedad/18166/.

directly onto concepts of martial politics discussed earlier, where war-like relations are enacted on anyone who threatens the established civil order (e.g., racialized, *campesino*, feminist, or LGBTQ+).[55] The FARC women were acutely aware of this; they knew after disarming that their fight was far from over. Indeed, the concept of "militarization" itself underestimates the level at which most societies live with war and especially how marginalized populations are consistently subject to war-like (i.e., martial) politics.[56]

The loyalist women spoke of gender equality at length, as did their male counterparts. Most women loyalist respondents maintained that not being commanders did not bother them, and that this was a choice – a common narrative that fits the overall frame. One woman, in an informal conversation over coffee, became visibly frustrated with my questions about the lack of female commanders and pointed out that their feminism did not mean that women had to be commanders or had to take on "masculine" roles – it meant that they could *choose* what they wanted to do. If women chose not to be commanders, she said, that was still feminism. The FARC's leadership structure had strategically contained insurgent feminism within established militarized masculinities, so as not to upend carefully constructed gender hierarchies. But what about the women who wanted to be commanders and could not advance?

Women's choices were clearly constrained, not only in terms of the "glass ceiling" of rank, but also with evidence of a clearly gendered division of labor. For example, the women in this sample most commonly said that they were nurses, *economas* (i.e., in charge of distribution and managing food and supplies), and radio operators, while men discussed roles as commanders, military trainers, political leaders, spies, explosives specialists, and so on. Several respondents said that women were always sent with units who did community relations, because they were less threatening and could talk to women in the community. By justifying these gendered roles as *choices* (which they may have been, in some cases), the women could maintain their insurgent feminism even within these confines. It was a highly effective form of dissonance reduction.

These conversations also illustrated that the presence of women in the FARC is very utilitarian: not only did women create a fully self-contained army where men did not need to look elsewhere for female companionship and sex, but the group placed women front and center as symbols of a humane, community-focused, rights-focused, "army of the people." The

[55] Howell, "Forget 'Militarization'."
[56] Howell, "Forget 'Militarization'."

large presence of women also helped to counter government accusations that FARC men were rapists and child molesters. Because, as loyalist and even some deserter respondents reiterated, why would any woman stay if that were true? But this gendered trope erases generations of women who have stayed with their abusers for myriad complex reasons.

And while the men realized that transitioning to civilian life would be particularly difficult for their female comrades, they often placed the responsibility for changing societal gender norms directly on the women themselves, just as the government did:

> I think that there will be woman comrades, who will go to get their companions, who hopefully do not eat their words and then end up being newly enslaved in *machismo*. And that can happen. Or to the others who go and get, for example, a civilian ... [who] is going to directly subject them to *machismo* because he does not know everything that they were taught. But I think that more than that, it is they [the women] who have to be valued. Support them as well, but they have to value themselves and along the way defend themselves and ... not allow themselves to submit to that place. And the women know, they know why they learned, yes? What they were taught. (Rafael, FARC, B46)

In turn, many women loyalists embraced this responsibility, explaining how, now that they had disarmed, it was their job to teach *campesino* women about their rights, and to protect these women from spousal and state abuse. I was invited to observe a meeting of women FARC leaders at one of the ETCRs, where they had gathered dozens of women from the surrounding communities and spoke at length about women's rights, the importance of women in politics, and how to organize and improve women's lives. It was an impressive and inspiring meeting. These ex-combatants saw themselves as responsible for changing gender norms in rural Colombia. They often expressed concern that most *campesino* women were uneducated in this regard, and that it was their responsibility as insurgent feminists to change the misogynist culture:

> If we do not organize, we won't accomplish [change]. Because it's like the saying goes: "One swallow alone does not bring rain, you need to have many."[57] This is our message. And with the women it's the same. The women submit to the husbands, to the beatings, and those you see most among the *campesinos*, because it is a culture that we have brought from many years ago. It's a culture, well, here I don't want to lay blame, whether it's the mother or the father, no. It's a culture that came from long ago. (Mafe, FARC, B29)

[57] The English equivalent is "one swallow does not make a summer" – meaning that the return of many swallows signals the beginning of warmer weather (or, in Colombia, of the rainy season), and metaphorically that you need more than one person to make real change.

Some of these women, however, did express concern about reincorpo-
rating into a traditional society that would not necessarily accept their
progressive values. A few acknowledged that they would need to tread
carefully when educating civilian women about their rights. Others worried that their awareness of – and insistence on – gender equality might
present new challenges:

Well, on the one hand, it's beneficial for us, the women, to have this liberty
because, well, one had to submit to the ... to the rules and to follow orders every
day. But on the other hand, now we, we've already emerged with this conviction
and that, that knowledge that the man has to learn to participate, as much in the
house with the children and with the housework. (Laidy, FARC, B34)

This view that gender equality was primarily about men sharing in housework and childcare was common among both men and women loyalists.
Equality was about equal duties; there was very little discussion about
equal *opportunities*.

Nonetheless, with this firm belief that their group was fighting for gender equality and women's rights, most of the FARC loyalists, and quite a
few of the deserters, said that media stories of sexual abuse in the FARC
were preposterous. Several women deserters from the FARC and the
ELN also embraced the language of gender equality and expressed dis-
appointment that gender equality was better inside the guerrilla groups
than in civilian life.

But women deserters who talked publicly about abusive experiences
were (and still are) a serious threat to the credibility of the overall revolution frame of both the ELN and the FARC – and especially to the
FARC's credibility as a political party. As a result, these women deserters are met with forceful dissonance reduction strategies. When I asked
the FARC women about the widespread media coverage about violence
against women within the ranks,[58] nearly all of them denied that this ever
happened, claiming that the women who told those stories had been paid
by the government to lie:

For me, it's that they paid [the women] to say that. That's one thing. And the
other, for me, is that those women are not ex-guerrillas ... I cannot go and say, or
have the luxury to say, that they obliged me [to have sex] in the guerrilla or that

[58] Recognizing the sensitivity of these issues and the fact that many ex-combatants suffer
from post-traumatic stress disorder, I did not ask any women directly if they had had an
abortion or if they had been sexually abused; rather, we spoke about their children and
their families, and these topics sometimes arose organically. I did, however, ask women
directly what they thought about the media stories describing them as victims of their
own group.

they mistreated me ... and I'm carrying a rifle, how am I not capable of defending myself? So, that is a great slander that they invented in order to discredit us as guerrillas. (Paula, FARC, B24)

This idea that women who told stories of sexual violence in the FARC were paid by the government was common, and sometimes repeated nearly verbatim, in interviews in the ETCRs. It was a forceful dissonance reduction strategy in the face of clear threats to the frame. But whether they truly believed this or were trained to give this answer, or a combination of both, was unclear. As with the accusations where women reporting abuse were discredited or even killed, several respondents said that women who told stories of abuse were government infiltrators, whose job was to enlist in the FARC and then desert in order to tell false stories of mistreatment. To further address the cognitive dissonance that abuse stories generated, some loyalists also claimed that *if* the women were not infiltrators, then they were weak-minded and had been brainwashed:

Well, this follows the falsehoods that the police have created with relation to [sexual abuse]. Because there was a number of women who demobilized and the first ones who helped them were the armed forces. So, well, they have always had their ways to create falsehoods, right? You know about the false positives and all those things. So, one time they give you a letter saying what you had to tell the media. And they put that in your head. And if [the women] would not say that, then [the army] would not give them the help that they supposedly provided, the guarantees. And there are people that are easily brainwashed. So, many, many, many women that left [the FARC] to say things was because, in some way, they were brainwashed. (Roberto, FARC, B25)

Another primary tension in the insurgent feminist identity was the topic of pregnancy. While many loyalist women discussed how careful they were about birth control because they did not want children while in the group, pregnancy was the leading reason that women deserters cited for leaving both the FARC and the ELN, which has also been identified by other researchers as a key motivator for women's desertion from the FARC.[59] In addition, several male deserters cited the pregnancy of a partner as their reason to leave the group, and as noted earlier, couples often deserted together. Several woman loyalists mentioned that they had had pregnancies while in the group, or that they had given birth or had abortions, but some made it very clear that they were not willing to discuss this. Others, however, showed visible sorrow when they discussed having

[59] Gutiérrez Sanín and Carranza Franco, "Organizing Women for Combat."

to give up their babies, even while maintaining that they did not regret any choices they had made.

Clearly, the insurgent feminist identity was difficult to reconcile with motherhood in a post-demobilization world. Several loyalist women in the ETCRs discussed how challenging it was to take advantage of the reintegration education and work training programs when they did not have adequate childcare, or simply because they wanted to spend time with their children instead – this was often mentioned in conjunction with the guilt they felt over not spending time with their first children. As one loyalist woman said: "I do not [study here], for example. Here they come to teach and all that stuff, and I have never gotten into studying stuff here because I said, 'no, I'm going to spend time with my daughter'."[60] Another woman said that she was simply too tired from taking care of her children to be involved in politics the way she used to be. With the introduction of pregnancy and children into the group, and the increased demands this placed on women (many of whom were single mothers), this partial return to traditional gender norms was clearly weakening the insurgent feminist identity for some women, resulting in reduced frame resonance around the ongoing "revolution."

CONCLUSION

Overall, the guerrilla men's support of insurgent feminists within the clear hierarchies of their militarized masculinities was both intriguing and problematic. The men used the presence of insurgent feminists as evidence that they were better than the misogynistic military and paramilitary organizations – they portrayed themselves as enlightened, modern men who saw women as equals and also pitched in with cooking, laundry, childcare, and other domestic tasks. Indeed, as other research has found in different Latin American guerrilla groups, the gender equality narrative opens space for men to exercise different forms of masculinity outside the confines of *machismo*.[61] On the other hand, they had seemingly convinced themselves that equal duties were sufficient, using explanations like "capacity" and women not wanting to lead as reasons why more women were not commanders. The insurgent feminism embraced by the FARC did not challenge male dominance within the group where it mattered, but it still allowed the men to claim a form of masculinity

---

[60] Gutiérrez Sanín and Carranza Franco, "Organizing Women for Combat."
[61] Dietrich, "Looking Beyond Violent Militarized Masculinities."

that was more progressive than their rivals – and it convinced women to embrace the revolution frame as their own.

Once recruits are deeply indoctrinated, they are more likely to avoid information that contradicts the group (and thus its frame) in order to decrease cognitive dissonance.[62] Similarly, while frame resonance is partly reliant on empirical credibility, social movement research suggests that this credibility is largely "in the eyes of the beholder."[63] Thus, while it was clear that many FARC loyalists knew that the militarized masculinities structuring their group clashed with the group's frame of an egalitarian revolution, this juxtaposition did not damage the credibility of the frame in their eyes. They were entrenched in the martial politics they claimed to be fighting against, but they had found ways to explain and justify it. The combined effect was that both men and women loyalists felt that the group supported their goals and identities, which strengthened their overall commitment to the group.

The FARC loyalist women, on the other hand, refused to be reduced to government narratives of sexual violence and fought to be recognized as willing insurgents. Their insurgent feminism was thus a critical aspect of carving out space for female political participation. They may not have had many leadership positions in the guerrilla military structure, but many of them saw space for leadership post-disarmament. It was thus critical that they refute stories of sexual abuse; not only did these stories not reflect many of their experiences, but it also reduced them to sexualized victims and erased them as political agents. As Gowrinathan articulates, the focus on the sexualized condition of women in the developing world "at best detracts from and at worst overshadows the larger forces of political subordination that perpetuate all forms of violence against women."[64]

Understanding the frame of revolution as reliant on the identity of "fighters for justice" – and recognizing the tensions within this frame – is critical to understanding how organizational framing affects individual decision-making and experiences. Not only is the fighter identity strong inside the guerrilla groups, but it also extends across respondent

---

[62] Leon Festinger, *A Theory of Cognitive Dissonance* (Evanston: Row, 1957); Leon Festinger, *Conflict, Decision, and Dissonance*, Vol. 3 (Stanford: Stanford University Press, 1964).

[63] Benford and Snow, "Framing Processes and Social Movements"; James M Jasper and Jane D Poulsen, "Recruiting Strangers and Friends: Moral Shocks and Social Networks in Animal Rights and Anti-Nuclear Protests," *Social Problems* 42, no. 4 (1995): 493–512, 496.

[64] Gowrinathan, *Radicalizing Her*, 83.

categories and often persists long after disarmament and demobilization. This can make it difficult for some ex-combatants to let go of their war mentality and truly reintegrate as civilians.

Those that have convinced themselves that this is a fight worth fighting can endure painful, traumatic, and contradictory experiences if they can organize or at least justify these experiences inside the revolution frame. This does not mean, however, that deserters are weak, as many loyalists paint them to be. On the contrary, to speak out against violence, and/or to leave an armed group to save your own life or that of someone else, takes a great deal of courage. While these people may have fled their groups, they too see themselves as fighters – as fighters for justice, for peace, for their families. What this predicts for reintegration is that those who still see themselves as fighters may be more resistant to traditional DDR programming and may struggle more with the transition to civilian life – especially if they are expected to go back to their former life of as poor, disregarded, disrespected *campesinos*. Or, for women, if they are expected to drop their fight for equality and return to patriarchal gender roles.

In addition, the tensions between insurgent feminism and militarized masculinities within the revolutionary frame appear to have at least two distinct outcomes in terms of desertion decisions: (1) those that can organize their insurgent feminism within the framework of dominant militarized masculinities (i.e., by reducing cognitive dissonance through narratives that women did not want to be commanders, and/or that all stories of sexual abuse or exploitation came from infiltrators) were much more likely to stay committed to the group – or, at least, to feel like it was the safest place for them to be; and (2) those who could not reconcile insurgent feminism – or any aspect of the revolution frame – with the abuses and exploitation they experienced or witnessed inside the group were much more likely to leave.

A more difficult question is why some recruits found it more difficult to reconcile these tensions. I offer a few potential explanations. First, militia women seem to have had more exposure to the guerrillas' criminal income-generating activities, which affected their perception of the group as a whole and weakened the empirical credibility of the revolution frame and the overall credibility of the frame-makers. Second, women who could not reconcile the revolution frame with the abuses they witnessed (i.e., irrefutable credibility issues) were more likely to reach out to sympathetic networks both inside and outside the group – which often helped them to escape.

In other words, not all ex-combatants cling to their fighter or insurgent feminist status; but finding a way to reconcile their new identities as civilians with their identity as revolutionaries (rather than obliterating the old identity) is critical. The loyalist FARC women were willing and active dissenters, but when they are raped by soldiers or reduced by government narratives to sexualized victims, they are forcefully reminded that they are women.[65] And the FARC women actively resisted this framing in multiple ways, including by adopting masculine traits. As one FARC woman said: "Of course … we said the fight was the revolution, that we were revolutionaries. We are still revolutionaries, but [now] we are also civilians."[66]

[65] Gowrinathan, *Radicalizing Her.*
[66] Author interview B30.

VII

Countering the Revolution Frame

We're not witnessing the birth of a new guerrilla army, but rather the criminal threats of a band of narco-terrorists who have the protection and support of Nicolás Maduro's dictatorship ... We won't fall into the trap of those pretending to shield themselves behind false ideological clothing to sustain their criminal structure.

Iván Duque, former president of Colombia[1]

Well, I can't feel happy with rapists of children here, obviously, coming to lecture about peace.

María Fernanda Cabal, Colombian senator,
Democratic Center Party[2]

COLOMBIAN MILITARY TIME

In one of my first meetings with military officers in Bogotá, the colonel in charge of the GAHD strode into the room, his booming voice instantly overriding any conversation taking place at the time. After a brief discussion about my research, he said the military would pick me up at six the next morning and escort me to the first safe house I would visit. They joked it was probably too early for me. I assured them it would be fine. He repeated: six. *Sharp*. I wrote it down and underlined it twice. This colonel was the one who had previously given me the Ministry of Defense newspaper celebrating

[1] Joshua Goodman, "Colombia FARC Negotiators Say They Are Taking up Arms Again," *Associated Press*, August 29, 2019, https://apnews.com/article/0c222740688f49e3bb1d4572fceb7524.

[2] Maria Cartaya, "FARC Members Join Colombia's Congress," *CNN*, July 21, 2018, www.cnn.com/2018/07/21/americas/farc-members-join-colombias-congress/index.html.

fifteen years of demobilization, and he said to me, yet again, that he wanted me to share Colombia's stories of demobilization success with the world. I smiled but said nothing. At the time, I had not yet seen the poverty and poor housing conditions in the FARC reintegration camps (ETCRs), and I had not yet heard first hand the angry feelings of betrayal that many ex-combatants had toward the government. But I knew that both recidivism and reintegration program dropout rates were high, and that the country was far from achieving "post-conflict" status. Colombia provided lessons to be learned, that was certain – but the success part was less clear.

The next day, a military escort showed up not at six but at four thirty in the morning. The doorman had rung up, waking my host, who knocked softly on my door: "Rachel, the Colombian military is here."

These are words that nobody wants to hear at four thirty in the morning. I have never been ready so fast in my life. Ten frantic minutes later, I was downstairs in the lobby, hair in a tight bun, hoping I had not forgotten anything. Despite what I thought was impressive haste, the officer looked annoyed.

"We said five," he said to me curtly.

For the record, "six" in Spanish is *seis* and "five" is *cinco* – it is virtually impossible to confuse the two. I gave my best half-awake, apologetic smile and stumbled across my words, explaining that the colonel had said six. He shook his head in firm disagreement and ushered me into the van.

As we drove off, I heard the officer arguing with the driver over what the colonel had said the day before. They had to leave at five, he insisted, to beat the *trancón*. It was a word I would hear often during my research, one that exemplified so many of Bogotá's problems: traffic jam. I was not about to point out that regardless of their debate, they had not arrived at five *or* six. They had gone out of their way to pick me up at home on the way to the safe house, and I had somehow made an error on the very first day. About twenty minutes later, we stopped to pick up the GAHD psychologist who had spoken to me the day before. We waited at the side of the road for what felt like a very long time. Finally, the officer called him, and I could hear his irate voice, insisting that they had told him they were picking me up at six and him at six *thirty*, and they would just have to wait because he was not ready. The psychologist soon got into the car, shaking his head and smiling, lamenting to me that he had not even had time to make coffee. I told him they had arrived at my apartment at four thirty. He burst out laughing, punching the officer playfully on the shoulder and chiding them for giving me such a shock.

I felt vindicated, but the officer never wavered: they had said five. They had *always* said five. That same psychologist later warned me that

whatever time the military said to me, always assume half an hour earlier. Colombian military time, he said, was the opposite of the rest of the
country – always early. But I long wondered if coming so much earlier
than agreed had been deliberate, to knock me off balance and show me
who was in charge. In any case, I learned a memorable lesson that day
about trying to contest the military's version of the truth.

COUNTERING A REVOLUTION

The Colombian government has long framed guerrillas as criminals and
terrorists to discredit any legitimate political grievances that the FARC,
ELN, and multiple other guerrilla groups may have had. This framing
was also integral to Uribe's claims that the country was not experiencing
a civil war. The state later discredited guerrilla grievances even further by
placing successor paramilitary groups into that same "narco-terrorist"
frame. Despite the previously discussed collusion between high-level politicians and paramilitaries, and the later discovery that the Colombian
military murdered thousands of civilian men and boys in extrajudicial
executions, the government has mostly held fast to this framing of the
guerrillas (and later, paramilitaries) as criminals and terrorists, even in
the immediate aftermath of the peace accord. While Santos did try to
move away from this framing during the peace negotiations, his successor, President Duque, wasted no time in returning to it.

This chapter discusses the state's counter-frame to the guerrillas' revolution frame. In the government frame, the guerrillas are labeled as
terrorists – and later, "narco-terrorists" – which helped the Colombian
government gain more US support to fight the guerrillas as part of both
the "war on drugs" and the "war on terror," while also delegitimiz-
ing the guerrilla cause. This longstanding framing of the guerrillas as
terrorists has informed disengagement and reintegration policy, where
ex-combatants who deserted their groups are treated as criminals and
encouraged to abandon former fighter identities to become peaceful,
law-abiding citizens. The chapter later turns to the stories of Tobias and
Hugo from the AUC, looking at how ex-paramilitaries challenge both
government and loyalist framings of the conflict, positioning themselves
as protectors of the people and wrongly maligned allies in the government's counterinsurgency. The chapter concludes with an analysis of
what this multipronged framing contest means for disengagement decisions and what it predicts about reintegration, arguing that prolonged
maligning of ex-combatants and dismissing the strong commitment of

many ex-combatants to a fighter identity – even when they have will-ingly disarmed – is impeding effective reintegration.

A Humanitarian Counterinsurgency?

The Colombian government's framing of the conflict goes far beyond fram-ing guerrillas and other opponents as terrorists. The government, especially under Uribe, invested considerable funds into framing its counterinsurgency as humane and benevolent, in a form of "brand warfare."[3] In fact, framing its opponents may have been the least important element of this strategy.

In 2006, the Ministry of Defense contracted the marketing firm MullenLowe SSP3 to brand and publicize its demobilization program, as part of an overall effort to present an image of a "humanitarian coun-terinsurgency."[4] This branding was still apparent in my meetings with military and police officials twelve years later, several of whom told me how unique it was that their soldiers were trained to reach out and assist their enemies, whereas most militaries were trained only to kill their opponents. I could not help but wonder what my *campesino* respon-dents would think of this narrative, given the thousands of extrajudicial executions perpetrated by Colombian soldiers – and sanctioned by upper levels of command – at the exact same time this campaign was promot-ing a supposedly humanitarian military. I wondered how they would feel about this government expenditure on marketing itself, when the govern-ment had all but abandoned their regions.

One of the most publicized campaigns designed by MullenLowe SSP3 for the government began in December 2010 – purportedly to encour-age guerrilla desertion by sharing messages of hope – and was dubbed "Operation Christmas."[5] The PR firm, whose clients include Red Bull and Unilever, worked with the military to select trees along known guerrilla pathways and cover them with thousands of Christmas lights, along with signs that said: "If Christmas can come to the jungle, you can come home. Demobilize. Anything is possible."[6] Another phase of

[3] Fattal, *Guerrilla Marketing*.
[4] Fattal, *Guerrilla Marketing*.
[5] Anna-Maria Hollain, "'Desmovilícese, En Navidad Todo Es Posible,'" *El Pais*, December 24, 2010, https://elpais.com/internacional/2010/12/24/actualidad/1293145201_850215 .html; Emily Steel, "The Ads Making Colombian Guerrillas Lonely This Christmas," *Financial Times* (December 2013), www.ft.com/content/3dc53856-4ddc-11e3-8fa5-00144feabdco.
[6] Steel, "The Ads Making Colombian Guerrillas Lonely This Christmas."

FIGURE 7 Operation Rivers of Light, campaign funded by the Military of Defense to encourage guerrillas to desert.
Photo credit: TONKA.

this marketing campaign was the release of plastic, floating globes lit with LED lights into rivers ("Operation Rivers of Light") known to pass through FARC territory (see Figure 7). These globes, released with much fanfare and carefully staged photographs, had notes inside encouraging guerrillas to demobilize. A third component ("You Are My Child") involved posters on trees that had pictures of guerrilla combatants as children (reportedly collected from their mothers) with the message: "Before being a guerrilla, you are my son/daughter."[7]

Throughout this multiyear campaign, the government positioned itself as a benevolent savior for the guerrillas, in an attempt to create the image of a humanitarian military and to counteract the very poor public opinion of the Colombian armed forces and its well-known links to paramilitary death squads and "social cleansing" operations.[8] At the same time, however, the military was also mounting a massive counter-offensive

[7] Author interview Co1; Steel, "The Ads Making Colombian Guerrillas Lonely This Christmas."
[8] Fattal, *Guerrilla Marketing*; Human Rights Watch, "The 'Sixth Division'."

operation that was decimating FARC ranks – slaughtering those same guerrillas they were purporting to rescue, in addition to killing and displacing thousands of civilians.[9] Indeed, the military killed four members of the FARC Secretariat between 2008 and 2011 – a massive blow to the group in terms of both military planning and overall morale.[10] Many FARC respondents told me of their heartbreak when these leaders were killed, events which made many of them even more resolute to resist the government. While the strategy behind Operation Christmas and related campaigns was to complement these military assaults by "attacking the heart" of the guerrillas,[11] the effectiveness of this campaign was questionable at best and the promises of reconnecting with loved ones often impossible to fulfill. In fact, in my interviews, many FARC and ELN members either had never heard of the GAHD demobilization program or had heard of it but assumed it was a trick to lure them out and kill them. Given the thousands of extrajudicial executions documented in the "false positives" scandal, this fear was not unfounded.

Arguably, this campaign's main focus was not the guerrillas themselves, and the marketing firm even emphasized that its main goal was to target the "national mood."[12] To underscore the true target audience of this campaign, advertisements ran in multiple forums, including YouTube, radio, and television. One video commercial even featured an American pop artist singing in English,[13] clearly intended for international audiences, as rank-and-file guerrillas in the mountains did not have access to television or internet (except when strictly controlled by commanders) and generally did not speak English. In fact, one of the commercial producers won an award for that 2010 Christmas commercial and reportedly traveled to London to receive it from a black-tie audience that was "moved to tears."[14] This award and the fanfare surrounding it could not have been more removed from the lived realities of guerrilla combatants.

The Colombian media portrayed Operation Christmas as highly effective, stating that 2,435 guerrillas deserted the FARC in 2010 alone due to this strategy.[15] The strategy was to bring Christmas to the jungle, with the campaign promising guerrillas that they could spend Christmas

---

[9] Rojas Bolaños and Benavides, *Ejecuciones Extrajudiciales En Colombia, 2002–2010.*
[10] Fattal, *Guerrilla Marketing.*
[11] Fattal, *Guerrilla Marketing*, 83.
[12] Fattal, *Guerrilla Marketing*, 87.
[13] Fattal, *Guerrilla Marketing.*
[14] Fattal, *Guerrilla Marketing.*
[15] Hollain, "'Desmovilícese, En Navidad Todo Es Posible'."

at home.[16] But in many of my conversations with FARC loyalists, their favorite memories were the Christmas parties that they would have every year with the group when multiple fronts came together – in fact, for many of these respondents, their first Christmas after demobilization had been profoundly disappointing. They told me how, in 2017, many ex-combatants went home to their families for Christmas and reported interpersonal conflict with family members – especially with children left behind – and painful silences, while others stayed in the ETCRs and felt lonely and abandoned by their former comrades, nostalgic for the parties they used to have. The plan to "bring Christmas to the jungle" did not consider that many FARC combatants already enjoyed Christmas in the jungle and had little desire to go home. While many guerrillas certainly had violent and traumatizing experiences in the ranks, others like Junior and Mari felt that the ELN and FARC were their families – taking them in and protecting them when no one else would.

The promise that combatants could demobilize and safely go home again was also wholly false: the government has thus far been unable or unwilling to adequately protect deserters. Nearly all of the deserters that I interviewed said that after they demobilized, they realized that they could never go home, because that is the first place their former group would look for them. As noted earlier, thousands of ex-combatants have been murdered or have returned to criminal activity.[17] Recidivism rates are likely even higher when considering those who desert without registering in government demobilization, and those who demobilize but do not enter reintegration programs. One study found that ex-combatants who remain in areas where there are active armed groups are 158 percent more likely to return to armed activity.[18] Since guerrilla and paramilitary members primarily come from these areas, sending them back home not only puts them and their families in danger – it is also a recipe for recidivism. Most deserters that I spoke to had not, in fact, reunited with their parents and did not plan to, either because it was unsafe or because they had never told their parents that they had joined the guerrillas and did not want them to know. Even many FARC loyalists that I spoke to had not reunited with their families after demobilization – often because their parents had disowned them for being guerrillas or,

---

[16] Fattal, *Guerrilla Marketing*.
[17] ARN, "La Reintegración En Colombia – Cifras"; FIP, "Retorno a La Legalidad o Reincidencia de Excombatientes En Colombia."
[18] Kaplan and Nussio, "Explaining Recidivism of Ex-combatants in Colombia."

in several cases, because they had never told their families that they had joined the FARC.

Also, ARN statistics show that overall desertion, as measured by yearly entrants into the reintegration program, was already declining before Operation Christmas was launched at the end of 2010 and continued to decline over the next several years. In 2010, 2,227 total combatants from various groups demobilized and entered the ARN program, in 2011 there were 1,368, and in 2012 there were 961.[19] Based on the government's own statistics, significantly fewer combatants demobilized after the launch of Operation Christmas, not more. This decline is also likely related to the start of the peace negotiations in 2012 – the cost-benefit calculation of desertion may have shifted with the possibility of a collective demobilization on the horizon. In fact, many former guerrillas that I spoke to – especially those from the ELN – had no idea that a government demobilization program even existed until after they fled the ranks. Granted, demobilization cannot be fully equated with reintegration, as the programs are run separately by different agencies; however, if combatants demobilize and then do not enter the reintegration program, it certainly puts the veracity of their demobilization – and of the government's promises – into question.

The marketing firm's creative team was proud of the fact that they spoke to deserters to design this campaign,[20] but this approach did not seem to consider that (1) deserters often do not tell the government, or people associated with the government, the truth about their experiences and have strong incentives to lie; and (2) loyalists generally have a very different perspective than deserters. For example, many deserters told me that they had lied to the government about their reason for deserting, their rank, and/or about the amount of time that had lapsed between deserting and reporting to the military. Sometimes months or even years had passed between desertion and registering for demobilization benefits, but to avoid prosecution, combatants generally told the military that they had "just" deserted and only hours had passed. When I first met Andrés, he told me a highly edited story about his guerrilla experiences and why he deserted. After we spent more time together and the real story unfolded, it became clear that Andrés had largely enjoyed his militant experience and was somewhat nostalgic for the life he once had. When I later asked

[19] ARN, "La Reintegración En Colombia – Cifras."
[20] Fattal, *Guerrilla Marketing.*

him why he did not tell me the truth about his rank in our first interview, he said: "You showed up with the colonel, in a military van! I had to tell you the same story that I gave to the military." Despite my documentation and reassurances that I was an independent researcher and that his interview transcript or my notes would not be shared with anyone, Andrés did not initially trust me because I showed up with a military escort – which made perfect sense. Why, then, would a PR firm hired by the military ever assume that deserters were telling them the truth?

Some of these campaigns were also remarkably tone deaf to the FARC women's claims of insurgent feminism – or, more likely, deliberately ran against the group's purported feminist ideology. A clear illustration of this disconnect was a campaign directed specifically at women's demobilization in 2012, where a poster depicted shades of lipstick named "freedom," "love," and "happiness" alongside phrases encouraging female guerrillas to demobilize so they could "feel like a woman again" and "become the mother [they've] always dreamed of being."[21] But this type of narrative rang hollow with most female guerrillas that I interviewed (including deserters), as many were already mothers before demobilization because they either had babies while in the group – and often left them with another family to raise – or left babies behind with family members in order to join the group.[22] These women had chosen the cause over motherhood. Once demobilized, some women had difficult and conflicting emotions about their choices to abandon children or whether to reunite with them. In contrast, several women in this study stated that they never wanted to be mothers. Many others (mothers or not) also strongly identified as "insurgent feminists" and did not feel that their choice to be guerrillas was opposed to their womanhood – on the contrary, as stated in Chapter VI, they felt that the presence of women was crucial to the FARC's goals.[23] In addition, women who were militia members in either group may have lived with their children for the entire time that they were part of the group. Thus, stereotypical messaging imploring female guerrillas to "feel like a woman again" could, in fact, have had the opposite effect as intended because it did not consider the varying gender identities among women guerrillas.

In fact, this messaging clashed so strongly with the FARC's insurgent feminism that it seems likely this campaign was not truly intended

---

[21] Alpert, "To Be a Guerrilla, and a Woman, in Colombia."
[22] Author interviews B48, B50, B51, B53, B56.
[23] Author interviews B07, B29, B40, B45, B50, B51, B53, B56, B61, B62.

for guerrilla women at all. First of all, at the most rudimentary level, women insurgents already had lipstick in the jungle; my female respondents asserted that they had everything they needed in this regard if they wanted it, including makeup, nail polish, and hair accessories. In fact, several women in the GAHD safe houses complained to me about the poor quality of shampoo, soap, and other hygiene products provided by the program, compared to what they used in the ranks. It was an unexpected but surprisingly common complaint. But more importantly, most women guerrillas that I spoke to did not see their militancy as running counter to their womanhood. This strategic messaging to "become a woman again" thus seemed intended for the Colombian public – not the guerrillas themselves – to reinforce the government's framing of its "humanitarian counterinsurgency." That is, it was another portrayal of the guerrilla women as victims of their own group and of a destructive "gender ideology," with the government framed as heroic in helping these "deviant" women return to socially acceptable gender norms. Indeed, all of the MullenLowe SSP3 campaigns portray the government as benevolent toward guerrilla combatants and the guerrillas as victims trapped in guerrilla life who would go home, if only they could. But for many guerrillas, this was simply not true. A core strategy of this campaign was to urge guerrillas to leave the revolution behind and to consider family life, childrearing, and traditional gender roles instead.[24] The lipstick campaign in particular was so off the mark in terms of women guerrillas' lived experiences that it seemed blatantly focused on winning public support for a costly internal conflict, rather than a genuine attempt to get women guerrillas to disarm.

But none of that mattered for the government's frame of a humanitarian counterinsurgency, because arguably this frame was never really about the guerrillas at all. Even civilians in conflict-affected areas did not buy into this scheme, as many were wary of demobilization promises as a political strategy that rewarded violent actors and did nothing to address victims' experiences.[25] The government's counter-frame to the guerrillas' revolution frame was multifaceted but transparent in its aims, portraying its counterinsurgency efforts as benevolent and humanitarian while painting its enemies as drug traffickers, terrorists, and rapists. This frame, of course, while slick, expensive, and sophisticated, had a major credibility issue: it denied the existence of an armed conflict, took no

---

[24] Fattal, *Guerrilla Marketing*.
[25] Fattal, *Guerrilla Marketing*.

responsibility for the state's own role in perpetuating armed violence, and did nothing to address the poverty, insecurity, and inequality at the core of many guerrillas' reasons for taking up arms. Instead, it focused largely on humanizing the army while demonizing the rebels – a highly salient and credible frame in some circles, but certainly not in others.

The Power of Labeling: From Narco-Guerrillas to Narco-Terrorists

Former President Álvaro Uribe once made a now infamous comment that Colombia did not have a civil war but had only "narco-terrorists."[26] Not only did this statement allow him to dismiss calls for unwanted international intervention in terms of peacebuilding or peacekeeping, but it also allowed for increased assistance from the United States in terms of massive counter-narcotics and counterterrorism military funding.[27] The state's longstanding refusal to acknowledge that the guerrillas had *any* legitimate grievances ironically contributed to the environment in many Colombian departments of government absence, lawlessness, and insecurity in which the guerrillas could grow – especially the FARC.[28] This refusal to accept the existence of a civil war paradoxically exacerbated the armed conflict – and then spilled over into prematurely declaring "peace" before there truly was any.

A key component in the government framing of the guerrillas and its denial of armed conflict came when the term "narco-guerrillas" was coined in the 1980s by a US ambassador to Colombia.[29] This term was quickly adopted by the Colombian government, as it conveniently implied that the FARC, ELN, and other guerrilla groups did not have ideological goals and were merely drug-dealing criminals.[30] It also subsumed all the guerrilla groups under the same label, despite clear differences in their strategies, organizational structures and goals, and combat success. While there is certainly substantial evidence of guerrilla involvement in the drug trade to fund their operations, the political implications of this label were significant: the terminology deliberately conflated Colombia's internal armed conflict with international organized crime, allowing the

---

[26] Semana, "Sí Hay Guerra, Señor Presidente."
[27] Castrillón Riascos and Guerra Molina, "A Deep Influence."
[28] Ramírez, *Between the Guerrillas and the State.*
[29] Carlos Gustavo Arrieta et al., *Narcotráfico En Colombia: Dimensiones Políticas, Economicas, Jurídicas e Internacionales* (Bogota: Ediciones Uniandes y Tercer Mundo Editores, 1990).
[30] Arrieta et al., *Narcotráfico En Colombia.*

state to receive military counterinsurgency assistance from the USA in the name of the "war on drugs."[31] In addition, in heavy coca-producing departments, such as Putumayo, the state deliberately framed coca cultivation not as a social problem and/or a lack of government presence or alternative employment, but as a narco-guerrilla problem.[32] This framing was still evident with President Duque's stated intention to bring back coca fumigation in 2019, and the near total impunity for the execution of social leaders who continue to be killed by paramilitaries or drug traffickers for suspected ties to the guerrillas.[33] That is, if the government frame maintains that the guerrillas (and by extension, their supporters) are all criminals and that there is no war, politicians can comfortably justify ignoring calls for accountability if the violence is (theoretically) confined to criminals killing each other.

Notably, Uribe's linguistic shift from narco-guerrillas to narco-*terrorists* was an important labeling mechanism for this frame. Replacing the word "guerrillas" with "terrorists" further erased the implications of war and any potential link to a legitimate rebel cause. The word "terrorist" heightens public outrage – and tolerance for a heightened security response – connected with any use of the word "terrorism." In fact, conflating everyone "undesirable" into this criminal/terrorist framing is a convenient way to justify securitized policy choices (e.g., militarized security, disarmament, policing, repression) over community development, sustainable reintegration, and psycho-social assistance. And for many guerrilla ex-combatants in this study, the state effort to frame them as narco-terrorists only reinforced their suspicions that the government was fighting a dirty war against them, solidifying their convictions that they were fighting the "good fight" against a corrupt and lying state.

While the state could no longer publicly call the FARC "narco-terrorists" once the peace agreement was signed, the arrest and detention of Jesús Santrich (aka Seuxis Paucias Hernández) – one of the key negotiators of the peace accord – for drug trafficking *after* the peace agreement was signed was arguably another method to do just that. When the JEP ruled that there was insufficient evidence to extradite Santrich to the USA, and that he should be freed and subsequently judged in Colombia,

[31] Arrieta et al., *Narcotráfico En Colombia.*
[32] Ramírez, *Between the Guerrillas and the State.*
[33] El Tiempo, "'Se Necesita La Fumigación Aérea Contra La Coca': Duque a La Corte," *El Tiempo*, April 3, 2019, www.eltiempo.com/politica/gobierno/duque-reitera-que-se-necesita-la-fumigacion-aerea-contra-la-coca-345554; Felbab-Brown, "Death by Bad Implementation?"

Colombia's attorney-general stepped down in protest, maintaining that there was "conclusive, unequivocal" evidence of Santrich's guilt.[34] Upon release, Santrich disappeared and Colombia's Supreme Court issued a new arrest warrant for his capture.[35] Shortly thereafter, Santrich and two other key leaders of the FARC publicly announced that they were returning to arms and retaining the original FARC acronym – creating a significant intragroup framing dispute within the former ranks.

This return to arms by two of the lead negotiators of the peace accord (Santrich and Iván Márquez) and their alleged partnership with the ELN – who had, earlier that same year, bombed a police academy in Bogotá and killed twenty-one people – was vindication for anyone who claimed that the FARC was always, and would always be, a group of narco-terrorists. In fact, the peace agreement, the arguably premature Nobel Peace Prize, and the government's quick declaration of "post-conflict" processes reinforced this framing that those who returned to arms were nothing but criminals. After all, there was never a war, but even if there had been a war, it was now over. Thus, anyone still fighting was certainly not a legitimate combatant. Indeed, Colombia's ambassador to the United States almost immediately said that the combatants who returned to arms were "just a miniscule element – more the ones who are involved in drug trafficking, who've got their hands in the cookie jar. And that's why they decided to jump the ship. And they will be treated as such, as criminals."[36]

In what seemed like a potential agreement with this framing, Rodrigo Londoño (aka Timochenko), the current leader of the FARC political party, announced in May 2020 that he was considering changing the name of the political party.[37] The retention of the FARC acronym was highly controversial at the time of the peace accord, and the return to arms of key FARC commanders – who are now clashing with various other groups of FARC dissidents – made political leaders of the FARC reconsider their attachment to the name. In 2021, party members voted to change the name to "Comunes" ("Commons" in English). This tension

34 BBC News, "Colombia Peace Process: Ex-rebel Santrich to Be Freed," *BBC News*, May 16, 2019, www.bbc.com/news/world-latin-america-48294827.
35 BBC News, "Arrest Warrant Issued for Farc Ex-Rebel Jesús Santrich," *BBC News*, July 10, 2019, www.bbc.com/news/world-latin-america-48932019.
36 Anna Gawel, "Envoy Says Government Is Sticking by FARC Peace Deal – and Venezuelan Refugees," *Washington Diplomat*, October 31, 2019, https://washdiplomat.com/index.php?option=com_content&view=article&id=20737&Itemid=413.
37 Semana, "¿No Más Farc? Timochenko Plantea Cambio de Nombre Para Su Partido," *Semana*, May 2020, www.semana.com/nacion/articulo/timochenko-plantea-cambiar-nombre-de-partido-farc/673747/.

is an illustrative example of intragroup frame disputes, where the leaders do not agree on key aspects of the frame, splitting their followers and creating a rift in what was once a highly durable and cohesive narrative. But Lina's husband, Johan, explained to me that this internal dispute had always existed. According to Johan, the three commanders who returned to arms (Santrich, Márquez, and Velázquez) had always been the top commanders primarily involved in drug trafficking, while Londoño and the others remaining in their political seats had been the ideologues.[38] While this assertion struck me as odd, given that Santrich and Márquez were lead negotiators of the peace accord and widely considered to be key FARC ideologues, it was clear by 2019 that the group's leadership had come to a crossroads. This split also placed ex-combatants who genuinely wanted to continue with the peace process in a precarious position. The state immediately dismissed the commanders' accusations that the government had not fulfilled the peace deal and mounted a full military offensive to pursue the three commanders and their followers.[39] Márquez – who had been head of the FARC delegation in the peace negotiations – publicly declared that Duque himself was the problem, accusing Duque of having an illegitimate mandate to eliminate legitimate social movements.[40] Reports also suggest that the numbers of FARC dissidents may have doubled between 2019 and 2020.[41] Now, all ex-combatants from the FARC risk being suspect as potential criminals, as the state cannot be sure which ex-combatants are loyal to the rearmed commanders and which ones are committed to peaceful reintegration. As this conflict has been marked by repeated infiltration and propaganda wars on all sides, any suspicions of misrepresented intentions are hard to confirm or deny. Thus, on the government's side, the narco-terrorist frame remains intact, the military offensive can continue, and counter-narcotics and/or counterterrorism funding will keep coming.

The government is well aware that ex-combatant retention of a fighter identity can be problematic for the transition to the subservient civilians that the state would prefer. In the reintegration process, there is

[38] Author interview B31.
[39] BBC News Mundo, "FARC: Abaten a 9 Guerrilleros En La Primera Ofensiva Militar Contra Iván Márquez y Su Grupo En Colombia," *BBC News*, August 30, 2019.
[40] Semana, "'Duque Debe Irse': La Polémica Reaparición de Iván Márquez," *Semana*, September 2020, www.semana.com/nacion/articulo/tras-meses-de-silencio-reaparecio-el-guerrillero-ivan-marquez/202044/.
[41] Jorge Cantillo, "Preocupación En Colombia: Las Disidencias de Las FARC Duplicaron Sus Miembros Armados En El Último Año," *InfoBae*, 2020, www.infobae.com/america/colombia/2020/06/07/preocupacion-en-colombia-las-disidencias-de-las-farc-duplicaron-sus-miembros-armados-en-el-ultimo-ano/.

psychological counseling that – while wildly inconsistent across the demobilized population – is supposed to help ex-combatants shed this combatant identity and "reinvent themselves" as civilians.[42] However, as noted earlier, this focus on reinvention emphasizes ex-combatants' criminal background and does not take into account valuable skills that they may have learned in the armed group. It also once again falsely reinforces the binary of war and peace. Despite clearly needing mental health support, several respondents also told me that only ex-combatants with "obvious" psychological issues were referred to psychologists. And for some ex-combatants, the program can be somewhat infantilizing, as it places, for example, eighteen-year-olds who may have only spent a few months in an armed group in the same classes and programs as forty-five-year-olds, who may have been high-ranking commanders with a wealth of knowledge and skills. As one deserter said:

> At the ARN they are always in the position that they are ones who know. I think these guys [in the ARN] end up getting very comfortable because they earn good money, and so it's worth almost nothing ... whether they learn [from us] or don't learn. Simply, "you are a brute, a *campesino*, and you will learn what I teach you." (Caleb, ex-FARC, B68)

One loyalist respondent told me that she resented the government narrative that they were all illiterate, uneducated *campesinos* when she had undergone medical training in Cuba and had taken communications courses, along with having other key skills for which she had no formal documentation. Other respondents told me about being trained in explosives and intelligence by Israeli ex-special forces officers or about being sent undercover to Bogotá to attend university. Still others quoted Clausewitz and various other scholars and philosophers. In other words, the range of skills and education that respondents received in the guerrilla ranks was incredibly diverse. Yet, while some individuals working in the DDR programs admitted to me that a one-size-fits-all approach was sometimes problematic, others insisted that equal treatment across the board – regardless of age, rank, education, gender, or time in the group (with the exception of minors) – was the only way to deliver this programming.

Due to the increased costs and logistical complexities of individualized programming, this may indeed be true. However, these deliberate choices that homogenize the ex-combatant population end up reinforcing both the criminal framing and social stigma of ex-combatants as crude, barbaric, uneducated, and dangerous. Recently, the government shifted to

---

[42] Author interviews C01, C02.

using the term "residual groups" over "dissidents," choosing the Spanish acronym "GOAR" for "Residual Organized Armed Groups."[43] This is yet another reframing that attempts to erase the failures of the peace process by eliminating the links of these resurgent groups to the demobilized FARC, similar to the relabeling of paramilitary successor groups.

Not Paramilitaries, Only BACRIMs

The government framing and reframing of the paramilitaries – and their successor groups – has been more complex than its framing of the guerrillas but just as rife with corruption and controversy. First, despite concerted efforts to obscure or ignore paramilitary-government connections, it is well established that the Colombian military and the national police assisted and funded the paramilitaries and worked with them on counterinsurgency missions and, in some cases, drug-trafficking operations.[44] The "para-politics" scandal made it clear that high-ranking politicians were also involved in AUC operations, and the "false positives" scandal revealed that paramilitaries had assisted the Colombian military in the systematic misrepresentation of civilian murders as guerrilla combat deaths.[45] Thus, even though the AUC was a pro-state, politician-supported force, upon demobilization and amid widespread condemnation and evidence of mass atrocities, the government needed to shift public perception of its connection to this reviled group. This, too, is connected to the persistent denial of the existence of an armed conflict.

Because the AUC demobilization agreement did not require the dismantling of criminal networks or surrendering of assets, there were few obstacles to the resurgence of many paramilitary successor groups – and the Colombian government was widely condemned for this oversight.[46]

---

[43] Sebastian Pacheco Jiménez, "¿Cómo Los Llamamos: Paramilitares, Disidencias, Grupos Residuales, Terroristas?," *El Espectador*, November 24, 2019, www.elespectador.com/colombia2020/opinion/como-los-llamamos-paramilitares-disidencias-grupos-residuales-terroristas-columna-892676/.

[44] Human Rights Watch, "The Ties That Bind"; Human Rights Watch, "Smoke and Mirrors"; Human Rights Watch, "Paramilitaries' Heirs"; Sontag, "Colombia's Paramilitaries and the U.S. War on Drugs."

[45] Roa, "Guía Práctica Para Entender El Escándalo de La 'Para-Política'"; Rojas Bolaños and Benavides, *Ejecuciones Extrajudiciales En Colombia, 2002–2010*; Semana, "Las Cuentas de Los Falsos Positivos."

[46] Alfredo Campos García, "New Drivers of Displacement in Colombia," *Forced Migration Review*, no. 56 (2017): 34; Porch and Rasmussen, "Demobilization of Paramilitaries in Colombia"; Sontag, "Colombia's Paramilitaries and the U.S. War on Drugs."

The government thus made a concerted effort to avoid all blame for these failures and to distance itself from these criminal groups – and any connection they had to the former AUC – by calling them "emerging criminal bands" (BACRIMs).[47] The easiest way to do this, given that the Colombian public already had a poor opinion of AUC combatants, was to place the paramilitaries into the same narco-terrorist frame as the guerrillas. This was a deliberate and strategic labeling choice, as the term BACRIM placed the paramilitaries and guerrillas under the same criminal label, making them all legitimate military targets. This labeling also obscured former government ties to paramilitary violence and attempted to absolve the government of responsibility for the failed demobilization process. Given the international condemnation and related investigations of the AUC, along with the government's demobilization agreement with the group – which included top leaders serving prison sentences (albeit short ones) – the government was largely successful in placing the paramilitaries into the "narco-terrorist" frame.

But many of the paramilitary respondents that I spoke to contested this framing, noting how important they had been to the government's fight against the guerrillas and discussing how the government had betrayed them, pointing to the guerrillas as the "real bad guys" but also blaming the state for the protracted war.

POETRY, RUM, AND THE "REAL" SELF-DEFENSE FORCES

I first met Tobias after a disorienting walk through a poor urban neighborhood in central Colombia. Although he would never admit it, I think my local research assistant got a bit lost that day. After asking many different people for directions – and likely alerting the entire neighborhood to the rare appearance of a tall, blonde, blue-eyed foreigner – we found the right address and entered the nicest apartment inhabited by an ex-combatant that I had seen thus far, ushered in by Tobias' lovely and beaming wife. Tobias' wife was very chatty and immediately wanted to know everything about Canada. I showed her pictures of me and my children ice skating, as those had been particularly popular photos thus far, and she served us pudding and coffee

[47] Ávila, "Bacrim, Neoparamilitares y Grupos Post-Desmovilización Paramilitar"; El Espectador, "Las Bacrim Crecen En Todo El País," *El Espectador*, February 19, 2012, www.elespectador.com/noticias/judicial/bacrim-crecen-todo-el-pais-articulo-327595; García, "New Drivers of Displacement in Colombia."

while Tobias watched me carefully. He was a large man – one of the few Colombian men I had met that was taller than me – with sharp and wary eyes. He had dark skin but, like many other respondents, did not identify with any specific race or ethnicity. Unlike his wife, Tobias was not quick to smile and was not initially interested in learning about Canada (though later he would ask me lots of questions regarding how to send his son to university there). He had a fluffy little dog, which he observed carefully as she approached me. Perhaps the dog was his early warning system, a type of instant character assessment, because as soon as she snuggled up to me on the sofa and wagged her tail, Tobias chuckled and visibly relaxed. In fact, the devout attention lavished on me by that little dog became a joke every time I came over. In fieldwork, it is hard to know who (or what) will open doors for you, but with Tobias and his community of AUC ex-combatants, it was undoubtedly that little dog.

Tobias first told me that he had been part of the ACCU. As noted in Chapter II, this group was formed in 1994, preceding the AUC by about three years, and was collapsed into the AUC structure in 1997. Minutes later, however, Tobias said that he had been in the AUC ranks for less than a year – from September 10, 2004 to September 7, 2005. Besides being remarkably specific (many ex-combatants that I interviewed often could not recall the year they joined, much less the exact day), the math did not make sense. How could he have joined a group in 2004 that no longer existed at that point? I also knew from other participants that Tobias had been a commander of relatively high rank – something he also denied but that was apparent in the way other respondents deferred to him and the way he exerted authority in the community. But this comment was early in our interview, and I let it slide. Sometimes what people lie about is much more revealing than the truths they tell.

In any case, my conversation with Tobias was about to get much more interesting. During our interview, he told me about his childhood in a *campesino* family, how he had completed his mandatory military service, and how his life had been very "normal." So many ex-combatants said this to me that it became an interesting trust-building dance: they would almost all tell me at first that their lives were "normal." And then, over time, they would disclose childhoods full of forced displacement, poverty, violence, and/or abuse. Was this what "normal" meant to them? Tobias, for example, told me that he had enrolled in the ACCU because he had "nothing to live for":

When my mother died, there was nothing else, because what else [was there] to hold on to, yes? And anyway, from my military life ... I saw the things that other [armed] groups were doing and at some point I thought that being there [in the paramilitaries], I was going to help counteract those other things. I thought I was going to do something right.

This was a narrative that many ex-AUC combatants shared: they thought they were doing something "right." Without leaving me space to ask another question, Tobias launched into a long soliloquy about how he did not think he did anything wrong, and how in his unit they were under a very thoughtful and strategic commander. And then, again before I could ask another question, he said something fascinating:

Many people are unaware ... but both guerrillas, paramilitaries, common criminals, drug traffickers, armies, policemen, and everyone else is like football teams, [they] have fans ... No matter how bad a person is, there is always someone who admires or feels appreciation, or others have other feelings [but] do not externalize them ... But they all have followers.

I sat with this for a bit when I read the transcript later: "Everyone else is like football teams." This comment was only six minutes into my interview with Tobias, and in my prior interactions with him I had not said a single word about the paramilitaries' reputation for *gratuitous* violence. Yet he had wasted no time trying to convince me that he was not a bad guy, even though I had never implied any such thing. In fact, I had asked only four questions at that point – what group he had been in and for how long, if he self-identified as any specific ethnicity, and what his life was like before joining the group. His comment implied a somewhat apolitical and equivalent nature of all the groups that he named. He was suggesting that they were all generally the same – the army, paramilitaries, guerrillas, criminals – they just played on different "teams." Indeed, he said that when he met ex-guerrillas as part of the reintegration program, he realized that they were all very similar, they just had grown up in different places and thus were recruited into different groups. This was startlingly close to what Johan had told me, about how all the armed groups were basically just different departments of the same company.

Yet, Tobias went on to list some key differences. He told me that there was more discipline in the paramilitary ranks, compared to his military experience. He also told me that they were never "paid" to fight in the AUC but rather that they received "bonuses" – then he laughed, as if he had just told a joke (the AUC explicitly recruited people by promising monthly salaries, but when those salaries did not materialize, they often told recruits that they would receive "bonuses" of double or triple the monthly rate when money was available). He said that while he did not want to disparage the army or the police, the AUC had better discipline and treated people (both civilians and troops) better, and that in the ranks they were like a family. This stood in direct contrast with what many other paramilitary respondents told me – that intragroup violence was common, that middle commanders were frequently killed and replaced by the Central Command, and that rank-and-file combatants were regularly abused by superiors. Indeed, when I asked Tobias if he had had friends in the group, his story of being a "family" changed slightly:

Within the group many people know each other, within the group many people know each other, [but] what we cannot say is who is a friend or who is not a friend, yes? You cannot say that. We interacted with each other, and while we were together, we always seemed like a family. But we were all unpredictable, for a single reason: because there [in the ranks] men are unpredictable and women are unpredictable, because we are under a command, yes? So, we do not know at what moment the command will give us what order.

Thus, while on the surface they may have all *acted* like a family, there was very little real trust between AUC combatants, as they never knew what the commanders would order them to do. Many other paramilitary respondents told me different versions of the same story – that they had learned not to trust anyone, that they had lost all their friends, that commanders had tricked them, and that no one told anybody the truth. Indeed, Tobias soon became visibly sad while telling me a story of a comrade who died, and then he said:

In conflict there cannot be many emotional attachments, because that can cost one wealth, too. Truly, like this and truly in conflicts, in wars man adapts to that. In war, man adapts to the fact that you fell and, and you turned around and you forgot [long pause] ... part of human sensibility is lost, yes? ... there begins to be a process to meet those feelings again, to meet again with that feeling and with that human part that you forgot for a moment and left you, but you did not know where.

On a different day, after passing around shots of cheap rum, Tobias read to me a four-page, single-spaced, typed poem that he had written about the war and everything that he had lost – both tangibly and spiritually. When he finished reading, no one in the room knew what to do. Then his wife started applauding loudly so we all followed suit. It was strange, awkward, and utterly unforgettable. My research assistant later joked that if we had not clapped loudly enough for the poem, Tobias might have killed us. Macabre jokes aside, the entire experience was surreal. What do you say to a warlord who is clearly traumatized by his war experiences and wants your sympathy, but takes no responsibility for the trauma he inflicted on others?

While I do not have permission to share that poem here, he did give a copy to me, among other poems. He was clearly a conflicted man – one day full of proud *machismo* and the next, deeply lost, poetic, and emotional about events that had happened over fifteen years previously. He was even sometimes whimsical, showing me the many wooden children's toys that he had made and dreaming of a better future for his son.

Tobias' framing of his former group and of the war, like many of his ex-AUC colleagues, was much less clear than that of the guerrilla loyalists – he seemed unable to stick to the narrative that they were the unquestionable good guys, even though he clearly wanted to. He was proud of his involvement and yet he had lost himself; he had been in the army and fought the guerrillas and yet the government had abandoned him. Whenever he realized he had contradicted himself, he always went back to the key message – they were fighting the guerrillas because they did not agree with them, to uphold the status quo:

The clear objective, the objective of the group … was to counteract the other groups that, that were outside our philosophies, yes? That did not share our ideas, yes? And that did things differently. So, as an ex-military man … I had my own philosophy, that was always to counteract the belligerent groups, yes? That was my philosophy, yes? So given my own philosophy, it strongly fit my philosophy and behavior. That's why I had no difficulties within the organization.

He later told me directly that so many crimes had happened in Colombia that no one was ever going to admit to everything they had done.

Hugo, on the other hand, was much clearer in his framing. First of all, he never once tried to tell me that his life was normal. In the first thirty seconds of our interview, he told me that when he was a young child, his father had been killed in a park and he had seen it happen. This tragedy precipitated a life on the streets, addicted to drugs and surrounded by criminals, not really knowing how to find a way out. "It is not only knowing *what* to do," he told me, explaining the overwhelming challenges of escaping street life. "It is not only doing but knowing *how* to do it."

When I asked him how long he had been in the AUC, he did not answer directly but instead went on a long soliloquy about how he was proud of the work he had done in the group, and how he was proud to have fought for peace. This was common with AUC respondents – they often answered an entirely different question than the one I had asked. In fact, like Mafe, Hugo spoke with me for two and half hours and I barely asked him a single question. What he did say, however, was that he was seventeen and living on the streets, addicted to drugs, when he was recruited. He told me that the AUC recruited "that type of kid" to be assassins – presumably because these youth were desperate and would do almost anything to access more drugs. But he admitted right away that most people were wary of young men like him, and that this first job with the AUC put him on a path where armed violence became his only option. From a very young age, he felt that there was no one to set him or anyone around him right:

And there were no human rights, no NGOs, no parents, no priests, no churches, or presidents who told you not to kill that soldier who is unarmed, no. There was no one there who had that, that sensitivity of "I throw down the weapons, brother, because I don't I want to kill, I've changed." No. No one wanted to do that, no one wanted to stick his neck out to say: "no more." But to shoot? Everyone sticks his neck out, yes?[48]

In the end, most paramilitary respondents had a similar take on their own part in the war, refusing to accept blame for Colombia's violence and pointing to the state (or the state's absence) as the main driver of the conflict. They said they stepped in because the state had no ability to stop the violence, so they had to take up arms and do it themselves. While they claimed to be the "real" self-defense forces, they also admitted to very serious crimes, often with a shrug of the shoulders – these were just things that had to be done in the course of war. Their counter-frame was not anchored on whether they were good or benevolent or victimized people – though they used these narratives sometimes, it was not consistent. Instead, this counter-frame seemed to hinge primarily on one thing: that they had stepped in to fight the guerrillas when the government could not. And to them, whether they used drug profits to do that did not matter. For example, one ex-AUC combatant said: "The state, directly, indirectly, obligates one to kill, like, to provoke wars, do you understand? ... It is the state that in these moments is provoking wars."[49] Thus, while many of the paramilitaries in this sample used the government's "narco-terrorist" label when discussing their fight against the guerrillas, they rejected this framing for themselves specifically due to the "terrorist" element – especially as many admitted to having been involved (and in some cases, still involved) with drug trafficking. They believed they had done something important, and their lack of status

---

[48] Author interview B86.
[49] Author interview B73.

FIGURE 8 Interview with paramilitary respondent by the river, western Colombia. Photo credit: Alejandro Carlosama (research assistant).

or respect in post-demobilization life was weighing on many of them over a decade later (see Figure 8). Indeed, previous research in Colombia shows that a sense of having lost status or power is highly correlated with recidivism in male paramilitaries specifically.[50] But even this ongoing criminal activity they blamed on the government, who in their view was too incompetent to notice their illegal operations and did not care to help them find legitimate work. As one ex-paramilitary respondent said, in reference to the illegal activity happening in the community we were in at the time: "The government still doesn't know what's going on."[51]

CONCLUSION

In the individual disengagement and reintegration efforts, the government tries to capitalize on deserters' sense of being on the wrong path or wanting to be a different person. The attempts via programming to

---

[50] Kaplan and Nussio, "Explaining Recidivism of Ex-combatants in Colombia."
[51] Author interview B97.

"break" ex-combatants of their identity as fighters and/or revolutionaries is deliberate and overt – all ex-combatants in the individual reintegration programs receive the same benefits regardless of group, rank, age, or gender, and in the safe houses, ex-combatants of various groups are all housed together in order to resocialize them as civilians and not combatants.[52] But the terrorist/criminal label is sticky and makes it difficult for ex-combatants to obtain work, which in turn keeps them dependent on government benefits and contributes to their overall stigmatization in society.

Indeed, the tensions between the revolution frame and the government's narco-terrorist frame still persist years after the peace agreement. It was very important for loyalist respondents to reiterate to me that they were not what the media had portrayed them to be, that they were not terrorists, that people should not be afraid of them, and that they were normal people who had feelings and dreams. They were preoccupied with combating false stories about them – especially stories about terrorism or sexual violence. In contrast, when the FARC delegation took up their seats in Congress and the House of Representatives, Senator María Fernanda Cabal of the Democratic Center Party called them child rapists, as quoted at the beginning of this chapter.[53] While some ex-combatants perhaps deserved this stigma, *all* of them felt it.

The government's individualized approach to DDR has also clashed with the FARC insistence on collective reintegration, which deliberately retains the revolution frame and a sense of being fighters against the state. In the collective reintegration efforts with the FARC, the state has had much less success in erasing the fighter-revolutionary identity, and some of its efforts to do so have backfired. The FARC has insisted that their "reincorporation" (to distinguish it from "reintegration" of deserters and paramilitaries) be done differently than prior DDR efforts. And the related renaming of the Colombian Reintegration Agency to the Agency for Reincorporation and Normalization is an interesting outcome of two different framing contests: first, the contest between the revolution frame and the government's narco-terrorist frame, which the FARC loyalists appear to have partially won in this case of renaming the ACR; and second, the framing contest between loyalists and deserters, which is further discussed in Chapter VIII.

---

[52] Author interviews Co1, Co2, Co3, C14, C15.
[53] Cartaya, "FARC Members Join Colombia's Congress."

VIII

Deserters versus Loyalists

I tell you, I never thought of [deserting] because since I left my house – my
dad was a soldier too, and he said: "The war is for men, and if you leave
for the war, *never* do I want to see that you demobilized or deserted."
Manuel, FARC, B32 (joined at age eleven)

My research assistant and I were sitting in a small building under a hot
plastic roof when I was first explicitly introduced to the name-slinging
discursive contest between FARC deserters and loyalists. We were in
the first ETCR camp that I had received permission to visit, after a
long trip via taxis, a ferry, and dirt bike "moto-taxis" through territory bordering Ecuador that was actively contested by various armed
groups. On that long and stressful journey, and especially when my
research assistant roared out of sight and I clung to my dirt bike seat
as we rumbled through paths in the Amazon jungle, I admittedly questioned what on earth I was doing. This anxiety was not alleviated as I
sat at a table with four male FARC commanders and one woman who
hovered in the background. I had spread all my paperwork in front of
them: consent forms, interview questions, my letter of permission from
the Colombian government, my business card, passport – everything
I could think of to prove my identity and credibility. They perused
the documents carefully, and then they asked what *exactly* this study
was about.

This is where I took a critical misstep.

"I'm interested in studying different groups of demobilized combatants," I said in my clearest, most carefully rehearsed Spanish. It was, after
all, a phrase I had already repeated dozens of times. "For example, I am

comparing those who demobilized collectively compared to those who demobilized individually."

"We are *not* demobilized!" one of the former commanders immediately roared. I shared a worried glance with my research assistant. The commander continued: "We are *reincorporated*. We have *not* demobilized. We negotiated a deal. We did not surrender."

Like President Duque's framing of massacres as "collective homicides," and the paramilitaries calling themselves "self-defense forces," language and labels were critical here. And I had used the wrong words. But this was early in my interviews, and no one up to that point had advised me that the FARC loyalists did not call themselves *desmovilizados* ("demobilized"). If demobilization signified handing in weapons and disbanding as an armed insurgency, then they had, in fact, demobilized – had they not? But I quickly learned that this is not what that word meant to them.

While the main framing competitions in the previous chapters were carefully constructed strategies between insurgent group leaders and the government, this last contest that I focus on takes place between different categories of former combatants, specifically deserters and loyalists. While this contest is much less structured and the frames emerged more organically – particularly as the deserters do not have a clear leadership constructing a strategic frame for them, nor a clearly defined audience – it was still having a powerful influence on reintegration experiences. As previous chapters have made clear, guerrilla deserters and their stories are critical to the credibility of the government's counter-frames and the delegitimization of guerrilla claims, making it imperative for loyalist guerrillas to challenge and discredit those deserters. In this last contest, which overlaps with all the others, language and labeling are key, as these components both create stigma and help ex-combatants fight against it. While ex-AUC respondents eschewed their paramilitary label and instead called themselves *autodefensas* ("self-defense forces") and *desmovilizados* ("demobilized"), the deserters generally called themselves *desmovilizados* but rarely *desertores* ("deserters"). And while I was warned by reintegration and military officials not to use the term *desertor* in my interviews because of the negative stigma,[1] it was not until I visited the first ETCR (see Figure 9) that I learned the FARC loyalists were

---

[1] While I avoided using the term "deserter" in the interviews, for analytical clarity I chose to use the term "deserter" throughout this book to refer to any person who has left their armed group without permission – with modifications or explanations added where necessary.

FIGURE 9 Moto-taxi in the Amazon, southern Colombia.
Photo credit: Alejandro Carlosama (research assistant).

adamantly against the use of the word *desmovilizado* to refer to themselves. I found it interesting that no one in the government had warned me about that.

In fact, the FARC loyalists were so insistent that they not be subsumed in reintegration programming and language designed for, in their view, "traitors and criminals" (i.e., deserters and paramilitaries) that they negotiated with the government to call their program something else entirely: "reincorporation."[2]

This distinction was critically important for the loyalists, and the differences were readily apparent. For example, some reintegration staff expressed the opinion that combatants in the reincorporation stream were much more "difficult" (i.e., less cooperative with authorities) than those who had deserted their groups.[3] But this result seems fairly logical: combatants that took great risks to flee their groups and faced significant military pressure to cooperate clearly have greater motives to

---

[2] Information obtained during a background meeting with ARN officials in October 2018, Bogotá.
[3] Author interviews C01, C03.

reintegrate through the government model compared to combatants who were ordered to disarm and – as previous chapters have shown – often still see the government as the enemy.

This chapter and Chapter IX examine the identity construction and related stigmatization within the framing contest of *desmovilizados* versus *reincorporados*. While this contest is primarily among groups of ex-combatants themselves, the government also plays a role not only by encouraging desertion but also by contesting both sides, grouping all ex-combatants under the same criminal label, and discrediting any frame constructed by combatants and/or ex-combatants.

THE DESERTER FRAME

The FARC loyalist framing of deserters is constructed on three primary factors: labels, othering, and gender. As deserters have been key detractors to the credibility of the FARC's and ELN's revolutionary frames – especially in the government's strategic use of their stories – it has been important for the FARC leadership to discredit deserters. FARC leaders thus forcefully reduce cognitive dissonance among their troops caused by deserters' stories by silencing stories of abuse, producing counter-information, and in some cases killing those who threaten the frame's credibility. The loyalist narrative thus requires a carefully constructed frame that deserters are cowards, liars, and informants – in other words, a narrative which insists that deserters were never "true guerrillas" from the start. This framing allows group adherents to accept the elimination of such traitors without guilt and without invalidating the frame of the noble revolutionary. But it also clearly contradicts substantial evidence of internal threats that push combatants out of their groups and highlights the effects of intragroup disputes about reality.

Desmovilizados versus Reincorporados

In my first round of fieldwork in the military safe houses, the government staff, and the guerrilla ex-combatants themselves (FARC and ELN), referred to all demobilized combatants as *desmovilizados*, so I quickly adopted the same terminology in these interactions. While they distinguished between the two ARN programmatic streams (i.e., reintegration and reincorporation), they still frequently referred to *desmovilizados* in both streams. Later, in my first AUC interview, that respondent also referred to himself as a *desmovilizado*. This consistent use of the word "demobilized" across different populations was why I did not realize my mistake in that first FARC camp until I was reprimanded. One loyalist later explained the problem to me, emphasizing that to him, the demobilized were never true guerrillas:

The "demobilized" ... the "demobilized" is what? That which is a harmful, a pig, a degenerate. That, yes, is an infiltrator sent by the enemy to do damage. The infiltrator does what? He kills guerrillas in fights; he damages the pots or breaks them so that water passes through; he kills people in their beds. That is the infiltrator, that comes from there to "sap" the civilians, those who support our economy, to get them put in jail. They go with their faces covered and walk around hurting the poor peasants who have soothed our hunger. So that's why we are fed up here; they made us kill guerrillas, [in the] bombings. That's why I don't agree with them being here [in the ETCR]. Because no, because if we were at war, they were not with us, and as we are not at war right now, that is, this is over according to the government. Yet they [the demobilized] are here and they take benefits as though they are guerrillas, and I don't know what. Lies; for me they are nothing, for me they are civilians. And that [word] pains me because I am *not* demobilized. (Adrián, FARC, B44)

Similarly, Pablo explained why the term "demobilized" could not be applied to loyalists:

Demobilization was a program that the government drew up when some groups of paramilitaries broke up. Fine. Then, there they classified it as "demobilization." So, we said no, we did not, we are not demobilized, because demobilizing is to disintegrate. But we did not disintegrate, we left there, from a stage of struggle, and we settle here to another stage of struggle, in other conditions that are already in political conditions, [but] not with weapons in hand. (Pablo, FARC, B47)

While this distinction had not been signaled to me by any of the military or government contacts that I had interacted with up to that point – clearly, the military did not make this distinction between types of ex-combatants – this labeling was very important to the FARC loyalists. It seems unlikely, however, that government officials were completely unaware of this difference in terminology, given their claim that many FARC members from the ETCRs had been switching to the individual program, in addition to the enormous emphasis that all ex-combatants in this study put on these labels. Why, then, had no one told me? When I made this small change in word choice, it made an immediate and noticeable difference in establishing trust with loyalist respondents.

Indeed, FARC ex-combatants in the ETCRs went to great lengths to discuss how, for them, the term *desmovilizados* also referred to the AUC paramilitaries that demobilized in an agreement with (in their view) the same government who had paid them to fight in the first place. These committed combatants saw the paramilitary demobilization as a farce and argued that the term was problematic because many "demobilized" AUC combatants never actually demobilized. The FARC ex-combatants in the ETCRs also applied this label of *desmovilizados* to deserters who turned themselves in to the military, but (to confuse matters further) *not* to deserters who simply left the group and went back home.[4] FARC loyalists were quite clear that combatants who left the group but did not demobilize via the military and otherwise did not harm the organization (i.e., by sharing intelligence, stealing supplies, or handing in weapons) were not considered *desmovilizados*. These were simply combatants who left the group – some were even referred to as having "retired," though it was unclear under what circumstances this was permitted. In fact, despite the insistence of government staff that I should not use the term "deserter" in the safe houses, one loyalist respondent explained that, in his mind, deserters were just people who left, and they were very different from *desmovilizados*:

Infiltrators. Look, for me, all the demobilized, for me, are infiltrators. They are our enemy. For this reason, I am not in agreement with deserters nor the infiltrators. Nor the demobilized. Yet the deserter, the deserter is very different than the demobilized because there are deserters that left the organization, they got tired, they didn't want to know anything about the fight, they were frustrated with it. They left and they left to work. (Adrián, FARC, B44)

This framing came directly from the top: Pablo said the group was careful to distinguish between people who left to work and people who surrendered to the army. People who did not surrender to the army, he said, would receive "a small sanction" and then some "education."[5] Another respondent agreed that this distinction was important, but he specifically used female pronouns (e.g., la/ella) in this passage to emphasize female deserters (even though I had not asked about women in particular):

Of course, there was a terrible difference [between deserters and demobilized]. First because one [woman], she might have gone because she wasn't capable to adapt to the fight. And the other [woman], that she left because "I'm not capable either" but she also left for her weak ideology in service to the enemy. So, that person, well yes, her degree of crime is worse. (Rafael, FARC, B46)

---

[4] This is similar to some of the disengagement literature that distinguishes between desertion, understood as simply leaving the group, and defection, which is going to "the other side."

[5] Author interview B47.

In addition, according to Pablo, there was a process of appeal where one could ask to leave the group, or to "retire," and these people were not considered deserters; in fact, several loyalists told me that there was an established process in which members could request to leave. For example, another loyalist said, about a female recruit who had wanted to leave:

> It was a lot for her, and she wanted to go. Once, she told me, "look, I want to go." And so, I respected her, and I said, "love, here no one is going to force you. If you want to go, then go." That is what I told her, "if you want to go, then go." And yes, this girl, she left. (*Ricardo*, FARC, B26)

These portrayals of the group as benevolent toward dissatisfied recruits are critical to the overall deserter frame, as they emphasize that members simply had to ask permission to leave – making desertion not only traitorous but also unnecessary. Deserters refuted this, saying that requests to leave were never granted.

Of course, a lackadaisical attitude toward desertion also does not match official FARC statutes, where the group demands lifetime membership and the punishment for desertion is death. But this contradiction was framed as benevolence by loyalists. And yet, despite this insistence on benevolence or indifference toward deserters, several respondents said that some former members who had officially demobilized (i.e., entered the government program), had tried to come back and it was very clear that this type of deserter was not welcome. I was told multiple stories of former deserters who asked to be admitted into the ETCRs, and the loyalists scoffed at this, clearly incredulous that any deserter would dare try to return to the group. As one respondent said:

> Well ... it depends on how they leave, right? ... If a person leaves without anything and doesn't take anything from the organization and is not going to present himself to the army to betray us, and he is just working normally, [then] nothing happened ... . If [a deserter] had taken something from the organization, then I would feel rage, because those are things that we had obtained in the collective, for everyone. Because if a person took a rifle, and that rifle had just been recovered in combat, and two or three people had died to recover that rifle, and then for another to come and take it away? So, you get angry with a person like that. (Paula, B24)

In this frame, deserters who surrendered to the army were traitors, *sapos* (informants), cowards, and liars. As one FARC loyalist said, "that is why we never took part in 'demobilization,' because demobilization is giving up the principles we were fighting for."[6]

---

[6] Author interview B25.

Othering: Infiltrators and Benevolent Justice

The deserter frame – and its reinforcement of the revolutionary frame – is stronger if loyalists can portray deserters as weak, lazy people who could not handle the revolution, or as evil people who betrayed the cause, while portraying themselves as tough and dedicated but also benevolent. Note the mirroring here with the government's campaign of a "humanitarian military": both sides were still trying to show themselves as benevolent despite waging a brutal war. While labeling is certainly a component of the "othering" process, the maligning of deserters went far beyond labels. A small number of loyalist FARC members admitted that the group had made some mistakes, but most said that they had no regrets and that their time in the group – and all the violence, death, loss, and displacement involved – had been worth it. Indeed, this commitment to the group and to the maintenance of the frame was so strong among some loyalist respondents that they blamed any mistakes the groups made, and any mistreatment by commanders, on the work of infiltrators: "Yes, the group made mistakes … mistakes where they killed people who they shouldn't have killed, but like I was saying, all that was done by infiltrators in order to harm [the group]" (Magdalena, FARC, B61). Indeed, denigrating the character of deserters by calling them infiltrators, while portraying themselves as forgiving and loyal individuals, was a recurring pattern in the loyalist interviews. These respondents would say that people left because they were not committed to the cause, because they were weak-minded, because they were afraid of sanctions, because they misinterpreted sanctions as mistreatment, and because they were military or paramilitary infiltrators who had joined only to sow discontent in the ranks and then desert. Multiple respondents told me that any commanders who mistreated their subordinates were clearly military informants who had joined the group to demoralize members and inspire desertion. And even though several deserters expressed ongoing commitment to the guerrilla cause and said they had only left because of threats to their lives, loyalist respondents said that those who deserted were never truly committed to the cause:

The people who enter, how do I say, were not, they came in, but with another thought, not saying "I'm going to achieve something." They thought that entering FARC was to shoot and no more. That is, there is a conception and a political ideology in that struggle that those lives and those dead were for something, that is, it was not because they wanted to die. But then they went and committed outrages against the communities or against, well things like that … there was not a real political conception in these people, and because of that they decided not to accept that or those laws, they decided to get out of the movement. (Mafe, FARC, B29)

While no respondents articulated exactly where this framing of deserters came from, it was clear that these narratives had been repeated in multiple forums, such as the FARC "cultural hour," military meetings, and in informal conversations. Other respondents told me about the significant fear and inconvenience caused by desertion:

Oh, we were upset because we would have to move. For example, say you are here, quiet, in the downpour, in your bunk, and you are relaxed, and then you hear the news: "A guy left." Rain or not, you pack and "ciao." Because you don't know what the person was thinking, right? If he deserted and decided to be caught or whatever, the army comes here tomorrow and finds us, and in many cases that happened. So, it was always a pain, change the plans, things we were going to do, if a person deserted. So, yes ... it interrupted all the tranquility and all the plans, so it was a very, very complicated component [of guerrilla life]. (Reina, FARC, B40)

However, even though the loyalists had significant resentment and specific labels for deserters that had entered the government demobilization programs, they were also careful to make distinctions between deserters who had simply left to go home and had not, in their words, "caused damage to the organization." This definitional clarification was a clear pattern throughout all three ETCRs. In fact, in my sample, there were several deserters who had left the group for various reasons – for two of the women, it was pregnancy – but had been welcomed back into the ETCRs with their children as members entitled to benefits. While there were incidences of both men and women being welcomed back, most of the stories that loyalists told me about their benevolence were related to women – even though many of the stories of betrayals and infiltration were also related to women.

And while many of the loyalists said that desertion was inconvenient, they maintained that it was perfectly normal in any armed group. For example, one respondent said:

For me it was hard because, not because they had left, but because of the knowledge that a person who left had. For another man who arrived, it was going to be much harder. For example, a man who already had four of five years, he had a lot of experience. Do you understand? That's what was hard, that I had to teach people all over again ... that's what was hard. But was it hard because they left? No, normal. (Carlos, FARC, B22)

Another FARC loyalist echoed this sentiment that desertion was not a significant issue: "The war is like getting on an urban bus: in one block someone gets on, and in another block someone else gets off, and the bus keeps going, full of people."[7] As with blaming violence against women on infiltrators and liars, this response about the bus was repeated so often in different variations that it seemed like a rehearsed script. And despite the high level of fear among most deserters in this study about being hunted down (and deserters were indeed found and executed by both the FARC and ELN), when I asked some loyalists about this, they said that sometimes they looked for deserters but often they did not. For example, one loyalist said:

Yes, I heard, I heard that yes, that people said: "Well, I'm going home," or: "I'm going to hurt the organization." Well, that's it, they're gone, it's normal. But if they did not hurt us then why would we hurt that person? Because it was not our idea to kill people. (David, FARC, B43)

Indeed, despite the vehement rejection of deserters by some loyalist FARC respondents, and deserters' legitimate fear of being killed, many loyalists maintained that desertion was fairly normal, that it happened in all armies, and that it was not really a big deal. Of course, this relaxed view about desertion directly contradicts the strategic and concerted efforts that the FARC leadership made to prevent desertion – such as bringing in more women recruits to create a self-contained fighting unit, forcefully reducing cognitive dissonance by silencing stories of abuse, and physically separating couples because they tended to desert together. And while this sanguine response to desertion also stood in contrast to some respondents' articulated rage at deserters, it was hard to determine if the relaxed attitude was practiced or genuine. There was an obvious tension in the loyalist interviews in that they wanted to portray themselves as both victims and as noble, benevolent fighters for justice, and they knew that telling the truth about what often happened to deserters was a threat to the credibility of these frames.

However, stories about sometimes applying the rules and sometimes not did not match these same respondents' emphasis on how important it was to *always* follow the rules. In fact, they would go to great lengths to explain to me that deserters often left because they could not handle the rules. And nearly all the loyalist FARC respondents skirted around the fact that the punishment for desertion was death – listed clearly in the organization's own rule book – even when I asked about this directly. In fact, that question made many respondents visibly uncomfortable, and they insisted that this was a discretionary policy and not always applied. But this discrepancy between emphasizing the importance of rules and

---

[7] Author interview B23.

then insisting that some rules were inconsistently applied was problematic to the empirical credibility of their framing.

There were, however, a few exceptions: some loyalists openly discussed the punishment for desertion when explaining why they had never heard anyone talk about leaving. For example:

No, in our organization the regulation said that whoever left, the punishment was *ugly*. So, then a person never talked about it. It's like, a person would arrive when it was already getting dark and then it was his turn to guard. He would stand guard, then discard [his weapon] and leave. But I never heard anything [about it], like, "listen, soon, I am going to leave." (Jhon, FARC, B35)

In addition, a few loyalist respondents also gave slightly different variations on deserters, admitting that they had friends who had left, and saying that they felt sad, felt a vacancy when someone left: "One felt the emptiness left by that person. At least if a person left who was a hard worker, then one missed her, felt the emptiness there."[8] Similarly, another loyalist said:

A person left, one left, the emptiness remained. The emptiness remained because, because we were already accustomed to these people; the sharing, the way of being, the treatment, yes? And, well, we all worked together with that force to move forward, everyone, and that was beautiful. To feel the emptiness ... (Laidy, FARC, B34)

Another loyalist admitted that often desertion was a surprise, because people they did not suspect would leave so suddenly: "No, they thought about it and when they left, one was shocked, one said 'he was a guy that I never imagined would leave.'"[9] These admissions that good people – and not just liars, traitors, and cowards – also deserted were important, as they indicated some intragroup frame dispute in the narrative around deserters. That is, such stories challenged the dominant frame that all deserters were military infiltrators, weak cowards, people who liked violence, or people not dedicated to the cause. These stories allowed for the possibility that "good," loyal people might have had legitimate reasons for leaving, and that perhaps the guerrillas were not always so benevolent. This contradiction indicates an intragroup dispute over how to represent reality – based on an obvious problem with empirical credibility – as clearly not all loyalists agreed that deserters were uniformly bad or incompetent people.

---

[8] Author interview B30.
[9] Author interview B39.

Gendering Deserters: Men as Traitors, Women as Liars

In previous chapters, I discussed how women deserters were labeled by FARC loyalists as brainwashed and deceitful for telling stories about sexual abuse, and how this narrative allowed the group to uphold militarized masculinities and insurgent feminism within the revolution frame. But this discourse also serves the deserter frame in reinforcing that all deserters were traitors and liars, and that the women were especially bad. When loyalists spoke about desertion in general, it was always in terms of whether the person had "done harm to the organization" by, for example, giving up their location or taking weapons or money with them. But when they spoke specifically about women deserters, they almost always discussed the lies women deserters told.

There was also disagreement about whether men or women deserted more frequently, even though this was not a question I ever asked – nor could I find verifiable data on rates of male versus female deserters, especially once the ARN blocked public access to their detailed reintegration statistics. A few loyalist men discussed how women who got pregnant would often desert the group, or they would leave and convince their male partners to desert with them. One commander was clearly quite bothered by the large number of women that had deserted the group:

In Colombia there were thousands and thousands of women who deserted. Why? Because they wanted to solve money problems for their family, because they wanted to solve their health problems with money. But it was a betrayal of their group, and they talked all kinds of garbage against my group. That is what happened in Colombia, and the press here, yes, they do publicize it, and they are in the newspapers, like: "No, that this woman was raped, that she was mistreated by the commanders," that, I don't know. "And that this woman had to give her services to her commander." ... That was what they did: portray us like we were, like we were people from mental institutions, that we were the worst, that we commanders were rapists. But that is a farce. That was a farce. (Adrián, FARC, B44)

What was the most telling is that female deserters were most frequently described as liars, whereas male deserters were *sapos* (informants) and traitors. Men's betrayals threatened military operations, but women's betrayals threatened the overall credibility of the revolution. Perhaps most illustrative in this regard is the story of "Karina" (aka Elda Neyis Mosquera) – the only recorded female front commander in the FARC's history who surrendered to the army in 2008.[10] While I did not

---

[10] Orth, "She Was Colombia's Most-Feared Female Revolutionary."

ask about her, several men mentioned her by name as a "lying traitor" who helped craft false stories of sexual abuse in the ranks. While government statistics indicate that far more male commanders deserted to the army and gave harmful intelligence than female ones – due to the fact that there were far more male commanders in general – Mosquera was the only one who came up in interviews by name. And while I certainly asked questions about women guerrillas, I asked questions about both men and women commanders and never about Mosquera specifically. This singling out was undoubtedly influenced by the fact that she was the only female front commander. Her betrayal was a convenient confirmation, based on a sample of one, of gendered expectations that women were not fit to be commanders and could not be trusted. Her betrayal was also framed as far worse than that of male commanders because, according to loyalists, she *lied*. Other (male) commanders were accused of being traitors because they gave up information, but not because they allegedly fabricated damning evidence. And based on the reactions in my interviews, FARC respondents seemed to feel that Mosquera's testimony, which they alleged falsely supported government propaganda, was the far greater betrayal.[11]

Women deserters were thus routinely dismissed as not having been real guerrillas and blamed for reinforcing the government narrative of the FARC as terrorists and abusers. At the same time, stories of benevolence toward deserters were often focused on women. Gendered narratives, then, seemed to be employed whenever they were the most useful to reinforce the dominant frame – even if they were contradictory.

CONCLUSION

What this frame demonstrates most clearly about desertion and the personal decision-making of combatants is how compelling frames can affect perceived alternatives. The deserter frame – as with the victimhood frame – calls into question whether it is the actual alternatives that matter or simply the perception of alternatives. And resonant organizational frames are highly effective at justifying experiences and influencing

---

[11] I have no way of personally confirming or negating the specific testimony of Elda Neyis Mosquera; while her version of events was certainly refuted by many respondents in this study, it was also supported by many others. In addition, Mosquera's testimony has been supported by independent human rights investigations, reports from the National Center of Historical Memory, and by interviews with two staff members in the Colombian Victims' Unit (author interviews C10, C13).

individual perceptions. The FARC and ELN leadership try to convince combatants that they can never go home again to keep them dependent on the group. Indeed, as shown in this and previous chapters, several loyalists said that they had never considered deserting because they had nowhere else to go.

While the FARC appears to have won at least one framing victory in getting the government to recognize a distinct stream of "reincorporation" for the collectively disarmed troops, the credibility of the group's frame that deserters are all traitors, military plants, and liars does not hold when loyalist members know the people who have left and know that this frame does not represent all deserters. This leaves open the possibility that some people may indeed have had good reasons to leave and even committed recruits can change their minds. Since it appears that at least some deserters were able to return to the ranks simply by joining a different bloc also damages the claim that the group knew everything about where deserters have gone and what they have done or said. In addition, in terms of societal stigmatization, the general public does not differentiate between ex-combatants who deserted and ex-combatants who stayed loyal – they are all just ex-combatants. Therefore, does the FARC's deserter frame actually help to maintain group cohesion, as it is clearly designed to do?

While the deserter frame certainly reduces the appearance of alternatives (e.g., by making recruits too scared to leave and/or by convincing them that they have nowhere else to go), it is not sufficient in and of itself to keep people inside the group. Even this perceived lack of alternatives can be overcome if the threats against someone are credible and large enough, especially if the would-be deserter has networks in the group – and outside the group – willing to collaborate in the escape. And the intragroup disputes about this frame are exacerbated by deserter and government contestations around how deserters are depicted, which is explored in Chapter IX.

IX

Contesting the Deserter Frame

I am working with [the prosecutor's office]; we are catching people who rape children, people who recruit children, because that is against humanity. Recruiting a child as they recruited me, I do not want that, I do not want the same thing to happen again, that another child relives what I lived. Because I lost my youth, I lost my childhood, I lost the opportunity to study, I lost the opportunity to be someone in life. That is a mark that lasts a lifetime, because due to this [history], you are discriminated against.

Nathaniel, ex-ELN (B74)

There are two main counter-frames that challenge the loyalist frame about deserters. The main challenge comes from the deserters themselves, who refused to be labeled as traitors and do not want to be identified as ex-combatants, in addition to fearing being hunted down by both loyalists and FARC dissidents. The secondary challenge arises from the government, which continues to place all ex-combatants into the same category of *desmovilizado* and whose neglect of the collective economic projects promised in the peace agreement is creating mass abandonment of the protected reincorporation zones – thus dismantling the FARC hierarchy and putting the group's stated revolution project into further jeopardy.

"WE ARE NOT TRAITORS": DESERTER CONTESTATIONS

While many deserters that I interviewed still thought of themselves as "fighters" in terms of being tough and resilient, they were also actively seeking to shed their combatant identity – and in fact, many were afraid of being "outed" as an ex-combatant. Michael[1] was one such respondent. A *campesino* like most guerrilla members, Michael was working on a farm at age seventeen when he was forced into the ELN ranks. He had never been interested in fighting and said he could not care less about guns, unlike many of his friends. But he told me that while working on the farm, he took up with some "bad company" and ran into problems, which caused the ELN to come looking for him. They said he had to join the ranks or they would kill him. As we spoke over several meetings, the rest of the story slowly came out: several times before this forced recruitment, the ELN had tried to recruit him and his mother had held them off, refusing to let the group take her son. But then, Michael told me, gesturing to his many tattoos like they might somehow explain, he got involved in a bad crowd and had "a problem" (he never told me what that problem was), which gave the ELN an opportunity to threaten him: "They took advantage [of the situation] to tell my mom … 'If you don't give us your son, we will kill him.' And so, my mom, well, she said yes so that they wouldn't kill me." At first, however, his mother tried to convince Michael to do his military service instead, but he felt like that was a riskier choice:

Well, on the one hand, she first told me not to leave, to go to military service, here in Colombia. But then I said no because, because as soon as I left [for the army] they would kill me – one because I was joining the military and two, because I ran away from them … Then she calmed down and at last we agreed. Then she spoke [to the ELN] … they told her that around there, in about two years they [would] release me again, and what a pure lie. After that, I was inside [the group] for three years until I demobilized.[2]

After being recruited, Michael could only speak to his mother if they went into town on errands, where he would sneak off and ask civilians for a minute on their cell phones.

While Michael's story of forced recruitment was rare among the ex-combatants that I interviewed, the issue of being tricked into joining, or being lied to about the level of commitment, was very common – especially among former ELN members. While commanders from the FARC, ELN, and AUC assured me that they never tricked anyone into joining, this was not true for those groups in general. While forced recruitment into Colombian insurgent groups has been rare, many respondents reported being tricked into joining with false promises. In fact, most of the ex-ELN combatants told me that ELN official rules permit combatants to

---

[1] Author interview Bo8.
[2] Author interview Bo8.

take leave, or to retire entirely, but that in reality these leaves are rarely granted. Junior, who was still deeply committed to the ELN despite having deserted, assured me that the ELN was very different from the FARC and that the group was quite reasonable in terms of granting leave. But Michael and other former *elenos* (slang for ELN members) said that, similar to the FARC, once you joined the ranks it was nearly impossible to leave. If you never wanted to be there in the first place, or if you had planned to stay only for a short time, deserting became the only option.

But when deserters surrender to the military and enter a safe house, they are coerced by the military to cooperate and share information or face prison time. That is, to be eligible for benefits, they must participate in at least three military intelligence interviews.[3] Thus, deserters' incentives to cooperate with government officials, and the consequences for not doing so, were high, which also made the costs of desertion high. Indeed, almost all of the deserters in this sample were well aware of how loyalists in the FARC and ELN were framing them (i.e., as cowards, liars, traitors, etc.) and many went to considerable effort to dismantle this framing. To me, however, it was unclear who the audience was for this counter-frame. Who were they trying to convince, given that most of the Colombian public did not differentiate between deserters and loyalists? Who, besides researchers like me, was even listening?

Several respondents maintained that they never participated in military interviews and wanted to make it clear that they were not the traitors that their former group made them out to be. They maintained that they had never intended to share intelligence or betray their group but had left for other reasons – usually to protect their own safety or that of someone else. However, government officials confirmed that participating in military intelligence interviews was a fixed requirement for deserters to receive DDR benefits.[4] (One military official later told me that these interviews were voluntary, but that was clearly not the case.) If demobilized combatants refused to "voluntarily" participate, they could not obtain DDR benefits and would be prosecuted for rebellion, sedition, terrorism, and other related crimes. Several loyalists who had served prison time, including Mari, confirmed this, saying that they had been sentenced to seventy years or longer due to their refusal to cooperate. Many deserters also confirmed this requirement, but several stated that they had been surprised when they demobilized that they had to share intelligence with the military in order to avoid prison time; that is, many combatants surrendered to the military not fully understanding the costs.

[3] Author interviews C01, C05.
[4] Author interviews C01, C05.

This unexpected requirement caused a significant amount of fear and resentment among the deserter population, who did not want to be labeled as snitches. And while they all called themselves *desmovilizados*, they rejected the negative associations that loyalists had placed on this label. Several said that despite the required interviews, they had not given up any legitimate information and that their decision to leave their armed group never included betraying their former comrades in this way. One FARC deserter who left when he was a company commander (mid-level, in charge of fifty-four guerrillas) explained how deserting was very difficult for him, even though he knew it was the right decision. He had many friends in the group and so was distressed about leaving them that he had called his commander after he had surrendered to warn him:

And I demobilized, I called the commander here in Bogotá right away … and I said to him: "Friend, I am demobilizing."
[Me: Really? And what did he say?]
"No! How can this be?" [laughs] And I said, "yes, comrade, I am demobilizing." "No, brother, how can this be? Don't do this to me! … No, no, no, no, my son, don't do this to me. We'll do something," he told me. "We'll do something. Think about it a few days, do what needs to be done, because there is already a lot of money in it, do it." And I said to the man, "no, comrade, no, no. I'm going to advise you not to move that money because … you'll lose that money, and you'll blame me, and I don't want any responsibility." … And I said, "no, call and cancel the delivery of this money, because it's a lot of money and it will be stolen, and you will blame me, because later they are going to say that I handed it in, and this is why I'm telling you. I don't want to continue." "My son, stay there a few days, go and pick up the money, think about it, rest, and later, my son, do the mission, and think and return here and there will be no problem." And me: "No, no. Comrade, I'm telling you no. Listen, the truth is I'm grateful, I'm grateful for all the time I shared with you all, the truth is I learned a lot with you, comrade, but no more. Listen, the truth is that I'm telling you this with pain in my soul, the truth is this is very hard for me, but no. No more." (Caleb, ex-FARC, B68)

This story, and others like it, challenge the loyalist frame that deserters are all military spies or people who did not believe in the cause or did not like hard work. The FARC and the ELN knew they had desertion problems and were losing good people – but admitting this would damage their carefully constructed frame around desertion, so they doubled down on the narrative that all deserters were informants and infiltrators.

In a similar effort to portray himself as loyal, one former ELN militia commander said that he had endured eighteen military intelligence interviews and five polygraph tests, but said that he finally drew the line at betraying the commander who had protected him as a child recruit:

I won the trust of the commander ... he loved me as a son, of all the children there, because I took care of him, because I was very responsible in my things and I never went ... I never failed him. Anything he asked me to do, I did it. So that's why I gained his trust, and right now the army is telling me that I delivered him [to them], and I'm not going to hand him in, because he is like my dad, the one who raised me, the one who taught me. He taught me what was good, what was good, bad ... so I did not hand him in. (Nathaniel, ex-ELN, B74)

Many deserters professed some level of loyalty to people within their former group and remorse at betraying their friends. Indeed, some deserters struggled with their decision to leave, and some even found a way to go back. For example, one loyalist told me how he had demobilized, enrolled in the government reintegration program, and then left the program after a year and rejoined the FARC – but he joined another bloc where the group did not know him.[5] This was fascinating, given that commanders told me that they *always* knew where all deserters were, including whether deserters had cooperated with the government or not. Deserters in this sample also repeatedly refuted the framing that they were liars and traitors, often saying that they had no choice but to run. It was the level of threat – or more importantly, the *perception* of the threat – that mattered when it came to the decision to stay or go, not the type or level of commitment to the group. And this perception was clearly influenced by strategic and carefully constructed organizational framing.

In fact, in my interviews, disillusionment in the ideology or tactics of the group were much less influential in desertion decisions than threats (perceived or actual) from within the group, or from the government. Indeed, as noted earlier, many FARC deserters still believed in the group's professed cause of fighting for equal rights, land redistribution, and ending government corruption, and still clung to some form of the fighter-revolutionary identity. Many even said they were grateful for their experiences, but they had left for other reasons, often because they felt their life was in danger. In addition, a few "deserter" respondents were not true deserters at all – four had been captured by the military and, in their words, had been completely abandoned and stigmatized by their own group. When intensely pressured by the state (with some saying they were tortured), these prisoners cooperated with the government to shorten their sentences. But because they officially "demobilized" by cooperating with the government, they were subsequently rejected by the loyalists. One FARC respondent spent seventeen years in prison (but had been sentenced to forty) and was released in 2018 under the JEP. He said that during his time in the group he had never

5 Author interview B36.

once thought of deserting. When I asked why he had not entered an ETCR upon his release (as other FARC members released from prison had done), he said that he could not accept the group's treatment of comrades who had cooperated with the government once imprisoned:

So here I have a strong criticism against them, because they should, if they want to grow their ideological and political ranks, they should make a reconciliation not only with the army or the national police, but also with their former combatants. We gave good parts of our lives as militia, fulfilling duties ... many years lost due to the duty and fulfillment of those orders. And if there were many people who ... looked for some laws [to help them], it was because at the time they were favorable and because we were already subject to the state regime ... So, they cannot label people, who are all here for the same reason to say that they are traitors, because many are not. They are firm and not traitors ... because now I realize, what I see with more clarity, now that I have regained my freedom and I have been out more than a year, I realize that [the peace agreement] was not a negotiation. It was like a surrender, that was more like a surrender and some commanders have settled now that they are legal, they have been accommodated, they have been given [political] seats, they have been given a security scheme ... that, for me, could be called a betrayal. Because they handed over their ideology, their movement in arms, and now those troops are disintegrated, disintegrated and are being discriminated against by the state, without work. Then I do, yes there I would make that criticism. (Jaseph, ex-FARC, B70)

It was clear that these respondents were torn. The counter-frame that deserters were nobler and/or were victims of their own groups was not salient for this subgroup as it did not match their lived experience. They had never made a distinctive choice to abandon their comrades; they had gone to prison because of their membership in the group, and now they were discriminated against not only by society and by the state but also by their own former comrades.

Other deserters admitted fleeing the group but justified their actions as protecting themselves or protecting a loved one, and they vehemently contested the loyalist frame that all deserters who had entered a demobilization program were traitors. Some were quite distressed at having caused harm to their former group, while others were terrified of the consequences of sharing intelligence that they had never intended to share. They placed the blame for any actions perceived as "traitorous" (such as sharing intelligence) on the government, and several expressed regret, like Lina had done – not at having left the group but at having entered the demobilization program at all. Lina felt that the demobilization program had publicly "outed" her as an ex-combatant, which she had previously managed to avoid. Until she had been forced to enroll, there had been a clear disincentive for her, and many like her, to enroll in the DDR program due to stigmatization, which was exacerbated by the government's framing of guerrillas as narco-terrorists, rapists, and rape victims, and the loyalist framing of deserters as liars and traitors. Again, her calculations of the costs and benefits of demobilization – and of enrolling in the DDR program – were strongly influenced by these framing contests. And the persistence of these discursive battles continued to negatively affect her transition to civilian life for years after demobilization.

But deserters who had no ongoing loyalty to their group often made considerable efforts to show how and why they were better than the loyalists – a direct rebuttal of the loyalist frame that they were worthless traitors. Indeed, these deserters directly contested the image of benevolence that FARC loyalists had constructed regarding deserters. For example, several deserters were eager to discuss their experiences in order to debunk what they had seen loyalist FARC ex-combatants saying in the news; they seemed intent on telling me gruesome stories of civilian murders and violent drug deals in order to dismantle the guerrilla frame of the noble, benevolent, and victimized revolutionary. One ex-FARC commander struggled with the tension between revealing what the loyalist guerrillas were doing to deserters and the very real danger of exposing himself to threats. He said explicitly that the demobilized ex-combatants, the deserters, were the "real victims" in this conflict: "I don't want them [the demobilized] … to disappear. On the other hand, if we … make ourselves known to the world, the world will know that there are some people who are being persecuted, not only by the state but by the guerrillas themselves" (Rob, ex-FARC, B01).

Although I did not directly ask any respondents about their involvement in drug trafficking or other illegal activities, a few higher-ranking deserters volunteered significant amounts of information around their roles in buying and selling drugs for the FARC, partly because they explicitly wanted to refute claims that the FARC was never directly involved in narco-trafficking. Andrés, who had initially refused to demobilize and continued fighting as a dissident – and working, by his own admission, as a drug trafficker – often regaled me with stories of how much cash he would handle on any given day. He missed the money, and he clearly missed having people respect or fear him. One day, while having coffee, he asked me: "I'm a nice guy, right? You think I'm a nice guy? What kind of person do you think I was, in the FARC?" I shrugged, knowing he wanted to tell me. "I was badass. I was pretty hard on people," he said, laughing. "People were scared of me sometimes." But he was not ashamed of this. He was clearly nostalgic for the days that he had power and money.

One combatant who deserted from the FARC (and then later also deserted from a group of EPL dissidents) expressed his frustration with the FARC's failing ideology:

Drug trafficking is something that … I mean, I never liked it when the FARC started working with drugs. Because the FARC, when Comrade Manuel Marulanda was alive, the FARC was FARC, it was a beautiful organization, where they fought for an ideal of a real people. Truly one … things were done for the people, they helped the people. But after he died, everything became the mafia – mafia, mafia, mafia, mafia. (Fabian, ex-FARC/ex-EPL, B19)

Some deserters also seemed eager to demonstrate that they had had status in the group – and in society – due to their levels of command, but at the same time they wanted to dismantle the mythology of the FARC's ideological intentions. In fact, while these commanders were very willing to expose FARC's drug-trafficking activities, they did not cite these illicit activities as their reason for leaving the group. Several of them dropped big names in an apparent bid to impress me:

Once I arrived at a dispatch by order of Raúl Reyes, by order of my narco-commander, by order of Commander Sonia,[6] to arrive and load and unload the cars of [a high-ranking police officer].[7] And he witnessed what was being done. The road police arrived and provided security while loading and unloading. So, what is the truth in this country? Here there will be no complete truth. (Johan, ex-FARC, B31)

The use of "narco-commander" was clearly deliberate here, indicating an adoption of the government narco-terrorist frame. Despite having spent decades in the group, Johan was bitter about his experiences and, in our repeated interactions over the course of a year, took any chance he could to debunk the revolution claims of the FARC. This too seemed to be a form of forceful dissonance reduction, but in the opposite direction: adopting the government framing of former comrades as criminals and abusers in order to make sense of his desertion.

While being involved in drug trafficking might change one's self-perception as a noble warrior or just revolutionary (evidenced by the fact that most of the loyalist FARC members vehemently denied involvement

---

[6] Referring to Omaira Rojas Cabrera (alias "Sonia"), a high-level female commander who was charged in the USA for running a drug network that earned the FARC tens of millions of dollars. Jeremy McDermott, "Colombia Extradites Rebel 'Sonia,'" *BBC News*, March 9, 2005, http://news.bbc.co.uk/2/hi/americas/4331673.stm. She was convicted in Washington, DC in 2007. Reuters, "Court Convicts Colombian Rebel on Drug Charges," *Reuters*, February 20, 2007, www.reuters.com/article/us-colombia-farc/court-convicts-colombian-rebel-on-drug-charges-idUSN2019514720070220.

[7] Name and identifying details withheld as to my knowledge this person has never been charged or prosecuted for drug trafficking.

in drug trafficking), this did not seem to play a significant role in desertion decisions – at least not for deserters I interviewed, nor the ones they
knew. Actually, for some deserters, the loss of the power and money they
had from being high-placed managers of drug operations was clearly a
painful loss. Retaliation against their former group by revealing details
of drug operations and deriding the group in general may have been one
way to compensate for this loss of status. Andrés and many other deserters derided the peace process as a sham and wanted to completely destroy
the revolutionary frame by providing testimony that FARC leaders were
primarily interested in profits from criminal activities. But they lacked a
critical ingredient to presenting an effective counter-frame: an audience.

   In the ETCRs, people in positions of power often retained that power
even after demobilization, but in the individually demobilized population,
former commanders had to grapple with the return to being regular – and
usually very poor – civilians once again with no status and no power.
To battle discrimination and counter the loyalist framing of deserters as
traitors, some deserters tried to reframe themselves and take their power
back by comparing themselves to the opposing guerrilla group, or to the
paramilitaries, in order to show how they were better. Two ELN former commanders, for example, asserted that their group's ideology was
"truly to fight" for the people and for equality, unlike the FARC, which
they derided as a "group of murderers."[8] On the other hand, one FARC
deserter said: "At least in the FARC you would not prostitute a female
guerrilla for any reason, while in the army and the police, yes."[9] He then
went on to detail multiple graphic abuses of minors that he primarily
attributed to the military but also to Colombian society in general, stating that "this would never happen in the FARC." And while some ELN
deserters cited violence from the FARC as the reason why they joined the
ELN, many deserters from both guerrilla groups spoke about the paramilitary or military violence that had driven them to join the guerrillas or
had caused the death of loved ones. Others spoke about being targeted
in "social cleansing" missions as children, specifically mentioning the
Colombian military. One FARC deserter explained that – despite loyalist
narratives of revolution and protecting children who had nowhere else to
go – many of them had joined simply for the guns:

I came primarily, we say, without knowing, because I did not know the structure
of the FARC well. My story was not ideological. My story was the weapons. I

---

[8] Author interviews B17, B74.
[9] Author interview B68.

liked to have weapons. I liked how they dressed, I liked the power that they had, and that is what I wanted. (Caleb, ex-FARC, B68)

This story, of course, fits with the loyalist frame that deserters were people who joined just because they wanted to shoot guns. What the loyalists did not say, however, was that *many* people who joined as children – including loyalists – had little concept of the ideology and cited that very same love of weapons as a primary reason to join. That is, what made them stay was often quite different to what initially brought them in.

Finally, many deserters spoke about the death threats they had received from their former group (including the demobilized FARC), which challenged the FARC loyalist narrative of having transformed to a peaceful and legitimate political party and having left violence behind. These deserters spoke at length about how they were afraid of being discovered and afraid of meeting new people or building new relationships, because they never knew who might be an informant. Indeed, many deserters told me that they stayed within close circles of other deserters that they had met in the safe houses and hardly spoke with anyone else. Andrés and these other deserters made significant efforts to hide their former guerrilla identities when seeking work or participating in school, and they talked about how being an ex-combatant was a significant impediment to moving forward in their lives – not only because of the stigma against them and the resulting difficulties in finding work and housing, but also because of the fear and insecurity that followed them everywhere. ELN deserters were, understandably, the most nervous about being identified and found due to the group's active status. But deserters from the FARC also dealt with threats and significant levels of insecurity, not only due to the rising numbers of FARC ex-combatants that have been killed since the peace agreement, but also because some deserters – including Andrés and Johan – were receiving ongoing threats from dissidents. Several deserters from the FARC also felt that the demobilized loyalists were still hunting them. One female FARC deserter who had opted to demobilize individually rather than enter an ETCR felt that once she left the government safe house, the FARC would actively hunt her – a threat she did not want to think about:

The FARC has many contacts, and they can send someone to kill you anywhere. Because I was there in the commissions … and I realized many things. And the FARC has a lot of contacts at the national or international level. There are many people left and sometimes you go around, and you don't know if it is possible that someone is working with them or not, and they could harm you. And even more so if you're a deserter who said something, that is certain. The FARC has a lot of national and international contacts and can harm you. This is life now, and it's also a reason not to think [about it]. (Carmen, ex-FARC, B02)

Some of the deserters that I interviewed, such as Namona and her husband, had been assigned a protective detail by the government due to their ongoing testimony for the prosecutor's office and/or the continuation of credible threats, while others never left home without a bulletproof vest. Indeed, despite the loyalist portrayals of benevolence and their assurances that members could ask permission to "retire," one of these respondents recalled how, when he joined the FARC at twelve years old, his recruiters told him he could never leave: "And on the way, they said to you, like, 'listen, because you have already arrived in the camp, this implies that you already know, now you cannot return. The only form of leaving is death or if you flee. But if you flee, you can't let yourself be caught because we'll kill you.'" (Caleb, ex-FARC, B68). For all of these respondents, revealing their ex-combatant identity meant accepting large amounts of risk; they lived with the suspicion that anyone could be an informant, and for many FARC deserters, the peace agreement had not assuaged their fear of being hunted. Thus, even those who still agreed with the group's revolutionary mission (and many did) talked about the measures they were taking to remain anonymous and to pass as civilians.

Most of these respondents felt that the government was not doing enough to protect them; many reported feeling abandoned by the government despite having taken significant risks to demobilize and provide testimony about crimes committed by their former group. In fact, several felt that since the peace agreement, all national and international attention was focused solely on the collectively demobilized FARC, and everyone had essentially forgotten that they (individually demobilized combatants) existed. These deserters voiced significant resentment against the collectively demobilized FARC for receiving better benefits than they did, especially as most deserters felt that they had done "the right thing" by leaving their violent groups, whereas the combatants who kept fighting until ordered to demobilize received a higher monthly allowance, a food allotment, and free (though temporary and shoddy) housing.

However, while threats from within the group were important motivators for a person to leave, they rarely were the sole reason for deserting. Often, a respondent would cite one reason for desertion early in the interview, and then over the course of the conversation, new details would emerge. For example, Namona's husband – an ELN commander – originally said that he left because Namona had been sexually assaulted by other combatants in the group. He later revealed that he had a relative in the military who helped him escape and got the couple into the safe house program. Then, later in the interview, he said they had started to plan their escape when they got a new commander, who was "more grotesque and stricter" than their previous one, and that he had started to witness more recruitment and sexual abuse of children, which he did not want to be part of.

As the previous chapters have also shown, this multilayered experience that eventually led to desertion was not an exception. While a few respondents reported that their decision to leave was quite sudden, this trajectory was rare; most deserters reported multiple interacting factors that built up over time. For example, Michael initially said that he escaped because he missed his family and was bored, but then later added that he was almost killed in a bombing in 2016, a traumatic event that made him want to leave. One female FARC deserter said that she had accidentally killed a comrade when her gun went off, a traumatic event that triggered thoughts of leaving – but she did not actually leave until she got pregnant.[10] Junior said that his entire family – mother, father, cousins, uncles – were still in the group and he would never have left if he had not lost a large sum of the group's money: "I did not demobilize because I wanted to, only because I had this problem with the group ... otherwise I would not have demobilized ... there are lots of people here [in the safe house] like that."[11] It appears that, for some, even incredibly strong ties to the group may not be enough to prevent desertion if the threat to personal safety is large enough. But, as the paramilitary desertion patterns will show, this threat must be greater than the perceived costs of leaving the group in order to inspire action.

Overall, deserters used many different strategies to combat the loyalist narratives that they were all traitors, liars, and infiltrators – including denying that they had given intelligence to the state, hiding their ex-combatant status, and maligning their former group. But without credible leadership to coordinate and amplify this framing, and without an attentive audience, these attempts were reactive, uncoordinated, and ineffective. Some ex-combatants had formed collectives of deserters, taking to social media and self-publishing newsletters to counter the loyalist narratives, but they simply did not have the same reach as the guerrilla leadership or the government. It was also dangerous to speak out publicly. Loyalist guerrillas tended to erase any involvement in drug trafficking or violence against civilians, but deserters rejected the idea of being traitors or cowards and emphasized the idea of "being someone" and wanting to do something good with their lives. Many of them wanted to prove that they were someone worth helping. Nonetheless, in the eyes

---

[10] Author interview B11.
[11] Author interview B17.

of the government and the general public, distinctions between deserters, paramilitaries, and loyalists did not really matter. They were all in
the stigmatized category of ex-combatants with all other ex-combatants.
These counter-narratives thus had limited effect; without strategic coor-
dination and wider dissemination, they hardly amounted to a real frame
at all. Deserters knew that the safest and most effective way to amplify
their side of the story and reach a wider audience was to work with the
government – even if it meant adopting the government's negative framing of themselves.

"THEY MARK YOU": THE GOVERNMENT ENTERS
THE DEBATE

> There is a characteristic of the demobilized population, one is that they
> don't have tolerance for frustration, and also they don't know how to
> delay gratification. They want everything now, and if it isn't now, well
> then you haven't done what you promised. And the structure and the way
> that demobilized people think, they can't stand waiting for things. They
> want it *now*.
>
>   GAHD psychologist (C01)

The renaming of the ARN mentioned earlier might suggest that the government accepted the FARC's deserter frame – or at least the distinctions
between the two groups of ex-combatants. It was certainly a significant move on the government's part to accept the FARC's insistence on
a different type of reintegration programming. However, the fact that
several government officials still called all ex-combatants *desmovilizados* in their interactions with me indicates that while the name change
may have been a conciliatory signal by the ARN, it was not adopted
universally across government departments – especially not in the military. While it is possible that some reintegration officials were unaware
of the loyalists' strong preference for not being called *desmovilizados*,
that seems unlikely, given how adamant the FARC loyalists were about
this preference. In fact, to conflate all demobilized actors together in
the same category of *desmovilizados* had a similar effect as the government's efforts to put combatants and ex-combatants from all groups
into the narco-terrorist frame: it delegitimized all combatants, former
or otherwise.

    I am not suggesting that the government did not see the difference. In
fact, as noted earlier, there were two distinct reintegration programs, and
several military and ARN officials said that the FARC members who had

been ordered to demobilize were much more "challenging" to reintegrate than those who had deserted. Nonetheless, all ex-combatants were placed under this label of *desmovilizado*. And, in fact, the government's failure to implement collective economic projects caused mass abandonment from the ETCRs (something that only became worse after this fieldwork was conducted), which meant that many collectively demobilized FARC members were switching to individual reintegration programs – or leaving the reintegration process altogether. By early 2020, out of the 13,104 FARC members accredited in the peace process by that time (10,129 men and 2,975 women), 70 percent were already living outside an ETCR and only 23 percent lived inside of one.[12] In 2018, one GAHD official even mentioned to me as a point of pride how many FARC members they were getting in their demobilization program who had "deserted" the ETCRs. He clearly saw this as a success, presumably because leaving the designated and protected reintegration zones was dismantling the FARC hierarchy and cohesion. It also pointed to a failure of FARC leadership if their former followers were choosing the military program. But many ex-combatants who left the ETCRs were not reporting to the government at all; in fact, while the ARN stated in 2018 that 739 ex-combatants were designated as "location unknown," by then the UN was already reporting that the dispersion of ex-combatants out of the territorial areas was hard to track and was causing significant challenges to reintegration.[13]

Having ex-combatants leave the collective reintegration of the ETCRs and, essentially, follow the individual reintegration path, fit exactly into the government frame of *desmovilizados*. Aside from the financial differences in the benefits, once ex-combatants leave the ETCRs their process becomes nearly identical with that of the other demobilized combatants. Placing all ex-combatants together and removing distinctions of groups and rank fits with the government counter-frame that nothing the ex-combatants did before is relevant, and they are all just ex-criminals. Having ex-combatants dissipate and reintegrate individually is certainly more effective at dismantling group cohesion and the overall group frame (whether it be revolution or self-defense) than allowing former comrades to live together in collective communities.

---

[12] ARN, "Reincorporacion En Cifras"; Guterres, "United Nations Verification Mission in Colombia: March 2020."

[13] ARN, "Reincorporacion En Cifras"; Guterres, "United Nations Verification Mission in Colombia: April 2018."

This government framing of all ex-combatants as being the same is also echoed in the media and in the general public. Indeed, the stigma against ex-combatants in general is quite high in Colombia, especially in urban centers, and all deserters spoke about this. While the loyalists in the ETCRs had experienced less interaction with the general public, and most had not lived in the major cities, the deserters had distinctly different experiences. The paramilitaries in particular felt public discrimination deeply, even fifteen years after demobilization. As one ex-AUC woman said:

It's still terrible … . they "mark" you, it's what we say, right? No, that to be in the category of "demobilized," people think the worst of you … and for being a woman here too, they discriminate more … I am not proud of it, nor am I proud to say I was [AUC]. No, for nothing, because that is a bad thing. I never even killed a moth, by God! (Clara, ex-AUC, B82)

While some women guerrilla deserters used a similar justification – that they had not participated in violence and thus should not be discriminated against for their ex-combatant status – they all agreed that the stigma was impossible to escape. Some deserters expressed surprise that people somehow "just knew" that they were ex-combatants, when they thought they could emerge from the safe house as anonymous and normal civilians. Indeed, many of the deserters in this study had very simple goals: to blend in and erase their past so that they could secure employment. One deserter from the ELN articulated this discomfort:

I went out [of the safe house] and people look at you … they give you nasty looks … you know, that they discriminate against you for having been of that [armed group], but they do not understand that one has already demobilized, and wants to start a new life, a correct life. And then what they do is to discriminate against one many times … I have heard them, it happened that the [demobilized] are denied employment, they are denied housing, they cannot get a lease or anything because they were demobilized, yes? … They try to discriminate against people, without knowing them, without knowing their good plans, that they want to have a good future, or anything else. (Sofia, ex-ELN, B03)

In other words, once a person is publicly known to belong to the category of ex-combatant, their chances for a normal life are low, as is their ability to find work or housing. When layering on racial, class, and gender discrimination against Indigenous and Afro-descendant populations, *campesinos*, women, and displaced people, these challenges become even more profound. While many loyalists in the ETCRs – who remained somewhat separate from the general population (see Figure 10) – said that they had not experienced discrimination, many deserters voiced frustration at not being able to find work because they had no references and no official work experiences: "That the army is going to give us work references,

FIGURE 10 Walking with a FARC ex-combatant in an ETCR, northern Colombia.
Photo credit: Alejandro Carlosama (research assistant).

that the ARN is going to find work and give us references, that is a lie. We have had many interviews and [employers ask]: 'But what have you done in your life, tell me.' What do they want me to say, lies?" (Johan, ex-FARC, B31).

Indeed, many of the deserters in this sample were only working part-time because they could not find anything else, or because they did not have affordable childcare. And while the ARN reports that 79 percent of collectively demobilized FARC ex-combatants are "optimistic about their future,"[14] that was certainly not the case for the deserters in this sample, nor for the ex-AUC respondents – all of whom were frustrated about their options and with the government for what they felt were false promises. And while this societal stigmatization and lack of employment may be the combined effect of the government framing all combatants as narco-terrorists and placing all ex-combatants under the same label of *desmovilizado*, the end result is a profound failure of reintegration.

THE AUC ANTI-FRAME

The fact that this sample only contains one successful AUC deserter may not be significant given the size of the sample, but other researchers have indicated that desertion in Colombia has been predominantly from the guerrilla groups – with some deserters fleeing to the AUC for protection but almost never the other way around.[15] Three male respondents from this sample had deserted a guerrilla group and shortly thereafter joined the paramilitaries. Indeed, research data and the government's own data show that the majority of deserters (i.e., individual demobilizations) were guerrillas.[16] Throughout this research process it proved very difficult to find respondents who had deserted the AUC – or at least those who would admit to it. Due to large variations among paramilitary units in different areas – compared to the highly regimented FARC structure – it is likely that desertion patterns depended on commanders and the level of structural control in each particular unit. In addition, as noted earlier, the AUC paid their recruits and gave them many opportunities for personal enrichment, while the guerrillas did not. Thus, even if people wanted to leave, respondents in this sample indicated that they were hesitant to abandon their income, which directly contradicts theories that economically motivated recruits are more likely to desert or switch sides.

---

[14] ARN, "76% de Los Excombatientes FARC-EP, Optimista Sobre Su Futuro En Proceso de Reincorporación," Resultados del Registro Nacional de Reincorporación, 2019, www.reincorporacion.gov.co/es/sala-de-prensa/noticias/Paginas/2019/El-76porciento-de-los-excombatientes-farc-es-optimista-sobre-su-futuro-en-proceso-de-reincorporacion.aspx.

[15] Gutiérrez Sanín, "The FARC's Militaristic Blueprint."

[16] Oppenheim et al., "True Believers, Deserters, and Traitors"; ARN, "La Reintegración En Colombia – Cifras."

Although this sample had only one successful paramilitary deserter, as noted earlier there were many ex-paramilitaries in this study that fell into the category of "would-be" deserter – that is, they would have left if they could have. Testimonies from these respondents indicate that the AUC did not really have a frame about deserters versus loyalists at all – in this study, no one told me stories about AUC deserters sharing intelligence or lying about sexual assault. There was no framing of deserters here, largely because there were no deserters – brutal violence appears to have made the construction of a frame unnecessary. The paramilitary respondents were fairly transparent that they had been fighting for money and that the group's main goal had been profits from narco-trafficking. While a few maintained that they were fighting to protect Colombia, only Hugo noted a difference in labeling between loyalists and deserters: "It is the same as the difference between the reinserted and the demobilized: the reinserted is the one that flees and surrenders, and the demobilized is the one who plans to surrender, plans, that is, as a complete group, you see?" (Hugo, ex-AUC, B69).

Unlike the ELN, which allegedly permitted people to withdraw under certain conditions, or the FARC, which made distinctions between deserters who simply left the group and those that surrendered to the army, the AUC was structured more like a mafia than an army and had zero tolerance for desertion. Those that left were killed, or if they could not be found, their families were killed. And would-be deserters were well aware of that:

And I thought of running, I thought of running but I couldn't … I couldn't because my mom lived in the village … my mom lived there, my mom, my dad, my siblings. And if you run, they kill your mom, they kill your dad, your siblings, so I couldn't. For one to leave, your family has to live somewhere else, you have to get your family out before you do this, out of the village. Because if you have them there, nothing will be left. And because of that, I did not run. (Pedro, ex-AUC, B77)

Thus, while there were not many successful paramilitary deserters in my research or in general, it is not difficult to see why. Anyone who successfully deserted from the paramilitaries would not only need to hide themselves, they would need to hide their whole families – and given the number of still-active paramilitaries, these deserters would need to stay hidden indefinitely. This did not seem as significant a concern for the guerrilla deserters, however, who said they could not go home because the guerrillas would find them but did not voice concern that the guerrillas would also kill their entire families.

Overall, the ex-AUC respondents did not speak much about desertion at all. When asked about it, they mostly asserted that it never happened because people were too scared, or they shared stories of people who had been brutally punished for trying. There was no attempt to portray their group as benevolent toward deserters, as no respondents took responsibility for this behavior or claimed leadership roles (despite evidence indicating at least a few had more senior ranks). The "anti-frame," then, was exactly that: no frame was needed for deserters because anyone who deserted was, in their minds, probably dead.

CONCLUSION

In the framing contest of deserters versus loyalists, there are no clear winners or losers. The FARC loyalists' depiction of deserters may be compelling within their own circles, but testimony from deserters has been extremely damaging to the FARC's overall image and to the credibility of the group's revolutionary frame. In addition, the government's counterframe places all ex-combatants into the same stigmatized category of terrorists and criminals. As a result, despite what loyalists and deserters say about each other, the general public does not really differentiate between ex-combatants who deserted and those who did not. When these groups speak badly about each other, they create a feedback loop in which narratives about the "other" ricochet back and morph into narratives about *all* ex-combatants. For example, when women deserters share stories of sexual abuse in government PR campaigns, this not only stigmatizes the loyalists but also reinforces public belief that guerrilla men in general (deserters or not) are rapists and that guerrilla women are rape victims who likely have had multiple abortions.

What these contests demonstrate most clearly is that the stigmatizing effect on deserters in particular is a threat to their successful long-term reintegration. In their efforts to encourage desertion, the government tries to convince combatants that they can go home again, that anything is possible – and some believe it, only to realize later that this promise is a lie. This breach of trust heightens their resentment toward the government, and some feel that if they are going to be treated like criminals anyway, then they might as well embrace it and make some money. Women deserters are especially stigmatized in this contest: not only are they socially rejected for being ex-combatants, but FARC loyalists – some of whom are now political leaders – have framed them as liars and infiltrators, while the government frames them as rape victims. This compounded stigma from public officials – who have a large platform to disseminate information – makes it very difficult for women deserters to move forward as civilians with gainful employment and free from fear.

In addition, the government campaign to encourage desertion did not appear to have a significant role in this framing contest between different categories of ex-combatants. In fact, many of the deserters (especially in the ELN) had no idea that a demobilization program even existed until after they had fled the group. This calls into question not only the government's campaign but also other "counter-narrative" efforts made by governments across the globe in an effort to stop recruitment into terrorist and insurgent groups. In addition to the lack of evidence on the efficacy of these counter-frames, and virtually no evidence on how they work for women,[17] the Colombian case shows that these frames can backfire by entrenching oppositional narratives of former insurgents rather than encouraging collaboration. As a result, ongoing hostilities between loyalists and deserters threaten the reintegration of all ex-combatants and may even encourage recidivism, especially if deserters feel hunted by former groups and rejected by the general public. In this multilayered framing contest, then, it does not necessarily matter who "wins." It is the contest itself, and the persistence of these discursive battles, that threaten sustainable peace.

---

[17] Amy Jane Gielen, "Exit Programmes for Female Jihadists: A Proposal for Conducting Realistic Evaluation of the Dutch Approach," *International Sociology* 33, no. 4 (2018): 454–72; Andrew Glazzard, "Losing the Plot: Narrative, Counter-Narrative and Violent Extremism" (The Hague, 2017), https://doi.org/10.19165/2017.1.08; Alex P Schmid, "Al-Qaeda's 'Single Narrative' and Attempts to Develop Counter-Narratives: The State of Knowledge" (The Hague, 2014), www.icct.nl/download/file/Schmid-Al-Qaeda's-Single-Narrative-and-Attempts-to-Develop-Counter-Narratives-January-2014.pdf.

X

Framing Reintegration

It's an entire lost generation ... the return to armed groups is primarily about a lack of opportunities. They lose their jobs because of rejection, and there is lots of recruitment of kids into gangs. But this gets much less attention, even though a lot of these groups are contracted by the FARC. This is a big issue, but very hidden ... and then a lot of these kids aren't eligible for the demobilization program.

Social Worker, Central Colombia (C12)

There are people who have never picked up a gun but did far more damage.

Alejo, ex-FARC (B85)

When I first conceived of this research project, my first step was to go through official reintegration programming channels and contact the ARN. While at the time I took this route because it seemed to be the safest and most legitimate option (and the least likely to get me kicked out of the country), I did not adequately reflect upon the fact that this trajectory could lead me down a road of overemphasizing carefully constructed state narratives – something I certainly had no intention of doing. The ARN has a very specific process through which one can request permission to conduct research with ex-combatants, and I followed it to the letter. As other scholars have written, the ARN is a very protective institution that tries to guard its reputation and access to ex-combatants carefully, but at that time I did not know how else to access ex-combatants.[1] My first written request – which included a lengthy research prospectus, among other official documentation – was returned to me with requests to change

---

[1] Fattal, *Guerrilla Marketing*.

certain sections. I did so and sent it back. It was returned to me again, months later, with different requests. I complied and sent it back. This process happened four more times, for a total of six revisions in which I complied with the agency's ever-changing requests, over the course of twelve months. In the meantime, worried that my research objectives were being diluted and reframed by the ARN, I had obtained a contact at the Ministry of Defense through dauntless persistence and, admittedly, a decent dose of good luck. After much negotiation, I obtained permission to conduct research in the GAHD safe houses, starting in February 2018. As a result, I was already in Colombia when the ARN conditionally approved my proposal, but it took six more months for ARN officials to agree to an in-person meeting, and another month after that to actually get that meeting. I was well into my interviews and had been to two military safe houses and two ETCRs (the latter of which was facilitated through FARC ex-combatants directly and not with the government at all) when I finally sat down with four women at the ARN. They did not know that I had already conducted dozens of interviews (with both Ministry of Defense and FARC leadership approval), and I could instantly sense that their answer would not be good.

"We have read your proposal," said one woman, after the introductions were over and we were all sipping tiny cups of rich coffee. "But we do not understand the value of your question. We already know why combatants leave their groups."

Her Spanish was perfect in the way Bogotá Spanish often is: clipped, articulated, clear. I understood her perfectly, yet I was still confused. This proposal had already gone through a full year and six rounds of revision, where I had complied with every single change request. What more could they want? I carefully explained that while the government had summaries of the main reasons that people deserted, there were no systematic comparisons of collective versus individual demobilizations, nor of the desertion pathways of men ex-combatants compared to women. Not only that, but not everything the ARN did research on was publicly available. There was a significant research gap, I insisted politely. And I had made all the requested changes.

"We already have a strong grasp on gender," the woman said firmly. I began to wonder why I was there at all. Why had they bothered to ask for all those revisions to my proposal, if only to shut me down after a year of negotiations? I tried again, explaining that while they may indeed have information on gender and DDR, it was not always publicly available or in English for international audiences. In a last-ditch attempt to boost my own credibility (in a way that I admittedly question now), I explained that the Ministry of Defense had approved my study and had given me access to GAHD safe houses. When that did not work, I reluctantly resorted to flattery, echoing the words of the GAHD colonel by suggesting that this research could help "share their reintegration successes with the world." They told me that they could not help me to access the ETCRs, as their relationship with the FARC leadership was quite strained. But by this point I had already been inside two ETCRs with the permission of FARC leadership and had leads on the third, so that did not affect my plans. They did, however, promise to help me obtain interviews with former paramilitaries across Colombia. I was thrilled, because that was one ex-combatant population where I did not yet have contacts.

That excitement, however, was wildly premature.

*

As the preceding chapters should make clear, there is a great deal of over-lap between the various frames used by the guerrillas, paramilitaries, and government. The victimhood frame overlaps with the revolution frame, and both of these depend on the deserter frame to reinforce the idea of guerrilla benevolence and justice. The government's framing of the guer-rillas as victimizing their own troops is reinforced by the narco-terrorist frame, and then further reinforced by the conflation of all ex-combatants into the same category of the stigmatized *desmovilizado*. Clearly, these framing contests matter a great deal to the ones creating them and have lasting effects long after demobilization.

When studying insurgency and civil war, understanding different exit pathways from violence could, ideally, help to prevent the resurgence of that violence. But criminologists have long stated that desistance from violent groups is notoriously difficult to measure: people might disengage from violence but still be committed to their group in other ways, or they might disengage temporarily, only to rejoin the group or commit violence in other ways or with different groups later on.[2] In Colombia, these failures of reintegration and repeated resurgence into conflict have been illustrated over and over again. Millions of international dollars have been poured into the country for the "war on drugs," and later the

---

[2] John H Laub and Robert J Sampson, "Understanding Desistance from Crime," *Crime and Justice* 28 (2001): 1–69; Gary LaFree and Erin Miller, "Desistance from Terrorism: What Can We Learn from Criminology?" *Dynamics of Asymmetric Conflict* 1, no. 3 (2008): 203–30.

"war on terror," and still later for the peace process – but the country remains mired in a multitude of active armed groups, many of whom have disarmed only to rearm again. Understanding why people join violent rebellions is not enough to understand the full trajectory of participation in armed activity – especially when a lot of that understanding is built on why men join violent rebellions. It is also critical to understand why both men and women stay, why they leave, and/or why they return after having disarmed. Desertion, perceptions of threat, and armed group fragmentation also cannot be understood at only the organizational level, nor at only the individual level. These phenomena must be examined by looking at how they are linked together: how these groups frame reality and threats to build cohesion and collective identities, and how their recruits interpret or dispute these frames.

Ex-combatants generally all face many of the same hardships upon demobilization (e.g., poverty, discrimination, violence, insecurity), so understanding how armed groups frame their rebellions, and how opposing actors contest these frames, is critical to understanding how disengagement trajectories and armed group identities affect reintegration experiences. As the Colombian case shows, some counter-narratives coming from the government can backfire if they do not adequately consider the powerful components of the rebel frame that they are competing with. These framing contests are also important in understanding how different exit pathways from violence (e.g., deserting versus being ordered to demobilize versus being captured) affect reintegration experiences and, in particular, affect future encounters with government officials, regular civilians, and active armed actors.

Andrés' story is particularly illustrative in this regard. First off, Andrés was not a typical FARC recruit. While he did grow up in a rural area, he did not identify as a *campesino*. He had a high school diploma, his mother was a teacher, and he had siblings that were urban professionals. One of his relatives was in the army. But like many of the deserters, Andrés told me he had always been a rebel – he did not like taking orders, he said, which seemed odd to me given how long he had stayed with the FARC. He first got involved with the FARC as militia, working logistics, obtaining food and supplies, and so on. But the group soon promoted him to other tasks because, in his words, he was "great at talking to people and could get along with anyone." Andrés ended up in two different fronts and finally in one of the "mobile columns" of the FARC, which were elite fighting units. But when the FARC officially disarmed, Andrés did not – he continued fighting with a group of dissidents, for profit and not for any sort of revolution. Andrés never cared about the revolution; in fact, he made fun of it frequently. Indeed, within five minutes of our first interview, he was telling me how he skimmed off the top of the organization's profits:

I made good money ... I always handled the money; I went out to buy drugs and ... for example, if a *campesino* arrived and had a cake of base [for cocaine], an example, and it weighed a kilo and ten grams, I would tell him "you only have a kilo" and I paid him a kilo and I kept ten grams. And so, square and square. He earned good money. Then I went to get it crystallized and I provided my people with security, and they paid me 30 or 40 million [pesos] in eight days, fifteen days. In other words, in [US] dollars that would have been $10,000 for fifteen days.[3]

I understood then his comment about not taking orders. Even when he was within the strict hierarchy of the FARC, Andrés flouted the rules. Of course, this level of profit almost defied belief and certainly may have been exaggerated. But even if it was only a quarter of that, it was still more money in two weeks than some Colombians would earn in an entire year. Seeing the poverty and employment insecurity that most deserters faced once they left their groups, it was easy to understand Andrés' decision to stay on with the dissidents. He was accustomed to money and power. When we first spoke, however, he was very worried about leaving the safe house, because for the first time in over a decade, he was going out into the world with nothing:

You don't leave with work, you don't leave with anything. You ... you aren't prepared to just leave here right away. I have family. But there are comrades here who leave ... And they said: "I don't know where I am going to go." There are people who say they don't know where they will go.[4]

Over the months after he left the safe house, encouraged by the ARN's emphasis on turning ex-combatants into entrepreneurs, Andrés started pitching new business ideas to me over endless WhatsApp messages. I could invest, he said, and share profits. He could be a guide, he suggested, for people who wanted to travel to Colombia. He could book group trips to the FARC "tourist camps" that the group had created (see Figure 11).

He could buy a food cart. He could export coffee to Canada, he told me excitedly once, and I could help import it. He could *grow* coffee. He could start a collective with other ex-combatants. He could buy a

[3] Author interview B18.
[4] Author interview B18.

FIGURE 11 FARC "ecotourism" project, northern Colombia.
Photo credit: author.

hotel – he even found a woman who was selling one and asked me to
invest. Never mind that he knew nothing about running a hotel. He
could drive for Uber – he just needed a car, and could I help with that?
The list went on. He had dozens of these ideas, always asking me to
invest with large amounts of cash that I did not have. But even though
he knew a lot about the drug trade and was excellent at calculating how
to skim off the top, he had no idea how to run a small business. While I
am no business expert either, every time I asked him to consider details
and expenses – insurance and interpreters for tourists, or import/export
fees and trade regulations, for example – he would become frustrated
and switch to a new idea. And, as mentioned earlier, the ARN confirmed that most ex-combatants do not even claim their start-up funds
because they do not understand or cannot meet the conditions to access
that money. And when they do access that money, my research and that
of others indicates that most of these start-up businesses fail due to lack
of training, knowledge, or insufficient capital.[5]

---

[5] Fattal, *Guerrilla Marketing*.

Like I felt with Junior, within ten minutes of first meeting Andrés in that safe house, I worried he would not last long as a civilian. And for both of them, in different ways, I was right.

UNDERSTANDING FRAMES: WHY CONTESTS MATTER AND HOW THEY OVERLAP

Employing the concept of frames focuses on how people organize and interpret knowledge,[6] which is arguably a critical component of under-standing people's perceptions of risk, their calculation of options, and the way ex-combatants navigate their post-demobilization experience. Importantly, frames as socially constructed objects are not only inside people's minds – they are also "embedded in social routines, practices, discourses, technologies and institutions."[7] As such, frames exist both inside people's minds as constructs and externally as social practices and discourses – and this combination of individual and organizational fac-tors is what makes the study of frames critical to understanding armed group cohesion and post-demobilization experiences. That is, studying individual processes of desertion has provided nearly as many different answers as there are deserters – while there are certainly patterns, every person's story, and how they interpret and explain their decisions, is dif-ferent. But studying only the "type" or structure of an armed group also does not adequately explain varying patterns of desertion and cohesion within that group or similar groups. Understanding frames – and the framing contests that challenge the way people have organized knowl-edge and constructed both individual and collective identities – brings both individual-level and organizational-level analysis together, arguably contributing a stronger understanding to patterns of disengagement from violent groups and how these patterns affect combatants' transition to civilian life. In addition, understanding how frames influence exit path-ways from violence – and how certain frames negatively affect the post-conflict experiences of ex-combatants – can improve our understanding of reintegration successes and failures.

Framing is a continuous and dynamic process; over the course of a movement, frames will be repeatedly contested and reinvented, or even replaced.[8] For dissidents like Andrés that kept fighting, for example, the

---

[6] Autesserre, "Hobbes and the Congo."
[7] Autesserre, "Hobbes and the Congo," 252.
[8] Benford and Snow, "Framing Processes and Social Movements."

TABLE 5 *The three main framing contests*

Frame	Primary counter-frame
Victims	Perpetrators
Revolution/self-defense	Narco-terrorists
Loyalists	Deserters

revolutionary frame was replaced with one about profit and power. In this book, I identified three core framing contests in the Colombian conflict, illustrated in Table 5. While there was certainly evidence of other frames, these are the three contests that appeared most influential on rebel group cohesion and disengagement trajectories in Colombia.

Within the guerrilla victimhood frame, there were several core components: the *campesino* identity, the gendered dimensions of victimhood, and the claim of acting in self-defense. But there was also a hierarchy of victimhood in this frame, particularly among the women guerrilla loyalists, where they viewed *campesino* women as more victimized than they were. This chapter identified racialized aspects of the supposedly "nonethnic" *campesino* identity, showing how shared experiences of discrimination and marginalization – and, specifically, of repression from the state – had contributed to a cohesive frame around the concept of victimhood. The chapter also demonstrated how victimhood was experienced differently by men, who largely discussed their victimization in regard to land, compared to women, who emphasized the gender-based and sexual violence perpetrated by paramilitary and state forces. This aspect of women's victimhood in particular kept many women inside the group, as they were convinced it was the safest place that they could be. These narratives of victimhood led to a third component of the frame – that of claiming self-defense. All of these components legitimize the victimhood frame for combatants, and indeed many deserters also adhered to this framing.

The government and the paramilitaries, on the other hand, challenged this victimhood frame with a counter-frame of the guerrillas as perpetrators – and, more specifically, as perpetrators against their own troops. This, too, was highly gendered, as the most discrediting stories the government used about the guerrillas – and about the FARC in particular – came from female deserters who shared stories of sexual abuse and forced abortions in the ranks. Indeed, this contest was primarily about who was the "real" victim, who was the "real" perpetrator, and thus, who was legitimately acting in self-defense.

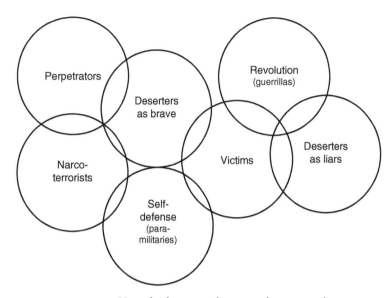

FIGURE 12 How the frames and counter-frames overlap.

Here it again becomes clear that many of the frames identified in this book overlap (see Figure 12), and they all have gender(ed/ing) norms woven throughout. Indeed, these contests are not isolated in themselves – they are frequently reinforced by other frames, in a form of "frame bridging," defined as the linking of two or more ideologically congruent frames regarding a particular issue or problem.[9]

This brings us to the second competition, that of *revolutionaries versus narco-terrorists*. The victimhood frame is important in justifying the use of violence and claiming to be acting in self-defense, and it is particularly critical in convincing women guerrillas that they have nowhere else to go. The revolution frame, on the other hand, is critical in demonstrating that self-defense is not enough, and that in fact the group must act offensively in order to overthrow the government and transform society. This frame has several key components that are critical to group cohesion: the fighter identity, militarized masculinities, and – for the guerrillas – insurgent feminism. While the fighter identity helps give combatants status and makes them feel like they matter, and that their cause matters, militarized masculinities reward male aggression and emphasize a gendered division of labor, while creating a "guerrilla glass ceiling" in which women are

[9] Benford and Snow, "Framing Processes and Social Movements."

included (and lauded) in the group while also being kept under strict control. Indeed, the insurgent feminism that is a critical component of the revolution frame and the overthrow of traditional society is still firmly bounded within military masculinities. But, in this sample, some women who were critical of the bounds of insurgent feminism still remained in the group – often because they felt that even within these constraints, the limited gender "equality" of the group was still better than in Colombian society. That is, they still believed in the revolution, and their perceived alternatives outside the group were worse than staying inside, especially when they knew how women deserters were framed by the group. For these women, both disengagement and reintegration were (and continue to be) particularly challenging, as they disarm into a society that stigmatizes them not only for being "narco-terrorists," but also for not fitting into traditionally gendered expectations of being peaceful, maternal women. They are not good victims, but nor are they peaceful resisters. The revolution frame, especially for women, shows that when considering commitment to one's group, the alternatives are highly gendered and perceived alternatives matter just as much as real ones.

Indeed, the government's counter-frame of all Colombian combatants as "narco-terrorists" has highly limited the perceived alternatives of combatants who may want to disengage. This durable and society-wide counter-frame also contradicts the government's own campaign that encourages combatants to demobilize so they can go home again. Deserters reported being consistently treated like criminals and harassed by law enforcement, even when lawfully demobilized. Thus, the government's "narco-terrorist" frame may influence combatants to stay in their groups, as was the case with Andrés, or it might drive ex-combatants to rejoin armed groups because of the lack of alternatives.

The perpetrator and narco-terrorist frames clearly overlap, as the guerrillas, and later the paramilitaries, are framed by the government as violent criminals in both frames. These frames also reinforce the framing of deserters as brave for having escaped these groups – especially as many deserters shared stories of narco-trafficking and violence that contributed to both the perpetrator and narco-terrorist framing. The paramilitary frame of being "protectors" of the people and self-defense forces overlaps with the narco-terrorist frame (because they stated frequently that they were helping the government fight the terrorists and protecting the people from the guerrillas), but it also overlaps with the victimhood frame, because of the assertion that they were only acting in self-defense. In addition, the "deserters as brave" framing overlaps with the guerrilla

victimhood frame, because most deserters retained a narrative of also
being victims of the government. In turn, the victimhood frame overlaps
with the guerrilla revolution frame (i.e., overthrowing the government in
the name of justice and equality), but both the victimhood and revolution
frames are threatened by stories told by deserters, which necessitates (for
the loyalists) the framing of deserters as liars.

This last framing contest – that of *loyalists versus deserters* – is between
the ex-combatants themselves, though the government does play a role
by discounting all ex-combatant frames and grouping them all together
into one category. Labeling and othering were prominent in this contest,
where the guerrilla loyalists had a very different definition of *desmovilizado* compared to the deserters and the ex-paramilitaries. While all
the ex-combatants in this sample had technically demobilized, the FARC
loyalists were insistent that they had not, in fact, demobilized – because
to them, demobilization meant surrender and disintegration. Instead,
they had simply shifted to a new strategy and were persisting with their
revolutionary goals without weapons. The deserters and ex-AUC respondents, however, argued that the FARC had not demobilized at all because
they were still persisting with their criminal activities.

LINKING FRAMING CONTESTS AND DISENGAGEMENT
PATHWAYS TO REINTEGRATION

Like several of the other male deserters in this study, Andrés finally demobilized when his wife convinced him to leave. He had been assigned a
dangerous mission: while I had no way to verify this and Andrés certainly
had a tendency to exaggerate, he told me he had been ordered to assassinate Rodrigo Londoño Echeverri, aka "Timochenko," the former leader
of the FARC and now a senator. Knowing this mission could very well
end in his death or capture, he spent a few days with his wife and kids
before leaving. While there, his wife begged him not to go, to think of
his children, to leave all the violence behind. On the way to complete the
mission (what he often called "running an errand" or even more vaguely,
"doing a thing") he changed his mind and called his wife: "And then I
decided. I [had] told her that they should go back home, and I would
go run my errand. And no, when I called, I told her: 'No, I'm going to
Bogotá to desert.'"[10] But then he realized he had no idea how to do that.
He told me that he searched for "how to demobilize" on the internet but

[10] Author interview B18.

could not find any helpful information; eventually, his mother helped him connect with relatives who were in the military, whom he had never met before:

[*Me: Were you scared?*]
 Of course I was scared! Because when one goes to surrender, without knowing what they will do to him … And I called [the relatives] and they said: "They are going to call you from a number." Well, and they called me: "No, that you have to do directly with the GAHD." And I said: "What the hell is the GAHD?" You don't know! And no, at the other end the man told me: "No, make the decision, get to Bogotá, and I will send someone to pick you up." I told him: "No, I will not be picked up. I will surrender myself in a large, public place," I said. "They are not going pick me up and [then] kill me." And I arrived at the place to surrender.[11]

This, however, was far from the end of Andrés' problems. The dissidents that he had abruptly abandoned, in the middle of a critical mission, were furious. He knew everything about their operations; he had also demobilized with cash for the mission that was surrendered to the military. A high price was put on his head; he received constant death threats via WhatsApp messages, even after he changed his number repeatedly. He never explained to me how they kept finding his number, or at least, he did not want to explain it to me. In fact, there was a lot that Andrés did not explain – like how he managed to get pictures of the bodies of deserters who had been assassinated. But Lina had a theory about this.

Lina knew Andrés – in fact, Andrés had introduced Lina and her husband to me, many months after I had first met him. While Lina's husband and Andrés had been comrades in arms, there was no love lost there. It was clear that Lina and her husband did not like or trust Andrés. Why, then, had they trusted him enough to come and meet me? They were curious, it seems, and hopeful. They wanted to tell their stories to someone who would listen. But Lina eventually told me that she did not believe that Andrés had ever actually demobilized. She told me that he was a criminal for life, and that there was no way he would ever leave drug trafficking behind. Lina said that she and her husband had deserted ten years before Andrés had demobilized (I later confirmed that it had actually been five years), and she found it hard to believe that it was sheer coincidence that he had shown up in the safe house at the same time that they had been forced to enter the demobilization program by the military. She said that when Andrés came in, full of swagger

---

[11] Author interview B18.

as always, none of the deserters could believe it: "Everyone was like: '*Andrés?*'" She mimicked a gasp. "'No! How can this be?' He was in it for life," she told me. "He would *never* leave voluntarily." Her theory was that he falsely demobilized in order to get access to the safe houses and report back to the dissidents about who was there. Why else, she asked me, did so many deserters start dying after that, and how did he get pictures of them? It was a fair question – one I already had been wondering myself.

But if that were true, why would Andrés introduce me to Lina's husband – a high-ranking deserter who was hunted by the FARC for years – instead of just executing him? If he really did demobilize falsely to kill FARC deserters, why were Lina and her husband still alive? I never told Andrés about Lina's theory, but Andrés later warned me not to trust anything they told me, just as they had told me not to trust him. It was like Lina's husband had told me months before: "There is no truth here."

But that is the thing about frames. They do not have to be fully true, or fully credible. They just have to be *mostly* true and/or highly credible – but perhaps more importantly, they have to help people make sense of their experiences. Information that contradicts strong frames is, as FARC loyalists illustrated, often met with forceful reduction strategies. Lina and her husband had a strong framing that they and other deserters were noble for having walked away from illegal armed groups. But she knew that Andrés had remained in arms as a dissident even when the FARC signed a peace agreement. She knew he was a drug trafficker and that he had liked it. She told me that he had not treated people well. She needed me to be on her side, to trust her, to believe her. And Andrés did not fit into her frame that deserters were good people and victims of the FARC. Andrés *was* the FARC; he was not a good person. In her frame, he was the perpetrator that treated subordinates badly and made lower-ranking guerrillas desert.

What is perhaps most notable about all of these frames is that they have persisted for decades and continue to persist years after the official peace agreement with the FARC was signed. Indeed, the durability of these three framing contests predicts continued conflict, ongoing recidivism, and recurring problems with reintegration – especially for troops who were ordered to demobilize and for insurgent feminist women who are challenging patriarchal gender norms. Arguably, the government's insistence on the narco-terrorist frame even after signing the peace accord was a contributing factor to the three top FARC leaders returning to arms in 2019.

The ARN never did help me to obtain any interviews. I had to leave Colombia long before any came to fruition, and follow-up emails to them went unanswered. Andrés told me that this was "very Colombian." He told me that Colombians "always" promised things they could not do, because it was rude to say no. That had not been my experience, so I was skeptical. Perhaps the ARN had politely promised something they truly could not deliver. But I think they were simply not interested in what I was trying to learn. In contrast, ex-combatants seemed quite keen on exploring these questions. The disconnect between the ARN and the ex-combatants they were supposed to be helping was strong indeed.

The contests examined here are, of course, not unique to Colombia, and the lessons here go far beyond borders. These discursive battles are archetypal of frame disputes found in many internal armed conflicts. Thus, while from this one case it is difficult to predict with certainty how framing might influence desertion decisions and resulting reintegration trajectories in other cases of armed conflict, the evidence presented here does suggest a few potential effects.

First and most importantly, framing contests clearly limit perceived alternatives, and in Colombia those contests and alternatives are highly gendered. Rampant stories about women infiltrators and testimonies from women who were accused of being liars about in-group violence confirm that all three guerrilla frames (i.e., victimhood, revolution, deserters as liars) had a marked influence on women's choices: they kept many women in the group and kept them from challenging authority. And the government's counter-frame of portraying guerrilla women as ignorant, sexually abused, and failed mothers only reinforced for many women the idea that staying inside the guerrilla ranks was the safest place to be. While these frames also limited men's options, the overall vitriol against and stigmatization of male guerrilla deserters was different, and it did not remove men's agency as it did for women. In fact, the government's narco-terrorist framing likely gave men too much agency (by ignoring that some of them were indeed victims) and gave women too little (by assuming they were *all* victims).

Second, the frames enabled both loyalists and deserters to reduce cognitive dissonance quickly; for the loyalists, this dissonance reduction aided in group cohesion, but for deserters it helped to justify choices about which many were conflicted. Combatants who had experienced some form of victimization from their own comrades were more likely to leave or consider leaving. Of course, this makes sense – people who experience in-group violence should be more likely to leave. But why, then, do other people in the same overall circumstances choose to stay? Why does this in-group violence not weaken the frame's credibility and disillusion other combatants? And this is where the frame is key: as framing influences how people organize experiences and interpret reality, highly resonant frames can be useful to suppress conflicting information and address cognitive dissonance, or at least to organize conflicting information in a way that does not threaten the overall frame.

For example, when combatants who have not directly experienced abuse can organize dissonant information to fit the experiences of others into the dominant frame (i.e., insisting that the combatants reporting abuses are liars, paid informants, not "real" guerrillas, etc.), it reduces cognitive dissonance and allows them to stay without guilt. Alternatively, some combatants might choose to stay in the face of adverse experiences for other reasons – economic needs, relationships, or, as some attested, simply having nowhere else to go. In this case, the frame helps to justify their choice to stay. Given that these interviews were done *after* demobilization, it is hard to say with certainty whether some frame adoption – particularly those of deserters – influenced the choice to leave or were adopted afterward in order to justify the choice to leave. Either way, the frames are clearly important in helping ex-combatants to make sense of their experiences.

For example, a highly resonant frame could shift a person's type of commitment: even if a person joined because of the guns or because of economic need, for many respondents being immersed in the victimhood and/or revolutionary frame (i.e., indoctrination) eventually shifted – or expanded – their type of commitment to the group. This is inextricably linked to ideology, as ideology informs both the articulation and amplification of the frame (even with the paramilitaries, where the ideology was simply to quash rebellion and maintain the status quo). Framing, after all, is how the group communicates its ideology to the world and to its recruits. In the Colombian case, this link is readily apparent in how each frame operationalizes gender norms, where the guerrillas use insurgent feminism to show that they are more enlightened and progressive than the state, and the state exploits gender stereotypes of women as victims to discredit the guerrillas and win public support. Perhaps most importantly, framing contests between rebels and the government can actually reinforce the group's framing of their ideology – such as reinforcing the belief that the government is the "real terrorist" and/or that gender equality is better inside the group than outside of it.

In addition, the *campesino* victim and the insurgent feminist are linchpins in the guerrilla framing of their cause, and the protector or *autodefensa* identity is critical in the paramilitary frame that insists they were never the aggressors in Colombia's conflict. Discursive battles around the competing identities of revolutionaries versus terrorists is a core framing contest not only in Colombia, but in civil wars all over the world.

The framing contests in this case also influenced the calculation of the costs and benefits of membership versus the costs and benefits of leaving the group, not only by creating an echo chamber of reinforcing information but also by discrediting or threatening anyone who spoke against the credibility of the frame (e.g., women who accused commanders of abuse). This effect was also highly gendered, where many women were convinced that membership in the guerrillas was the safest place to be due to widespread sexual violence and gender inequality in Colombian society, and many men could not see viable alternatives to group membership due to the inability to obtain land for farming and/or a general fear of having to find work in the cities.

Network effects, on the other hand, seem to go both ways: networks are influenced by the frame but also influence the resonance of the frame. That is, being inside the group "en el monte" (as opposed to being a militia member living at home) restricted the amount of information available to recruits, thus reducing cognitive dissonance and making the frame more credible and salient (i.e., relevant to daily life and experiences). Also, those that were known to be highly committed loyalists were less likely to hear anyone discuss deserting. Thus, commitment to the frame is influenced by network connections, but a strong commitment to the frame also influences who is in one's most direct network – it is a self-reinforcing loop.

Finally, government demobilization and/or amnesty promises do not appear to have convinced deserters to leave, or at least none of the deserters in this sample, but they certainly affected ex-combatants' post-demobilization trajectories and resentment. This is largely due to the government's credibility problem (i.e., combatants simply did not believe government promises). This credibility problem was especially pronounced for women, many of whom had experienced or witnessed gender-based violence perpetrated by the military and paramilitaries and also felt maligned by government portrayals of women guerrillas. Thus, the framing contests between the government and the armed groups did not seem to convince combatants to desert, but they did have the effect of reducing perceived alternatives for some combatants who might have considered desertion under different circumstances. And these ongoing contests almost certainly affected the post-demobilization transitions for all ex-combatants.

This research raises several implications for ongoing research on disengagement, desertion, and reintegration. First, the persistent government framing of insurgents as criminals and terrorists may prevent disengagement and impede long-term reintegration. Second, framing contests between armed groups and the government reduce perceived alternatives, which may make combatants less likely to desert, or less likely to enter government programs if they do desert. Third, cost–benefit calculations for combatants are highly dependent on societal gender norms, and gendered frames exacerbate the lack of perceived and actual alternatives for women combatants in particular. Fourth, highly resonant frames reduce cognitive dissonance among recruits and help to maintain group cohesion, even in the face of serious frame credibility issues. And finally, "genderwashing" (i.e., using the language of gender equality without actually implementing it) obscures gendered hierarchies within armed groups and makes women combatants less likely to challenge internal patriarchal structures.

POLICY IMPLICATIONS: IMPROVING REINTEGRATION

Can the study of frames improve the implementation of disengagement and reintegration policies? I believe it can, in several ways. First, understanding the durability of particular frames and the identities constructed within them, such as collective claims to victimhood, insurgent feminists, and the fighter identity, can guide reintegration practices that validate ex-combatants' experience and capitalize on skills that many combatants have acquired in armed groups. While treating all ex-combatants equally may have its advantages for the government in dismantling hierarchies within armed groups, it can also backfire if highly educated and/or accomplished ex-combatants feel that they are being patronized or discounted. That is, rather than treat all ex-combatants as criminals or as deviants that need reeducation, reintegration programs need to acknowledge skills and knowledge that many ex-combatants have acquired and parlay these skills into employment training and other reintegration options. Rather than destroy the "fighter" identity, reintegration programs should try to redirect the fighter identity, showing ex-combatants how to fight for their rights and for equality without the use of violence. Of course, this shift requires acknowledging that many ex-combatants have legitimate grievances rather than treating them all like ex-convicts – but this means the government would have to acknowledge that it too is responsible for the sustained violence.

Second, understanding how frames can shift perceived alternatives, especially for women, appears to be critical to successful reintegration. As the preceding chapters have shown, reintegration is particularly challenging for women who have adopted a feminist stance, as they are often returning to the same patriarchal status quo in civilian life that they had been fighting against. Reintegration processes also affect men's identities related to stereotypical gender norms of *machismo* and militarized masculinities, but psycho-social assistance and job retraining for them to cope with these changing identities continue to be lacking in all versions of Colombian reintegration. For men in particular, the inability to find adequate or dignified work after demobilization in order to provide for their families has been a significant motivator to consider rearming or to become involved in other illicit activities. A program with a 55 percent male dropout rate clearly needs a better assessment of what is not working. Both men and women suffer from the failure of DDR to adequately consider what gender means to combatants who are trying to become civilians – especially in a country with ongoing conflict and myriad opportunities to obtain power and money through armed violence and militarized masculinities.

Reintegration Trajectories: Andrés and Lina

A few weeks before I left Colombia, Andrés sent me a picture of a funeral wreath that had appeared on his doorstep, with a note on it that said *sapo* ("snitch"). He had immediately abandoned his apartment, packed up his family, and relocated to a different department entirely. He changed his number and sent me a new one, but he would not tell me where he had gone. He had been receiving death threats since he deserted the dissidents in 2017, often as voicemail messages or pictures of official letters from FARC dissidents, offering a reward for his death or capture. How the dissidents kept getting his phone number was a mystery he never explained.

Then, a year after I finished my fieldwork, Andrés disappeared. He would normally send WhatsApp messages several times a month, telling me stories of how difficult reintegration was, how insufficient the program was for someone supporting a family, or how scared he was. The ARN's solution to the repeated death threats was to provide him with a bulletproof vest. That was the extent of the government's protection. Despite campaigns that promised protection in exchange for information, despite promising combatants they could go home to their families, what really happened was this: a Kevlar vest.

Andrés' fear was highly justified. Deserters were being picked off, one by one. He knew, because he somehow had photos of their dead bodies. (The ex-combatant networks were odd like that – graphic pictures of death and violence seemed to circulate rapidly among them.) So, when I heard that Junior was dead, I had a sinking feeling it was true. Only a few months after Junior left the safe houses, shortly after I left Colombia, I received word that he had been killed: executed by the ELN, on the orders of his own father. I still remember talking to Junior in that safe house, where he proudly showed me a picture of his two-year-old daughter and confessed his fears about going into the world. But he had been determined to figure it out, while also regretting that he had left the group he loved so much. He had fled to the army not because he wanted to betray his group, but because he needed protection. Protection that was promised but not provided.

He had been right: there was no justice either way.

Unsurprisingly, after I left Colombia, Andrés was often very despairing in his messages to me, hinting or outright asking me to send money or to help him get his children out of the country. The situation had deteriorated in his department, and dissident groups were forcibly recruiting children, he said. When the messages stopped completely, I feared the worst. I could tell from WhatsApp that my messages were not even going through to his number. And while it is common for ex-combatants to change their phone numbers often (something the ARN encourages them to do), it was out of character for Andrés to disappear completely. Through social media, I managed to get in contact with his son, who put me in touch with Andrés' mother, who gave me the number of Andrés' ex-wife. And this is where everything got a bit weird. At first, she told me that Andrés was sick in the hospital, and that was why he was not answering messages. But something was off – she would not tell me what was wrong with him, and I knew that if he was in the hospital, he would have called to ask me for money. Finally, after several days of messaging back and forth, she told me the real story: he had been arrested and was in jail. But she would not tell me why. His young son thought his father was on a work trip.

After many months of calls and messages and being barraged daily with WhatsApp messages from Andrés in prison, I finally obtained official documentation from the public defender on the case. Andrés had been arrested for a violent crime he had allegedly committed while working with the FARC dissidents. Since he had formally demobilized, he thought he had amnesty (though he later changed his story and claimed total innocence for that particular crime), but the prosecutor's office argued that this specific offense was personal and had nothing to do with the armed conflict. This is the tangled web of the current transitional justice system in Colombia: in addition to being rife with corruption and bureaucratic ineptitude, the system is structured so that many ex-combatants do not fully understand which crimes are covered under amnesty agreements and which are not. And how do they prove that a crime was done under orders? I spent months trying to get Andrés proper legal representation and trying to find a way to at least post bail so he could be reunited with his family while awaiting trial. Andrés was stuck in no man's land between multiple competing frames – the dissidents were hunting him, the FARC had disowned him, society had shunned him, and the government wanted to lock him up forever.

Eventually, due to my constant pleading and the good will I had built up, the FARC political party offered some logistical assistance and Andrés' family managed to pay for a proper lawyer. But it took over a year for Andrés to get a real hearing, and after two of these (which were rescheduled twice due to the Covid-19 pandemic), a judge determined that the prosecution did not have enough evidence to go to trial and ordered him released. But it would be several more months before Andrés was actually released, because he had to pay the balance for his prison stay. How could he do that, he asked me, when he had been locked up for a year and unable to work? He had spent over a year in prison without trial, sleeping on the concrete floor because he could not afford a bed in his cell; he contracted Covid-19 while there, and then had to pay the balance of his medical expenses before he could be released. At least, that is how he tells it. I never quite knew how much of his stories were true.

But after his release is where the failures of reintegration became even more profound. As the charges were fully dropped, there was no proof that Andrés had violated any terms of his demobilization. He was therefore still entitled to his reintegration benefits. In fact, because the charges were dropped, he should have been entitled to a year of withheld monthly payments while he was held in prison without trial. When I told him that, he laughed: "That's never going to happen." Instead, Andrés was released from prison with no money, no belongings, no phone – not even any identification. His national ID card had been taken from him when arrested and, inexplicably, he never got it back; he needed fifty thousand pesos (approximately US$13) to get another one. But since he did not have ID to accept money transfers from his family or otherwise, and no money in the bank to withdraw, he had no idea how to get this seemingly impossible sum. He would need to "run errands," he said. And we both knew what that meant. His reintegration officer, according to Andrés, was uninterested in helping him even though he had not legally violated any terms of his demobilization. He had clearly been presumed guilty. How could he get fifty thousand pesos, he asked me, when they had thrown him onto the street with literally nothing? He did not even have enough money for bus fare to get home. How does a man like this, with no work experience except trafficking drugs and fighting wars, start over with literally nothing but the clothes on his back? The arrest and imprisonment had set him back to the point of breaking. He told me he wanted to kill himself.

Now, I realize that there are more sympathetic characters than a man who spent ten years running drugs, refused to demobilize when the peace accord was finally signed, and, by his own account, killed at least a few innocent civilians. A year in prison is likely far too small a price to pay. But the point of sharing this story is not to garner sympathy for Andrés. The point is to illustrate the failure of a demobilization program that promises fighters they can leave violence behind, that they can go home and start families, that promises them protection in exchange for information, but then does very little to equip them to live law-abiding, healthy, and safe lives. In fact, by persecuting and harassing them – as happened with many of my respondents – the government may be pushing many of these ex-combatants back to arms.

Lina, of course, is a far more sympathetic character – and not only because of her gender. Tricked into joining the FARC, raped repeatedly, ordered to use sex to collect intelligence, and then finally escaping with her future husband, only to have her child kidnapped two years later to try to force her husband back into drug trafficking – Lina had lived ten lifetimes by the time I met her. And many years after she fled, when she thought she was finally getting her life back, she was outed as an ex-combatant and forced to enter the demobilization program. Four years after that, she had already lived in three different cities and still struggled to establish any sort of normalcy. She and her husband could not even get cleaning jobs without references – but where would they get references? Her husband had spent twenty-five years with the FARC. What kind of work references could he possibly provide?

Lina and Johan had a folder full of certificates from courses they had taken with the Victim's Unit and with the reintegration program

– certificates that Lina only realized in retrospect were completely useless in terms of actually getting a job. Due to their background – and the inability to certify their medical training or other types of guerrilla education – many ex-combatants worked in construction or as security guards (though they were not allowed to be armed). But women were never hired for those jobs. "How am I not a victim in all of this?" Lina wondered out loud, more than once. Of course she was a victim. Her husband, recruited at age ten, was too – though he had clearly also been a perpetrator for decades. Their daughter, kidnapped and abused and moved around to multiple cities, certainly was a victim. But so were over nine million other people – most of whom got nothing at all while Lina and her husband will receive their monthly reintegration allowance for years. How do these ex-combatants reintegrate into a society that has both been harmed by their actions and openly resents the assistance they receive to rebuild their lives? How do they reconcile with victims who never took a side or picked up a gun?

As I was finishing the first draft of this book in the middle of the Covid-19 pandemic, I received a message from Lina's husband. They were doing well, he told me. With the help of the ARN, they had made plans to start a fast-food restaurant of some kind, specializing in chicken. They were very excited about it, he said, rattling off a long list of chicken dishes they planned to serve. They wanted me to come visit so I could eat there. I immediately felt a pit in my stomach. While of course I wish them all the success in the world, I could not shake the feeling that this was the same story all over again: the same cycle of underprepared, underfunded, doomed-to-fail entrepreneurship that thousands of other ex-combatants had been through.

But I really hope that I am wrong.

Remobilized: Michael

About a year after I left Colombia, I checked in with Michael – the young and charming ELN deserter who had been forcibly recruited. For over a year, he had been moving around, receiving threats from the ELN, falling in and out of work, and being repeatedly evicted for not paying rent. He had often been quite despondent. Right before I left, he had become desperate and tried to register as a victim with the Victim's Unit – he had been forcibly recruited, after all – but he was ineligible as he was already registered as an ex-combatant. One could not, officially, be both a victim and an ex-combatant. However, when I checked in this time, Michael's messages were dotted with exclamation points and happy face emojis. He was working with the military, he said, doing intelligence like he had always wanted to.

This brought me up short. The military demobilized him and then remobilized him? Michael did not quite see it that way, though I sure did. But I should not have been surprised. The military's main goal in demobilizing combatants is not to turn them into productive citizens nor to protect them from their former group – that is, in theory, the job of the ARN. The military's main objective is to disarm combatants and then turn them into information sources to help the government win the war. And while military officers are not supposed to contact combatants once they leave the safe houses, this rule is regularly flouted.[12]

But Michael did not see himself as being exploited; it was a job, he was getting paid, and it was work he had always wanted to do – even if the military had moved him to a very "hot" area (i.e., active with armed violence). "Aren't you scared?" I asked him. The ELN, after all, had put a price on his head. And yet here he was, going on missions with the military deep into ELN territory. But he assured me that he liked the work. This sweet young man with a thousand-watt smile, who never liked guns and dreamed of being a tattoo artist, was now reassuring me that he liked working for the military in the middle of the same conflict zone he risked his life to escape.

I sat with this for a long time, thinking about what I knew about Michael, and what I knew about the Colombian military. I thought about the thousands of "false positive" murders of young men just like Michael. I thought about the widespread sexual assault perpetrated by soldiers and proven military collusion with paramilitaries and drug traffickers. I thought about the police who were paid off by armed groups to look the other way, and the multinational corporations that paid these same armed groups for "protection." And then I thought about Michael, falling into this complex web of bribery and violence, after finally escaping the ELN. Then again, he was doing far better than Andrés or Lina or any other deserters that I stayed in touch with. He had not been arrested, and he didn't have children or a wife to support – he never begged me for money or said he wanted to die. In fact, of all the ex-combatants that I stayed in touch with, Michael was the only one openly working with the military and seemed to be the only one who was even close to content. He had a place to live, a regular income, and a job he was proud of.

---

[12] Fattal, *Guerrilla Marketing*.

Of course, Michael was faring decently in reintegration compared to so many others is because the program was specifically designed for him: he was young, male, single with no children, and deserted voluntarily.

But he was still deeply involved in the war. He may have technically demobilized, but he had certainly not left violence behind – he was very much mobilized and militarized. If the main ways that ex-combatants can survive financially in their civilian lives was either to work with the military or to return to some form of illegal activity, what did that say about the reintegration program as a whole?

THE LONG-TERM REPERCUSSIONS OF FRAMING CONTESTS

I still remember one Indigenous woman ex-combatant from the ELN talking to me in her room, on the second story of a brick house with a plastic and tin roof that she shared with several other women, on a steep hill on the outskirts of Bogotá. I remember her adorable baby crawling around underneath our feet. At one point, she motioned to a plate of change on her dresser. "The ARN tells us to save, always save," she said. "But what can I save? Each month I try to put something aside, but I usually only have a few coins left. That is what I've been able to 'save.'" In other words, they are conditioned to think of themselves as failures for not being able to meet program expectations – even though these expectations are impossible for most.

All of the stories presented here – not just the twelve I have explored in detail, but also the eighty-seven other ex-combatants – suggest that framing matters profoundly in terms of how combatants see the costs and benefits of armed participation, and how they calculate alternatives. But the effects of framing go beyond that. The Colombian case shows that framing contests – both within the groups and with adversaries – have long-term repercussions long after the signing of peace agreements. The military's often coercive use of deserters to gain counterinsurgency intelligence, and the exploitation of these ex-combatants' narratives in propaganda that encourages desertion, solidifies the guerrilla loyalists' frame that deserters are liars and traitors. But deserters are still ex-combatants and thus also subsumed into the government's narco-terrorist frame. As a result, they are maligned by all sides, rejected by society, and unprepared for entrepreneurship, and they often struggle from gig to gig, finding informal and precarious employment where they can. For those with dependents, studying full time while also working in order to maximize their ARN benefits and improve their chances in the marketplace was virtually impossible. And while men were most maligned by the narco-terrorist, child rapist narrative, women deserters were affected differently. Framed as liars and traitors by their own group, and as uneducated victims by the government, they may receive more sympathy from the general public. But once they demobilize, they too are rejected – for being too sexual, for being the wrong kind of feminist, for violating gender norms, for being too "badass" (*berraca*).

Of course, when former guerrillas or paramilitaries called me *muy berraca*,[13] they meant it (and I took it) as a compliment. However, I could tell by my conversations with reintegration professionals and other civilians that *berraca* was not, in their minds, a good thing. *Berraca* to civilians working in reintegration usually meant brash, dauntless, aggressive, deviant, adventurous, even reckless – all things that women integrating into civilian life in Colombia "to become women again" should not be. The ARN program wants ex-combatant women to be orderly, obedient, simple, demure – but also independent and economically successful. To be *berraca* is to be a female fighter, and that does not fit with traditional gender norms nor with the reintegration requirements of dropping the fighter identity and abandoning the revolution to focus on entrepreneurial goals.[14] (I would argue, however, that one must be incredibly *berraca* to survive as both a single mother and an ex-combatant in Colombia.)

But women who can barely make ends meet to feed their children – with some continually getting pregnant because they cannot afford contraception – have a hard time focusing on the insurgent feminist fight. This shift of focus from the collective to the individual that comes after disengagement often causes deep isolation. But initial disarmament coupled with an inability to return to the revolution appears far more important to the Colombian government than long-term, sustainable, and productive reintegration. In fact, one reintegration official said that children were a key factor in preventing ex-combatants from returning to arms, implying that there was little incentive for the program to assist women with contraception needs – especially when the various reintegration streams do not offer additional stipends for dependents. Keeping them pregnant kept them peaceful. Ex-combatants' mental health is included (or at least listed) as part of the DDR program, but it is most certainly not a priority.

[13] Note that *berraca*, sometimes spelled *verraca* (which literally translates to "boar"), has many meanings in Colombia and can also mean "very capable" or "intelligent." Amongst the guerrillas, it was generally (though not always) used to indicate being tough, risk-taking, courageous, and/or "badass."
[14] Fattal, *Guerrilla Marketing*.

To make reintegration effective and sustainable, ex-combatants would need dignified jobs with living wages, tools to deal with their trauma from the war, and proper training and education on how to run businesses successfully. Those that are parents (especially single parents) would need assistance with childcare. They would also need protection from the exploitation of armed militias operating as the de facto authorities in rural areas and urban slums, groups that Andrés informed me are now charging exorbitant fees for so-called "work permits." For real success, ex-combatants would need better options than being remobilized with the military or paramilitaries – both of which, at present, give ex-combatants the highest financial return and the most stable economic situation, even if they provide little physical or psychological security. While these options are sometimes open to women, they are more commonly offered to ex-combatant men – especially in terms of remobilizing with the military.

I want to close by discussing the Colombian government's emphasis on success stories. About halfway through my fieldwork, two of my research participants brought me to an ARN graduation in central Colombia. One of them wore a bulletproof vest. We sat in the back, with both of them whispering to me the entire time. The graduation is a ceremony to celebrate demobilized combatants who have completed the reintegration program – usually about six years of benefits and education or training, depending on each person's adherence to the criteria. One of the participants I was with had completed the program years ago; the other was one year into it. What they were whispering were sarcastic comments about the ARN's self-congratulatory speech about how remarkable the program was. "Graduating with what?" said one under his breath, as demobilized combatants walked up to get their certificates. "Graduating with *nothing*. What is that diploma good for?" Then, articulating each syllable for extra emphasis: "Ab-so-lu-ta-men-te *nada*." The other man laughed wryly, earning us a few reproachful glances.

Absolutely *nothing*.

I watched the pomp and circumstance of the diplomas being handed out, the smiling and hopeful faces of the "graduates," the speeches from ARN reps, the children watching their parents proudly. For most of them, I could predict what was coming – poverty, struggle, pressure from the military, pressure from other armed groups, constant fear of being hunted down, a life of stigmatization. Now, a few years later, I think of Michael, working for the military, and of Lina and her husband, constantly struggling to find work, optimistically starting their chicken restaurant. I think often of Andrés, out of prison and scraping by from gig to gig. I cannot help but wonder what the rest of them are doing and how many of them are doing well. Or how many have returned to arms.

To fully understand desertion and the impact of exit pathways on reintegration experiences, it is clearly not enough to study why some people abandon armed groups – we must also seek to understand the nature of the violence they are resisting and why some people stay in the fight, including how they make sense of those choices, even in the face of in-group violence, the loss of leader credibility, and intense pressure from government and other opposing forces. Understanding variance in troop commitment and how combatants organize dissonant experiences in order to stay loyal – something this book has aimed to do – could improve demobilization and reintegration programs by improving our understanding of pathways out of armed violence, the gender norms that affect those pathways, and the impact of these trajectories on long-term reintegration. Most importantly, the evidence presented in this book illustrates that the extension of these discursive battles into the "post-conflict" environment only prolongs war mentalities on all sides and does not allow ex-combatants to move forward into new identities and new lives – even when they desperately want to.

Appendix A

Ex-combatant Interviews

INT #	Gender (man/ woman)	Group/ former group	Ethnicity (self-identified)	Age of initial enlistment	Time in armed group(s)
B01	M	FARC/M-19		13	20+ years
B02	W	FARC		13	Unknown
B03	W	ELN		17	1 year
B04	W	ELN		20	Unknown
B05	W	FARC	Indigenous	17	2 years
B06	W	ELN		37	2 years
B07	W	ELN	Afro-descendant	15	Unknown
B08	M	ELN		17	3 years
B09	M	ELN/AUC	Indigenous	Unknown	Unknown
B10	M	FARC	Indigenous	12	15 years
B11	W	FARC		21	3 years
B12	W	FARC		35	7 years
B13	W	FARC		25	6 months
B14	W	FARC		20	7 years
B15	M	ELN	Indigenous	18	6 years
B16	M	ELN		16	3.5 years
B17	M	ELN		11	14 years
B18	M	FARC		18	10 years
B19	M	EPL/FARC		12	12 years
B20	M	FARC		Unknown	17 years
B21	M	FARC		22	30 years
B22	M	FARC		21	18 years
B23	M	FARC	Indigenous	30	24 years
B24	W	FARC		16	14 years

(*continued*)

(continued)

INT #	Gender (man/ woman)	Group/ former group	Ethnicity (self-identified)	Age of initial enlistment	Time in armed group(s)
B25	M	FARC		45	13 years
B26	M	FARC		16	16 years
B27	M	FARC	Indigenous	13	30 years
B28	M	FARC		Unknown	30 years
B29	W	FARC		20	10 years
B30	W	FARC	Indigenous	12	6 years
B31	M	FARC		10	25 years
B32	M	FARC		11	37 years
B33	M	FARC	Indigenous	14	24 years
B34	W	FARC	Indigenous	20	11 years
B35	M	FARC		13	5 years
B36	M	FARC		15	16 years
B37	W	FARC		14	4 years
B38	M	FARC		13	6 years
B39	M	FARC		13	9 years
B40	W	FARC		16	10 years
B41	M	FARC		38	5 years
B42	W	FARC	Indigenous	14	7 years
B43	M	FARC	Indigenous	12	9 years
B44	M	FARC		21	11 years
B45	W	FARC		14	7 years
B46	M	FARC		20	22 years
B47	M	FARC		25	47 years
B48	W	FARC		18	20 years
B49	W	FARC		16	30 years
B50	W	FARC	Indigenous	14	20 years
B51	W	FARC		18	43 years
B52	W	FARC		12	16 years
B53	W	FARC		13	29 years
B54	W	FARC	Mulatto	14	19 years
B55	M	FARC		18	37 years
B56	W	FARC		14	28 years
B57	M	FARC		32	33 years
B58	W	FARC		14	27 years
B59	M	FARC		16	37 years
B60	W	FARC		12	20 years
B61	W	FARC		18	30 years
B62	W	FARC	Indigenous	15	21 years
B63	W	FARC		22	4 years
B64	W	ELN	Indigenous	18	3 years

(*continued*)

INT #	Gender (man/ woman)	Group/ former group	Ethnicity (self-identified)	Age of initial enlistment	Time in armed group(s)
B65	W	ELN	Indigenous	12	6 years
B66	M	ELN	Indigenous	23	2 years
B67	M	ELN	Indigenous	16	2 years
B68	M	FARC		12	13 years
B69	M	AUC		17	7 years
B70	M	FARC		21	4 years
B71	M	FARC	Afro-descendant	29	2 years
B72	M	FARC		13	25 years
B73	M	FARC/Black Eagles		14	10 years
B74	M	ELN		10	18 years
B75	M	ELN		13	11 years
B76	M	AUC		17	21 years
B77	M	AUC		21	6 years
B78	M	AUC/EPL		42	7 years
B79	M	AUC		Unknown	4 years
B80	M	AUC/M-19	Afro-descendant	21	8 years
B81	M	AUC		30	2 years
B82	W	AUC	Afro-descendant	30	1.5 years
B83	W	FARC		17	6 years
B84	M	FARC		13	11 years
B85	M	FARC		12	8 years
B86	M	AUC/army		30	1 year*
B87	W	AUC		38	5 years
B88	M	AUC	Afro-descendant	13	12 years
B89	M	AUC		41	6 years
B90	M	AUC/army		30	16 months*
B91	M	AUC/FARC	Afro-descendant	11	19 years
B92	M	AUC/army		24	2 years
B93	M	AUC/army		28	1 year*
B94	M	AUC		28	3 years
B95	M	AUC		24	5 years
B96	M	AUC/army		24	4 months*
B97	M	AUC/army		39	5 years
B98	M	AUC		23	1 year*
B99	W	AUC		26	3 years

Note: * Based on other available information, this respondent was very likely underrepresenting the actual time spent in the group.

Appendix B

Expert Interviews

INT #	Profession	Affiliation
C01	Psychologist	GAHD
C02	Safe house supervisor	GAHD
C03	Reintegration officer	ARN
C04	Researcher	Independent
C05	Head of military interviews (of defectors)	GAHD
C06	Head of child recruitment prevention program	Colombian National Police
C07	Researcher/community liaison	National Center of Memory
C08	Representative	International organization (name withheld)
C09	Government representative	Donor country (name withheld)
C10	Departmental director	Colombian Victim's Unit
C11	Regional director	Undisclosed human rights NGO
C12	Social worker	Local government
C13	Lawyer	Colombian Victim's Unit
C14	Reintegration officer	ARN
C15	Reintegration officer	ARN

Bibliography

ACR (Colombian Reintegration Agency). "Reseña Historíca Institucional." Bogota, 2016. www.reincorporacion.gov.co/es/agencia/Documentos de Gestin Documental/Reseña_Historica_ACR.pdf.

Albuja, Sebastián, and Marcela Ceballos. "Urban Displacement and Migration in Colombia." *Forced Migration Review* 34 (2010). www.fmreview.org/sites/fmr/files/FMRdownloads/en/urban-displacement/albuja-ceballos.pdf.

Alison, Miranda. *Women and Political Violence: Female Combatants in Ethno-National Conflict.* New York and London: Routledge, 2009.

Alpert, Megan. "To Be a Guerrilla, and a Woman, in Colombia." *The Atlantic,* September 2016. www.theatlantic.com/international/archive/2016/09/farc-deal-female-fighters/501644/.

Alsema, Adriaan. "Rape in Colombia Tripled over Past 20 Years; 87% of Victims Are Minors." *Colombia Reports,* 2019. https://colombiareports.com/rape-in-colombia-tripled-over-past-20-years-87-of-victims-are-minors/.

Altier, Mary Beth, John G Horgan, and Christian N Thoroughgood. "In Their Own Words? Methodological Considerations in the Analysis of Terrorist Autobiographies." *Journal of Strategic Security* 5, no. 4 (2012): 85–98.

Altier, Mary Beth, Emma Leonard Boyle, Neil D Shortland, and John G Horgan. "Why They Leave: An Analysis of Terrorist Disengagement Events from Eighty-Seven Autobiographical Accounts." *Security Studies* 26, no. 2 (2017): 305–32.

Altier, Mary Beth, Christian N Thoroughgood, and John G Horgan. "Turning Away from Terrorism: Lessons from Psychology, Sociology, and Criminology." *Journal of Peace Research* 51, no. 5 (2014): 647–61.

Alto Comisionado para la Paz. "Acuerdo Final de Paz." 2016. www.altocomision adoparalapaz.gov.co/procesos-y-conversaciones/Documentos compartidos/24-11-2016NuevoAcuerdoFinal.pdf.

Alzate, Monica. "Adolescent Pregnancy in Colombia: The Price of Inequality and Political Conflict." In *International Handbook of Adolescent Pregnancy,* edited by Andrew Cherry and Mary Dillon. New York: Springer, 2014.

Anctil Avoine, Priscyll, and Rachel Tillman. "Demobilized Women in Colombia: Embodiment, Performativity and Social Reconciliation." In *Female Combatants in Conflict and Peace: Challenging Gender in Violence and Post-conflict Reintegration*, edited by Seema Shekhawat. Basingstoke: Palgrave Macmillan, 2015.

Arango, C. *Farc Veinte Años de Marquetalia a La Uribe.* Bogotá: Aurora, 1984.

Arias, Luis Alberto. *Familias En Situación de Desplazamiento En Altos de Cazucá.* Bogotá: Fundación Educación y Desarrollo, 2003.

Aristizábal Farah, Lorena. "Devenir Civil/Devenir Mujer: Una Mirada a Las Subjetividades de Mujeres Excombatientes En Proceso de Reinserción." In *Desafíos Para La Reintregración: Enfoques de Género, Edad y Etnia*, edited by Centro Nacional de Memoria Histórica. Bogotá: Imprenta Nacional, 2013.

ARN (Agency for Reincorporation and Normalization). "76% de Los Excombatientes FARC-EP, Optimista Sobre Su Futuro En Proceso de Reincorporación." *Resultados del Registro Nacional de Reincorporación*, 2019. www.reincorporacion.gov.co/es/sala-de-prensa/noticias/Paginas/2019/El-76porciento-de-los-excombatientes-farc-es-optimista-sobre-su-futuro-en-proceso-de-reincorporacion.aspx.

ARN. "La Reintegración En Colombia – Cifras." ARN, 2019. www.reintegracion.gov.co/es/la-reintegracion/Paginas/cifras.aspx.

ARN. "Reincorporacion En Cifras." ARN, 2020. www.reincorporacion.gov.co/es/reincorporacion/Paginas/La-Reincorporación-en-cifras.aspx.

ARN. "Reseña Histórica." ARN, 2019. www.reincorporacion.gov.co/es/agencia/Paginas/resena.aspx.

ARN, Director General de la. *Resolución 1356.* Bogotá: ARN, 2016.

Arrieta, Carlos Gustavo, Luis Javier Orjuela, Eduardo Sarmiento Palacio, and Juan Gabriel Tokatlian. *Narcotráfico En Colombia: Dimensiones Políticas, Economicas, Jurídicas e Internacionales.* Bogotá: Ediciones Uniandes y Tercer Mundo Editores, 1990.

Arvelo, Jose E. "International Law and Conflict Resolution in Colombia: Balancing Peace and Justice in the Paramilitary Demobilization Process." *Georgetown Journal of International Law* 37, no. 2 (2006): 90–108.

Autesserre, Séverine. "Hobbes and the Congo: Frames, Local Violence, and International Intervention." *International Organization* 63, no. 2 (2009): 249–80.

Ávila, Ariel. "Bacrim, Neoparamilitares y Grupos Post-Desmovilización Paramilitar." *Semana*, March 30, 2016. www.semana.com/opinion/articulo/ariel-avila-bacrim-neoparamilitares-y-grupos-post-desmovilizacion-paramilitar/467330.

Barnett, Michael, Hunjoon Kim, Madalene O'Donnell, and Laura Sitea. "Peacebuilding: What Is in a Name?" *Global Governance* 13, no. 1 (2007): 35–58.

Barnett, Michael N, and Martha Finnemore. *Rules for the World: International Organizations in Global Politics.* Ithaca: Cornell University Press, 2004.

BBC. "Colombia's Uribe Wins Second Term." *BBC News*, May 29, 2006. http://news.bbc.co.uk/2/hi/americas/5024428.stm.

BBC. "BBC Colombia Timeline." *BBC News*, August 8, 2018. www.bbc.com/news/world-latin-america-19390164.

BBC. "Colombia Farc: Election Candidate Timochenko Taken to Hospital." *BBC News*, March 1, 2018. www.bbc.com/news/world-latin-america-43251435.

BBC News. "Arrest Warrant Issued for Farc Ex-rebel Jesús Santrich." BBC News, July 10, 2019. www.bbc.com/news/world-latin-america-48932019.

BBC News. "Colombia Peace Process: Ex-rebel Santrich to Be Freed." BBC News, May 16, 2019. www.bbc.com/news/world-latin-america-48294827.

BBC News Mundo. "FARC: Abaten a 9 Guerrilleros En La Primera Ofensiva Militar Contra Iván Márquez y Su Grupo En Colombia." BBC News, August 30, 2019.

Beltrán, William Mauricio, and Sian Creely. "Pentecostals, Gender Ideology and the Peace Plebiscite: Colombia 2016." *Religions* 9, no. 12 (2018): 1–19.

Benford, Robert D, and David A Snow. "Framing Processes and Social Movements: An Overview and Assessment." *Annual Review of Sociology* 26, no. 1 (2000): 611–39.

Bjørgo, Tore. "Processes of Disengagement from Violent Groups of the Extreme Right." In *Leaving Terrorism Behind: Individual and Collective Disengagement*, edited by Tore Bjørgo and John Horgan. New York: Routledge, 2009.

Blair, Erik. "A Reflexive Exploration of Two Qualitative Data Coding Techniques." *Journal of Methods and Measurement in the Social Sciences* 6, no. 1 (2016): 14–29.

Bloom, Mia. *Bombshell: The Many Faces of Women Terrorists*. Toronto: Viking Canada, 2011.

Bluradio. "Nueve Exjefes 'Paras' Que Estuvieron Presos En Colombia Ya Están Libres." *Blueradio*, 2016. www.bluradio.com/nacion/nueve-exjefes-paras-que-estuvieron-presos-en-colombia-ya-estan-libres-119450.

Bouta, Tsjeard, Ian Bannon, and Georg Frerks. *Gender, Conflict, and Development*. Washington, DC: World Bank, 2005.

Bouvier, Virginia M. "Gender and the Role of Women in Colombia's Peace Process." Peacewomen.org, 2016. www.peacewomen.org/sites/default/files/Women-Colombia-Peace-Process-EN.pdf.

Bovenkerk, Frank. "On Leaving Criminal Organizations." *Crime, Law and Social Change* 55, no. 4 (2011): 261–76.

Bray, Laura A, Thomas E Shriver, and Alison E Adams. "Framing Authoritarian Legitimacy: Elite Cohesion in the Aftermath of Popular Rebellion." *Social Movement Studies* 18, no. 6 (2019): 682–701.

Brodzinsky, Sibylla. "Colombia's 'Parapolitics' Scandal Casts Shadow over President." *The Guardian*, April 23, 2008. www.theguardian.com/world/2008/apr/23/colombia.

Bubolz, Bryan F, and Pete Simi. "Disillusionment and Change: A Cognitive-Emotional Theory of Gang Exit." *Deviant Behavior* 36, no. 4 (2015): 330–45.

Burnyeat, Gwen. *Chocolate, Politics and Peace-Building: An Ethnography of the Peace Community of San José de Apartadó, Colombia*. London: Palgrave Macmillan, 2018.

Cantillo, Jorge. "Preocupación En Colombia: Las Disidencias de Las FARC Duplicaron Sus Miembros Armados En El Último Año." *InfoBae*, 2020. www.infobae.com/america/colombia/2020/06/07/preocupacion-en-colombia-las-disidencias-de-las-farc-duplicaron-sus-miembros-armados-en-el-ultimo-ano/.

Carpenter, R. Charli. "Gender Theory in World Politics: Contributions of a Nonfeminist Standpoint?" *International Studies Review* 4, no. 3 (2002): 153–65.

Carpenter, R. Charli. "'Women, Children and Other Vulnerable Groups': Gender, Strategic Frames and the Protection of Civilians as a Transnational Issue." *International Studies Quarterly* 49, no. 2 (2005): 295–334.

Carpenter, R. Charli. "Recognizing Gender-Based Violence against Civilian Men and Boys in Conflict Situations." *Security Dialogue* 37, no. 1 (2006): 83–103.

Cartaya, Maria. "FARC Members Join Colombia's Congress." *CNN*, July 21, 2018. www.cnn.com/2018/07/21/americas/farc-members-join-colombias-congress/index.html.

Castrillón, Javier Alberto, and René Alonso Guerra Molina. "A Deep Influence: United States–Colombia Bilateral Relations and Security Sector Reform (SSR), 1994–2002." *Opera*, 20 (2017): 35–54.

Castro, María Clemencia, and Carmen Lucía Díaz. *Guerrilla, Reinserción y Lazo Social*. Bogota: Almudena Editores, 1997.

Celis, Luis Eduardo. "Diez Años de Enfrentamientos Con Las Farc." *El Espectador*, August 7, 2008. www.elespectador.com/impreso/politica/articuloimpreso-diez-anos-de-enfrentamientos-farc-0.

Centro Nacional de Memoria Historia. "Exilio Colombiano: Huellas Del Conflicto Armado Más Allá de Las Fronteras." Bogota, 2018. www.centrodememoria historica.gov.co/informes/informes-2018/exilio-colombiano.

Chant, Sylvia, and Nikki Craske. *Gender in Latin America*. New Jersey: Rutgers University Press, 2003.

Cheldelin, Sandra, and Maneshka Eliatamby. *Women Waging War and Peace: International Perspectives of Women's Roles in Conflict and Post-conflict Reconstruction*. New York: Continuum International Pub. Group, 2011.

Chernov Hwang, Julie. *Why Terrorists Quit: The Disengagement of Indonesian Jihadists*. Ithaca and London: Cornell University Press, 2018.

Cohen, Dara Kay. *Rape during Civil War*. Ithaca, NY: Cornell University Press, 2016.

Cohn, Carol. "Women and Wars: Toward a Conceptual Framework." In *Women and Wars*, edited by Carol Cohn. Cambridge: Polity Press, 2013.

Cohn, Carol. *Women and Wars*. Cambridge: Polity Press, 2013.

Colombian Ministry of Defense. "15 Años Transformando Historias." *Las Fuerzas: Periódico Del Comando General de Las Fuerzas Militares de Colombia* 47, September 2017.

Colombian Ministry of Defense. "Llevando La Navidad a La Selva Mindefensa Invita a La Desmovilización," 2010. www.mindefensa.gov.co/irj/go/km/docs/documents/News/NoticiaGrandeMDN/909f5a16-31ec-2d10-b0a3-cb86ef098c23.xml.

Congreso de la Republica de Colombia. Ley 975 de 2005, Pub. L. No. 45.980, 1 (2005). www.fiscalia.gov.co/colombia/wp-content/uploads/2013/04/Ley-975-del-25-de-julio-de-2005-concordada-con-decretos-y-sentencias-de-constitucionalidad.pdf.

Connell, Raewyn. "Masculinities in Global Perspective: Hegemony, Contestation, and Changing Structures of Power." *Theory and Society* 45, no. 4 (August 2016): 303–18.

Connell, Raewyn, and James Messerschmidt. "Hegemonic Masculinity: Rethinking the Concept." *Gender & Society* 19, no. 6 (2005): 829–59.

Corte Constitucional de Colombia. Sentencia T-478 de 2015 (2015). www.corte constitucional.gov.co/inicio/T-478-15 ExpT4734501 (Sergio Urrego).pdf.

Costa, Dora L, and Matthew E Kahn. *Heroes and Cowards: The Social Face of War*. Princeton: Princeton University Press, 2010.

Coulter, Chris. "Female Fighters in the Sierra Leone War: Challenging the Assumptions?" *Feminist Review* 88, no. 88 (2008): 54–73.

Courtheyn, Christopher. "De-indigenized but Not Defeated: Race and Resistance in Colombia's Peace Community and Campesino University." *Ethnic and Racial Studies* 42, no. 15 (2018): 1–20.

Cragin, Kim, and Sara A Daly. *Women as Terrorists: Mothers, Recruiters, and Martyrs*. Santa Barbara, CA: Praeger Security International/ABC-CLIO, 2009.

Crenshaw, Kimberlé. "Demarginalizing the Intersection of Race and Sex: A Black Feminist Critique of Antidiscrimination Doctrine, Feminist Theory and Antiracist Politics." *University of Chicago Legal Forum* 1 (1989): 139–67.

Dahal, Swechchha. "Challenging the Boundaries: The Narratives of the Female Ex-combatants in Nepal." In *Female Combatants in Conflict and Peace: Challenging Gender in Violence and Post-conflict Reintegration*, edited by Seema Shekawat. Basingstoke: Palgrave Macmillan, 2015.

Daniels, Joe Parkin. "Peace Is War as Armed Groups Roil Colombia's Lawless Border Region." The Guardian, July 20, 2019. www.theguardian.com/world/2019/jul/20/colombia-guerrillas-peace-war-catatumbo.

Demant, Froukje, Marieke Slootman, Frank Buijs, and Jean Tillie. *Decline and Disengagement: An Analysis of Processes of Deradicalisation*. Amsterdam: IMES, 2008.

Denov, Myriam. "Girl Soldiers and Human Rights: Lessons from Angola, Mozambique, Sierra Leone and Northern Uganda." *The International Journal of Human Rights* 12, no. 5 (2008): 813–36.

Departamento Administrativo Nacional de Estadística. "Censo General 2005." DANE, 2005. www.dane.gov.co/index.php/estadisticas-por-tema/demografia-y-poblacion/censo-general-2005-1.

Dietrich, Luisa Maria. "La Compañera Guerrilla as Construction of Politicised Femininity: A Comparative Study of Gender Arrangements in Latin American Insurgencies and New Paths for Gender Responsive Demobilisation of Combatants." PhD dissertation, University of Vienna, 2017.

Dietrich, Luisa Maria. "Looking beyond Violent Militarized Masculinities: Guerrilla Gender Regimes in Latin America" *International Feminist Journal of Politics* 14, no. 4 (2012): 489–507.

DNP. "Política Nacional de Reintregación Social y Economíca Para Personas y Grupos Armados Ilegales." Bogotá, 2008. https://colaboracion.dnp.gov.co/CDT/Conpes/Económicos/3554.pdf.

Drissel, David. "Reframing the Taliban Insurgency in Afghanistan: New Communication and Mobilization Strategies for the Twitter Generation." *Behavioral Sciences of Terrorism and Political Aggression* 7, no. 2 (2015): 97–128.

Duncanson, Claire. "Forces for Good? Narratives of Military Masculinity in Peacekeeping Operations." *International Feminist Journal of Politics* 11, no. 1 (2009): 63–80.

Ebaugh, Helen Rose Fuchs. *Becoming an Ex: The Process of Role Exit*. Chicago: University of Chicago Press, 1988.

Edel, Mirjam, and Maria Josua. "How Authoritarian Rulers Seek to Legitimize Repression: Framing Mass Killings in Egypt and Uzbekistan." *Democratization* 25, no. 5 (2018): 882–900.

EFE. "El Ex Número Dos de Las FARC, Iván Márquez, Anuncia Que Retoma Las Armas." *La Vanguardia*. August 29, 2019. www.lavanguardia.com/internacional/20190829/47349585577/farc-guerrilla-vuelta-armas-ivan-marquez.html.

Eichler, Maya. "Militarized Masculinities in International Relations." *The Brown Journal of World Affairs* 21, no. 1 (2014): 81–93.

El Tiempo. "La Del Plebiscito Fue La Mayor Abstención En 22 Años." *El Tiempo*, October 2, 2016. www.eltiempo.com/politica/proceso-de-paz/abstencion-en-el-plebiscito-por-la-paz-36672.

El Tiempo. "En Estos Diez Departamentos Hacen Presencia Los Carteles Mexicanos." *El Tiempo*, January 28, 2018. www.eltiempo.com/justicia/investigacion/fiscalia-alerta-de-presencia-de-mafia-mexicana-en-10-zonas-de-colombia-175974.

El Tiempo. "Cuatro Fichas Claves En El Plan Contra La Escuela de Cadetes." *El Tiempo*, January 20, 2019. www.eltiempo.com/justicia/conflicto-y-narcotrafico/los-hombres-del-eln-tras-atentado-con-carro-bomba-en-escuela-general-santander-316580.

El Tiempo. "Apoyos y Críticas a Decisión de Duque Sobre Ley Estatutaria de La JEP." *El Tiempo*, March 12, 2019. www.eltiempo.com/justicia/jep-colombia/apoyos-y-criticas-a-decision-de-duque-sobre-ley-estatutaria-de-la-jep-336988.

El Tiempo. "'Se Necesita La Fumigación Aérea Contra La Coca': Duque a La Corte." *El Tiempo*. April 3, 2019. www.eltiempo.com/politica/gobierno/duque-reitera-que-se-necesita-la-fumigacion-aerea-contra-la-coca-345554.

El Universal. "Cronología Del Proceso de Paz Con Las Farc En La Habana." *El Universal*, November 6, 2013. www.eluniversal.com.co/colombia/cronologia-del-proceso-de-paz-con-las-farc-en-la-habana-cuba-140970.

ELN. "El Enfoque de Género y La Equidad," 2016. https://eln-voces.com/el-enfoque-de-genero-y-la-equidad/.

ELN. "El Camino Es La Solución Política Del Conflicto." eln-voces.com, 2019. https://eln-voces.com/el-camino-es-la-solucion-politica-del-conflicto/.

Enloe, Cynthia H. *Maneuvers: The International Politics of Militarizing Women's Lives*. Berkeley: University of California Press, 2000.

Escobar, Daniel Mendendorp. "Colombia Guerrilla Group EPL Wants to Join Peace Dialogues." *Colombia Reports*, 2014. https://colombiareports.com/colombia-guerrillla-group-epl-wants-join-peace-dialogues/.

Esguerra Rezk, Juanita. "Desarmando Las Manos y El Corazón: Transformaciones En Las Identidades de Género de Excombatientes (2004–2010)." In *Desafíos Para La Reintregración: Enfoques de Género, Edad y Etnia*, edited by Centro Nacional de Memoria Histórica, 116–77. Bogotá: Imprenta Nacional, 2013.

Espectador, El. "Las Bacrim Crecen En Todo El País." *El Espectador*, February 19, 2012. www.elespectador.com/noticias/judicial/bacrim-crecen-todo-el-pais-articulo-327595.

Espectador, El. "Cristianos y Farc 'Solucionan' El Tema Del Enfoque de Género En Los Acuerdos." *El Espectador*, October 29, 2016. www.elespectador.com/noticias/paz/cristianos-y-farc-solucionan-el-tema-del-enfoque-de-gen-articulo-663030.

Espectador, El. "Las Masacres Aumentaron Un 30% En Los Primeros Dos Años Del Gobierno Duque." *El Espectador*, August 7, 2020. www.elespectador .com/colombia2020/pais/la-guerra-en-los-dos-primeros-anos-del-gobierno-duque/.

Fattal, Alexander F. *Guerrilla Marketing: Counterinsurgency and Capitalism in Colombia*. Chicago: University of Chicago Press, 2018.

Felbab-Brown, Vanda. "Death by Bad Implementation? The Duque Administration and Colombia's Peace Deal(S)." Brookings, 2018. www.brookings.edu/ blog/order-from-chaos/2018/07/24/death-by-bad-implementation-the-duque-administration-and-colombias-peace-deals/.

Ferguson, Neil, Mark Burgess, and Ian Hollywood. "Leaving Violence behind: Disengaging from Politically Motivated Violence in Northern Ireland." *Political Psychology* 36, no. 2 (April 2015): 199–214.

Finn, Luke. "Military Recruitment Breeds Inequality for Colombia's Teenage Boys." NACLA, 2014. https://nacla.org/blog/2014/2/11/military-recruitment-breeds-inequality-colombias-teenage-boys.

FIP. "Retorno a La Legalidad o Reincidencia de Excombatientes En Colombia: Dimensión Del Fenómeno y Factores de Riesgo." Bogota, 2014. http://cdn .ideaspaz.org/media/website/document/53c8560f2376b.pdf.

Fujii, Lee Ann. "Shades of Truth and Lies: Interpreting Testimonies of War and Violence." *Journal of Peace Research* 47, no. 2 (2010): 231–41.

Galvis, Nicolás, Omar David Baracaldo, Miguel García, and Catalina Barragán. "Barómetro de Las Américas Colombia 2016." Bogota, 2016. https:// obsdemocracia.org/uploads/related_file/Informe_Paz_2016.pdf.

García, Alfredo Campos. "New Drivers of Displacement in Colombia." *Forced Migration Review* 56 (2017): 34.

García Duque, Juana, and Juan David Martínez. "Cooperación Internacional, DDR y Los Retos de La Reincorporación." In *Excombatientes y Acuerdo de Paz Con Las FARC-EP En Colombia: Balance de La Etapa Temprana*, edited by Erin McFee and Angelika Rettberg. Bogotá: Universidad de los Andes, 2019.

Gawel, Anna. "Envoy Says Government Is Sticking by FARC Peace Deal – and Venezuelan Refugees." *Washington Diplomat*, October 31, 2019. https:// washdiplomat.com/index.php?option=com_content&view=article&id=20737 &Itemid=413.

Gentry, Caron E, and Laura Sjoberg. *Beyond Mothers, Monsters, Whores: Thinking about Women's Violence in Global Politics*. London: Zed Books, 2015.

Ghilarducci, Dario. "Víctimas y Memoria Histórica. Las Madres de Plaza de Mayo y El Movimiento de Víctimas de Crímines de Estado En Colombia." *Análisis Político* 93 (May–August 2018): 189–207.

Gielen, Amy Jane. "Exit Programmes for Female Jihadists: A Proposal for Conducting Realistic Evaluation of the Dutch Approach." *International Sociology* 33, no. 4 (2018): 454–72.

Glazzard, Andrew. "Losing the Plot: Narrative, Counter-Narrative and Violent Extremism." The Hague, 2017. https://doi.org/10.19165/2017.1.08.

Goffman, Erving. *Frame Analysis: An Essay on the Organization of Experience*. Cambridge, MA: Harvard University Press, 1974.

Goldstein, Joshua S. *War and Gender: How Gender Shapes the War System and Vice Versa.* Cambridge: Cambridge University Press, 2001.

Goodman, Joshua. "Colombia FARC Negotiators Say They Are Taking up Arms Again." *Associated Press*, August 29, 2019. https://apnews.com/article/0c2227 40688f49e3bb1d4572fceb7524.

Gouldner, Alvin Ward. *The Coming Crisis of Western Sociology.* New York: Basic Books, 1970.

Gowrinathan, Nimmi. *Radicalizing Her.* Boston: Beacon Press, 2021.

Grupo de Memoria Histórica. "Basta Ya! Colombia: Memorias de Guerra y Dignidad." Bogotá, 2016.

Guterres, Antonio. "United Nations Verification Mission in Colombia: Report of the Secretary General, April 2018." New York, 2018. https://reliefweb.int/sites/ reliefweb.int/files/resources/N1808241.pdf.

Guterres, Antonio. "United Nations Verification Mission in Colombia: Report of the Secretary General, July 2018." New York, 2018. https://doi.org/S/2010/579.

Guterres, Antonio. "United Nations Verification Mission in Colombia: Report of the Secretary General, September 2018." New York, 2018.

Guterres, Antonio. "United Nations Verification Mission in Colombia: Report of the Secretary General, December 2018." New York, 2018. https://colombia .unmissions.org/sites/default/files/n1845592.pdf.

Guterres, Antonio. "Conflict Related Sexual Violence: Report of the Secretary General S/2019/280." New York, 2019. www.un.org/sexualviolenceinconflict/ wp-content/uploads/2019/04/report/s-2019–280/Annual-report-2018.pdf.

Guterres, Antonio. "United Nations Verification Mission in Colombia: Report of the Secretary General, March 2019." New York, 2019. https://doi.org/10.1017/ S0020818300001107.

Guterres, Antonio. "United Nations Verification Mission in Colombia: Report of the Secretary General, October 2019." New York, 2019. www .securitycouncilreport.org/atf/cf/%7B65BFCF9B-6D27–4E9C-8CD3- CF6E4FF96FF9%7D/s_2019_780.pdf.

Guterres, Antonio. "United Nations Verification Mission in Colombia: Report of the Secretary General, December 2019." New York, 2019.

Guterres, Antonio. "United Nations Verification Mission in Colombia: Report of the Secretary General, March 2020." New York, 2020.

Guterres, Antonio. "United Nations Verification Mission in Colombia: Report of the Secretary General, June 2020." New York, 2020.

Guterres, Antonio. "United Nations Verification Mission in Colombia: Report of the Secretary General, December 2020." New York, 2020.

Gutiérrez Sanín, Francisco. "Telling the Difference: Guerrillas and Paramilitaries in the Colombian War." *Politics & Society* 36, no. 1 (2008): 3–34.

Gutiérrez Sanín, Francisco. "The FARC's Militaristic Blueprint." *Small Wars & Insurgencies* 29, no. 4 (2018): 629.

Gutiérrez Sanín, Francisco, and Francy Carranza Franco. "Organizing Women for Combat: The Experience of the FARC in the Colombian War." *Journal of Agrarian Change* 17, no. 4 (2017): 770–8.

Gutiérrez Sanín, Francisco, and Antonio Giustozzi. "Networks and Armies: Structuring Rebellion in Colombia and Afghanistan." *Studies in Conflict & Terrorism* 33, no. 9 (2010): 836–53.

Gutiérrez Sanín, Francisco, and Elisabeth Jean Wood. "Ideology in Civil War: Instrumental Adoption and beyond." *Journal of Peace Research* 51, no. 2 (2014): 213–26.

Hafner-Burton, E, and M A Pollack. "Mainstreaming Gender in Global Governance." *European Journal of International Relations* 8, no. 3 (2002): 339–73.

Hayon, Alejandra. "Feminismo Insurgente: Cómo Las Exguerrilleras de Las FARC Piensan Su Rol En La Sociedad." *Latinoamérica piensa*, 2019. https://latinoamericapiensa.com/feminismo-insurgente-como-las-exguerrilleras-de-las-farc-piensan-su-rol-en-la-sociedad/18166/.

Hegghammer, Thomas. "Should I Stay or Should I Go? Explaining Variation in Western Jihadists' Choice between Domestic and Foreign Fighting." *American Political Science Review* 107, no. 1 (2013).

Heitlinger, Alena. "Framing Feminism in Post-Communist Czech Republic." *Communist and Post-Communist Studies* 29, no. 1 (1996): 77–93.

Hollain, Anna-Maria. "'Desmovilícese, En Navidad Todo Es Posible.'" *El Pais*, December 24, 2010. https://elpais.com/internacional/2010/12/24/actualidad/1293145201_850215.html.

Horgan, John. *Walking Away from Terrorism: Accounts of Disengagement from Radical and Extremist Movements*. Abingdon and New York: Routledge, 2009.

Howell, Alison. "Forget 'Militarization': Race, Disability and the 'Martial Politics' of the Police and of the University." *International Feminist Journal of Politics* 20, no. 2 (2018): 117–36.

Human Rights Watch. "The Ties That Bind: Colombia and Military–Paramlitary Links." New York, London, Washington, Brussels, 2000. www.hrw.org/reports/2000/colombia/.

Human Rights Watch. "The 'Sixth Division': Military–Paramilitary Ties and U.S. Policy in Colombia." New York, London, Washington, Brussels, 2001. www.hrw.org/reports/2001/colombia/.

Human Rights Watch. "'You'll Learn Not to Cry': Child Combatants in Colombia." New York, 2003. www.hrw.org/reports/2003/colombia0903/colombia0903.pdf.

Human Rights Watch. "Smoke and Mirrors: Colombia's Demobilization of Paramilitary Groups." New York, 2005. www.hrw.org/report/2005/07/31/smoke-and-mirrors/colombias-demobilization-paramilitary-groups.

Human Rights Watch. "Paramilitaries' Heirs: The New Face of Violence in Colombia." New York, 2010. www.hrw.org/sites/default/files/reports/colombia0210webwcover_0.pdf.Human Rights Watch. "World Report 2017: Colombia." New York, 2017. www.hrw.org/world-report/2017/country-chapters/colombia.

Human Rights Watch. "World Report 2018: Colombia." New York, 2018. www.hrw.org/world-report/2018/country-chapters/colombia#84a68b.Hunt, Scott, and Robert D Benford. "Identity Talk in the Peace and Justice Movement." *Journal of Contemporary Ethnography* 22, no. 4 (1994): 488–517.

Idler, Annette. *Borderland Battles: Violence, Crime, and Governance at the Edges of Colombia's War*. New York: Oxford University Press, 2019.

InSight Crime. "ELN Profile," 2017. www.insightcrime.org/colombia-organized-crime-news/eln-profile.

Isaacson, Adam. "Colombia's Victims' Rights Act." Latin America Working Group, 2008. www.lawg.org/colombias-victims-rights-act/.

Jacobson, M. "Terrorist Dropouts: Learning from Those Who Have Left." Washington Institute, 2010. www.washingtoninstitute.org/uploads/Documents/pubs/PolicyFocus101.pdf.

Jennings, Kathleen M. "The Political Economy of DDR in Liberia: A Gendered Critique." *Conflict, Security & Development* 9, no. 4 (2009): 475–94.

Jervis, Robert. "Understanding Beliefs." *Political Psychology* 27, no. 5 (2006): 641–63.

Kalyvas, Stathis N.. *The Logic of Violence in Civil War*. Cambridge: Cambridge University Press, 2006.

Kalyvas, Stathis N. "Ethnic Defection in Civil War." *Comparative Political Studies* 41, no. 8 (2008): 1043–68.

Kaplan, Oliver, and Enzo Nussio. "Explaining Recidivism of Ex-combatants in Colombia." *Journal of Conflict Resolution* 62, no. 1 (2018): 64–93.

Keck, Margaret E, and Kathryn Sikkink. *Activists beyond Borders: Advocacy Networks in International Politics*. Ithaca, NY: Cornell University Press, 1998.

King, Anthony. "The Female Combat Soldier." *European Journal of International Relations* 22, no. 1 (2015): 122–43.

Kline, Harvey F. *State Building and Conflict Resolution in Colombia: 1986–1994*. Tuscaloosa: University of Alabama Press, 2002.

Koehler, Kevin, Dorothy Ohl, and Holger Albrecht. "Disaffection to Desertion: How Networks Facilitate Military Insubordination in Civil Conflict." *Comparative Politics* 48, no. 4 (2016): 439–57.

Krystalli, Roxani. "'We Are Not Good Victims': Hierarchies of Suffering and the Politics of Victimhood in Colombia." PhD dissertation, Tufts University, 2019.

La Calle, Humberto de. "Enfoque de Género." *El Tiempo*, October 15, 2016. www.eltiempo.com/archivo/documento/CMS-16727692.

LaFree, Gary, and Erin Miller. "Desistance from Terrorism: What Can We Learn from Criminology?" *Dynamics of Asymmetric Conflict* 1, no. 3 (2008): 203–30.

LaRosa, Michael, and Germán Mejía P. *Colombia: A Concise Contemporary History*. Lanham: Rowman & Littlefield Publishers, 2012.

Laub, John H, and Robert J Sampson. "Understanding Desistance from Crime." *Crime and Justice* 28 (2001): 1–69.

Lazala Silva Hernandez, Yira Carmiña. "From Home Gardens to the Palais Des Nations: Translocal Action for Rural Women's Human Right to Land and Territory in Nariño-Colombia." Graduate Institute of International and Development Studies, 2020.

Lederach, Angela J. "'The Campesino Was Born for the Campo': A Multispecies Approach to Territorial Peace in Colombia." *American Anthropologist* 119, no. 4 (2017): 589–602.

Leech, Garry M. *The FARC: The Longest Insurgency*. London, New York, Halifax: Fernwood, 2011.

Leliévre Aussel, Christiane, Graciliana Moreno Echavarría, and Isabel Ortiz Pérez. *Haciendo Memoria Y Dejando Rastros: Encuentros Con Mujeres*

Excombatientes Del Nororiente de Colombia. Bogota: Fundación Mujer y Futuro, 2004. http://bdigital.unal.edu.co/45755/1/9583369004.pdf.

Leongómez, Eduardo Pizarro. *Cambiar El Futuro: Historia de Los Procesos de Paz En Colombia (1981–2016)*. Bogotá: Penguin Random House, 2017.

Livingstone, Grace. *Inside Colombia: Drugs, Democracy, and War*. New Brunswick, NJ: Rutgers University Press, 2004.

Londoño, Luz María, and Yoana Fernanda Nieto. *Mujeres No Contadas: Procesos de Desmovilización y Retorno a La Vida Civil de Mujeres Excombatientes En Colombia, 1990–2003*. Bogota: La Carreta Editores, 2006.

López, Claudia Maria. "Contesting Double Displacement: Internally Displaced Campesinos and the Social Production of Urban Territory in Medellín, Colombia." *Geographica Helvetica* 74, no. 3 (2019): 249–59.

Lyall, Jason. *Divided Armies: Inequality and Battlefield Performance in Modern War*. New Jersey: Princeton University Press, 2020.

Lynch, Michael. "Against Reflexivity as an Academic Virtue and Source of Privileged Knowledge." *Theory, Culture & Society* 17, no. 3 (2000): 26–54.

MacKenzie, Megan. "Securitization and Desecuritization: Female Soldiers and the Reconstruction of Women in Post-conflict Sierra Leone." *Security Studies* 18, no. 2 (2009): 241–61.

Mance, Henry. "Colombia's Campaign to Win Rebel Minds." *BBC News*, January 23, 2008. http://news.bbc.co.uk/2/hi/americas/7194377.stm.

Mancuso, Salvatore. "Discurso de Salvatore Mancuso Ante El Congreso de La República." Bogotá, 2004. www.telam.com.ar/advf/documentos/2013/11/529 66a9d7950c.pdf.

Mapping Militants Project. "National Liberation Army (Colombia): Mapping Militant Organizations." Stanford, 2015. http://web.stanford.edu/group/mapping militants/cgi-bin/groups/view/87.

Marulanda, Manuel. *Resistencia de Un Pueblo En Armas*, Vol. 1.Havana: Ocean Sur, 2015.

Mazurana, D, and K Carlson. "From Combat to Community: Women and Girls of Sierra Leone." Peacewomen.org, 2004. www.peacewomen.org/assets/file/ Resources/NGO/PartPPGIssueDisp_CombatToCommunty_WomenWage-Peace_2004.pdf.

McDermott, Jeremy. "Colombia Extradites Rebel 'Sonia.'" *BBC News*, March 9, 2005. http://news.bbc.co.uk/2/hi/americas/4331673.stm.

McEvoy, Kieran, and Kirsten McConnachie. "Victimology in Transitional Justice: Victimhood, Innocence and Hierarchy." Edited by Susanne Karstedt and Stephan Parmentier. *European Journal of Criminology* 9, no. 5 (2012): 527–38.

McFee, Erin, and Angelika Rettberg, eds. *Excombatientes y Acuerdo de Paz Con Las FARC-EP En Colombia: Balance de La Etapa Temprana*. Bogotá: Universidad de los Andes, 2019.

McKay, Susan, and Dyan E Mazurana. *Where Are the Girls? Girls in Fighting Forces in Northern Uganda, Sierra Leone and Mozambique: Their Lives during and after War*. Montréal: Rights & Democracy, 2004.

McLauchlin, Theodore. "Desertion and Collective Action in Civil Wars." *International Studies Quarterly* 59, no. 4 (2015): 669–79.

McLauchlin, Theodore. *Desertion: Trust and Mistrust in Civil Wars.* Ithaca, NY: Cornell University Press, 2020.

McLauchlin, Theodore, and Wendy Pearlman. "Out-Group Conflict, In-Group Unity? Exploring the Effect of Repression on Intramovement Cooperation." *The Journal of Conflict Resolution* 56, no. 1 (2012): 41–66.

Meléndez, José. "Increasing Presence of Mexican Drug Cartels in Colombia." *El Universal,* October 2018. www.eluniversal.com.mx/english/increasing-presence-of-mexican-drug-cartels-colombia.

Méndez, Alicia Liliana. "Eln y Disidencias Se Unieron En Arauca Para Controlar La Frontera." *El Tiempo,* February 18, 2018. www.eltiempo.com/justicia/conflicto-y-narcotrafico/eln-y-disidencias-firman-pacto-de-control-en-arauca-327990.

Mendez, Andrea. "Militarized Gender Performativity: Women and Demobilization in Colombia's FARC and AUC." PhD dissertation, Queen's University, 2012.

Mesias Garcia, Liliana. "Relatos y Contrarrelatos de Los Actores Subalternos: El Campesino Organizado En La Construccion de Narrativas Democraticas En Colombia." *Cuadernos de Desarrollo Rural* 6, no. 63 (2009): 139–62.

Minority Rights. "Afro-Colombians," 2019. https://minorityrights.org/minorities/afro-colombians/.

Mironova, Vera. *From Freedom Fighters to Jihadists: Human Resources of Non State Armed Groups, Causes and Consequences of Terrorism.* New York: Oxford University Press, 2019.

Monblatt, Steven. "Terrorism and Drugs in the Americas: The OAS Response." OAS, 2004. www.oas.org/ezine/ezine24/Monblatt.htm.

Mora Lemus, Giovanni. "Memorias, Pluralidad, y Movimiento Social: La Experiencia Del MOVICE." MA dissertation, Universidad Javeriana, 2010.

Nacos, Brigitte L. "The Portrayal of Female Terrorists in the Media: Similar Framing Patterns in the News Coverage of Women in Politics and in Terrorism." *Studies in Conflict and Terrorism* 28, no. 5 (2005): 435–51.

New York Times. "Colombia's Capitulation." *New York Times,* July 6, 2005. www.nytimes.com/2005/07/06/opinion/colombias-capitulation.html.

Ní Aoláin, Fionnuala, Dina Francesca Haynes, and Naomi R Cahn. *On the Frontlines: Gender, War, and the Post-conflict Process.* New York and Oxford: Oxford University Press, 2011.

Nieto-Valdivieso, Yoana Fernanda. "The Joy of the Militancy: Happiness and the Pursuit of Revolutionary Struggle." *Journal of Gender Studies* 26, no. 1 (2017): 78–90.

Nussio, Enzo. "Learning from Shortcomings: The Demobilisation of Paramilitaries in Colombia." *Journal of Peacebuilding & Development* 6, no. 2 (2011): 88–92.

Ohl, Dorothy. "The Soldier's Dilemma: Military Responses to Uprisings in Jordan, Iraq, Bahrain, and Syria." PhD dissertation, George Washington University, 2016.

Oppenheim, Ben, Abbey Steele, Juan F Vargas, and Michael Weintraub. "True Believers, Deserters, and Traitors: Who Leaves Insurgent Groups and Why." *Journal of Conflict Resolution* 59, no. 5 (2015): 794–823.

Orth, Maureen. "She Was Colombia's Most-Feared Female Revolutionary. Can She Help It Find Peace?" *Vanity Fair*, August 2018. www.vanityfair.com/news/2018/08/colombia-civil-war-farc-female-revolutionary.

Pacheco Jiménez, Sebastian. "¿Cómo Los Llamamos: Paramilitares, Disidencias, Grupos Residuales, Terroristas?" *El Espectador*, November 24, 2019. www.elespectador.com/colombia2020/opinion/como-los-llamamos-paramilitares-disidencias-grupos-residuales-terroristas-columna-892676/.

Porch, Douglas, and María José Rasmussen. "Demobilization of Paramilitaries in Colombia: Transformation or Transition?" *Studies in Conflict & Terrorism* 31, no. 6 (2008): 520–40.

Rabasa, Angel, and Peter Chalk. *Colombian Labyrinth*. Santa Monica: RAND Corporation, 2001. www.rand.org/pubs/monograph_reports/MR1339.html.

Ramírez, María Clemencia. *Between the Guerrillas and the State: The Cocalero Movement, Citizenship, and Identity in the Colombian Amazon*. Durham, NC and London: Duke University Press, 2011.

Rapoport, A. *The Origins of Violence: Approaches to the Study of Conflict*. Second. London: Transaction Publishers, 1994.

Reuters. "Colombian Paramilitary Chief Admits Getting Backing from Businessmen." *CNN*, September 6, 2000. www.cnn.com/2000/WORLD/americas/09/06/colombia.paramilitary.reut/.

Reuters. "Court Convicts Colombian Rebel on Drug Charges." *Reuters*, February 20, 2007. www.reuters.com/article/us-colombia-farc/court-convicts-colombian-rebel-on-drug-charges-idUSN2019514720070220.

Reyes le Paliscot, Elizabeth. "La Oportunidad de La Paz." Fundación Ideas para la Paz, 2015. https://doi.org/10.15713/ins.mmj.3.

Roa, Élber Gutiérrez. "Guía Práctica Para Entender El Escándalo de La 'Para-Política.'" *Semana*, April 10, 2007. www.semana.com/on-line/articulo/guia-practica-para-entender-escandalo-para-politica/84455-3.

Rojas Bolaños, Omar, and Fabian Leonardo Benavides. *Ejecuciones Extrajudiciales En Colombia, 2002–2010: Obedencia Ciega En Campos de Batalla Ficticios*. Bogotá: Universidad Santo Tomás, 2017.

Rojas, Cristina. "Securing the State and Developing Social Insecurities: The Securitisation of Citizenship in Contemporary Colombia." *Third World Quarterly* 30, no. 1 (2009): 227–45.

Roldán, Mary. *Blood and Fire: La Violencia in Antioquia, Colombia, 1946–1953*. Durham, NC: Duke University Press, 2002.

Romero, Mauricio. *Paramilitares y Autodefensas*. Bogotá: IEPRI, 2003.

Rusbult, Caryl, Christopher Agnew, and Ximena Arriaga. "The Investment Model of Commitment Processes." In *Handbook of Theories of Social Psychology*, edited by Paul Van Lange, Arie Kruglanski Higgins, and E Tory. London: Sage Publications, 2012.

Salazar, Miguel, and Mariana Araujo Herrera. "The Silences of Sexual Violence: Commission Faces Truth Deficits in Colombia." Council on Hemispheric Affairs,2015.www.coha.org/the-silences-of-sexual-violence-commission-faces-truth-deficits-in-colombia/.

Salvesen, Hilde, and Dag Nylander. "Towards an Inclusive Peace: Women and the Gender Approach in the Colombian Peace Process." Reliefweb.int, 2017.

https://reliefweb.int/sites/reliefweb.int/files/resources/Salvesen_Nylander_
Towards_an_inclusive_peace_July2017_final.pdf.

Schemo, Diana Jean. "Colombia's Death-Strewn Democracy." *New York Times*,
July 24, 1997. www.nytimes.com/1997/07/24/world/colombia-s-death-strewn-
democracy.html.

Schmid, Alex P. "Al-Qaeda's 'Single Narrative' and Attempts to Develop Counter-Narratives: The State of Knowledge." The Hague, 2014. www.icct.nl/
download/file/Schmid-Al-Qaeda's-Single-Narrative-and-Attempts-to-Develop-
Counter-Narratives-January-2014.pdf.

Schmidt, Rachel. "Duped: Examining Gender Stereotypes in Disengagement and
Deradicalization Practices." *Studies in Conflict & Terrorism*, 2020. https://
doi.org/10.1080/1057610X.2020.1711586.

Schmidt, Rachel. *No Girls Allowed? Recruitment and Gender in Colombian
Armed Groups*. Ottawa: ProQuest Dissertations Publishing, 2007.

Schmidt, Rachel. "When Fieldwork Ends: Navigating Ongoing Contact with Former Insurgents." *Terrorism and Political Violence* 33, no. 2 (2020): 312–23.

Schmidt, Rachel, and Paulo Tovar. "A 'Post-conflict' Colombia? Analyzing the
Pillars (and Spoilers) of Peace." In *Post-conflict Peacebuilding*, edited by Monika Thakur. Montreal: McGill-Queen's University Press, forthcoming.

Schwitalla, Gunhild, and Luisa Maria Dietrich. "Demobilisation of Female Ex-
combatants in Colombia." *Forced Migration Review* 27 (2007): 58–9.

Scott-Samuel, Alex. "Patriarchy, Masculinities and Health Inequalities." Liverpool: University of Liverpool, 2008.

Segura, Renata. "Colombia Further Polarized by President's Action on Transitional Justice Law." New York, 2019. https://theglobalobservatory.org/
2019/04/colombia-polarized-president-action-transitional-justice-law/.

Semana. "Sí Hay Guerra, Señor Presidente." *Semana*, February 6, 2005. www
.semana.com/portada/articulo/si-guerra-senor-presidente/70763-3.

Semana. "La Fiscalía Acusa a Jorge Noguera de Haber Puesto El DAS Al Servicio
de Los Paras." *Semana*, February 1, 2008. www.semana.com/on-line/articulo/
la-fiscalia-acusa-jorge-noguera-haber-puesto-das-servicio-paras/90753-3.

Semana. "Ya Son 46 Los Jóvenes Desaparecidos Que Fueron Reportados
Como Muertos En Combate." *Semana*, September 26, 2008. www.semana
.com/nacion/conflicto-armado/articulo/ya-46-jovenes-desaparecidos-fueron-
reportados-como-muertos-combate/95578-3.

Semana. "Las Cuentas de Los Falsos Positivos." *Semana*, January 29, 2009. www
.semana.com/nacion/justicia/articulo/las-cuentas-falsos-positivos/99556-3.

Semana. "ELN, El Nuevo Enemigo." *Semana*, February 17, 2018. www.semana
.com/nacion/articulo/eln-en-venezuela-el-nuevo-enemigo/557445.

Semana. "¿No Más Farc? Timochenko Plantea Cambio de Nombre Para Su
Partido." *Semana*, May 2020. www.semana.com/nacion/articulo/timochenko-
plantea-cambiar-nombre-de-partido-farc/673747/.

Semana. "¿Cuál Es La Diferencia Entre Homicidios Colectivos y Masacres?" *Semana*,
August 24, 2020. www.semana.com/nacion/articulo/cual-es-la-diferencia-entre-
homicidios-colectivos-y-masacres/696762/.

Semana. "'Duque Debe Irse': La Polémica Reaparición de Iván Márquez."
Semana, September 2020. www.semana.com/nacion/articulo/tras-meses-de-
silencio-reaparecio-el-guerrillero-ivan-marquez/202044/.

Shaw, Ibrahim Seaga. "Historical Frames and the Politics of Humanitarian Intervention: From Ethiopia, Somalia to Rwanda." *Globalisation, Societies and Education* 5, no. 3 (2007): 351–71.

Shesterinina, Anastasia. "Collective Threat Framing and Mobilization in Civil War." *The American Political Science Review* 110, no. 3 (2016): 411–27.

Shesterinina, Anastasia. "Ethics, Empathy, and Fear in Research on Violent Conflict." *Journal of Peace Research* 56, no. 2 (2019): 190–202.

Simons, G L. "*Colombia: A Brutal History.*" London: SAQI, 2004.

Sjoberg, Laura, and Caron E Gentry. *Mothers, Monsters, Whores: Women's Violence in Global Politics*. New York and London; Zed Books, 2007.

Sjoberg, Laura, and Caron E Gentry. *Women, Gender, and Terrorism*. Athens, GA: University of Georgia Press, 2011.

Snow, David A, and Robert D Benford. "Ideology, Frame Resonance, and Participant Mobilization." *International Social Movement Research* 1 (1988): 197–217.

Söderström, Johanna. *Peacebuilding and Ex-combatants: Political Reintegration in Liberia*. London: Routledge, 2015.

Sontag, Deborah. "Colombia's Paramilitaries and the U.S. War on Drugs." *New York Times*, September 10, 2016. www.nytimes.com/2016/09/11/world/americas/colombia-cocaine-human-rights.html.

Speckhard, Anne. "The Emergence of Female Suicide Terrorists." *Studies in Conflict & Terrorism* 31, no. 11 (2008): 995–1051.

Stanfield, Michael Edward. *Of Beasts and Beauty: Gender, Race, and Identity in Colombia*. Austin: University of Texas Press, 2013.

Staniland, Paul. "Between a Rock and a Hard Place." *Journal of Conflict Resolution* 56, no. 1 (2012): 16–40.

Steel, Emily. "The Ads Making Colombian Guerrillas Lonely This Christmas." *Financial Times*, December, 2013. www.ft.com/content/3dc53856-4ddc-11e3-8fa5-00144feabdco.

Stekelenburg, Jacquelien van, and Bert Klandermans. "The Social Psychology of Protest." *Current Sociology* 61, no. 5–6 (2013): 886–905.

Stemler, Steve. "An Overview of Content Analysis." *Practical Assessment, Research & Evaluation* 7, no. 17 (2001): 1–6.

Summers, Nicole. "Colombia's Victims' Law: Transitional Justice in a Time of Violent Conflict?" *Harvard Human Rights Journal* 25 (2012): 219–35.

Tarnaala, Elisa. "Legacies of Violence and the Unfinished Past: Women in Post-demobilization Colombia and Guatemala." *Peacebuilding* 7, no. 1 (2018): 1–15.

Taylor, Laura K. "Transitional Justice, Demobilisation and Peacebuilding amid Political Violence: Examining Individual Preferences in the Caribbean Coast of Colombia." *Peacebuilding* 3, no. 1 (2015): 90–108.

Telles, Edward Eric. *Pigmentocracies: Ethnicity, Race, and Color in Latin America*. Chapel Hill: University of North Carolina Press, 2014.

The Economist. "*Colombia's President Iván Duque Undermines a Peace Deal.*" *The Economist*, March 2019. www.economist.com/the-americas/2019/03/16/colombias-president-ivan-duque-undermines-a-peace-deal.

The Guardian. "One Million Fled Economic Crisis-Hit Venezuela for Colombia in Past Year." *The Guardian*, May 9, 2018. www.theguardian.com/world/2018/may/09/one-million-refugees-entered-colombia-after-economic-crisis-hit-venezuela.

Theidon, Kimberly. "Reconstructing Masculinities: The Disarmament, Demobilization, and Reintegration of Former Combatants in Colombia." *Human Rights Quarterly* 31, no. 1 (2009): 1–34.

Theobald, Anne. "Successful or Failed Rebellion? The Casamance Conflict from a Framing Perspective." *Civil Wars* 17, no. 2 (2015): 181–200.

Trevizo, Dolores. "What Can Intersectional Approaches Reveal about Experiences of Violence?" OpenGlobalRights, 2020. www.openglobalrights.org/what-can-intersectional-approaches-reveal-about-experiences-of-violence/.

UARIV. "Registro Único de Víctimas (RUV): Unidad Para Las Víctimas." Unidadvictimas.gov, 2018. www.unidadvictimas.gov.co/es/registro-unico-de-victimas-ruv/37394.

Ugarriza, Juan Esteban, and Rafael Camilo Quishpe. "Guerrilla Sin Armas: La Reintegración Política de La FARC Como Transformación de Los Comunistas Revolucionarios En Colombia." In *Excombatientes y Acuerdo de Paz Con Las FARC-EP En Colombia: Balance de La Etapa Temprana*, edited by Erin McFee and Angelika Rettberg. Bogotá: Ediciones Uniandes, 2019.

UN Women. "Global Database on Violence against Women: Colombia." Global Database on Violence against Women, 2020. https://evaw-global-database .unwomen.org/en/countries/americas/colombia.

UNHCR (United Nations High Commissioner for Refugees). "UNHCR Fact Sheet: Colombia," 2017. https://reporting.unhcr.org/sites/default/files/UNHCR%20Colombia%20Factsheet%20-%20February%202017.pdf.

UNHCR. "ACNUR – Colombia," 2018. www.acnur.org/5b97f3154.pdf.

Valencia, León, and Ariel Avila. "La Compleja Estructura Detrás Del 'Clan Del Golfo.'" *El Tiempo*, July 14, 2018. www.eltiempo.com/justicia/conflicto-y-narcotrafico/como-funciona-la-estructura-del-clan-del-golfo-243522.

Vargas, Ricardo. "Colombia y El Area Andina: Los Vacíos de La Guerra." *Controversía* 169 (1996): 53–72.

Vertigans, Stephen. *The Sociology of Terrorism: People, Places and Processes.* London and New York: Routledge, 2011.

Viveros Vigoya, Mara, and Manuel Alejandro Rondón Rodríguez. "Hacer y Deshacer La Ideología de Género." *Sexualidad, Salud y Sociedad* 27 (2017): 118–27.

Wade, Peter. *Blackness and Race Mixture: The Dynamics of Racial Identity in Colombia.* Baltimore: Johns Hopkins University Press, 1993.

Watts, Jonathan. "Battle for the Mother Land: Indigenous People of Colombia Fighting for Their Lands." *The Guardian*, 2017. www.theguardian.com/environment/2017/oct/28/nasa-colombia-cauca-valley-battle-mother-land.

Weick, Karl E. *Sensemaking in Organizations.* Thousand Oaks, CA: Sage, 1995.

Weinstein, Jeremy M. *Inside Rebellion: The Politics of Insurgent Violence.* Cambridge and New York; Cambridge University Press, 2007.

Wilson, Scott. "Colombian Rebels Use Refuge to Expand Their Power Base." *Washington Post*, October 3, 2001. www.washingtonpost.com/archive/politics/2001/10/03/colombian-rebels-use-refuge-to-expand-their-power-base/88d8f638-24ea-4607-ac19-c4293bdac97e/?utm_term=.3e6fcb073e3c.

Wood, Reed M, and Jakana L Thomas. "Women on the Frontline: Rebel Group Ideology and Women's Participation in Violent Rebellion." *Journal of Peace Research* 54, no. 1 (2017): 31–46.

Index

For EU product safety concerns, contact us at Calle de José Abascal, 56–1°,
28003 Madrid, Spain or eugpsr@cambridge.org.